Hester Thrale Piozzi

Hester Lynch Thrale in the 1770s,
artist unknown, from James L. Clifford, *Hester Lynch Piozzi (Mrs. Thrale)*,
2nd ed., Oxford University Press, 1952.
By permission of Oxford University Press.

Mrs. Piozzi on her eightieth birthday, 27 January 1820,
after a painting by Hopwood, engraved by James Thomson,
from *Columbia Library Columns* 27 (no. 3): 11.
Rare Book and Manuscript Library, Columbia University.

HESTER THRALE PIOZZI

Portrait of a Literary Woman

WILLIAM MCCARTHY

The University of North Carolina Press
Chapel Hill and London

To
Paul Fussell
and
Rosanne Potter

© 1985 The University of North Carolina Press

All rights reserved

Manufactured in the United States of America

Design by Ron Maner

Library of Congress Cataloging in Publication Data
McCarthy, William, 1942–
Hester Thrale Piozzi, portrait of a literary woman.
Bibliography: p.
Includes index.
1. Piozzi, Hester Lynch, 1741–1821.   2. Authors,
English—18th century—Biography.   3. Johnson, Samuel,
1709–1784—Friends and associates.   I. Title.
PR3619.P5Z75 1986   828'.609 [B]   85-1097
ISBN 0-8078-1659-0

Contents

Preface

"MRS. PIOZZI can never be forgotten," wrote Edward Mangin in 1833, in the first book about Hester Lynch Piozzi, ". . . were it only because her name is closely connected with that of Johnson, whose reputation will endure as long as the language . . . he adorned." Certainly she has not been forgotten; she remains one of the best known women of her time and place. And yet we must say of her what Bertrand Bronson said some years ago of Johnson himself. There are two Johnsons, the Boswellian Great Clubman and the writer. The clubman is funny, cranky, and popular; the writer, a very different person indeed, is hardly known. There are likewise two Piozzis, or rather, a Piozzi and a Thrale. Thrale is the "light and lively" hostess of Streatham, a fixture in the Johnson Legend and even in some sense his possession—"Dr. Johnson's Mrs. Thrale," she has been called. Piozzi is one of his first memoirists and editors, remembered also as a letter writer and diarist. Her identity as an author is vague; traditionally she has been the object of a peculiar double vision, even a logical inconsistency. When Johnson the writer was eclipsed, his writings were treated accordingly; editors and critics lost interest in them. Not so with Thrale-Piozzi. Since her death, *Anecdotes* has remained in print, and the canon of her private writings—letters, diaries, marginalia—has grown. She cannot be numbered with those really forgotten women writers, the Catharine Cockburns and Mary Astells, whose work is only now being recovered. Yet the same people who were editing and reprinting her were also asserting that her importance lay in "her indefinable charm" and her "singular gifts" as a hostess.[1] They were keeping her writings alive, and asserting that she did not really count as a writer.

No doubt this doubleness has much to do with the strong pull of the Johnson Legend itself, which has sucked even Johnson into its vortex. Still, Piozzi's equivocal reputation is also consistent with the historical fortunes of early women writers. Historically women writers were not welcomed into the canon; they were forgotten in disproportionate numbers, or they were admitted on equivocal and belittling terms, as clever second-raters. Piozzi's reputation for "feminine" charm is comparable to Jane Austen's for miniature deftness in her "little bit of ivory." Piozzi herself had very strong feelings about the reception of literary women in her time. After the death-by-detraction of her own career she wrote a bitter remark about Joanna Baillie, whose plays had been well received on their first, anonymous publication: "What a Goose Joanna must have been ever to reveal her Sex & Name!! Spite and Malice have pursued her ever since."[2] Like Austen, Piozzi has had her Janeites; she has also had a goodly share of "Spite and Malice." Together they have obscured the actual range and merits of her writings; more, they have obscured the very perception that she is a writer.

To perceive her as a writer is the aim of this book. To that end I trace her career from its earliest recorded efforts to its demise, attempting at once a chronicle of her writing life and an exegesis of its products. My principal subjects, the subjects of chapters 4 through 8, are the books she published between 1786 and 1801. Her poems I have treated chiefly in one place, chapter 3; her diaries, memoirs, and letters, although drawn on throughout, are the main materials of chapters 1 and 9; her unpublished writings are treated in relation to the published or to whatever facet of her writing career I believe they best illustrate. The intent is to tell a generally consecutive story largely in her words and emphasizing what she chose to emphasize. "Story" suggests biography, and this book may indeed be read as a kind of literary biography. The emphasis, however, is on "literary." My subjects are the writer and her writings.

Thrale's traditional public has been Johnsonians, both professional and amateur; as an early woman writer, however, Piozzi has a claim to the interest of historians of women's writing. Unfortunately, these two publics do not often meet. (At the Modern Language Association in 1981, I brought members of them together in the same room. Perhaps not by chance, they sat on opposite sides of the room.) Nor do they always share the same knowledge; historians of women's writing, for instance, may not be specialists in eighteenth-century literature. I attempt to address both publics through the mediation of a third person, the general reader. The general reader resembles the Johnsonian in knowing little of Piozzi beyond her Johnson connection; the general reader also resembles some historians of women's writing (and even some admirers of Johnson) in not being an eighteenth-century specialist. The specialist reader will therefore find parts of my exposition familiar.

If Piozzi's double audience complicates exposition, so does the exceptional range of her interests. We must be as ready to follow her through the controversy over Pope's *Essay on Man*, early synonymy books, the French Revolution, and the Napoleonic Wars as through the well-known territory of Johnson's life and letters. Also, the subtleties of her literary relationships are such that in order to appreciate what she is doing we must often expound Johnson or Smollett or Burke or Wollstonecraft as well. For all these reasons my exegesis includes a fair share of context setting. Many of my readers will already know this or that context and would, perhaps, treat it differently than I do. My wish is to tell what is needed to make Piozzi intelligible.

For that purpose I also take account of the obstacles raised in her time against female success in literature. Piozzi's character as a writer is closely connected with those obstacles. If they account in certain obvious ways for her failings, they are equally a measure of her significance and strength. For I see her as a very strong writer, however flawed, and I agree with Hannah More in finding her rather more strong than sweet. If I sometimes find her less pleasant than others have, I also find her weightier. By canonical standards she was not a "great" writer, but those standards, as I suggest in chapter 2, are not innocent of bias. More relevant statements about her are that she was intelligent, brave, unstuffy, and resourceful. Her confusions and failures speak less of her personal character than of the extreme psychic difficulty of doing, then and there, what she set out to do. Her achievement, estimable in any case, appears only more impressive when we admit the odds against it.

The starting points for this book were, as they must be for anyone who aims to look long at Piozzi, James Clifford's biography and Katharine Balderston's great edition of *Thraliana*. As an interpreter of her I have found my best hints in the broodings of Harold Bloom on Poetic Influence. I had already begun to revise them in a way more suited to a female writer when, embarrassingly late, I came to Sandra Gilbert's and Susan Gubar's revision of Bloom, *The Madwoman in the Attic*. That book gave me the courage to keep swerving.

For patient and generous support of my work I am grateful to three agencies of my home institution: the Iowa State University Research Foundation and the Sciences and Humanities Research Institute for grants and salary in the summer of 1980, and the Graduate

College for repeated grants between 1978 and 1983. I want also to
thank the Department of English and Professor Frank Haggard for
frequent awards of released time during those years. Additional support came from the Penrose Fund of the American Philosophical
Society and from the National Endowment for the Humanities in the
form of a Summer Seminar at Princeton University in 1981. I am
grateful to these bodies and to the seminar's director, Professor Alvin
Kernan.

It is a pleasure to record my thanks to libraries and their staffs:
to Glenise A. Matheson, Keeper of Manuscripts at the John Rylands
University Library of Manchester, who gave friendly and patient assistance both in person and by mail, and to Dr. M. A. Pegg, University Librarian, for generous permission to quote from and reproduce
manuscripts in the Rylands collection; to Richard M. Ludwig, Assistant Librarian for Rare Books and Special Collections at the Princeton University Library, for answering queries and for permission to
quote from manuscripts at Princeton; to Rodney G. Dennis, Curator
of Manuscripts at the Houghton Library, for permission to quote
from manuscripts there; and to Aldo Cupo, Public Services Assistant
at Yale University Library, for materials from periodicals. To Donald
Pady, Humanities Librarian at Iowa State University, I am grateful
for his ready willingness to procure books. And how can I sufficiently
thank the Inter-Library Loan staff at Iowa State University, Susan
Rafter, Martha Richardson, Rod Henshaw, and their colleagues present and former, who during five years persevered in tracking down
obscure and rare items?

For encouragement, ideas, information, criticism, and all the
nameless helps that people give, I am happy to thank Robert Bataille,
Edward and Lillian Bloom, Martine W. Brownley, Bill Fowler, Aubrey
Galyon, Harry Giuditta, Kathleen Hickok, Carren O. Kaston, Joan
Klingel, Linda Koenig, Virginia McCarthy, Sylvia Myers, Lee and Susan Poague, Janet Reed, Sarah Smith, and Michael Stugrin. For some
particularly feisty and pointed criticism, of which I hope I have made
good use, I am grateful to Germaine Greer, formerly of the Tulsa
Center for the Study of Women's Literature. My thanks are also due
to Kathleen Felt for research assistance and to Sheryl Kamps and
Carol Palmquist for expert typing of a difficult manuscript, and I
deeply appreciate the editorial insight and support of Sandra Eis-
dorfer of the University of North Carolina Press.

In addition I wish to name my sister, Elizabeth Johnson, for indispensable help in the summer of 1980 and for much else, and my father, Stuart McCarthy, who believed in this book but did not live to see its publication.

To two other people I owe especially much. The first was my teacher at Rutgers University; the second is my colleague and my dearest critic. For these reasons, and in memory of a conversation among the three of us at Princeton in July 1981, I dedicate this book to them.

Hester Thrale Piozzi

The Profession of Ladies
Education and Marriage

*Life is a Magic Lanthorn certainly, and I think more so to
Women, than to Men: who often are placed very early in a
Profession which they follow up regularly, & slide on;—Labitur
et labetur almost unconsciously:—but We Females
(myself for Example,) . . . .*

*Not that I consider my Life as an unhappy one—Oh God forbid!
. . . but bitter to* Remembrance, *& hateful to* review.[1]

THE WOMAN WHO, in her sev-
enty-eighth year, wrote these words had already become a legend. To
young people who sought her out in their visits to Bath, she represented the bygone Age of Johnson, Burke and Reynolds, envisioned
as the drawing room at Streatham, a brightly lit scene of pastoral
nostalgia. Like all pastoral visions this one is deeply attractive; however, its simplifying charm banishes most of Hester Lynch Piozzi's
experience, the life that she found "hateful to review." In that life she
had outlived eight children, two husbands, and most of her income.
She had also outlived what she prized perhaps more than any of
these, her literary career and fame. Being canonized as a hostess did
not compensate her for that loss.

In her life Johnson had been an accident, but writing was a necessity. When she had nothing new to write she rewrote or recopied
the old. Thus it was that, however hateful the task, she reviewed her
life at least four times in some detail: in *Thraliana* in 1778, anticipating childbirth and its attendant possibility, her death; in a collection
of her poems made in 1810 for her nephew; and in memoirs written
in old age for two young men whose admiration she sought to relieve
her loneliness. The story she tells is one of promise and betrayal. Her

theme is her intellectual precocity, its initial encouragement by her elders, and its eventual betrayal by them. Her memoirs are tart, bitter, melodramatic; they deal in broad strokes. Her biographer advises scholarly caution in their use, and as to niceties of fact he is right. To feel the emotional curve of her life as she felt it, however, we will turn above all to them.

"Half a Prodigy"

She was born 27 January 1741, at a farmhouse near the village of Pwllheli in remote northwest Wales, the only child of John and Hester Maria Salusbury. Both parents were of old Welsh family, decayed on her father's side to genteel poverty. Their daughter retained much family pride and a lifelong affection for Wales, returning to live there fifty-four years later. She thought of herself emphatically as a Welshwoman—that is, in accordance with the persistent notion of the "Celtic type," as impetuous, cranky, and passionate. "Her Temper," she wrote of herself in *Thraliana*, "is warm even to Irascibility; Affectionate and tender, but claiming such returns to her Tenderness & Affection, as busy People have no Time to pay, and coarse people have no Pleasure in paying: She is a diligent & active Friend," but "by Nature a rancorous and revengeful Enemy." Elsewhere she speaks of her "Temper sarcastic." These are the makings of a formidable character, one who will not tamely settle for second place. They are also the makings of literary aggressiveness. In these traits she resembled her father, of whom she gives a striking sketch. "My Father was a Man of quick Parts, much Gentleman like Literature, and a Vein of humour very diverting and seemingly inexhaustible: his Conversation was showy however, not solid; few Men were ever more certain to please at Sight; but though his Talk did not consist in telling Stories, it fatigued his Hearers, who as he was not rich—made no Ceremony of letting him see it. His Sensibility—quickened by Vanity & Idleness was *keen* beyond the *Affectation* of any other Mortal, and threw him into Hypocondriack Disorders in spite of a Manly Vigorous Person, & of a Constitution eminently strong." It was part of John Salusbury's sensibility that he could not keep an employment, that he was prompt to quarrel with his associates, that he habitually felt ill-used, and that he had some literary ambitions of his own and tried his hand at writing a novel.[2]

About her father Hester could write precisely and pungently. Her mother, however, she remembers in the mode of sentimental fiction: "She was for all personal and mental Excellence the most accomplished Female that ever my Eyes beheld. Her Shape so accurate, her Carriage so graceful, her Eyes so brilliant, her Knowledge so extensive, & her Manners so pleasing." This largely misses the truth of Hester Maria Salusbury, although in its way it attests to her power. Mrs. Salusbury, tied to improvident and touchy John, assumed the role of a martyr. Hester also recalls her self-denying domestic energy: "sick or well, [she] had me to get up & put to Bed always, My Father to sit up for to all Hours of ye Night & Morning, his Bed to Warm [,] his Shirts to iron [,] the Linen to mend & the Stocks to pleat. . . . I was . . . Tutored in dancing, History, Geography & Language & She attended to my Translations & Studies as if She had had nothing else to do."[3] Capable and determined, Mrs. Salusbury exacted her daughter's lifelong reverence.

Hester's parents taught her to be precocious. At age four she was given a copy of Ogilby's Homer; when not yet seven she was already, her uncle supposed, "over-stockd" with French books (these included translations of Livy and Plutarch, and Rapin's history of England); by fifteen she had gone through Tasso in Italian, and a year after that we find her translating out of Spanish a certain "Dissertation on the God Endovellicus," apparently a self-imposed task. She remembered her precocity for the pleasure it gave her elders: she "lov'd them, and was desirous to learn." She remembered also, with mingled pride and resentment, being regarded as a sort of toy: "*I* was their Joynt Play Thing, & although Education was a Word then unknown, as applied to Females; They had taught me to read, & speak, & think; & translate from the French, till I was half a Prodigy." That she grew skillful to please is certain, and she delights to remember proofs of it, such as her having become "a Favourite with The Duke & Duchess of Leeds, where I recollect often meeting the famous Actor Mr Quin, who taught me to speak Satan's Speech to the Sun in Paradise lost." This was in London; she was perhaps ten. Like other forward children, she had more success with adults than with playmates. She recalls being "always the Dupe to my Playfellows, who used regularly to cheat me at Cards, & then hoot me for being cheated; cram Cake into my Cup of Tea & then call my Mother to shew her how naughty little Miss Salusbury had been."[4]

She thus learned the ambiguous joy of performing, and performing specifically for men. Although she seems never to have pondered its ambiguities, she would probably have appreciated Mary Gordon's meditation on them, in her essay "The Parable of the Cave." Like Hester, Gordon learned to be her father's daughter. "I had a charming father. . . . He wanted me to be like him. He was a writer, an unsuccessful writer, and my mother worked as a secretary to support us. . . . He wanted me to be a writer too. . . . So I was taught to read at three, taught French at six, and taught to despise the world of women, the domestic. I was a docile child. I brought my father great joy, and I learned the pleasures of being a good girl." The rewards of performing, for Hester as for Gordon, were "by no means inconsiderable: safety and approval." They were also, however, delusive. The experience that Gordon articulates was to be Hester's as well. Taught to esteem herself by men's standards, she then finds that men do not, after all, take her seriously. "I have been told by male but not by female critics that my work was 'exquisite,' 'lovely,' 'like a watercolor.' They, of course, were painting in oils. They were doing the important work."[5] Brought up to despise the world of women, Gordon is nevertheless directed, implicitly, to enter it. Hester's experience, similar in form, was sterner in quality. Cultivated, flattered, brought forward, and promised much, she was not only to miss her reward but also to be ordered to dwindle into a wife.

The reward of her precocity was to be an inheritance, and she lost it not once but twice. Needing money and hoping that Hester might be the means of getting it, her parents first introduced her to a wealthy, childless uncle, Sir Robert Cotton. Charmed by little Hetty's accomplishments, Sir Robert promised to make her his heir, supplied her family with clothes, and settled them in London.

He then died suddenly, having neglected to make his will. Thus stranded, the Salusburys contrived for a while to keep up genteel appearances. Again Hester was impressed by her mother's determination. Although at home she was tutor and servant, Mrs. Salusbury resolutely put on a face to meet the world: "She . . . kept up her Dignity too, visited her Quality Friends & dress'd while the Effects of Sir Rob[ts] Fondness continued wearable or in Fashion." This model must have been instructive. In it we have the prototype of Streatham, with its brilliant talk in the parlor and dying children in the nursery. Engrained in Hester's adult character was the habit of maintaining through every shock of circumstance the appearance of good humor, even vivacity. She soldiers on, resisting pain by sheer buoyancy of spirit. In this conduct she is not complying with mere decorum (Hester, to her great credit, was almost never decorous), nor is she euphemizing. She could contemplate pain with a clear, objective eye, and in reporting it her language is free of euphemism. She could write of Henry Thrale in his last illness that he "can scarce retain the Faeces." This refusal to euphemize is one of her temperamental strengths. At the same time, the strenuous gaiety by which she opposed pain was undoubtedly calculated to deceive outsiders, and it did deceive them. Once when she and Thrale were "agonizing with Apprehension" over money, Boswell came to dine: "we talked, we rattled, we flashed, we made extempore Verses, we did so much that at last Mr Boswell said why Mrs Thrale . . . you are in most riotous Spirits today—So I am reply'd I gaily, & actually ran out of the Room to cry."[6]

At length John Salusbury procured a government post in Nova Scotia; he went there alone, "and poor dear Mama was left sine Pane [without bread] almost I believe, . . . with her odd little Charge a Girl without a Guinea." Then came a second chance at the stratagem used on Sir Robert Cotton. Because this time it enjoyed greater immediate success, its eventual disappointment brought Hester much keener anguish. John's brother Thomas contrived to marry an heiress, and thus became the rich master of Offley Park in Hertfordshire. Hester was once more kissed and petted, once more put forth by her hopeful parents, and the charm worked again: Sir Thomas, childless like her other uncle, delighted in her and called her his heir. She remembered the years that ensued as a time of pastoral felicity. "I used to be my Father's Favourite, my Mother's Comforter and Companion, & my Uncle's Darling. . . . Sir Thos having No Joy except in his Dogs, his Horses and myself, I was looked up to—as the principal Person of the Family."[7]

At Offley Park during the later 1750s Hester flourished. Her education hitherto had been largely informal; now she was set to five years' study of Latin, logic, and rhetoric under the watchful eye of Dr. Arthur Collier, son of the philosopher Arthur Collier, and to advanced study of French literature under Dr. William Parker, later chaplain to George III. Collier was her general preceptor and closest friend. Old enough to be her father (he was 51 when she was 17), he became something between a second father and a platonic lover. Hester always declared afterwards that he, rather than Johnson as we assume, was the great formative influence on her mind: he "formed my mind to resemble *his*." We know far less about Collier's mind than about Johnson's (he was not a writer), but we have her sketch of him in *Thraliana*. It is another striking performance, utterly unsentimental, evenhanded, and quietly devastating.

> He was a Person of a most assimilating Temper, could live in any Family, conform to any Hours, & take his Share in any Conversation; he had such a Taste of general Knowledge, that he was not nice in his Choice of Company, & would make Talk with any one rather than be alone. . . . Yet to many, nay to most people the Doctor was no agreable Companion; he loved to talk better than to hear, & to dispute better than to please; his Conversation too was always upon such Subjects as the rest of Mankind seem by one Consent to avoid. Duration and Eternity, Matter & Motion, Whig & Tory, Faith and Works were his favourite Topicks; and upon these or other Metaphysical Disquisitions would he be perpetually forcing his Company— while by his Superiority in Logic, & constant Exercise in all the Arts of Ratiocination, he delighted to drive them into Absurdities they were desirous to keep clear of, & then laugh at the ridiculous Figures that they made: All this however being done with an Air of great Civility made him more a painful than an offensive Companion, & People generally left the Room with a high Opinion of that Gentleman's Parts and a confirmed Resolution to avoid his Society.[8]

Collier's "favourite Topicks" became Hester's also and remained close to her heart throughout her writing career. "Duration and Eternity, Matter & Motion, Whig & Tory" are among the topics of *British Synonymy* thirty-five years later; Whig and Tory appear in her earliest known publications and reappear in *Retrospection*; "Faith and Works" is the subject of a theological discourse she wrote in Italy in 1786. It may well have been from Collier that she imbibed her predilection for intellectual discourse generally, and for the combative mode of conducting it. Her sketch of him is itself combative; its cool satire charges against him the interests and skills that he had taught her. When she wrote it (1776) she had long been under Johnson's influence, and Johnson was inclined to deprecate these topics. At the same time, this combative treatment of Collier resembles her combative treatment of Johnson himself, in *Anecdotes of Johnson*. It may appear ungrateful, just as her similar treatment of Johnson has appeared ungrateful to many of his admirers. It will be a premise of the present book that we cannot understand the relations of writers to their mentors so long as we seek to idealize them; to understand Piozzi's literary behavior, we must be prepared to accept resentment against her instructors as a fair motive for writing. In any case, she eventually had reason to resent Collier.

Under his care and Parker's she advanced rapidly. She read Rousseau; she began to write poems, both translations and original pieces; she sent pieces to the London newspapers. How many and what they were, we will probably never know; "there was no Controversy about a Bridge, an Exhibition, or any such bauble," she writes in *Thraliana*, "but Miss Salusbury's Letters on the Occasion were printed under various Names & Signatures; so various, that She has long ago forgot them all." Among Collier's friends were the novelist Sarah Fielding and James Harris, eminent for the treatise *Hermes, or a Philosophical Inquiry concerning Universal Grammar*; he apprised them of Hester's abilities and engaged their interest in her progress. Another friend and instructor was the Rev. Bernard Wilson, translator of De Thou's *Historia sui Temporis*. Having read some of her poems (among them a Racine translation entitled "Essay on Man"), Wilson assured her that she possessed a gift for poetry "not to be equall'd by any of your own Sex, and which very few of ours if any can excell." Her French tutor Parker agreed, praising her "Essay" in the highest terms: "You do more than Justice to the Author. For I never saw any French Poetry that was so nervous [i.e., strong], or that pleased me so much as your Translation." The collective encouragement of these people must have animated Hester's ambition; certainly a young man so encouraged would have good grounds to elect literature as his calling. In later years Piozzi believed that the decisive event was her reading in 1760 of Joseph Warton's *Essay on the Genius and Writings of Pope* (1756): "this—shall I call it unlucky Volume . . . made a Writer & a Critic of H:L:P."[9]

In the *Life of Johnson*, Boswell asserts that Johnson disparaged Hester's learning in comparison with Henry Thrale's ("he has ten times her learning: he is a regular scholar"). Against this we also have from Boswell, but not in the *Life*, Johnson's reply to Hester when she declared that she would not choose to be Edmund Burke: "No, you would gain nothing but breeches." However, we need neither Boswell's nor Johnson's testimony to find out that Hester was a learned woman. We know that by age twenty-two she had four languages,

French, Italian, Spanish and Latin, and that in later life she added to them at least a smattering of Hebrew. French and Italian were conventional female accomplishments; Latin, however, was not, and she knew it well enough to translate Johnson's difficult Latin verses and the Meters of Boethius. We are further informed by Piozzi's catalogue of her library in 1806, a respectable collection of some 1,300 volumes. In that year she owned six Bibles: in French, Italian, Spanish, Latin, Hebrew, and Hebrew-Latin. She owned also the standard Latin classics, in multiple editions (including five Virgils). Of modern literature her collection was, to use her own phrase about Johnson's reading, "extensive and surprising." She knew the post-Renaissance English writers almost as well as he did, and the French writers better. Among seventeenth-century writers in her library we find Bacon, Browne, Bunyan, Burton, Butler, Camden, Thomas Fuller, James Howell, Locke, Raleigh, Selden, and William Temple; we find most of Restoration drama and virtually every poet, great and small, from Milton (three sets) to George Lyttelton. We find what would now be called a "special collection" of seventeenth-century French ana, and the complete works of Voltaire. We find three sets of Shakespeare, and we know that she could quote from memory even such peripheral plays as *King John*, for she does so in *Thraliana*. In early life she acquired the then antiquarian taste for Spenser, a taste that later extended to Chaucer and old ballads. Although she never confirmed herself in the methods of scholarship (an omission that was to prove ruinous to her career), she unquestionably possessed its appetites and indulged them in all seasons. Her later notebooks run rife with theologico-etymologico-antiquarian speculation, such as this: "possidet **A** numeros quingentos ordine recto. —from Baronius's Technical Verses. Ultima **Z** tenens, finem bis mille tenebit—& so perhaps it will; for God is indeed the Alpha & Omega the Aleph & Thau; and when the 2000 Years are out, will surely come again to judge the World— but was Baronius thinking on that?—I *fancy not.* א being a Leader, & ת a Patibulum, is however well worthy observation—Quere what Language did our Saviour converse in with St. John?" Long afterwards she wrote of her late adolescence, "My Head [was] full of Authors, Actors, Literature in ev'ry Shape."[10] Like Johnson she was saturated with books, and one could spend a lifetime tracing all her "sources."

Her first serious writings, between the ages of sixteen and

twenty, were poems. Because today she has no reputation, not even a bad one, as a poet, it has been easy for commentators to brush them aside as amateurish echoes of Pope, Milton, Gray, and half a dozen other precursors. A scrutiny informed in the evolution of young poets, however, will disclose in Hester's better attempts an active talent of large ambition. Every new poet starts as an imitator—indeed, as an "amateur," or lover—of a previous poet; the decisive question is whether the new poet becomes egotistical enough to insist on individuation, to struggle against the beloved precursor. Hester does, and she does early. In her first poems we do hear little besides a medley of other poets. One piece from 1758, "Forrester; or the old Hunter's Petition for Life addressed to Sir Thomas Salusbury," barely exists apart from the family occasion that called it forth; it opens as Gray's *Elegy* ("The setting Sun declar'd the Close of Day") and is soon in thrall to Pope's *Essay on Man* ("Tell me Philosophers why Man was made / Lord of the Wood and Tenant of the Shade?"). Another piece, however, an "Irregular Ode on the English Poets" dated New Year's day 1759, is deliberately a medley, and that is a very different thing. Explicitly it celebrates the poetical triumphs of "Britannias' Genius," illustrating them with imitations of Spenser, Shakespeare (or rather, Collins on Shakespeare), Milton, Dryden, and Pope; implicitly it is Hester's self-dedication to poetry, her own "Ode on the Poetical Character."[11]

By January 1760 she advanced to a poem as much superior to this ode as the ode is to "Forrester." It is a poem of some interest independent of its place in Hester Salusbury's career, for it is still the only English translation of an important poem by the French poet Louis Racine (1692–1763), son of the playwright and eminent in Europe for poems on religious and philosophical themes. Hester first wrote this translation probably as an exercise for Parker, but in a draft "Introduction" to it she implies an intention to publish. She anticipates criticism, parrying it in terms that are characteristically aggressive and nervous: "Another sort [of critics] . . . cries Heav'n protect me! a paltry Imitation! & y[e] best Lines in it palpably stole from Racine. However let 'em 1[st] try y[m]selves, next consider my Sex, want of School Learning, my manifest Disadvantages, in attempting a Translation never tho[t] of before, I shall then appeal to their Candour, & boldly give it y[e] Name of a free Translation."[12] A "free Translation," or "imitation," of the first of Racine's two *Épitres sur*

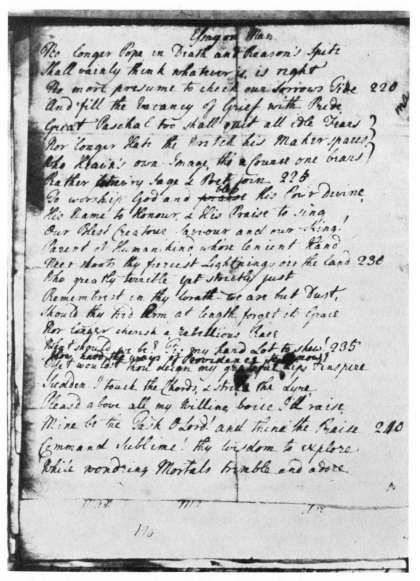

Hester Lynch Salusbury, "Essay on Man"
(Ry. 624, f41v) reproduced by courtesy of
The John Rylands University Library of Manchester.

l'homme (1747) is what this poem is explicitly; covertly it is Hester's quarrel with Pope, and the piece which sets the tone for all of her subsequent literary relationships.

In this poem the influence of Pope presides more than in any of her others: she even calls it an "Essay on Man." She opens herself to Pope, however, only to attack him, by the indirect method of making Racine appear to attack him. Racine had previously attacked Pope, but not in the poem Hester (mis)translates. In *La Religion* (1742) Racine had joined the Catholic assault on the alleged deism of Pope's *Essay on Man*, an assault provoked, as Pope complained in a letter to Racine, by unfaithful French translations of the *Essay*. Racine professed himself satisfied with Pope's explanation and publicly apologized.[13] In his two *Épitres* he resumed his attack on deism, this time taking care to disjoin it from Pope. Nevertheless, the effect of *Épitre I*, as Hester translates it, is that Racine attacks Pope once more, and employs as weapons Pope's own words.

She opens with lines which, she explains in a note, state the principles that Racine intends to refute:

> What have we lost, a mighty Genius cries,
> What would this man, and whither would he rise?
> Secure of all the Bliss that he can bear,
> Say shall he murmur at the scanty Share?
> On Nature's Throne below sublimely plac'd,
> With Pow'r, Authority, and Reason grac'd,
> While other Creatures are by Heav'n resign'd
> To Man, their Lord and Governor assign'd,
> Is Heav'n to him, and Him alone unkind?

These lines, we see, are a pastiche from Pope's *Essay on Man* (1.173, 286, 186). It is not Racine, however, but Hester Salusbury who quotes them, and it is Salusbury, not Racine, who thus interprets Pope as a fatuous optimist. Her strategy is to set him up to be blasted by the proofs of concrete human misery that Racine marshals, and that in Hester's translation are somewhat more concrete than in Racine's French. Those proofs include bad conscience:

> While rigid Reason whispers from within,
> "Can God's dread Judgments fall on ought but Sin?"

surgery:

> There See, how helpless on a noisome Bed,
> Th' unhappy Patient at his length is laid;
> See him the polish'd Instruments explore,
> Hear him the Surgeon's Cruel Hand implore
> A moment's time . . .

the lassitude that follows on our pleasures:

> In Wine we wallow, or in Love we burn,
> Till wearied out, our Inclination spent,
> They grow insipid, we indifferent;

shame, nausea, indigestion:

> The Drunkard blushes when fair Reason's Light
> Dispels the fumes of an uneasy Night;
> The Glutton too perhaps, when broken Rest
> Succeeds the Pleasures of too rich a Feast;

asthma and dropsy:

> While the proud Monarch frets beneath the Smart
> Of raging Fever and Her fiery Dart,
> Or cruel Asthma's, which alone deny
> The gasping Patient Privilege to sigh,
> Shall he by Med'cine:mocking Dropsy swell'd
> Be puff'd with Folly as with Water fill'd?[14]

Finally, she makes Racine conclude in direct rebuke:

> No longer Pope, in Death and Reason's Spite
> Shall vainly think whatever is, is right,
> No more presume to check our Sorrows Tide
> And fill the Vacancy of Grief with Pride.

This near quotation of Pope's *Essay* (1.293–94) does not occur in Racine's French, which, in fact, asserts opposite sentiments. Nor is it an innocent mistranslation, for Hester's first draft of these lines is perfectly accurate: "Let me with Paschal and with Pope agree / Man may be blest, but in a low degree." Her error is chosen, and is doubly audacious. She spurns her French original in order to steal Pope's strength; she then makes Pope pay for her theft by turning his strength against him. This turn is her hallmark as a writer; we will find her performing it again and again. Her attitude towards Pope was always to be ambivalent, like Joseph Warton's in the book that she says first inspired her to write. She delights to catch Pope copying his predecessors; she despises his authorial jealousy; she scorns his fussy perfectionism, exclaiming at the manuscript of his *Iliad*, "All Wood & Wire behind the Scenes sure enough!"; but also she faults him for technical carelessness.[15] She loves him unquestionably, but she will not allow him to win.

Also indebted to Pope, the Pope of *Windsor Forest*, is a 240-line poem in celebration of Offley Park (1761).[16] This poem, however, has a more complicated lineage, including Thomson's *The Seasons* and going back to Milton's *L'Allegro* and *Il Penseroso*, the grandparents of that major line of romantic poems that numbers, among Hester's precursors, John Dyer's *Grongar Hill* and William Collins's *Ode to Evening*, and among her successors, poems like Shelley's *Alastor* and much of early Yeats. "Offley Park" is recognizably of this company by virtue of the moves it makes, and it makes them in good health if not memorably. The power of Fancy, invoked at the opening as Milton invokes Mirth and Melancholy, conducts her through the pastoral landscape of Offley to a noontide grove, a "green Resort," where the higher power Imagination "holds his aery Court." Here she experiences a visionary moment:

> a Gleam of trembling Light
> Shot thro' the Trees, and play'd before my Sight
> Touch'd ev'ry Sense and fill'd me with Delight.

On this light she gazes "guiltless," that is, without imaginative shame. This is the most interesting word in the poem, and the best evidence of its health. The actual content of her vision is an apparition of the fifteenth-century builder of Offley, and this is rather a letdown. Still, the visionary gleam is sufficiently present in this poem to suggest that in Hester we are dealing with a potential romantic poet. In a later chapter we shall trace what became of her romanticism.

Alongside it she also had, even at this early date, the ironic or charnel-house vision. One of her earliest poems, "Moral Stanzas from Rousseau" (1758), Johnsonian without Johnson, surveys mankind not from China to Peru but from birth to death, and finds that his life is all vanity and vexation of spirit.

> Still He exists, in helpless, hopeless Age,
> Conscious of Guilt, he fears the Judgment nigh;
> Tir'd of his Part, yet loth to leave the Stage,
> Asham'd to live, and yet afraid to die.

This image of foolish, pathetic human tenacity, the veteran lagging (in Johnson's words) "superfluous . . . on the stage," hung on in Hester's imagination; sixty years later she would apply it bitterly to herself.[17]

In irony her chosen precursor was not Pope, nor even Johnson, but Swift, especially the Swift of *A Tale of a Tub* and the poems. (Her library in 1806 contained more Swift than Johnson: *A Tale*, the poems in ten volumes, the *Miscellanies* in six, *Gulliver*, and a broken set of the *Works*.) Superficially her prose appears anything but Swiftian, yet attentive reading will disclose a distinct stratum of Swift in it. In another early poem, "Pompey, or a Doggrel Epistle from Pompey in the Shades—to his Master" (1761), Swift is conspicuous. She draws her premise, that animals can speak and reason, from "The Beasts' Confession to the Priest," her satire on Descartes from *A Tale*, and her bright eyed octosyllabics from Swift's versification generally. Here she ridicules Descartes's idea that "Brutes were mere Machines":

> Automatons by secret Springs
> Made to perform surprizing Things,
> For as two Figures on a Clock
> Will play whole Days at Shuttle Cock,
> And neither of them tire—till
> The Clock goes down at maker's Will;
> So Brutes he wisely could maintain
> Knew neither Pleasure Fear nor Pain.[18]

Apparently none of these pieces was published, not even the Racine translation, which certainly merited publishing. Her first identified publications, printed in the *St. James's Chronicle* in 1762, are "an American Eclogue—imitating the Style of Fingal" (i.e., James Macpherson's prose-poem *Fingal*, 1761) and her "first Essay as a Political Writer . . . which was signed Thomas, and called . . . Memoirs of the Albion Manor." The first is less interesting for itself than for its one-sentence preface, in which, characteristically, she twits the author she is imitating: "I inclose you an *Indian* Fragment for your Chronicle, which I picked up in *North America* six Months ago, and got a Countryman of mine, a *North Briton*, to translate for me into *Fingalian Prose.*" (Macpherson, a Scot or "North Briton" in the then current euphemism, had claimed that *Fingal* was translated from an ancient oral epic.) The second piece, "Albion Manor," is a complaint against George III's unpopular prime minister, Lord Bute. It is detectably Swiftian in the homeliness of its allegory. England is Albion Manor; Bute, described as "a dirty Scotch Boy," is the new "steward," and Thomas is the faithful old steward, meanly cast off by the new "master." This reduction of politics to the level of estate management is of a piece with Swift's reduction of Church history to the adventures of three brothers. Hester's intended next step was a grand "Ode on the Blessings of Peace" to celebrate the end of the Seven Years' War (1762). As a career move this was logical; poets from Dryden's time forward had made debuts with poems on public events. In writing the "Ode" Hester had in mind the ceremonial anthems of Purcell and Handel. It was submitted to Thomas Arne "in order to be set & sung at Ranelagh for one of the grand Fêtes exhibited there in honour of the Peace."[19] Its performance, however, did not take place. Far..ily disaster intervened and appeared to blast Hester's career in the bud. She was abruptly called on to take up the real "profession of ladies."

Throughout her life Hester found, or made, herself attractive to men. Johnson nicknamed her "Rattlesnake" from the snake's supposed power of fascinating its prey, and she herself remarks, "when any Man likes me I never am surprized, for I think how should he help it? when any Man does *not* like me, I think him a Blockhead, & there's an End of the matter." As good an emblem of her life, in this respect, as her friendship with Johnson is the fact that in later years her correspondents always include at least one younger man for whom her letters are decidedly performances. At no time, however, did she enjoy male admiration—or rather, possessiveness—as at Offley Park. Not only was she her father's "Favourite" and her uncle's "Darling," but also, as an heiress, she was an object of suitors. She remembers them bitterly, as fortune-seekers for whom she was, exactly, an object, albeit a rich and rare one: "our House . . . was even *haunted* by Young Men, who made Court to the Niece, & express'd Admiration of the Horses. Eveɪy Suitor was made to understand *my* extraordinary Value—Those who could read were shewn my Verses, those who could not, were Judges of my Prowess in the Field." (Her prowess in the field was apparently always considerable, and next to books she seems to have loved riding and hunting most.) "It was my Sport to mimick some, and drive others back, in order to make D.ᵣ Collier laugh, who did not perhaps *wish* to see me give a Heart away, which he held completely in his hand." Her relationship with Collier, who in his letters was capable of addressing her as "my Dearest Angel," was comparable to Swift's with Vanessa. Worse, her father, seeing the train of suitors, grew pathologically jealous. He "was . . . so attached to me, who alone could please his very particular Temper; that the least mention of a Proposal to his Daughter put him in the most violent passion imaginable." Supplied thus with more than enough of Freud's "family romance," it is no wonder that she "used to keep clear of Solicitations to Marriage with more Assiduity than other Girls use to procure them."[20]

One suitor, a brewer in his early thirties, was introduced to Hester in 1761. Introduced, rather, to her mother: for Henry Thrale was a "Blockhead"—one man who, perversely, did not respond to Hester's charm, but only to her fortune. Her account of him, written fifty years after, still crackles with anger: "My Uncle had been to Town for a Night or Two & returned to tell us what an excellent, what an incomparable young Man he had seen—who was in short a Model of Perfection: ending his Panegyric by saying that he was a *real Sportsman.* . . . The next Day M.ᵣ Thrale follow'd his Eulogist: and applied himself so diligently to gain my Mother's Attention—Ay & her Heart too; that there was little doubt of her approving the Pretensions of so very shewy a Suitor—if Suitor he was to *me*; who certainly had not a common Share in the Compliments he paid to my Mother's Wit, Beauty & Elegance." There ensued a family quarrel in which Sir Thomas and Mrs. Salusbury leagued with Thrale, John Salusbury and Collier opposed him, and Hester, disliking him but afraid to disobey her mother and uncle, found herself belabored by everyone. The situation grew nastier still when Sir Thomas, his first wife having died, made friends with a new neighbor, a widow King. Disgusted by John's complaints and reproaches, "my Uncle . . . sought Relief from the Widow, & shewed us that our Absence would no longer . . . be a Concern to him." In this crisis Collier undertook to watch Sir Thomas's moves and report on them. His espionage, a secret between him and Hester, had an unexpectedly disastrous effect: "one Night [in December 1762] Collier having sent me a private

Letter to say my Uncle was next Sunday to go to Church with Mrs King, & I suppressing the Intelligence somewhat awkwardly perhaps, my Father charged me violently that I carried on a clandestine Correspondence with Mr Thrale, a charge I could not bear." He raged, she fought back, and the next morning John Salusbury "dropped down dead—of an Apoplexy!"[21]

Financial need now dictated to Mrs. Salusbury that Sir Thomas be appeased and Thrale secured; to those ends she exerted all her formidable energy. In hopes of escape, Hester proposed to Collier that she try to earn money by writing. His answer, however, was bluntly practical: "Dont let your aspiring ambitious spirit be allways thinking of a Garret, I think a good nine Hundred pounds a year . . . may serve you and your mother pretty well till something better falls." Miffed, either from jealousy of Thrale or because Mrs. Salusbury had told him he would no longer be needed, Collier also put an end to the Latin lessons: "As to these same Verba Substantiva I . . . would not have you plague your self any more about the matter, for they won't make one a bit younger Richer, or Handsomer, and the only women that I ever knew made much of the matter all lived to be old maids."[22]

In so writing, Collier was only, at last, disclosing the truth of Hester's position. Despite the example of his friend, Sarah Fielding, he reverts automatically to the doctrine that a woman is not to make a career of literature. Her career is to be a wife. He but repeats the lesson urged by men and women alike—for instance, by the mother of Galesia, the bookish heroine of Jane Barker's novel *A Patch-Work Screen for the Ladies*: "My dear Mother now growing aged, began to be very desirous to see me established in a married State . . . urging, That I ought not to pass my Time in idle Dreams on *Parnassus*, and foolish Romantick Flights, with *Icarus*." Instead, "said she, you [should] . . . imploy your Parts in being an obedient Wife, a discreet Governess of your Children and Servants; a friendly Assistant to your Neighbours, Friends, and Acquaintance: This being the Business for which you came into the World, and for the Neglect of this, you must give an Account when you go out of it." The same lesson is urged by James Burgh, writing on a subject, "the Peculiar Management of Daughters," intensely canvassed during the century, and canvassed generally to the same effect. Literary amusements, he writes, "are utter ruin to young women. For, if they find any entertainment in them, they must unavoidably give their minds a cast, which can never be suitable to the useful part of a female character, which is wholly domestic." The lesson is still urged by Hannah More late in the century, and is urged in the teeth of her own immensely successful writing career: "Most *men* are commonly destined to some profession, and their minds are consequently turned each to its respective object. . . . The profession of ladies, to which the bent of *their* instruction should be turned, is that of daughters, wives, mothers, and mistresses of families." Even Mary Wollstonecraft, demanding better education for women, grounds her demand on "the peculiar destination of woman," which, she agrees, is "the rearing of children." Hester, then, did not need Collier to inform her of such a commonplace; yet she had been bred to think herself an exception to it, an exception de facto like Sarah Fielding. She had been bred to such hopes by the males in her family, at least. Her mother, who had been her earliest tutor, had also nagged her not to "ruin her figure" by study.[23]

Mrs. Salusbury soon came to agreement with Thrale, and Sir Thomas delivered him a suitable marriage portion. Collier was dismissed, and with him Hester's prospects of literary society. Hester dispatched one more poem to the *St. James's Chronicle*, a wistful fable of "Imagination's Search after Happiness." The nymph Imagination seeks happiness in love, ambition, and riches, all in vain. Ambition especially proves a bubble—"But when the Phantom she embrac'd, / It vanish'd, and was gone"—and the nymph finds repose only with Piety. This is the purgatorial lesson inculcated by Johnson's *Vanity of Human Wishes*, and a promising person of twenty-two must be among the least fit to accept or teach it. The marriage took place on 11 October 1763, and Hester found herself in the Thrale house at Streatham Park, left "to conciliate as I could—a Husband who was indeed much kinder than I counted on, to a *plain Girl* who had not *one* Attraction in his Eyes: & on whom he never had thrown five Minutes of his Time away,—in any Interview unwitness'd by Company—even till *After* our Wedding Day was done!!" Thrale proved not unbearable, but his notions of a proper wife were oppressively stodgy. When Hester tried to court him with verses, he was not impressed. When she offered to join him in the hunt, she was told that "it was Masculine for Ladies to ride." Even the housewife's last resort was closed to her: "*his* Wife was not to *stink of the Kitchen*." "I soon saw that I was married from prudential Motives, as a . . . well born & educated Girl; who would be contented to dwell in the Borough, which other Women had refused to do." "The Borough" was Southwark, on the dumpy south bank of the Thames, where Thrale's town house adjoined his brewery in a street inauspiciously named Deadman's Place. There he soon took her, and there she passed the vacant days of her first pregnancy. For company she had only her mother. "I re'd to her in the Morning, played at Back Gammon with her at Noon, & worked Carpets with her in the Evening." "After my Month was up . . . I [returned] to my Occupation of daddling after her, carrying the Child with me as I had the honour of suckling it, till I became a perfect Shadow; & they were forced for very Shame to let me off that Duty. . . . It was now Time to *teach* the little Girl my Mother said, & bring her forward as She had done by me; I was reproached with want of Attention to my Daughter, & told that I had now—*or ought* to have, something to amuse me without visiting or fooling at Places of publick Resort. . . . I therefore did buckle hard to my Business, taught this poor Infant twenty pretty Tricks . . . and so my Time was employ'd."[24] Meanwhile her uncle, Sir Thomas, had indeed married Mrs. King. When he died, ten years later, he left his estate to her.

Thus, at twenty-three, Hester Thrale found herself bereft of everything that she had thought promised her. She had been trained to literary ambitions, taught to value herself for her wit, and then delivered over to the only "profession" women were allowed: pregnancy. Her memories of this experience document the rage it engendered. Yet the documentation is not explicit; we find it, rather, in the cold fury of phrases like "daddling after her" and in her furious underscorings. The object of her rage is her mother, and with excellent reason, yet she can never bring herself to say so outright. On the contrary, she is more apt to take pride in her daughterly obedience ("For true Love of one's Mother & real preference of her to all human Kind, I believe I am a singular Example") and to insist that her mother is her best friend. There is surely some food for thought in the fact that the same person who, as a poet, does not shrink from combat with Alexander Pope can behave, as a woman, with such submissiveness to her mother. Insofar as Hester Thrale remained an unrealized writer, this submission is probably the original cause. "A slavish bondage to parents," Wollstonecraft writes in a moment of Bloomian insight, "cramps every faculty of the mind. . . . This . . . may in some degree account for the weakness of women; for girls, from various causes, are more kept down by their parents, in every sense of the word, than boys." Bloom speaks of the "Covering Cherub" (the phrase is from Blake), or that internalized figure who inhibits creation.[25] Hester's Covering Cherub would seem to have been her mother.

Hester's memory of the loss centers, however, not on her mother but on her lost inheritance. She did not finally lose it, legally and materially, until her uncle's death in 1773. It thereupon became a permanent anguish to her and a standing type of disappointment. Four years after the event she could write of it that "the Wound is still open"; forty years after that, she has made it the symbol of her girlhood—she had been "a Girl without a Guinea." Reminded of a quip by Goldsmith that he had known a man disinherited merely for not loving gravy, she thinks at once, pityingly, of herself: "I loved Gravy well enough—yet I got myself disinherited."[26] Although this sounds like an assumption of responsibility, it is more in the nature of a whimper against injustice by one who feels small, weak, and victimized. She had performed, she had pleased, yet these works were of no account; their reward had been withheld.

If Hester can indeed be said to have "got herself" disinherited, it would be nearer the truth to say that she did so by loving gravy too well, by being too ready to please. It remained a dangerous habit for her, and one of which she took long to grow weary. She is always "on stage" performing for others, always canvassing their responses. The drawing room was to be one of her theaters, and the snip-snap of repartee one of her favorite roles: "We have all been reading the Mysteries of Udolpho; 'tis very horrible indeed says one, very like *Macbeth* says another: Yes truly replied H:L:P. as like as Pepper-Mint Water is to good Brandy."[27] Her attraction in later years to the actual theater is perhaps the least of her theatricalizing; she is more truly theatrical on paper, where her characteristic modes are wit and melodrama. Anecdote, in itself a quasidramatic form, in her management approximates to melodrama; *Anecdotes of Johnson*, as we shall see, derives much of its power from melodrama. Melodramatic irony is a hallmark even of Hester's punctuation. She relishes, for instance, the mordant ironic jab, often setting it up with the melodramatic long dash ("his Talk . . . fatigued his Hearers, who as he was not rich— made no Ceremony of letting him see it"). To go on the stage, however, is to court applause at the risk of receiving boos; it is a perpetual flirtation with disinheritance. For a woman writer in her time the risk of boos was high, and Hester's writing career was to end with her getting herself disinherited once again, by the public for whom she performed.

During 1764, however, she had no hope of any career, even a failed one. She appeared condemned to domestic servitude, to be the ornament and childbearer of a man who valued her accomplishments only as earmarks of a lady and preferred to spend his time with other women. Clifford reports that for the year 1764 "very little" documentary evidence exists, and concludes that the year must have been uneventful.[28] For a person as insistently verbal as Hester, a different explanation suggests itself, and a grimmer one: withdrawal into deeply wounded silence.

Mistress of Streatham

In this bondage Hester could hardly foresee that she would soon meet and grow intimate with the leading writer of the age and that his friendship would make her famous. Henry Thrale was in no way a literary man; by sheer fortuity, however, his circle included the playwright, Arthur Murphy, who in turn was a friend of Samuel Johnson. Murphy's literary tastes made him sympathetic to Mrs. Thrale's, and he conceived the inspired idea of introducing Johnson to her. Accordingly, on 9 January 1765 Hester had the remarkable experience of facing Johnson across her dinner table. They liked each other at once and became friends. Soon Johnson engaged Mrs. Thrale in literary projects. He was meditating a translation of Boethius, and together they translated the poems in the *Consolations of Philosophy*. He had promised to publish the verses of his lodger, Anna Williams, and to augment the slender Williams oeuvre he asked Mrs. Thrale for contributions. She gave him "The Three Warnings" and a translation from Boileau, which in 1766 appeared in Williams's *Miscellanies in Prose and Verse*. A reprint of "The Three Warnings" in 1770 made that poem famous. It was the first appearance of Hester's name as an author.

Moreover Johnson, deeply conversant with the strategies of anger, perceived that Hester's resentment of her situation was crippling her. "After our Acquaintance ripened into Friendship," she writes, he "began opening my Eyes to my odd kind of Life." When she complained of "Mr Thrale's cold Carriage to me," Johnson took her up at once, sharply. "He said in Reply—Why how for Heaven's Sake Dearest Madam should any Man delight in a Wife that is to him neither Use nor Ornament? He cannot talk to you about his Business, which you do not understand; nor about his Pleasures which you do not partake. . . . You divide your Time between your Mamma & your Babies, & wonder you do not by that means become agreable to your Husband." Hester made good use of this rebuke; she declared to her mother that she wanted to learn Thrale's trade. Her mother scoffed and resisted: "I had my Children to nurse & to teach, & . . . She thought that was better Employment than turning into *My Lady Mashtub*."[29] Nevertheless, this was the indispensable first step towards self-assertion—towards, in fact, growing up. Slow, hesitant, often diverted or balked, the process pushed through to its aim only with her second marriage, and then not easily. Its first effect, indeed, was painful: Mrs. Salusbury grew jealous of Johnson's influence over Hester, as she had been of Collier's before, and for some years Hester had to mediate their frequently petty contentions.

Ironically, it was Johnson's own illness that introduced large changes into Hester's stultified existence. In 1766, his long labors on Shakespeare ended, Johnson experienced emotional collapse. For weeks on end he could not rouse himself to leave his room; gloom and guilt oppressed him. He had "often lamented to us the horrible condition of his mind, which he said was nearly distracted," she writes in *Anecdotes*; "when we waited on him one morning, and heard him, in the most pathetic terms, beg the prayers of Dr. Delap, who had left him as we came in, I . . . remember my husband involuntarily lifted up one hand to shut his mouth, from provocation at hearing a man so wildly proclaim . . . what, if true, would have been so very unfit to reveal."[30] On this occasion Thrale's bluntness was exactly the right thing. He and Hester packed Johnson off to Streatham and kept him there for three months. During the next sixteen years Johnson lived as much with the Thrales as he did by himself. He was given a room in each of their houses and became virtually one of the family, a sort of adopted child.

Johnson's presence transformed the Thrale parlor and turned its mistress into a saloniere. When Thrale built a new library wing at Streatham, he commissioned Sir Joshua Reynolds to paint for it the portraits of some of Streatham's guests. These trophies included Reynolds himself, Oliver Goldsmith, David Garrick, Edmund Burke, the Italian scholar Joseph Baretti, who tutored the eldest Thrale daughter, Sir Robert Chambers, Vinerian Professor of Law at Oxford, William Henry Lyttelton, brother of the poet and peer, and Edwin Sandys, second baron Ombersley. An introduction to Streatham came to be a badge of success in one's line. So Charles Burney thought it when, his reputation secured by the first volume of his *History of Music*, he was privileged to number the Thrales among his acquaintance. And so his daughter Frances thought it when her first novel, *Evelina*, earned her an invitation. Her Streatham debut was, she wrote, "the most consequential day I have spent since my birth."[31]

To give a fresh account of the Thrale éclat is hardly necessary, so many have been written; but it is certainly pleasant. One witness is the Irish clergyman, Thomas Campbell, who visited in 1775 and found himself in the Land of Cockaigne: "The dinner was excellent, first course soups at head & foot removed by fish & a saddle of mutton—second course a fowl they called Galena—at head, & a capon—larger than some of our Irish turkeys—at foot—Third course four different sorts of Ices viz. Pineapple, Grape, rasberry & a fourth—in each remove there were I think fourteen dishes—The two first courses were served in massy plate." He was also impressed by his hostess: "She is a very learned Lady & joyns to the charms of her own sex the manly understanding of ours." The conversation over which Hester presided was, it need hardly be said, eminently literary. Fanny Burney, socially anxious and a bit flustered by it, had to keep her memory on the stretch, for "I hardly ever read, saw, or heard of any book that . . . has not been mentioned here." Streatham talk was distinguished also for easy playfulness, an elevated frivolity that bespeaks the utmost sophistication. Burney recorded much of it, to such good effect that her *Diary* remains the cornerstone of the Streatham legend. All Johnsonians have their favorite bits, such as Johnson's encouragement to Fanny in the face of an impending interview with Elizabeth Montagu: "always fly at the eagle!"; or his unexpected answer to Henry Thrale's question whether he would not buy a spit for his kitchen as well as a jack: "No, sir, no; that would be superfluous; for we shall never use it; and if a jack is seen, a spit will be presumed!"[32]

Delightful as all of this is, it represents only the public face of Hester's experience in these years, a brilliant stage performance. The contrast between it and her private sensations is almost too sharp. Privately, she pours out resentment and lamentation. "God give us a quiet Winter! My Mother's Death, no; the Uproar in the Trade & the Story in the Newspapers 1772—was the beginning of my Miseries; then came my Mother's death; then came Lucy's, then S.ᵗ Tho.ˢ Salusbury's, then the Election, then the Fall, then Ralph's Smallpox; Oh when, when, shall I ever know peace & Happiness again." "The Uproar in the Trade" was an effect of Thrale's propensity to tinker with his beer. He had been persuaded (so Hester tells us) that he could brew "without the *beggarly Elements* of Malt & Hops." In 1772, upon tasting the results of that or some other experiment his customers forsook him. Thrale sank into helpless dejection; only Hester's intervention saved the trade. She wheedled large loans, pacified mutinous employees, and convinced estranged customers by "unwearied solicitation" to put their trust in next year's beer. In this public relations work she at first took satisfaction, and from her success she drew something of a feminist inference: "Women have a manifest Advantage over Men in the doing Business; every thing smooths down before them, & to be a Female is commonly sufficient to be successful, if She has a little Spirit & a little common Sense."[33] Thrale, impressed, assigned her an upper-management position in the firm, and it may be that for eight or ten years Hester Thrale was the highest placed female executive in English business. Her pleasure in the work faded, however; she felt degraded from her rank by it, and also Thrale's lust of speculation demanded continual watching—sometimes she had to enlist the force of Johnson against him. Between them they got the trade intact through the depression years of the American Revolution, and after Thrale's death she sold it.

If the brewery story has a comic side, the history of her children is simply grim. Of twelve born eight died, a high mortality even for the eighteenth century. There were also miscarriages. For fifteen years Hester was almost constantly pregnant—the "pleasures" of her marriage, she wrote mordantly long afterwards, "consisted in holding my head over a Bason Six Months in the Year"—and this in an age when every pregnancy was potentially fatal. She has acquired some fame for this alone, a circumstance on which she would probably have made a devastating comment. (We may judge what it might have been from a comment she did make much later about the fatal lying-in of Princess Charlotte, a lying-in which lasted two days before it finally, to everyone's surprise, killed her: "Every Female must feel not only afflicted, but indignant at one Express coming here after another, telling us all how Charmingly the Business was going on—a Charming Labour truly of **48** Hours *Agony!*") The men in Hester's family showed no particular concern for her usual condition. Thrale's care was for the outcome, and while awaiting that he would amuse himself with city mistresses; Hester had the mortification, one year, of finding his escapades written up in the newspapers. Johnson was not unsympathetic, but to him pregnancy was one of the routine ills of marriage and of life, to be endured like any other. Hester fell back on private lamentation, such as this heartcry from March of 1773, during her mother's long last illness: "nobody can guess what a Winter this has been to me, & big with Child too again God help me!"[34]

Despite her anger at being degraded to maternal chores, Mrs. Thrale took some pleasure in supervising her first child's education. She began for the purpose the first of her many notebooks-cum-diaries, which seems also to have been the very first baby book ever— the "Children's Book." It opens with a "Memorandum" of Queeney's "Corporeal & Mental Powers at the Age of two Years, to wch She is arriv'd this 17: Sept: 1766." There follow details of what the children were learning; the brightest were Queeney, who at six was reading Dryden and Pope, and Harry, who at five could rattle off the Latin declensions and verbs. There are remarks on the children's characters and anecdotes of their performances.

I asked him this morning what part of Speech *ring* was? I don't know now says he whether you mean the Noun or the Verb. He reads English well enough to be pleased with the Scripture History & Pilgrims Progress—& dearly loves a *dismal* Story in the Newspapers. I set him yesterday however to Nelson's Feasts & Fasts—this says he little Ma'amey to be sure is a very good Book; all about our Saviour & the Apostles, but it is *monstrous dull Fun.* I saw a little Boy yesterday whose beauty I was admiring—Oh mighty fine says Harry, but if you set him to Decline Via, I warrant he'd not do that so prettily.[35]

This is already a highly characteristic piece of writing, little different in manner from *Anecdotes.* It is at once bookish and familiar—bookish in its subject, familiar in its diction. It is intellectual, in that it centers on speech rather than action, and witty, in that the speeches are essentially one-liners and are set up as rejoinders. It is seemingly, but not really, artless. As a mother, Mrs. Thrale is cultivating the skills of a raconteuse.

For ten years the "Children's Book" was her principal verbal occupation, the one way in which she could be both a mother and a writer. Most of the time, however, it is a painful reminder of the insufficiencies of eighteenth-century medicine. It chronicles smallpox and pustulent ear infections and worms and tin pills and futile draughts of this or that potion, and always death. "This house smells like a Hospital," she writes one day in 1774; she is talking about Streatham Park. Two of the daughters, Lucy and Anna, died of brain disorders; so did the second son, Ralph. Upon autopsy "the Brain was found almost dissolved in Water, & something amiss too in the original Conformation of the Head." Hester began to feel superstitious horror whenever a child complained of a headache and to wonder whether the deaths were a punishment. "Has the flattery of my Friends made me too proud of my own Brains? & must these poor Children suffer for my Crime?" Commentators from Joseph Baretti to Lawrence Stone have canvassed the defects of Hester's mothering; one is tempted to say that *they* did not bear twelve children and lose eight. Defects of course there undoubtedly were. She had not wanted to be a mother, and she overcompensated by being a fretful, demanding mother. She teaches the children to perform, just as she had been taught to perform; she hovers around them, teasing herself and them at every sign of indisposition. She took Queeney along on a 1774 journey to Wales, with the result that she spoiled her own pleasure in the tour. At Lichfield she is worried lest Queeney catch cold and, moreover, angry because she must worry alone: "I had many feelings for Queeney which I was forced to suppress, as I was often told how little it signified whether she catch'd cold or no." On the road to Ashbourne she is suffering in silence: "Queeney breaks my heart and my head with her cough. I am scarce able to endure it." At Ilam Gardens Queeney soaks her feet and is waked in the night by her cough; at Ashbourne again she "had a miserable night . . . and so of course had I. I sat up with her till 3." Eleven days into the tour, Hester breaks down and weeps from sheer loneliness: "'tis so melancholy a thing to have nobody one can speak to about one's clothes, or one's child, or one's health, or what comes uppermost. Nobody but *Gentlemen*, before whom one must suppress everything except the mere formalities of conversation. . . . Here my paper is blistered with tears for the loss of my companion, my fellow traveller, my Mother, my friend, my attendant . . . who now have I to chat with on the Road? who have I to tell my adventures to when I return?"[36] We can perhaps appreciate after all what Hester valued in her mother, however vexed their relationship: female intimacy, the freedom to speak of her concerns.

The climax of the "Children's Book"—if it is right to speak in literary terms of such an affliction—is the utterly unexpected death of the favorite son, Harry, at age nine. On the day before, during a family outing, he had been lively and clever, and people remarked how fine a boy he was. ("Yes said I if the dirt were scraped off him.") At ten the next morning he began to act unwell. The doctors were summoned:

> Jebb came, & gave him 1st hot Wine, then Usquebaugh, then Daffy's Elixir, so fast that it alarmed me; tho' I had no Notion of *Death* having seen him so perfectly well at 9 o'clock. . . . The Child all this while spoke well & brisk; sate upright to talk with the D^{rs} ; said he had no Pain now but his Breath was short. . . . I was however all confusion distress & perplexity, & Mr Thrale bid me not cry so, for I should look like a Hag when I went to Court next Day—he often saw Harry in the Course of the Morn^g: and apprehended no danger at all. . . . But soon a universal Shriek called us all together to Harry's Bedside, where he struggled a Moment—thrusting his Finger down his Throat to excite Vomiting, & then—turning to Nurse said very distinctly—dont Scream so—I *know* I must die.

In the "Children's Book" a few months later Hester entered a short prayer: "Let me not, Oh let me not I most earnestly beseech thee follow any more of my Offspring to the Grave." Thereafter her interest in teaching the children flagged. "I have already spent my whole Youth at it & lost my Reward at last."[37]

The "Children's Book" closes, or simply stops, in 1778. By that year another book was in progress, a book which, it is safe to say, would have secured Hester Thrale some measure of fame had she never published a word. In September 1776 her husband, in an act of uncharacteristic insight for which he deserves the blessing of posterity, presented her with six beautifully bound blank volumes entitled—the title was his, not hers—*Thraliana*. She set at once to filling them. "It is many Years," she writes in her prefatory entry, "since Doctor Samuel Johnson advised me to get a little Book, and write in it all the little Anecdotes which might come to my Knowledge, all the Observations I might make or hear; all the Verses never likely to be published, and in fine ev'ry thing which struck me at the Time. Mr Thrale has now treated me with a Repository. . . . I must endeavour to fill it with Nonsense new and old. 15: September 1776." Except for her opinion that they were nonsense, these are precisely the things with which she filled it. Although conventionally called a diary, it is not one, not at least in the manner of Boswell's and Burney's diaries. (Hester's actual diaries, for she did keep diaries, are little more than memoranda, lists of engagements, and occasional exclamations.) Insofar as *Thraliana* belongs to any definable genre, that genre is chiefly a French one, the ana. Johnson's *Dictionary* defines ana as "loose thoughts, or casual hints, dropped by eminent men, and collected by their friends." In English literature works of this kind are uncommon; as Thrale herself notes, "Selden's Table Talk [1689] and Cambden's *Remaynes* [1605] are the only *Anas* in our Language; while France swarms with them."[38] She loved the French anas, and she elected one of them as the model for her own: the *Ménagiana* (1693), or the table talk of the French philologist, Gilles Ménage (1613–92). The topics of *Ménagiana* are etymology, criticism, history, and manners; impromptu verses and gossip also found a place in it. All these topics and modes have their counterparts in *Thraliana*. Its unconnectedness and occasional outcrops of topical arrangement likewise belong to the type.

Thraliana is at once a richly public and intensely private book. It is public in being a register of anecdote and comment on everyone she knew, and is thus a gold mine for biographers of her acquaintances. (Biographers not only of Johnson but also of Charles Burney have found it invaluable.[39]) Its later volumes are public in a more deliberate way as well, for after 1789 she makes it a witness for posterity of the horrors of the times, such as the high price of food: "Thraliana has to record its Writer's eating Bread in 1801 at 2 *Shillings and* 4^d—*the Quartern Loaf.*" In this mode she aims to make of it something like the last record of an expiring civilization. "I aver the Facts," she declares, and in doing so she saves them from the general wreck of things. In old age, long after the volumes had been filled, she kept them as one would keep vital documents, "in a Tin Box for fear of Fire." Assuredly this care was well employed, for *Thraliana* is one of the best records of an expired civilization. In the range of its reference it must have few equals: "From Cato to Cuzzona," she says, "& from Cuzzona to Cumberland!" More: from Goldsmith to *Antichrist in the French Convention*, and from Johnson to Napoleon Bonaparte; from London and Streatham to Milan, and from Milan to north Wales; from Latin epigrams to the price of a shirt in 1801. *Thraliana* is virtually encyclopedic, an *omnium-gatherum* of its age. In being so it is thoroughly characteristic of its author, a woman who preferred looking out upon the world to looking inside (and who, in consequence of that preference, has often been declared "shallow"). But perhaps the very writing of *Thraliana* encouraged her to look outward, to go foraging for things to put into it. She began the first volume perhaps in a mood of obligation ("I must endeavour to fill it"), and many of her early entries, such as "Odd medical Stories," have the air of filler.[40] It took her some months to learn how to fill *Thraliana*, to distinguish between the detritus of jest-books and the truly anecdotal. It took time, and imaginative boldness, to perceive that she could put the world into *Thraliana*, that it could hold her remarks on the American war as well as a recollected bon mot of her mother's. Even more than the "Children's Book" *Thraliana* seems artless and unpremeditated, yet in truth it is much less so. Only the acquired daring of long experience, the developed feel for data, can produce an entry such as "Thraliana has to record its Writer's eating Bread . . . at 2 *Shillings and* 4[d]," and only long experience in the disjunct, crystallizing statement can produce a sentence of such authority. "Thraliana has to record"—as if *Thraliana* were the eye of History.

Thraliana is also, to adopt her remark about Pope's manuscript, the "Wood & Wire" behind her scenes, and in more than one way. It was her writing workshop, the birthplace of *Anecdotes of Johnson*, of plans for other books, and of stray sentences which ended up in other books. It is also the place, after the "Children's Book," where she talks to herself about herself and her intimates. In it she makes a room of her own, articulating sentiments not welcome in the parlor and conducting a love affair with herself. She learns to delight in her book's variety, and to delight in it as her own variety: "strange Farrago as it is of Sense, Nonsense, publick, private Follies—but chiefly my own—& *I* the little Hero." She learns to relish her own agility and stamina: "My Mind is an active whirling Mind, which few Things can stop to disturb, & if disturbed, it soon recovers its Strength & its Activity." She learns to enjoy even her faults: "I am not used to People that do not worship me, & of course grow very fastidious in my desire of Flattery." She rises, indeed, to sublime arrogance: "Miss Owen & Miss Burney asked me if I had never been in Love; with mysel.^f said I, & most passionately"—a riposte worthy of Oscar Wilde. She enters also her resentments of family and friends—of Johnson, as we shall see in a later chapter; of Charles Burney ("a narrow

Souled Goose-Cap the Man must be" for not liking his daughter to learn Latin); of Henry Thrale ("he is obliging to *nobody*; & *confers* a Favour less pleasingly than many a Man *refuses* to confer one"). As her private book, *Thraliana* gave her power; she could make it whatever she wished, and no one could interfere. Everyone knew that she kept it, and people sometimes hinted a wish to read it, but she showed it to no one. She enjoyed the power of her secret and even in old age liked to make a mystery of it, asserting from time to time that the volumes might be read by her heirs but must never be printed.[41]

During the later 1770s the contradictions between the Thrales' public and private lives grew increasingly tense. Hester attained to glittering social eminence; in 1777 she was presented at Court. More, she was taken up by Elizabeth Montagu, leader of the Bluestockings. With this circle of literary-minded women Hester had much in common: social position, connection with eminent male writers, the faith that men and women could meet as intellectual equals. Yet by temperament she was never wholly a "Blue," the difference being her sense of humor, her Welsh "craziness," and their relentless high seriousness. She despised Montagu's attachment to causes and fads and her patronage of dubious poetasters like Edward Jerningham, the "harping bard." She perhaps resented being "taken up" by Montagu at all, for her own salon at Streatham was fully the equal of Montagu's. She was inclined to prefer her own Nature to Montagu's Art: "Mrs. Montagu's Bouquet is all out of the Hothouse—mine out of the Woods & Fields & many a Weed there is in it"—a good judgment on both counts. Nevertheless, she also rated Montagu very high, giving her a score of 101 on a rating system she devised in *Thraliana*, and giving herself only 76. She was pleased to be admitted to the hothouse, and admirers of both women were impressed by their conversational performances together. "Mrs. Montagu, Mrs. Thrale, and Lord Mulgrave talked all the talk," Fanny Burney reports of one performance, "and talked it so well, no one else had a wish beyond hearing them."[42]

Montagu has a minor role in one of Hester's private writings, "Three Dialogues on the Death of Hester Lynch Thrale," composed in August 1779 in emulation of Swift's verses on his own death. In them Thrale imagines how her associates will talk of her after her death. The irony—a bitter one—is that she will be only the topic of a moment. She, however, has something to say about them, and says it by brilliant and cutting parody of their speech. Johnson is loud, passionate, and petulant, Burke smoothly self-contained, Montagu abundant of arch witticisms, William Weller Pepys a fawning ass. In the second dialogue she has a go at two of Thrale's business associates, John Cator and a timber merchant named Norman. They are hilariously coarse, almost tongue-tied:

NORMAN.

Why tis a common Saying—& common Sayings is sometimes worthy observation—that the sensiblest persons does the foolishest Things, for that good Lady did not want for Wit hah Mr. Cator.—

CATOR.

No to be sure, on the contrary was always reckoned I believe above par: and had as I have been tould read a monstrous Sight of Books—but Books will not do Sir, not do every thing I mean to say—Books my Lord Bacon says—I think it is my Lord Bacon as says—Books will never teach the use of Books. A great man . . . Bacon & made very pertinent Observations for the time he lived in, very fine Things I have heard of his'n.

Johnson, in one of his own moods of deviltry, once proposed to write "Streatham—a Farce."[43] In "Three Dialogues" Mrs. Thrale writes "Society—a Farce." At no time in her life more than in the late 1770s was she socially on stage; here she takes a brief exit to contemplate with mocking eye the performances of her fellow actors.

Her offstage life was fast unraveling. Henry Thrale never recovered from his son's death, and his grief settled into that kind of despair that unleashes all the appetites. In his flirtations he grew extravagant, wounding Hester at her own table by his open preference of a family friend, the vapid beauty, Sophia Streatfeild. He began to spend extravagantly also; he formed a megalomaniacal ambition of outbrewing all his rivals and put up obstinate resistance to Hester's and Johnson's pleas for restraint. In 1779, finding himself bound for a huge debt, he suffered the first of several strokes. From it he emerged into dogged gluttony, gorging, as Hester lamented, "apparently in Defiance of Controul";[44] there followed two years of toting him back and forth around England in quest of health and diversion. For fifteen years he had sat as member of Parliament for Southwark; as the election of 1780 approached and it became obvious that he was too ill to campaign, Hester exhausted herself canvassing the borough for him. He lost, however, and this humiliation aggravated what was, in its sullen, torpid way, a case of insanity. On 3 April 1781 he ate the dinner that killed him. His death closed the great era of Streatham and freed Hester to meet her principal crisis.

"I was selfish *once*, and *but* once in my life; and though they lost nothing by my second marriage, my friends (as one's relations are popularly called) never could be persuaded to forgive it."[45] Piozzi's retrospective comment on the act that made her scandalous is accurate if touchy. In marrying Gabriel Piozzi she did nothing more remarkable than choose a husband for herself, a perfectly reasonable proceeding for a well-to-do widow of forty. Had she been less in the public eye, the marriage might hardly have been noticed. As it was, however, she was getting the sort of coverage that movie stars and former first ladies receive today, and she made the sort of choice that is always treated as scandalous in people who get that sort of coverage. She married, it was considered, beneath her, and because she married beneath her she made the inference inescapable that she was marrying purely for love. As a musician, Gabriel Piozzi was supposed to be her social inferior; as an Italian and a Catholic, he was one of the lesser breeds without the law. Also, as an Italian he was supposed to be oversexed; this gave rise to many newspaper jokes. At the same time, as a singer he was supposed to be effeminate; this gave rise to other newspaper jokes. Hester's choice was found additionally offensive, or at least problematic, on still another ground: in choosing Piozzi, she "abandoned" Johnson. This is the controversy that Boswell streamlined into an image of mean selfishness and embalmed in the *Life of Johnson*.

Hester first met Piozzi at a party given for him in 1778 by his patron, Charles Burney. The subject of Virginia Woolf's essay "Dr. Burney's Evening Party," it is probably the most famous failed party in history. No one enjoyed it; when Piozzi sang for the guests Hester mimicked him behind his back. She met Piozzi again at Brighton in 1780 and engaged him to teach her daughter. This was a logical choice, but also, she realized to her own surprise, an emotional one. "Piozzi is become a prodigious Favourite with me; he is so intelligent a Creature, so discerning, one can't help wishing for his good Opinion: his Singing surpasses every body's for Taste, Tenderness, and true Elegance; his Hand on the Forte Piano too is so soft, so sweet, so delicate, every Tone goes to one's heart I think; and fills the Mind with Emotions one would not be without, though inconvenient enough sometimes."[46] Piozzi's temperament was refreshingly soft and warm; moreover he was deferential, and Hester, overborne by the accumulated weight of Thrale and Johnson, had every inducement to appreciate a deferential man. In short, she fell in love with him.

She did nothing even faintly improper, however, not even after Thrale was dead and she was at liberty. Instead she spent an agonized two years trying to get clear with her conscience what she had a right to do. Contrary to all reasonable expectations, she had Johnson to worry about; she had her daughters to care for, although Queeney was almost of age and all were provided for by Thrale's will; she had unlooked-for money problems of her own, which in 1782 forced her to lease Streatham and live more cheaply; and she was being harassed by marriage offers and rumors of offers. One of those rumors concerned Johnson himself; as early as 1773 Hester had been romantically connected with him in the scandal sheets, and now even people who knew them entertained a notion that they would marry. For Johnson marriage to Hester would no doubt have been convenient, but there is no evidence whatever that he thought of seeking it; to her, fidelity to Johnson appeared to mean relinquishing Piozzi, and this, at age forty, she was not willing to do.

Entries in *Thraliana* show Hester's efforts to find rational sanction for her wishes. They amount to the most sustained and impressive feminist argument that she was ever to write, for at stake was the question of taking charge of her own life and fortunes. "A Woman of passable Person, ancient Family, respectable Character, uncommon Talents, and three Thousand a Year: has a Right to think herself any Man's *equal*; & has nothing to seek but return of Affection from whatever Partner She pitches on. To marry for *Love* would therefore be rational in me, who want no Advancement of Birth or Fortune." She is here asserting her right to companionate marriage, as distinct from marriage for family interest. This is an article of what Montagu once called "philosophical blue stocking doctrine," and is a theme of contemporary feminist thinking about marriage whether conservative, as in Hester Chapone's "A Matrimonial Creed," or radical, as in Mary Wollstonecraft.[47] In marriage one seeks a friend. On the other hand, Hester's phrase "to marry for *Love*" would have met with disapproval from all these women, as smacking too much of passion and too little of reason despite her claim that to marry for love would be rational. This distinction is symptomatic of the differences between Hester and her feminist, at least Bluestocking, contemporaries: Hester is more frankly impulsive and less "controlled" than they.

By September 1782 she has virtually made up her mind, and she anticipates objections: "But I am the Guardian of five Daughters by M[r] Thrale, and must not disgrace *their* Name & Family—Was then the Man my Mother chose for me of higher Extraction than him I have chosen for myself? No.—but his Fortune was higher—I wanted Fortune *then* perhaps, do I want it *now*? Not at all." Bitterly, she sees that the real issue is her own free agency—or the sacrifice of it, this time in behalf of Queeney's social standing. Queeney, having appointed herself conservator of the family honor, was strenuously opposing her mother's remarriage. "But I am not to think about myself, I married the first Time to please my Mother, I must marry the second Time to please my Daughter—I have always sacrificed my own Choice to that of others, so I must sacrifice it again:—but why? Oh because I am a Woman of superior Understanding, & must not for the World degrade my self from my Situation in Life." "Because I am a Woman of superior Understanding": thus bitterly does Hester confront the ethic of female honor promulgated by, perhaps more than anyone else, the Bluestockings themselves. It is the ethic that permits a woman "superior Understanding" only on condition that she use it in the service of highminded propriety and the general welfare, not in her own interest. It is an ethic of sacrifice and proto-Victorian obligation. It is the ethic that kept the polymath Elizabeth Carter at home making shirts for her father and stepfamily, and made her an object of sentimental veneration for that sacrifice. It is the ethic that drove Hannah More into the heartbreaking work of charity-school supervision so that the poor might receive, not a better life, but the Gospel. It is the ethic that eventually produced the Victorian Good Woman, the "angel in the house." Hester can see no practical difference between this doctrine and the unsentimental family interest that had sold her to Henry Thrale; either way, she must sacrifice her own choice to that of others. Against it, then, she bestirs herself magnificently to remember the true liberty of a human being, and her sentiments turn Miltonic—indeed, Wollstonecraftian: "But if I *have* superior Understanding, let me at least make use of it for once; & rise to the Rank of a human Being conscious of its own power to discern Good from Ill—the person who has uniformly acted by the Will of others, has hardly that Dignity to boast."[48] In two sentences this encapsulates the essence of the *Vindication of the Rights of Woman*. It is a great epiphany, even though it marked no transformation of its writer into a consistent or theoretical feminist. (Indeed, ten years later Piozzi was to find herself among the writers whom Wollstonecraft attacks for their degrading views of women.)

It is pleasing to report that events justified her decision. Besides being sensitive, Piozzi turned out to be prudent and stable; he appears to have made a generous husband and stepfather. Unfortunately, Hester was not able to carry out her decision cleanly; she let the panic atmosphere created by Queeney overwhelm her, and in January 1783 she and Piozzi were browbeaten into renouncing their plans. He withdrew to Italy, and she into sullen self-pity. In the meanwhile she had been backing away from Johnson, for she suspected (correctly) that if he knew her intentions he would oppose them. In June, while she was living miserably at Bath, Johnson suffered a stroke; when told of it she responded vaguely, as if to a distant acquaintance. This is the sole recorded act in which she may justly be charged with unkindness to him. Five months later she was sick herself, genuinely if psychosomatically. The doctors, for once knowing the right prescription, ordered Piozzi's return, and the marriage took place at last on 23 July 1784.

One month before it she nerved herself to inform Johnson, writing in anguish and asking his approval. Her plans, she says, were "concealed only to spare us both needless pain; I could not have borne to reject that Counsel it would have killed me to take. . . . The dread of your disapprobation has given me many an anxious moment. . . . I feel as if I was acting without a parent's Consent—till you write kindly to your faithful Servt." Johnson's response was a flash of violent insult: "you are ignominiously married. . . . If you have abandoned your children and your religion, God forgive your wickedness; if you have forfeited your Fame [i.e., honor], and your country, may your folly do no further mischief." To this she wrote a spirited and dignified reply. Her most famous letter, it has much the same place in her canon that Johnson's letter to Lord Chesterfield has in his:

> Sir—I have this Morning received from You so rough a Letter, in reply to one which was both tenderly & respectfully written, that I am forced to desire the conclusion of a Correspondence

which I can bear to continue no longer. The Birth of my second Husband is not meaner than that of my first, his sentiments are not meaner, his Profession is not meaner,—and his Superiority in what he professes—acknowledged by all Mankind.—It is want of Fortune then that is *ignominious*, the Character of the Man I have chosen has no other Claim to such an Epithet. The Religion to which he has been always a zealous Adherent, will I hope teach him to forgive Insults he has not deserved—mine will I hope enable me to bear them at once with Dignity & Patience. To hear that I have forfeited my Fame is indeed the greatest Insult I ever yet received, my Fame is as unsullied as Snow, or I should think it unworthy of him who must henceforward protect it.

To this Johnson responded more gently ("whatever I can contribute to your happiness, I am very ready to repay for that kindness which soothed twenty years of a life radically wretched"), but he did not forgive her.[49] In September the Piozzis left for France; Johnson died 13 December. It thereupon became a commonplace of gossip that his life had been shortened by "Signora" Piozzi's abandoned behavior. Hester herself continued to feel guilty; the tone of *Anecdotes* is partly colored by her wish to justify her conduct to her former friends.

Among the most striking features of the universal hiss that this marriage received was its thoroughgoing literariness. People wrung their hands in the style of tragedy and romance. "How *can* she suffer herself," exclaimed Fanny Burney, "noble-minded as she is, to be thus duped by ungovernable passions!" Burney assimilates poor Hester to Mark Antony in Dryden's rewrite of *Antony and Cleopatra*: "All for Love, she thinks, & the World well Lost." Even Johnson, for all his superb skepticism about people's readiness to read life in terms of literary fictions, in his last letter to Hester had to draw a parallel between her situation and that of Mary Queen of Scots, a parallel not less melodramatic for being taken ostensibly from history. What made this sort of declamation seem inevitable was the ready availability of a stereotype in cautionary novels, the Woman Who Succumbs to Passion. Women were believed to be naturally lubricious, and it was thought necessary to inculcate by constant precept and example the importance of female self-restraint: "Resist the impulse of inclination when it runs counter to the precepts of religion and virtue," one novelist exhorts her readers. On these grounds alone the Bluestockings universally repudiated Hester. In this contest Montagu may be awarded the prize. "I respected Mrs. Thrale, & was proud of the honour she did to ye human & female character in fulfilling all ye domestick duties & cultivating her mind with whatever might adorn it. I wd give much to make every one think of her as mad. . . . If she is not considered in that light she must throw a disgrace at her Sex." It followed, of course, that if a woman could once be supposed to have "yielded," no joke and no abuse were too low for her. Hester was a virtuous woman by any, even the mundane, standards, yet for many years thereafter she had to endure being the public butt of sexual innuendoes. As for Piozzi, since he was an Italian he seemed already a figure out of Gothic fiction. On their honeymoon in Italy Hester heard from London "that Mr. Piozzi has shut me up in a convent."[50] Actually, it was he who converted to her religion. He also preferred England to Italy, and he died a solid country squire.

T W O

The Celebrated Mrs. Piozzi

*PIOZZI, HESTER LYNCH. A Lady of considerable notoriety in
the literary world. . . . She is possessed of respectable talents, and
of an education superior to what commonly falls to the lot of the
fair sex; but . . . her vanity is so conspicuous . . . as to destroy . . .
any favourable impression which her abilities, or her attainments
might make.*

*In the walks of literature the female is distinguished with rather
unwilling admiration. She who yields to a powerful impulse, and
indulges either her fancy or her wit, with difficulty escapes from
the reproach of pedantry; and is suspected to resign, for literary
distinction, much of her proper charm, that graceful modesty,
which retires from even praise itself too vehemently pronounced.*

*Oh never wish Wit to a Lady:—that is indeed Superfluous; and
will draw nothing but Envy and Malice from 18 years old to 81.
I will not however wish mine away.*[1]

THE TRADITIONAL account of
Piozzi's literary career makes it appear an accident. She was not really
a writer, the story goes; she was only a friend of Johnson who, like his
other friends after his death, had "something to say" about him and
said it as best she could. When it turned out to be popular she fancied herself a writer and went on producing books without the talent
to do so, as the bumblebee is said to fly in defiance of its anatomy.
This account is tenacious, and is often accompanied by professions
of high regard for her in every other respect. One commentator, an
eminent New Critic, allows that Piozzi was "an extraordinary woman
. . . a woman in most respects unusually gifted," but asserts that she
had no "literary imagination"; in *Anecdotes*, he continues with an
air of gaping disbelief, "we encounter Mrs. Thrale-Piozzi . . . trying

to catch her impressions and recollections in a deliberate tissue of words—Mrs. Piozzi in short trying to be a writer." We might expect a high priest of New Criticism to apply exacting standards, but these remarks are normative for most criticism of her, old or New. A reviewer of *Anecdotes* in 1786, preferring it to Boswell's *Tour of the Hebrides*, simply assumes that Boswell is a writer and that Piozzi is not; he prefers *Anecdotes* to the *Tour* precisely because she is not a writer and therefore, presumably, tells the plain truth uncontaminated by literary embellishments. A standard modern account of the Bluestockings allots a chapter of twenty-seven pages to Piozzi, or rather to Thrale, for it treats mainly her Streatham years and mentions her writings only to dismiss them; the author may be suspected not to have read them. A highly esteemed feminist critic who has written several times on Piozzi nevertheless does not know what to call her, but only what not to call her: "Whatever Mrs. Piozzi was . . . she was no poet."[2]

What is striking in all this is not the judgment that she was a bad writer, but the decision, or rather assumption, that she was not a writer. Five published books do not count; the fact that she was known to her contemporaries as a writer does not count; the fact that her books have been reprinted, even recently, does not count. We are evidently dealing not with criticism but with a prior decision that she shall not be a subject of criticism.

The decision not to criticize a writer amounts to a decision not to notice a writer. It is a canon-making decision, one of the acts of selection and omission that, repeated again and again, compose a canon of literature and its associated pantheon of authors. Northrop Frye alludes to these phenomena when he ridicules "the literary chit-chat which makes the reputations of poets boom and crash in an imaginary stock exchange."[3] But the stock exchange is not imaginary; a canon of literature is a concrete social construction and a product of concrete social conditions. The institutional worlds of book publishing, reviewing, reading, teaching, and professional criticism all play a part in selecting the literary pantheon, and so do events in domains that seem to have nothing whatever to do with literature. Even Shakespeare owes his preeminence in part to the intense Anglo-French rivalry that fought itself out in three separate wars and, on paper, in the assertions of critics on both sides of the Channel that their national literature was the best. We may ask, perhaps fancifully, whether Shakespeare would enjoy the same canonical preeminence now had Napoleon succeeded in subjugating England, or whether he would take third place to Corneille and Racine.

Less fancifully, we may enquire what our singularly male-centered canon would look like if it had evolved in conditions more favorable to the production and reception of writing by women. I mean not only the original but also the ongoing reception, the reception that, for example, continues Gibbon in the canon but not his contemporary, the once-celebrated female historian Catharine Macaulay, that keeps *The Spectator* in the canon but not *The Female Spectator*, that preserves as "representative" eighteenth-century minor verse hundreds of pieces by males and almost none by females. Piozzi's disappearance as a writer is not a special case or a mere individual failure. It is a symptom. It has less to do with her merits as a writer, whatever they are, than with her sex.

For—as Piozzi herself well knew—in the social mythology that defines sex roles, women were not supposed to appear as writers. During the Restoration and eighteenth century they did appear, in large numbers. A bibliographical recovery of them now in progress, which promises to be a major work of literary archaeology, has already identified more than 450 writers and may yield two thousand. One of those writers, Mary Scott, in the preface to her poem *The Female Advocate*, argued that their appearance ought to put a dent in the social myth: "facts have a powerful tendency to convince the understanding; and of late, Female Authors have appeared with honour, in almost every walk of literature." In the very long run Scott was right, of course; today's women writers enjoy many, at least, of the marks of institutional acceptance. That acceptance, however, is only beginning to be extended backward to their foremothers, women who had to make such careers as they could in the face of institutional belittlement. Commenting in 1789 on the female violinist, Madame Gautherot, Piozzi predicts acidly what the critics will say: "a Violin is not an Instrument for *Ladies* to manage, very likely! I remember when they said the same Thing of a *Pen*."[4]

Whether or not she predicted Madame Gautherot's reception correctly (probably she did: public performances by women, except in the theater, were deemed most unladylike), Piozzi entirely grasped the general issue. In the institutional life of literature, the critics are the gatekeepers. They enforce the community's literary norms. In the eighteenth century those norms were male, as were the critics who enforced them. The norms that appear most often to have been invoked by critics were Learning and Correctness; both were presumed to be endowments of men, not of women. The presumption had a social basis, for men were usually better educated than women. Most women who did acquire learning acquired it unsystematically and were therefore prone to employ it in technically incorrect ways; they appeared inept, and the appearance was taken as proof of natural incapacity. Writing at the turn of the eighteenth century, Anne Finch bitterly acknowledges this social truth as she salutes three male poets: "Happy you three! happy the Race of Men! / Born to inform or to correct the Pen." At the turn of the nineteenth century, a reviewer of Piozzi's world history, *Retrospection*, writes of it exactly as one who has been "born to inform or to correct the Pen." Piozzi's reputation, he alleges, "induced us to entertain favourable expectations of the present work,—however unadapted such a labour might appear to a female pen, as requiring at once infinite and exact reading. We must ingenuously confess our disappointment, as the materials are not only . . . trifling or erroneous, and the arrangement confused, but as the style is often . . . abrupt and quaint." This depreciation is conducted entirely in terms of Learning and Correctness—rather than, say, imagination or insight, which women might possibly possess. A work of history appears "unadapted to a female pen" because it demands endowments alien to the sex. The very phrase "female pen" stands virtually as a synonym for error and ignorance. One might, to be sure, tolerate it in some circumstances; in reading *Anecdotes of Johnson*, say, where the "casual . . . escapes of a female pen" are acceptable for the sake of learning about Johnson.[5]

Against this systematic critical assumption of male competence and female incompetence, women writers throughout the century struggle in various ways, all more or less awkward. They apologize, they cajole, they entreat, they argue, usually in their prefaces. Katharine Rogers reports that female playwrights from the Restoration onwards, even those whose plays are inherently indistinguishable from plays by men, nevertheless felt compelled to write prefaces arguing their ability to write plays. Anne Finch, introducing her unpublished poems, writes a preface that has become a *locus classicus* of the early female writer's resentment and despair:

> Alas! A woman that attempts the pen
> Such an intruder on the rights of men,
> Such a presumptuous Creature is esteem'd
> The fault can by no vertue be redeem'd.

The threatened quibblings of reviewers are a source of torment even to successful writers like Hannah Cowley. Feeling teased beyond endurance by them, Cowley bursts out in a prefatory "Deprecation" to her blank-verse tale "The Maid of Arragon" (1780), "I entreat the Reviewers to have compassion upon me! From the beginning of my literary progress, though I may not have been unpraised, I have been teazed with the petty bickerings of Criticism." She goes on to imagine mockingly the terms in which Learning and Correctness will amuse themselves with her newest work: " 'Had this *Lady-Writer's* reading extended to a *Translation* of the Iliad, she would have found no example of such Liberties there.' " We have seen Hester Salusbury anticipating such criticism in her preface to the unpublished "Essay on Man" ("Another sort cries Heav'n protect me! a paltry Imitation!"). Almost thirty years later, Piozzi diverts a friend with the dismal joke of "reviewing" her own edition of Johnson's letters "and imitating the Style of those I expect to abuse it." The imitation is a remarkably exact parody of that style. "The Care and Attention with which we have review'd this Work, was rather excited by our long Expectation of it, than repaid by the Instruction or Amusement it affords . . . we should do the Publick double Injury in covering much paper with Criticisme upon what the Rambler himself would call *Pages of Inanity.* . . . If our fair Editress publish'd this Correspondence to shew with how much Insipidity people famed for their Wit & their Learning might maintain a twenty Years Intercourse by Letter . . . She has succeeded admirably." In the same spirit she anticipates how the critics will handle *Retrospection.* "Tho' we have been lately accustomed to the Style of *Female* Dramatists, *Female* Wits, Female Politicians, & Female Astronomers—It has not been quite in our Practice to travel wth y^{e} *fair* Creatures thro' the *Dark* Ages . . . or follow in their Train to present Times. . . . We still Observe Ignorance in Literature confident where Knowledge is most cautious . . . Mrs Piozzi upon the Strength of a three years Tour thro' Italy . . . bursts on us in the Character of *Serene Instructress* wth regard to Religion & Politics."[6]

These mock reviews capture the tone of real reviews with great accuracy, and in doing so they tell the kind of reception a woman writer could expect. She could expect to be patronized, to be told that she was out of her depth or that she was wasting the public's time. She would be told it in a style of lofty elegance and genteel banter, a style that makes a toy of her. It is an equivocating style, so that even when the reviewer gave praise she could not be sure that the praise was sincere. An extended review of *British Synonymy*, the most favorable that it received and in many respects an unusually candid one, still plays at this supercilious game. The critic begins with a fussy, but of course accurate, censure of its title, which should in pure usage be *English Synonymy*. Having thus asserted his own superior correctness by detecting an error of Piozzi's pen, he states that a work of this kind has long been needed in English literature. "We were glad," he avers, "to see that so useful and desirable a work was undertaken in our own country by a lady of a classical education, who had spent the chief part of her life in the study of literature and in conversations with the learned." But was he really glad? The next sentence, in a moment of uncommon candor, avows a different feeling. "We could not help being a little envious and ashamed that the honour of this enterprise should have been usurped . . . by a female, . . . and who shall say that this envy may not vent itself in a little severity, in our remarks on a work which has defrauded our sex of that superiority to which it has long laid claim?" Here certainly he is telling a truth, but he is not exactly giving praise. "Defrauded" implies a deceit or sleight of hand, not merit. "Usurped" takes us back to Finch's "intruder on the rights of men" and is hardly a word of welcome. Soon the reviewer's envy, or offended sense of sexual superiority, does indeed begin to vent itself. He finds fault with Piozzi's style; he calls her "this lively female Philologist"; he employs the characteristic reviewer's trick of oily gallantry ("We have . . . been so ungallant . . . as to point out some imperfections in [the book], though the work of a lady"). His review is a patronizing evasion, which takes away with one hand what it had seemed to give with the other. It tells truths but lards them with irony; an intelligent recipient of such a review could hardly know whether she had been complimented or ridiculed. Piozzi's comment after reading all the reviews of *British Synonymy* has an air of baffled suspicion, as well it might: "the Critics are all civil for ought I see."[7]

Fundamentally these reviewers are trading in irony. Irony is their defense against the social fact that women are indeed writing, publishing, getting paid for their work, and making it difficult to ignore them. But the social mythology does not lie down and die; the institutions of literature yield sullenly to the pressure. Women writers who force or cajole recognition in their lifetimes are allowed to drop out of literature after their deaths. The institutional norms of Learning and Correctness retreat, with literature itself, from the critical reviews to the academies, and there employ again the same defenses of ridicule, irony, and patronage. At the turn of the twentieth century we find an eminent Oxford Johnsonian scholar dismissing Piozzi with condescension as a "feather-headed lady" of "easy, irresponsible charm."[8] Ridicule is still the mode of the commentary with which the present chapter opened: "Mrs. Piozzi . . . trying to be a writer." Although it is no longer socially respectable to disdain new female aspirants to literature, the foremothers of today's women writers continue to lie posthumously under the same institutional odium that made their careers difficult in the first place. As a group, those women effected a social revolution in authorship—for that, surely, is the correct word for their insurgence into print during the eighteenth century. That they still remain mostly neglected or disparaged may be taken as a symptom of ongoing resistance, a sign of how profoundly unwelcome that revolution was.

"Her Original Taste"

Piozzi's career, then, will be more adequately described as interrupted: in 1784 she resumed the career that her first marriage had stifled. She resumed it before Johnson's death, and before she had any specific thought of writing *Anecdotes*. Leaving England for Italy in September, she began a journal of her tour, the journal from which she later worked up *Observations and Reflections*. Almost from the first, this journal is a draft of a travel book; it envisions an audience (e.g., "when I have told the Things I *see*, others may if they please relate the Things they *think*"). Indeed, even before Henry Thrale's death she had made her second appearance in print under her own name—a prologue to John Delap's tragedy *The Royal Suppliants*—and she was well known as the author of "The Three Warnings." Had she remained Mrs. Thrale she would probably have continued to publish from time to time, and more frequently as her children grew up and left her more leisure. Surely, however, the first cause of the burst of activity in 1784 was her second marriage. She was happy, "Happier at this Moment," she writes in her journal on 18 September, "than I have been these Two & Twenty Years." By leaving her daughters at home in the care of a governess she had freed herself at one stroke of all that fretfulness, and she was blissfully aware of the "utter Absence of Anxiety from my present Situation."

In her journal there is a feeling of returning life and avidity to write and think. This reawakening is the theme of a poem she wrote in Florence in July 1785. It is addressed "To Wm Parsons Esqr.," one of three literary Englishmen she met in Florence—the other two were Robert Merry and Bertie Greatheed—and it credits them all with reinspiring her dormant powers:

> Thus Fancy was stagnant I honestly own,
>   But I call'd that stagnation repose.
>
> Now wak'd by my Country-men's voice once again
>   To enjoyment of pleasures long past,
> Her powers elastick the soul shall regain,
>   And recall her original taste.

The advent of Parsons, Merry, and Greatheed was as nothing, however, compared to the absence of someone else. For the first time in nineteen years Piozzi was free of the overawing presence of Johnson. In her journal she allows herself explicitly to relish one implication of this freedom: "I shall let loose . . . in this Journey the Fondness for Painting which I was forced to suppress while Dr Johnson lived with me, & ridiculed my Taste of an Art his own Imperfect Sight hindered him from enjoying."[9] Also, it is noteworthy that the day on which she declares herself happier than she has been "these Two & Twenty Years," 18 September, is Johnson's birthday.

In view of what Johnson had done for her in 1765, and considering that her first two published books make capital of him, to suggest that she felt his exit from her life as a liberation may seem to accuse her of gross ingratitude. Gratitude, however, is not the emotion that dominates the relations of writers to their precursors. More relevant are feelings of identification and rivalry. Piozzi, who remarked often and intelligently on writer-precursor relationships, knew this hard truth better than most critics. We have seen how she treated her first love, Pope, in her youthful "Essay on Man." Among the many striking *obiter dicta* scattered throughout her last book, *Retrospection*, there occurs one on literary indebtedness and its animosities that is worth quoting in extenso. She is enumerating the literary achievements of the English Renaissance—enumerating them not as isolated glories (the sentimental critic's way of enumerating them) but as powerful influences on, or rather origins of, a later literature that must borrow from them and hate them for the borrowing. Her specific instance of that borrowing-with-hatred is posterity's treatment of Francis Bacon. Here is what she says:

> As from Edmund Spenser's prolifick muse sprung almost all the English poems which we now read and quote . . . so from Lord Bacon's Essays have proceeded Spectators, Tatlers, Observers, Worlds; . . . but whilst we borrow, we, like other creditors, seek to defame our lender's wild extravagance, and find a fault where we commend a virtue—
> If parts allure thee, think how Bacon shin'd,
> The wisest, brightest, *meanest* of mankind—
> says Mr. Pope: but had the charge of bribery been proved, he would have shared it with Edward the third and Henry the fifth. . . . Bribes had been openly given to every king and every chancellor for perversion of justice, until Sir Thomas More refused them, and *he* was blamed by his own family for so doing.

She is saying, correctly, that Bacon's taking bribes was fairly normal practice in his day and not a sign of personal meanness of character. (In saying this she is correcting Pope—yet once more; she is also correcting David Hume, who in his *History of England* asserts and laments Bacon's guilt.)[10] Why, then, has this myth of Bacon's meanness persisted? It has persisted, she asserts, precisely because his influence has been enormous, and its weight is intolerable to his debtors. Like all debtors, we seek to defame our lender. Where we must commend a virtue we will be sure to find a fault.

At the very least this is a true account of Piozzi's own literary behavior, which is marked from first to last by an incessant quarrel with her precursors. Among them Johnson was by far the most massive presence she had to contend with, not only by virtue of his literary stature but also because he had been so emphatically present in her life and because she had loved him. She had loved him as a human being, and she had loved him with the powerful identifying love of pupil for instructor. While Johnson was still living she could contemplate with narcissistic pleasure "our mutual Regard . . . founded on the truest Principles[,] Religion, Virtue, & Community of Ideas. . . . He has fastened many of his own Notions so on my Mind . . . that I am not sure whether they grew there originally or no: of this I am sure, that they are the best & wisest Notions I possess; & that I love the Author of them with a firm Affection." In this identifying love she feels herself enlarged by her community with him; it is a union in which she becomes Johnson and takes on his mind. Even here, however, she also feels uneasiness: "saucy Soul! Community of Ideas with Doctor Johnson." For is not Johnson really much larger than she? Some years later she was quite blunt about it: "in . . . Doctor Johnson's [mind] mine was swallowed up and lost." To feel swallowed up and lost in another is intolerable, especially to a writer. Hester was not a person to whom self-effacement came easily; her own egoism was considerably stronger and more demanding than average. There is, therefore, a sense in which Johnson's continual presence during those years must have been unbearably oppressive to her. Indeed, she herself says it was. "While Johnson lived whatever I wrote would have been attributed to *him* & I *could* not turn Author"; and again, "I would not accept help from Doctor Johnson . . . or I should not have waited for his Death before I commenced Authour—in good Time!" These statements, defensive though they are (the second pertains to her work on *British Synonymy* and has a specifically protective intent), are nevertheless also true, emotionally and even factually. In their work on Boethius in 1765, Johnson had taken to himself the role of schoolmaster, freely revising and correcting her drafts. Her own poem "The Three Warnings," the only piece for which she was uniformly praised by her contemporaries, was often attributed to him in all but name. As late as 1798 the author of a dictionary entry on Piozzi, calling that poem "a very masterly production," insinuates that the credit for it is not all hers: "it has been strongly suspected that Dr. Johnson either wrote it, or assisted in the composition of it. . . . That it has felt his correcting hand, we have little doubt."[11] (There is no evidence whatever that the poem felt his hand.)

Hester, possessed of a capable imagination but not of Johnson's massive one, had as a writer the double task of surmounting the social obstacles faced by all women writers and the imaginative obstacles embodied in Johnson's multifarious achievement. That she succeeded at all in this, even to a small degree, argues estimable toughness and courage. Moreover she did it in the most dangerous, indeed the rashest, way possible. She pursued her own interests right into Johnson's territory, throwing herself into direct competition with him and thus inviting comparisons. Comparisons were duly made, often, of course, to her discredit. She was pilloried sometimes for being too much his disciple ("she has imbibed all his prejudices, to which she is bigotted with an invincible obstinacy") and sometimes for being too little so: "Little indeed, do the lessons and example of her austere preceptor appear to have contributed toward making her more solid or more judicious!" Comparisons are still being made. A recent account of her career regards it as a parody of Johnson's: "Having produced her own version of the Life of a Poet in the *Anecdotes*, she proceeded to become an editor in the *Letters*, a writer of travels in the *Observations and Reflections*, a dictionary maker of sorts in the *British Synonymy*, and a political pamphleteer in *Three Warnings to John Bull Before He Dies*."[12] That is, she "recapitulates," respectively, Johnson's *Lives of the Poets*, edition of Shakespeare, *Journey to the Western Islands of Scotland*, *Dictionary*, and *False Alarm*. Certainly there is something to be said for the idea that Piozzi is only a parodic afterpiece to Johnson's drama. She takes care to remind her readers that she knew him, she does frequently shelter herself behind him, and in later life she made him into a personal property and herself into his repository. The Johnson of whom she was freed in 1784 was only the man; for years thereafter she carried an internalized Johnson whom she continued to reverence and with whom she had to quarrel. The first half of her career, as I read it, is the working out of that quarrel; in the mid 1790s she took a new direction.

The major phase of her career spans the first sixteen years of her second marriage. In these years she published five books, each more ambitious than its predecessors. Having begun the journal that was designed to be, and eventually became, a travel book, she heard of Johnson's death; she then set to work on *Anecdotes*. This undertaking was guaranteed to throw her into competition with male rivals. Johnson's death, as Arthur Murphy remarked in 1792, "kept the public mind in agitation beyond all former example"; the rivalry among biographers and would-be biographers was furious. Sir John Hawkins, Johnson's executor, was known to be planning the "official" biography; Boswell beat him into print with his *Journal of a Tour to the Hebrides* (1785), offered as a specimen of his own pretensions. Published early in 1786, *Anecdotes of the Late Samuel Johnson* was already the fifth sizable memoir to appear. Like Boswell's *Tour* and for many of the same reasons, it was an instant sensation; the first edition sold so fast that by nightfall of publication day the King's librarian could not find a copy on the stalls. Whether readers were chiefly entertained or chiefly scandalized by her portrait of Johnson would be difficult to say, for they themselves hardly knew. The newspapers generally extolled it, Horace Walpole despised it, Charles Burney attacked it, and the effect, as Hannah More remarked, was that "Mrs. Piozzi's book is much in fashion." A month before the appearance of *Anecdotes*, and in anticipation of it, a London magazine began to print her poems from *The Florence Miscellany*; soon other magazines and newspapers were printing them. In July, she was herself the subject of a biographical sketch in the *European Magazine*.[13]

In Italy, meanwhile, she continued to write her travel journal. She also recalled another of her original tastes, this one a taste for theological dispute; in Milan, in August, she wrote a short treatise "somewhat upon the Plan of Abbé Fleury's historical Catechism." It expounds Church of England doctrine for the use of "Youth in general, & chiefly . . . those who travel without a Tutour," and is designed "to shew the Necessity of that Union between Religion & Morality, which Bigots & Scepticks are alike diligent to destroy." This was her response to the persistent efforts of Italian clerics to make a convert of her; apparently she made no attempt to publish it, but many of its sentiments she transfused into *British Synonymy* and *Retrospection*. In March of 1787, back in London, she set to work editing Johnson's letters; they were published a year later and met a reception as noisy as that of *Anecdotes*. For *Anecdotes* she had been paid only £150, a poor sum considering that it sold four editions; for Johnson's *Letters*, however, she received £500. Two of her own letters in the collection, one describing a regatta and one advising a young man on his marriage, proved independently popular and went on to lead lives of their own; the second became a staple item in marriage manuals in the United States. She now, through her connection with Bertie Greatheed, met Sarah Siddons and turned her eye again to writing for the theater: an epilogue to Greatheed's rather successful tragedy *The Regent* (1788), in which Siddons acted. In the following year two other theater commissions came to her, a prologue for a theater at Exmouth and an epilogue for one at Dover.[14] In 1788 she secured an entry in a biographical *Catalogue of Five Hundred Celebrated Authors of Great Britain, Now Living*.

Having employed all her Johnson memorabilia, Piozzi now returned to her travel journal and carried out her original plan for it. *Observations and Reflections made in the Course of a Journey through France, Italy and Germany*, published in June 1789, represents the peak of her career. We do not know what it earned her (she asked £525); it was, however, warmly received despite murmurs against its style. It seems, in fact, to have extorted admiration even from readers who did not generally like her. One such reader was Charles Pigott, he of the ribald jest, who hated her Johnsonian "prejudices"; he allows nevertheless that "the account of her travels . . . is enriched by accurate observations, as well as by a faithful delineation of national character, and may be reckoned her best *literary* production" (as distinct from the Johnson books, which he evidently considers something else). A subsequent travel writer, James Edward Smith, in a bibliography of travel books appended to his own account of Italy, writes a guardedly generous appreciation in which, with rare candor, he allows that the male norms of Learning and Correctness may be inappropriate to judging Piozzi's achievement.

> This publication [he writes] is too well known, and its authoress too celebrated, to need a criticism here. It is stamped with the character of genius, and few books are more full of ideas. . . . I know not whether we have a right to censure the style of this publication, or to regret that passages of the most dazzling beauty are introduced amid inaccuracies of composition, which might be taken for carelessness, were they not evidently laboured to represent ease. The whole is so peculiar, and so masterly in its own way, we have no standard to judge it by, and had better, perhaps, submit to be pleased, though we do not know exactly why.[15]

This is perceptive and serious criticism, the best that she was to receive from any contemporary. *Observations* enjoyed the additional distinction of being translated (into German, 1790).

These first three books preserved her fame throughout the 1790s. In 1798 she was noticed again, albeit hostilely, in another dictionary of living authors; in the same year a magazine of current literature requested an autobiographical memoir for a series on contemporary writers. Although her theater career had proved abortive, in 1797 she was commissioned again to write for Siddons, this time a farewell epilogue for the close of the season. She should have conquered a new field, philology, with *British Synonymy* in 1794. This work earned her £300;[16] as we have noticed, it was greeted as "useful and desirable" but also as a "usurper" of the male prerogative of arbitrating language, and it was severely criticized for lapses from stylistic decorum. Also, more to Piozzi's dismay, its conservative, John Bullish politics were warmly reprimanded even by conservative reviewers. Moved by the French Revolution, however, Piozzi had committed herself to politics, and these reprimands did not drive her back. She turned her pen to patriotic uses, the most considerable being a pamphlet, *Three Warnings to John Bull Before He Dies* (1798), published anonymously. In 1796 she undertook an enterprise of epic proportions, a general history of the Christian Era designed to show that the French Revolution was the beastly outcome of material progress and irreligion. This great book, one thousand pages in two quarto volumes, appeared in January 1801. Perhaps *Retrospection* would have been her last work regardless of its reception; it is the kind of work which leaves its author nowhere else to go. However that may be, by the time the reviews had done with it Piozzi's career was effectively finished. She had encroached one time too many on the preserve of Learning and Correctness and had done so in a way that made her an easy target for their slaughter. Although strong, *Retrospection* is eccentric and undisciplined. The reviewers ignored its strengths (indeed, probably could not see them), seized on its eccentricities, damned them as the errors of a female pen, and laughed Piozzi off the stage so loudly and abusively that in the following twenty years she made but one attempt, and that half-hearted, to send a work to press.

To a modern reader, imbued with the prejudices of "specialization" and "expertise" (Learning and Correctness in modern dress), the variety of Piozzi's undertakings might suggest only dilettantism. True, her performance is sometimes dilettantish. Nevertheless, the prevailing literary assumptions of her age justify the scope of her endeavor. We need only recall Johnson's career to understand how various a thing an eighteenth-century writing career could be. He performed as poet, translator, publisher's hack, political satirist and analyst of current events, biographer, bibliographer, critic, philologist, editor, dramatist, essayist, and travel writer; he wrote fiction, sermons, legal briefs and law lectures, and prefaces to books by other people on virtually every subject. The range of his production is at least approximated in the works of Dryden, Swift, Defoe, Fielding, Goldsmith, Boswell, and innumerable writers of second, third, or tenth rank. The eighteenth-century writer functioned more as a general rhetorician than a specialist, and in so performing Piozzi was a perfectly representative specimen of the Age of Johnson. However variously her contemporaries judged her work, however they deprecated her ambitions, they had no trouble identifying those ambitions as professional. We may therefore amend our remarks on her literary relations with Johnson. In pursuing her own interests she did recapitulate his career; however, given her interests she would have done so inevitably, for Johnson's was the normative career, at least for a male writer. Piozzi's attachments to anecdote, philology, politics, and history are the normative attachments of late eighteenth-century writing from Johnson's *Life of Richard Savage* to Boswell's *Life of Johnson*, from Johnson's *Dictionary* to Thomas Warton's *History of English Poetry*, from the *Letters of Junius* to Burke's *Letter to a Noble Lord*, from Hume's *History of England* to Gibbon's *Decline and Fall of the Roman Empire*. This was Serious Literature, or "manly" literature as it was then called—with reason, for women took very little part in its production. By taking part in its production, Piozzi was demanding to be recognized as the equal of men. She was laying claim to membership in the republic of letters on the same footing with writers like Johnson, Hume, and Burke.

In speaking of Piozzi's relations with her precursors, I have been speaking more or less in the language of Harold Bloom's studies of poetic influence. As Sandra Gilbert and Susan Gubar have observed, however, Bloom's analysis of author-precursor relationships is calculated for male literary history and relationships among texts by men.[17] Men can plausibly be said to engage in Oedipal rivalry for a mother muse, but women cannot; nor have we a neatly inverse mythology of women engaging in Electral rivalry for a father muse. (In our mythology the muse is never a father because never male.) The new male writer, Bloom's "ephebe," is born in a primal experience of identification with some beloved precursor from whom he thereafter struggles to individuate himself. Gilbert and Gubar find no counterpart to this model among female writers, no struggle of the female ephebe to distinguish herself from an originally beloved foremother. Yet, nevertheless they find Bloom's model usable, by the inspired (and very Bloomian) method of swerving from it. The female ephebe, they argue, does not resist but rather seeks a literary foremother, and seeks her in order to resist a patriarchal literary culture that would smother her with forefathers. The woman writer needs a foremother to convince herself that a woman *can* write, in the face of a male literary culture that tells her again and again that a woman cannot write. The prime anxiety experienced by the male ephebe is the anxiety of influence; the female ephebe experiences an anterior and still deeper anxiety, the anxiety of authorship (or as I prefer to call it, of competence)—the fear that she cannot write at all. In the present book we shall encounter many instances of that anxiety and its consequences in the life and work of one woman writer. Piozzi's work is indeed deeply marked by a fear of incompetence.

Yet to the Gilbert-Gubar revision of Bloom we must enter our own qualifications. Gilbert and Gubar are chiefly concerned with nineteenth-century women writers, and also with novelists and poets. Piozzi was, or at least aspired to be, a poet, but she was never a novelist, and her predilections carried her into a line of country where the female literary subculture was tenuous indeed. As we have seen in considering her earliest writings, her elected precursors are all male, and for the most part they were to remain so. Among the several reasons for this choice, one is surely the fact that she had been educated by men and had learned how to please them. She had learned to identify with male literature and to behave literarily in competitive ways. When she talks about originality, for instance, as she often does, she sounds very much like a belated male poet: like Abraham Cowley lamenting the impossibility of gathering new poetical crops from the used-up ground of old mythology, or like Sir William Davenant wishing to spurn the imitators of the imitators of Homer, or like Johnson deploring "descriptions copied from descriptions, . . . traditional imagery and hereditary similes." Catching male authors—not just Pope—in their imitations becomes one of her pastimes, which she indulges with malicious pleasure. "I have been reading Gasparo Gozzi; 'tis inconceivable how Baretti imitated that Authour in all his lighter Pieces. . . . One would have sworne . . . Baretti's Dialogues; strange, whimsical and empty as they are, might at least have escaped the Charge of Servile Imitation; but No! you may have just such Stuff in . . . Gozzi's Letters—just such!" "There is no Original Wit in the World I fancy—reading an old Play of Dryden's I found Sir Tho[s] More's famous Bon Mot appropriated—'Tis a shame really to think how full y[e] Books are of Plagiarism—I marked y[e] Place, 'tis in the Wild Gallant." Even Johnson's parallel between Dryden and Pope "is imitated," she finds, "from the famous French one between Corneille and Racine; and that from an old classical comparison between the merits of Thucydides and Herodotus . . . *Oh imitatores! Servum pecus.*" This watchfulness to spy "plagiarisms" leads her at times to what looks startlingly like archetypal criticism in the mode of Frye—as in *Retrospection*: "The aukward imitators add a story of Alexander's *bugle-horn*, which no wight but himself could wield, and might be heard sixty miles. Boyardo and Berni enjoyed this horn too; it dropt to them, but not till Robin Hood had done with it."[18] The tone of this criticism, however, is not benign like Frye's but uniformly hostile.

This malelike competitiveness and fierce imprinting on male texts would, in some contemporary schools of criticism, get Piozzi expelled from the canon of women writers. She seems vulnerable to the charge of writing in male disguise, of being false to her sex. This charge, however, is fundamentally unhistorical in that it makes no allowance for the extreme cultural difficulty, then, of writing in any but a male guise. Moreover, if pressed home it would also discanonize George Eliot and the Brontes, who in taking male names unsexed themselves (symbolically, at any rate) to a greater degree than Piozzi did.

For although she elects male precursors, Piozzi never pretends to be male; she signs her books with her own name, and, as we shall note when we come to consider her style, she fills them with female "markers" of various kinds. In *Observations and Reflections* she tells a story that perfectly exemplifies her candor about her sex. At Venice, she writes, she was denied access to a painting housed in a monastery, for "no woman could be admitted." When she complained of this afterward "every body told me it was my own fault, for I might put on men's clothes and see it whenever I pleased, as nobody then would stop, though perhaps all of them would know me." This fraud she rejects with disdain. "If such slight gratifications . . . as seeing a favourite picture, can be purchased no cheaper than by violating truth in one's own person . . . it were better surely die without having ever procured . . . such frivolous enjoyments."[19] She will not violate the truth of her sex, not because it is her sex but because it is the truth. We may draw an analogy between the painting she could not see and literature. The painting she is willing to pass up, but literature she is not. She insists on access to it, and in her own dress. She does not pretend to be a man, but she demands to do what men are doing.

Yet, just because she is a woman who does not dissemble her sex, her very quarrelsomeness takes on distinctively female import. It enters into alliance with her female anxiety of competence and becomes an outsider's attack on the hegemony of the insiders. Her eagerness to catch male authors in their copyings can thus be read as female, as a revenge she takes on men for their social priority. It is also a compensation she gives herself for her own fear of literary barrenness, a fear which, as Gilbert and Gubar remark, must beset women writers in a culture which envisions serious writing as the result of male begetting upon a female muse. If the muse is female, how can a female writer beget? Or, as one male writer bluntly put it in 1702, "what a Pox have the Women to do with the Muses?" Piozzi had serious doubts of her own creative power, or genius: "I think the highest Flight of my Genius [is] to translate a Sonnet or an Epigram—nothing can I write of myself but a Letter."[20] If she can demonstrate that men are no more original than she is, she can make a kind of equality with them. Her behavior is amenable to Bloomian description, but because she is a woman its significance is different.

At the dawn of her career Hester Salusbury had elected to work in those genres that turn outward to the world of real people and events. As Hester Piozzi she continued to take for her province the real world, and in doing so she put herself into competition not only with Johnson but with all male writers. Undertaking to work in the major prose genres of her time, she undertook to perform in the then characteristically male roles of scholar, commentator, and judge. In these genres she had very few usable foremothers. She had female predecessors, to be sure: Mary Astell, who at the end of the seventeenth century had published successfully on religion and politics; Catharine Cockburn, who in the reigns of Queen Anne and George I had published defenses of Locke; Cockburn's contemporary Elizabeth Elstob, who managed to publish an Anglo-Saxon grammar; Constantia Grierson, who in the late 1720s published editions of Terence and Tacitus; Charlotte Lennox, a Johnson protégée, whose collection of Shakespeare's sources Johnson used in his edition. But these women, and some others like them, bequeathed no example; apart from Lennox, Piozzi seems unaware that they had existed. In France there had been Anne Dacier, eminent for translating Homer; of her Piozzi was aware. Very late in her career she also finds foremothers in Queen Elizabeth and the ladies of her court. In *Retrospection* she records with pleasure that the queen translated the Greek play *Hercules Oetaeus* and that "versifications of old poets by female hands, were then coming out every day"; she also quotes with dry indignation Puttenham's dictum, "We would not have girls be too precise poets, lest . . . they become hateful to husbands who love not fantastick wives." She asserts, however, and truly, that the learned women of Elizabeth's age have been surpassed by those of her own. "Though the princesses . . . read Plato, and Roger Ascham reproached the university with the court maidens' superior erudition, Eliza Carter, and Cornelia Knight, shrink not from the comparison; nor did the learned ladies of that age leave *us*, as those of this day will leave our posterity, works of acknowledged merit as remembrancers."[21] The confidence and dignity of this prediction are those not of a follower but of a conscious forerunner. For Piozzi and her literary sisters are themselves more important forerunners than any women they could look back to, and it is one of her distinctions to have prophesied truly.

Her sisters are the Bluestocking writers, and among them one, Elizabeth Carter, was venerable enough to be taken as a foremother. Carter's translation and life of Epictetus (1758) had been phenomenally successful, earning her £1,000; at the same time, her irreproachable domesticity and personal self-effacement disarmed criticism (almost) and secured her a kind of sainthood in her own lifetime. When William Hayley presumed to include her in his patronizing *Essay on Old Maids* (1785), Piozzi attacked him for daring to name "on his polluted Page / . . . the Glory of this Age / Our venerable *Carter*." When Carter died (1806) Piozzi wrote a touching and dignified elegy on her. If any woman writer figures as her chosen precursor, Carter is the one. Very late in her career Piozzi also elects to admire and emulate the even more phenomenally successful Hannah More, whose "fine Book about young Ladies & their Education" (*Strictures on the Modern System of Female Education*, 1799) she declares "admirable—Incomparable!" She knew More, and on her private rating scale she awarded her a total of 77 points, second only to Mrs. Montagu and just ahead of herself. Although she did not like More personally, she always speaks well of her writings. Indeed, one of Piozzi's conspicuous virtues is her loyalty to her literary sisters, and to women in general, even to those she had cause to resent for their prudish response to her second marriage. The poem in which she attacks Hayley is provoked not only by his mention of Carter but by his innuendoes against the sex generally, and she retaliates on behalf of them all:

> And trust me Sir, the World suspects
> You're little favour'd of our Sex,
>   We scorn your double Meanings:

Thin Irony's transparent Cloke,
The batter'd Theme, the studied Joke,
And Literary Gleanings.

She hails the poetical debut of Helen Maria Williams as a new ornament to the sex: "How the Women do shine of late!" On hearing
that the author of an acclaimed tragedy, *De Montfort*, is a woman,
she writes enthusiastically to her friend Penelope Pennington, "I am
delighted that we know the Author of De Montfort: she must be a
fine Creature. . . . I *felt* it was a Woman's Writing, No Man makes
Female Characters *respectable . . .* they only make them *lovely*." The
immediate cause of her literary quarrel with Boswell turns on a
question of female loyalty, her loyalty to Elizabeth Montagu despite
Montagu's abysmal behavior in 1784. In his *Tour* Boswell reported
Johnson's saying that neither he nor Mrs. Thrale had been able to
read through Montagu's *Essay on Shakespeare*. Although this claim was
probably true, in *Anecdotes* Piozzi made a point of denying it.[22] By
doing that she made herself a genuine martyr to sisterhood, for Boswell's revenge, long meditated and wreaked at last in the *Life*, has
constituted a standing blight on her reputation.

Her loyalty is the more admirable because loyalty was difficult.
The Bluestockings themselves maintained it to one another only at
the cost of something like paranoia, as is evident from their way of
being disloyal to Hester when she remarried. The marriage, wrote
Hester Chapone at the time, "has given great occasion to the Enemy
to blaspheme and to triumph over the Bas Bleu Ladies."[23] This is not
said facetiously. The Blues insisted on the utmost personal decorum
in intellectual women, for the Enemy was out there waiting for a slip.
A slip would demonstrate that intellectuality was dangerous to wom-
en's virtue, to that one virtue, sexual chastity, without which no
woman could be considered a lady. Moral conservatism was the Bluestockings' necessary defense of their activity as writers; faced with a
choice between loyalty to it and loyalty to any particular woman, they
repudiated the woman. To them a woman like Mary Wollstonecraft
was beyond the pale, not simply for the vice of her radical politics but
at least as much for her sexual irregularities. Piozzi herself eventually
dropped Helen Maria Williams for the same reason.

The Bluestocking dread of unchastity is itself but a facet of the
deep malaise experienced by women who attempted the pen, malaise
that tended to alienate them from one another and from themselves.

The source of this malaise is intimated by Mary Astell in a bitter reflection on the obstacles that must be overcome by girls who aspire to education. "If, in spite of all Difficulties, Nature prevails," she writes, ". . . they are stared upon as Monsters, censur'd, envied, and every way discouraged." Monsters: The learned woman is a freak of nature, with all its implications of uncleanness and moral wrong. The latent horror of unnaturalness probably underlies a good many female professions and disclaimers—for instance, Fanny Burney's superanxious care never to "do wrong": "A fear of doing wrong has always been the leading principle of my internal guidance." In Piozzi the horror bursts out on one occasion in full panoply. She is issuing a call for reformation of public manners, needful (she believes) if England is to survive the onslaught of French republican aggression, and she quotes approvingly a male writer's assertion "that if the women increase in boldness, *that* proves the men are turning soft and womanish." Moved, at least for the moment, by this conventional bit of male sexual mythology, she launches into a savage Biblical diatribe against her own sex. "The females are engaged, enlisted as seducers to bring *us* over to these curst [republican] opinions. The first consummate evil, and the last, are to be presented us by women—Eve or Pandora! from her fatal hand, has Satan sent us the infernal present . . . restless in curiosity as then, she *now* lends her assistance to the sinful project, and forwards the growth of that great poisonous tree, the very shade of which kills all who rest in it."[24] Although this blast is directed ostensibly against the conduct of "Ladies of quality," an object also of attack by Wollstonecraft and More, still one notes that the evil for which they are blasted is "curiosity," and the tree whose growth they are forwarding appears to be as much the Tree of Knowledge as the French republican tree of liberty. Piozzi, More, and their sisters in literature are all, unfortunately for them, Christians, which means that they are conscious of being daughters of Eve, weaker vessels, sources of error and sin.

Perhaps because they cannot be certain that their ambition of knowledge is not Eve's disobedience again, they shrink from recommending themselves as models for other women. Anna Laetitia Barbauld, although a highly successful writer and a liberal in politics, nevertheless explicitly declines to endorse a proposal for a women's college: "you may think that having myself stepped out of the bonds of female reserve in becoming an author, it is with an ill grace, I offer these sentiments, but my situation has been peculiar, and I would offer no rule for others." Like More, Barbauld regards herself as an exception from the female norm and asserts that other women should obey the norm: "Men have various departments in active life; women have but one, and all women have the same. . . . It is to be a wife, a mother, a mistress of a family." Declining, again, to take part in a literary journal to be managed by women, she declares that there is no "bond of union among literary women, any more than among literary men." Indeed there is not, when writers as eminent as More and Barbauld are urging their female readers in effect to do as they say, not as they do. "A female Polemic wanders almost as far from the limits prescribed to her sex, as a female Machiavel or warlike Thalestris," writes More in a work that is itself a polemic. More herself somehow contrived to live with this contradiction, indeed to thrive on it (she died worth £30,000); she seems to have been exceptionally adept at trimming, to have known exactly how far she could go. Unlike Piozzi she maintained excellent relations with the male literary establishment; Horace Walpole for instance, who sneered at Piozzi, published More at his Strawberry Hill press. A letter from More to Walpole thanking him for that honor suggests the skills that More deployed and the purpose for which she deployed them. She flatters Walpole's aversion to Piozzi by mimicking some of Piozzi's stylistic mannerisms, and comments, "you see I stand a good chance of adopting all her pretty colloquial familiarities." She continues, modulating with the nicest tact between praise and blame: "but as I am aware that I shall never be half so knowing and so witty [as Piozzi], I do not see what right I have to pretend to be as barbarous and as vulgar. I hope, however, *you* will confess that she has great strength of intellect, if I allow that she has rather too much of the worst property of strength, which is coarseness."[25] This is very nearly the arch tone of the male reviewers and must have been perfectly calculated to Walpole's taste. At the same time, More does contrive to insinuate that Piozzi deserves greater respect than Walpole has allowed her.

Piozzi had not this degree of tact or this willingness to dissemble. Her temper, as Fanny Burney lamented, was "fearless" and "incautious," and she was all too apt to rush in where the angel in the house knew better than to tread. Lacking dependable support from her literary sisters she incautiously provoked her male contemporaries, and in the end was beaten down by them. In a moment of great strength she could predict that she and her sister writers would leave posterity "works of acknowledged merit as remembrancers." Some years later, contemplating the wreck of her own career, she no longer had that confidence. "Tho' I would not lose my own little Sprig of Laurel," she writes to her nephew, "or exchange it for Queen Proserpine's Golden Bough; I would not advise *you* to breed your Girls to Literature: *My* Happiness was almost all made by it, but it is not the *natural* Soil, whence Females are likely to find or form a permanent Felicity. . . . No Severities could make me averse to Learning; but the *very—very* little Learning I obtained, made many People averse to *me*, who I certainly never offended."[26] In a word, a bitter word, for a woman the effort is just not worth the sorrows it brings in its train.

The Two Piozzis

When she died Piozzi was half a cultural anachronism. She outlived Keats and almost Shelley, carrying into the third decade of the nineteenth century a sensibility originally formed by the writers of Queen Anne's age. With her characteristic mixture of self-mockery and defiance she declared, after reading reviews of *Retrospection*, that "*my* learning, that the people laugh at so much more justly than they *think* they do, comes chiefly from the Spectators and Tattlers." She had other instructors also. One was Swift, whose writings, we have seen, got into her blood early and stayed there. Confronted by the scientific innovations of the nineteenth century she responds as Swift had responded to the Royal Society: "Dear me! 'tis a silly thing to try to extract sunbeams from cucumbers." Also Swiftian is the disgusted reductio ad absurdum of this remark: "Knowledge increases too in a wonderful manner, but the science ends in a wonder after all. Witness the aeronauts, the galvanists, the vaccinators, and a long etcetera of philosophers who turn the flame downwards, and burning our diamonds to death, find them to be *charcoal*. Never was poor Nature so put to the *rack*, and never of course was she made to tell so many *lies*."[27]

   This bitter repudiation of experiments is a late utterance, but it is not merely an effect of irascible old age. Nor is it uttered merely in ignorance; Piozzi read extensively in natural science and shared Johnson's fondness for chemistry. Rather, it betokens her allegiance to the tenets of eighteenth-century conservative ethics, which were in turn a bequest from Renaissance ethics; the works of Milton are their classic exposition. Speaking, in one of her many marginalia, of metaphysical speculations based on science, she employs language suggestive of Raphael's counsel to Adam in book 8 of *Paradise Lost* (except that it is noticeably more strident): "*I*, H. L. Piozzi do from my Soul abhor & condemn these Studies; produced from the rotten Fruit of the old *Forbidden Tree*. We were sent hither (after Adam's Fall & Punishment,) to *till* the Earth & not *examine it*. Our Business is to *labour*—we are not properly *now* Contemplative Beings." And she continues, in terms that echo not only Milton but also Johnson, in a famous passage in his *Life of Milton*: "it certainly does appear as if good & evil were given for Rational Creatures to chuse out of—as we cannot find any thing to exercise ye reasoning Power upon [anything proper, that is; for metaphysics is improper], excepting *Good & Evil*." Still another remark recalls the cautionary satire of Pope's *Essay on Man*: "When Death of Sense has set our intellect free, we shall I suppose be better Metaphysicians—but till then, let us fear God & mind our own business."[28]

Central to these ethics are three positions which deeply dye the character of eighteenth-century writing: first, that the corruption of human nature, which is taken to be a fact, obliges us to regard human passions and motives with habitual skepticism; second, that, at the same time, nothing in the world is either so interesting or so important as human conduct; and third, that literature ought to take for its chief subject the nature and state of humanity, so that readers may be assisted to understand themselves and thus (it was hoped) to attain to virtue. Piozzi shows commitment to all these positions. Although an avid reader of Rousseau, she did not draw from his writings the increasingly popular conclusion that man is naturally disposed to goodness and is corrupted by social intercourse; on the contrary, she supposes that man is naturally disposed to egoism, cannibalism, even affected sentimentality: "I do not think there is any such Thing as *natural Pathos*: Tho' Man is a Teardropping Animal; in a Savage State none fall I believe but for *himself*—The howls of Wild Irish or Canadians for their Dead is *gross Affectation of Refinement*. They would have *eaten* them had they been hungry." She steadily resists optimistic liberal ideology as a dangerous social delusion that panders to our natural vices. "Whoever preaches against authority is sure enough to find an audience, and every pitiful fellow is pleased to hear how he is independent of priest or presbyter, bishop or king. That pastors are superfluous and magistrates unnecessary to man, wise, good, and self-sufficient, are sounds in themselves delightful.

. . . [But] man not being either wise or good, or in any sense sufficient to himself, pastors are needful, teachers to be desired, and
rulers indispensable." As evidence of this position she can point, co-
gently, to the European rape of the Americas, an episode that demonstrates to her how feeble a hold Christian civilization has obtained
over the passions even of its apostles: "Crusading and chivalry had
much refined their manners, and Christianity taught lessons, which
they learned with difficulty; but soon as a new world opened itself to
their inordinate desires, they fell upon it like untaught children on a
toy-shop—tasting, and breaking, and knocking all in pieces. Robertson and Raynal, who love the dignity of human nature, may justly
shudder, but not wonder at this fury."[29]

Robertson is William, the Scottish historian and a leading advocate of liberal ideology; he is among the writers who, as Piozzi sees it,
are hastening the decay of Christianity "by reproaching their Christian brothers everlastingly with the superiority of savage virtues, till it
has at length become the mode to find out excellence in all *but* Christians." Along with most of the articles of liberal optimism, "the superiority of savage virtues" appears to her to be the whirligig of fashion, the plaything of a culture that is tired of itself, avid for novelty,
and on the brink of lightmindedly committing suicide. Others who
are engaged in the same destructive work are the skeptical philosophers from Locke onward, and chiefly Hume; in *British Synonymy*,
under the article "Identity and Sameness," she takes a Swiftian swipe
at them for "doubting, in good time! whether they are themselves
the same persons, who, before they became philosophers, readily believed that if they set an acorn an oak would come up." Hume's ultra-
sophistication she perceives as a vicious muddying of common sense.
Like Swift, she dismisses its logic and goes instead to its motive: "such
doubts and such doubters are best despised, as some of them may
possibly have a real interest in considering their existence to be dubious, that escape may be effected from accounting for its errors and
crimes."[30]

"The mind," Johnson wrote, "can only repose on the stability
of truth," and "truth" for eighteenth-century conservative writers
means truths about what people are like and how they act. Other
sorts of truth are of distinctly subordinate interest. So, speaking of
travel books of the type represented by James Bruce's *Travels to Discover the Source of the Nile*, in which the physical landscape takes pre-
cedence of the human one, Piozzi declares she "would rather read

two Pages of Rousseau's Confessions," goes on to quote Pope—"Let Bear or Elephant be e'er so white, / The People still—the people are the Sight"—and concludes with a flourish, "the Heart of Mortal Man is my *Topography*." The same considerations guide her preferences in novels. "I myself like Smollet's Novels better than Fielding's . . . there is more Rapidity & Spirit in the Scotsman: though both of them knew the Husk of Life perfectly well—& for the Kernel—you must go to either Richardson or Rousseau." Here, and in a similar passage in *British Synonymy*, the preference is for psychology over manners, as it was with Johnson ("a man must dive into the recesses of the human heart"). Often, again like Johnson, Piozzi expresses contempt for all fiction. "The Novel Reader lives in a Dream, till waked by positive & Illprepar'd for Anguish. —but Novels have another ruinous Tendency, they destroy all Taste for other Writing . . . the Mind saturated & debauched by perpetual Fiction, ends in believing every Fact a Falsehood." Her belief was that "the Romance of real Life beats all Fable & Fiction"; "the Mysteries of Carlton House surpass those of Udolpho" is one of her more memorable bon mots.[31]

That this sentiment was sincerely held is attested by her library in 1806. Replete with books on politics, travel, science, history and religion, it contained just seven novels: *Amelia, Rasselas, Tristram Shandy*, Beckford's *Vathek*, Burney's *Cecilia*, Cornelia Knight's *Dinarbas* (1790), and *Julia* (1790) by Helen Maria Williams. The presence here of three novels by women reminds us that the novel was the one genre in which women writers were allowed not just toleration, but absolute preeminence. Piozzi's contempt for novels was therefore ipso facto contempt for the generality of female writing. Certainly it was a healthy, indeed it was a feminist contempt, for the run of those fictions displayed as heroines women of a sickly, oppressive femininity and owed their popularity to this enforcement of stereotype. Also their subject matter, the trials of love and courtship, had virtually no connection with real life. On this point Piozzi is at one with Mary Wollstonecraft, who speaks disgustedly of "the stupid novelists, who, knowing little of human nature, work up stale tales, and describe meretricious scenes, all retailed in a sentimental jargon, which equally tend to corrupt the taste, and draw the heart aside from its daily duties." In a slightly paranoid mood after the debacle of *Retrospection*, Piozzi is even inclined to regard the female novelists as her enemies: "our Novel Writers have a Right to hate *me* who set my face so against Fiction, & who have endeavoured (tho' fruitlessly) to make Truth palatable."[32] More accurately, she has a right to hate them for confirming the social myth that women's writing must be vapid fiction in which truth has no place.

Throughout these remarks we notice a concern with what books do to readers. It is a chief premise of eighteenth-century literary ethics that writing of any sort ought, in Johnson's phrase, "to enable the readers better to enjoy life, or better to endure it."[33] In the background of this belief is Milton's claim that the function of serious literature is "to allay the perturbations of the mind and set the affections in right tune." That is, one reads not for "relaxation" (a bad word in fact), but to rectify one's soul. By the same token, one writes to rectify the souls of others. One reason why Piozzi wrote about Johnson is that Johnson, as everyone realized, was a great moral subject. Rectification of soul is also the true subject of her travel book, *Observations and Reflections*. *British Synonymy* conceives of linguistic usage in moral terms, and was by no means alone in doing so. *Retrospection* is expressly designed to provide matter for its reader's moral betterment.

Such is Piozzi the conservative eighteenth-century humanist. There is, however, another and quite different Piozzi. She is continuous with the passionate Welshwoman, the fledgling visionary poet of "Offley Park," and the melodramatist. This Piozzi did not scruple to read the books that the other one decried, and to like them—Beckford's camp Oriental thriller *Vathek*, for instance: "I have been reading Vathek, 'tis a mad Book to be sure, and written by a mad Author, yet there is a Sublimity about it." During the 1790s this Piozzi took up apocalyptic politics, working her Bible backwards and forwards to prove from it that the world would soon end; she read avidly in the extremist literature of the day and contributed to it herself. Against her own skeptical judgment she believed all the Gothic horrors related of the French National Assembly by its enemies. She not only believes, she repeats them, writing her own contribution to what is in effect Gothic fiction: "Authentic annals of the French Convention surpass all weak imaginative sallies of our confined ideas of their guilt. Where Satan's standard beaming . . . from the famed palace of great Lucifer attracts the astonished eyes of frighted Europe,—or where his hierophants in horrid cells howl the dark orgies of their mystic union . . . *There* might we learn, that all the acts we tremble at the bare recital of, are seriously approved by the Parisian legislature." Twenty years after this, referring in one grand gesture to British working class agitation, the manners of the age, and perhaps the assassination of Spencer Percival in 1812, she can summon up a visionary canvas of splendid horrors: "The Times *do* exhibit a frightful ForeGround—a black and Cloudy Offskip: Figures dancing a la Ronde, and Folly jingling Bells to put them more and more out of Time. . . . Female Cricketers make Room for Female Reformers, who will give Place to Poissardes: and a bad Day it will be for quiet Folk when Assassination becomes a Duty in the Daemons sworne to destroy us. . . . Girls, skipping in Ropes, & tumbling in Trowsers . . . What can it end in?"[34]

This Piozzi is in fact a romantic. She read *Werther*; she read "Monk" Lewis; she adored Sir Walter Scott and followed with avid if critical attention the career of Byron, thus concurring with two-thirds of Goethe's judgment that Scott, Moore, and Byron were the "literary heroes" of the age. Her comments on Byron are frequent, tolerant, and astute. Here is one, a splendid piece of criticism: "Lord Byron either knows, or affects to know (as if by Experience) the Horrors of unrepented Guilt; I . . . *suppose* 'tis mere Poetical Feeling— The fine Phrenzy &c. . . . His Taste leads him to *shock* his Readers, & leave an acrid Bitter in their Minds. If that Fellow had been permitted Access to the Tree of Life, he would only have chewed the Rind of its Fruit I fancy; unless the *Kernel* had perhaps yielded his *favorite Flavour*." Finally, she read *Frankenstein*, taking it as seriously as it should be taken and letting it set in motion all the contradictions of her sensibility. "I have never seen such an audacious, and I might add, such an ingenious, piece of impiety." "She confessed to me," Edward Mangin recalled, "that her objections were mostly founded on the . . . vast power which the novel exercised over her mind. She felt provoked on perceiving herself fascinated by a fiction, so wild, so bold, and improbable."[35]

Piozzi was alert to these contradictions in her sensibility and sometimes made play with them in the manner of Yeats's Self and Anti-Self. In a set of six dialogues she wrote in 1791 the speakers are "Una" and "Duessa," Una being Truth and Duessa specious falsehood. Between them Piozzi divides herself, putting into Una's mouth her humane and generous sentiments and into Duessa's her propensity for sarcastic "croaking." In a poem of 1808 she divides her sensibility between a female and a male who speak for Britain and for "Classic Taste" respectively. He swears constancy to "Schiller's Muse" and she to "Walter Scott, / Of Bardic Blood without a Blot;" but the poem ends by suggesting that Classic Taste and Britain break these vows and reunite with each other. It is not that Piozzi changed with the times, being humanist with the humanists and romantic with the romantics. Rather, she was a native of that half century that literary historians have never been able to pin down, calling it the Age of Johnson when they are thinking of its prose and the Age of Sensibility when they are thinking of its verse, and not describing it very well with either phrase. Her contemporaries included, after all, not only Gibbon but also William Blake. Her contradictions are representative of that age, and are themselves well represented by a notebook passage from 1814, in which she traces the history of her literary taste.

> How right is Doctor Young in his *Conjectures [on Original Composition]* . . . when he says originality is the only Thing for making sudden & powerful Impression. . . . This is so true, that I remember when Ossian's Poems first came out; I, who had never read any but the then fashionable Didactic Verses of Pope [,] Addison & the old Queen Anne School—was half frantic with admiration—& never till Walter Scott founded as it were a *new* Academy in Literature, *again* felt that Enthusiasm which Novelty alone can inspire. The Byromania succeeded . . . but I am not sure *any* of these Worthies—will like Pope, Addison, Swift & Young last their Century out, and become *Classical*.[36]

THREE

The Gods Had Made Her Poetical

Her "Three Warnings" have long been enshrined, and held
in universal admiration as a specimen of the precocity of her
talents; on graver subjects, those who knew her best will say
she most excelled.[1]

POETRY WAS Hester Salusbury's
earliest aspiration, and poems among the first things she published;
the last known publications of Hester Piozzi, in 1806, were poems.
Among her unpublished writings we find poems first, last, and
throughout. The corpus runs to some 465 pieces, of which she published in newspapers, in Anna Williams's *Miscellanies,* in *The Florence
Miscellany,* and in her five books less than a hundred. One of these,
however, was enough to earn her a substantial contemporary reputation as a poet. Whatever they say of her other writings—often, indeed, when they dismiss her other writings—her contemporaries always extol "The Three Warnings." Even Boswell, in the *Life* itself,
could not "with-hold from Mrs. Thrale the praise of being the authour of that admirable poem." Thomas Tyers called it "highly interesting and serious," affirmed that it "come[s] home to every body's
breast and bosom," and declared that "the gods had made her poetical." Its publication history suggests that "The Three Warnings" enjoyed that rare kind of success, circulation among all classes of readers from the literati to the barely literate.[2] *The Florence Miscellany,* a
more sophisticated production, was duly noticed by such sophisti-
cates as Horace Walpole; what is more telling is that every one of
Piozzi's contributions to it found its way into a London magazine or
newspaper, often in multiple printings.[3]

In the years of her fame she undoubtedly could have published
a volume of her verse. Yet she did not, and she seems never to have
thought of trying. Instead she hoped for publication at the hands of
her heir and executor. In 1810 she compiled a collection of "Poems

on several Occasions" to give to her nephew John Salusbury Piozzi with the hint that he might "think fit to publish" it after her death; later she asked Sir James Fellowes to choose from *Thraliana* such verses as he might think worthy of print.[4] Her hope was misplaced. When Fellowes attempted to execute her wish, Salusbury, whose aversion to literature his aunt had often bemoaned, locked up her papers and threatened with lawsuits any who sought to print them. During the first 120 years after her death, about ninety poems trickled into print from other people's collections; the scope of Piozzi's efforts in verse did not become public, however, until *Thraliana* was published in 1942, and by then her reputation as the author of "The Three Warnings" had faded. Although by no means complete, *Thraliana* is the nearest thing we have to the collected verse of Hester Piozzi. But *Thraliana*'s other attractions, principally its Johnsonian ones, elbowed the verse aside; she was by then so entirely a fixture in the Johnson Legend that her own writings seemed irrelevant. The poems are there, some 175 of them, but today she has no reputation as a poet.

In part this is a story of self-defeat, but it is not an untypical one for a woman poet of her century or even the next. Anne Finch, now reckoned the most considerable woman poet of the Augustan Age, left half of her poems in manuscript, to be published at last only in 1903; the most considerable of all women poets, Emily Dickinson, published virtually nothing. Gilbert and Gubar have remarked a tendency among woman poets to self-effacement. Yet eighteenth-century women poets, even those who published to contemporary acclaim, have in any case fared badly with posterity; had Piozzi published her volume, would she have been better remembered? Her contemporaries Anna Seward, More, and Barbauld were eminent as poets, yet today Seward is known for her sobriquet ("the Swan of Lichfield") and her acquaintance with Johnson rather than for her verse, More for her Sunday school work and her moral polemics, and Barbauld, if at all, chiefly for the quaintness of her married name. Going farther back we find Anne Killigrew, now known not for her poems but for Dryden's ode in praise of them, and Katherine Philips, long celebrated as "the matchless Orinda" and now forgotten. These women, and others still less known, have fared so badly with posterity that in the mid nineteenth century Elizabeth Barrett Browning could ask, "where are the poetesses?" and lament, "I look everywhere for grandmothers and see none."[5]

Piozzi's own comments on the pieces she sedulously copied and recopied tell all too plainly why she withheld them. She suffered from a debilitating sense of poetic inferiority. Her routine epithets for her verses are "trash" and "nonsense"; at times she subjects them to abuse that is embarrassing to read. "This trifling—perhaps meaner still than trifling Performance brought Tears into the Eyes of My Uncle." "Pope made *good* Verses at 12 years old, & Cowley better still; but how, or why should I at any Age write equal to Pope or Cowley." Unhappily, a good many remarks of this type deface the pages of *Thraliana* and "Poems on several Occasions." On the second of them Patricia Meyer Spacks has provided a feminist gloss: "The missing but implied term in [it] . . . is 'since I am only a woman.'" In poetry, being female has carried a special burden of anxiety. Gilbert and Gubar assemble an impressive array of remarks by male poets from Lord Rochester to Roethke, all tending to assert that poetry is a peculiarly male gift. Because poetry is the special domain of the muse, in it female anxieties of impotence would hold *a fortiori*. It was of poetry in particular that Mrs. Thrale lamented her lack of originality: "This is I think the highest Flight of my Genius, to translate a Sonnet or an Epigram—nothing can I write of myself but a Letter." If being female caused her to doubt her poetic competence, it also disposed her to expect less of herself. In *Thraliana*, thinking of poems by her contemporaries Erasmus Darwin and Edward Jerningham, she observes that "Writers now seem emulously desirous to *bend their Eye*, & that of their Readers—*on Vacancy*. . . . At present if all the Epithets are compounded, & the Periods elegantly arranged, it appears that all Meaning is needless, and Thought superfluous." Good criticism this, but she makes an equivocal application of it. "This Fashion makes well for us Women however, as Learning no longer forms any part of the Entertainment expected from Poetry—Ladies have therefore as good a Chance as People regularly bred to Science in Times when *fire-eyed Fancy* is said to be the only requisite of a Popular Poet."[6] This is less the seizing of an opportunity than the admission of a defeat. It takes the deliquescence of poetry for women to hope to be poets.

This self-denigration is to be deplored not only because Piozzi would probably have written stronger poems had she been free of it but also because its constant, nudging presence in the pages of *Thraliana* contaminates our impression of what she did write. The majority of her poems are indeed translations of sonnets and epigrams; poetry is the form in which she is least original. Some of them, however, are highly ambitious, albeit uneven in quality. In its total shape her canon resembles Johnson's; like his it includes a verse drama, a core of longish serious poems, several theater pieces, and a large penumbra of impromptus and jeux d'esprit. She worked in almost every eighteenth-century verse genre: the ode, essay, epistle, pastoral, locodescriptive poem, fable, satire, song, epitaph, and inscription. A selection of her poems printed apart, as she wished, would surely restore her to her lost rank among the minor poets, and unquestionably the best of them deserve inclusion in any comprehensive anthology of eighteenth-century poetry. Or of women's poetry: she survived till 1883 in anthologies of female poets, and she ought to be reinstated in the next such anthology.

Technique and Occasion

In verse, even more than in prose, there are two Piozzis, and they cannot be distinguished by period for they exist concurrently. Hester Salusbury wrote romantic poems in the line of vision, of which the best is "Offley Park," and an antiromantic poem in the mode of Johnson ("Imagination's Search after Happiness"), a mode which presupposes the romantic mode—indeed requires it, to fight against. She also wrote ironic and didactic poems, poems of argument and Popean rhetoric, much the best of them being her "Essay on Man." These two strains correspond to the two speakers in her late poem "Imitations," the woman who loves Scott and the male who is called "Classic Taste." In being thus in effect two poets she has precursors of course, notably Edward Young, whose work she highly esteemed. The Young who wrote Horatian satire, *The Love of Fame,* is bewilderingly unlike the author of *Night Thoughts,* with its blank verse and patches of graveyard Gothic, and of *Conjectures on Original Composition,* which virtually repudiates the entire system of "Classic Taste" within which the Horatian Young had written.

Much of Piozzi is also written within that system, a system of rhetorical proprieties and generic expectations. In that system, poems are distinguished more or less precisely by their purposes, their subjects, their size, their diction, and their versification. The poet is expected to know which diction and versification suit which subjects and purposes, for the aim of the poem is to provide its reader a certain sort of emotional experience. The poet is a rhetorician, a contriver of effects. Piozzi is working within this system when she remarks in *Thraliana* that "Triple Time in Musick has to my Ear an Effect like eight Syllable Rhyme in Poetry—adding Grace to light Compositions, but taking away Majesty from Sublimer Thoughts. —Parnell's Night piece on Death should have been in longer Measure."[7] She distinguishes as a matter of course between light and "Sublimer" compositions, each of which, she assumes, aims at a different sort of effect: the one at "Grace," the other at "Majesty." She assumes that different poetic means are needed to achieve these different effects, and her experience of reading verse tells her, as it does most readers, that octosyllabic couplets do not tend to produce majestic effects, although they are excellent for verse that is to move rapidly or easily. At first sight her objection to Parnell's octosyllabic "Night Piece" might appear to be based on the merely trite notion that a poem about death ought to be majestic, but it is subtler than that. She loved octosyllabic couplets; they are the prevailing measure of "The Three Warnings," which may be said to be about death. That poem, however, is a comic tale, and her choice of meter suits it perfectly. Parnell's "Night Piece" is quite a different matter, a graveyard horrors affair complete with charnel house, ravens, and "hollow groans." It is supposed to inspire awe.

Because different occasions are presumed to call for different styles of utterance, there is in a sense no such thing as "Piozzi's" poetic style. So long as she operates within the conventions of "Classic Taste" she is under no pressure to individuate herself in that way. The Hester Thrale who in a chatty anapestic epistle to her husband (1776) writes these lines:

> I ask'd of their Butler and heard he was nice,
> Possessing no Virtue, if charg'd with no Vice;
> Not an Englishman strong, nor an Irishman bony,
> But a Man half a Miss, a perfum'd Macaroni . . .

is not the Hester Salusbury who in the 1762 "Ode on the Blessings of Peace" wrote these lines:

> Beneath the Solemn Shade of some Old Oak,
> By Shepherds blythe, and Reapers long rever'd,
> . . . .
> There sat some rural Swains;

Who pleas'd to find their glowing Toil complete
Resolv'd to hymn the bounteous Hand that gave
Under fair Plenty's Name . . .[8]

not because Thrale has matured or otherwise changed, but because
the two poems are of utterly different kinds. The anapestic epistle is
a comic form, which swept the beau monde after 1766 when Christopher Anstey published *The New Bath Guide*, a series of verse letters
supposed to be written by gaping visitors to Bath and surveying with
mock naivete the follies of Bath tourism. In this genre locutions like
"nice," "bony," "a Man half a Miss," and the slang word "Macaroni"
are all felicitous; "glowing" in the "Ode" would here be "sweaty." The
"Ode" on the other hand, being designed to celebrate a great public
event, takes a lofty tone; since its occasion is a peace, the specific
idiom is heroic pastoral. "Glowing" is here correct; so are locutions
like "rever'd," "resolv'd," and "bounteous." With the syntactical inversions in both poems, discrimination becomes finer. In the "Ode,"
"Shepherds blythe" is straight heroic; in the epistle, with its pointedly
realistic context (an inquiry about a butler), "Englishman strong" is
mock-heroic. We no doubt prefer the epistle to the ode, but in each
case Hester performs appropriately.

A corollary of this concern with genre was a high degree of
craftsmanly attention to verse technique, regarded as interesting in
itself. Thus we find Hester recording in *Thraliana*, "This was the
first Time I ever tried my Skill at an Epitaph." (Cf. Johnson's remark to David Garrick: "An Epitaph is no easy thing.") Entering an
experiment in triolet, a French form, she notes its occasion and sizes
up the result: "we had been talking of Triolets the Night before, &
whether they would do well in English—they certainly do not well
at all." Many occasions of verse making recorded in *Thraliana* belong as much to the anecdotal as to the poetic, on the principle that
they exhibit a person's mental powers; they are instances of *sprezzatura*, or that trained mental readiness which can perform with impromptu virtuosity. It was as demonstrations of sprezzatura that Hester most consistently approved her own verses: "We had been talking
of the French rondeaux one day, and *both* doctors [Johnson and Burney] said they were impracticable in English, so I made *this*—Musa
loquitur."[9]

On this, at least, she rated herself justly. Virtuoso technique, em-

ployed as if impromptu, is one of her true poetic gifts. She is espe-
cially fond of the comic stunt of ringing changes on a single rhyme.
In English verse the best known achievement of this kind is probably
Johnson's poem to her on her thirty-fifth birthday:

Oft in danger yet alive
We are come to thirtyfive;
Long may better years arrive,
Better years than thirty five.

It continues through eighteen lines, a rondo on one note. Johnson's
feat is amusing, but it remained for Piozzi to demonstrate the expressive possibilities of this seemingly limited form. Her lines to her second husband on their anniversary (1803) show how a technical fa-
cility originally cultivated for sheer fun can be made to accommodate
substantial feeling. They are comedy hovering just on the edge of
something else:

Accept my Love this honest Lay
Upon your Twentieth Wedding Day:
I little hop'd our Lives would stay
To hail the Twentieth Wedding Day.
If you're grown Gouty—I grown Gray
Upon our Twentieth Wedding Day—
Tis no great Wonder;—Friends must say
"Why tis their Twentieth Wedding Day."
Perhaps there's few feel less Decay
Upon a Twentieth Wedding day:
And many of those who used to pay
Their Court upon our Wedding Day,
Have melted off, and died away
Before our Twentieth Wedding Day.
Those Places too, which once so gay,
Bore Witness to our Wedding Day;
Florence and Milan blythe as May
Marauding French have made their Prey.
The World itself's in no good Way,
On this our Twentieth Wedding Day.
If then—of Gratitude one Ray
Illuminates our Wedding Day,

Think midst the Wars and wild Affray
That rage around this Wedding day,
What Mercy 'tis—we are spar'd to say
We have seen our Twentieth Wedding-day.

In Johnson the preposterously copious rhymes are most of the show, and are meant to be; having recited them to her he bade Mrs. Thrale remark "what it is to come for poetry to a Dictionary-maker; you may observe that the rhymes run in alphabetical order exactly."[10] Reading her poem, one feels at once that the rhymes have an important place in its emotional scheme. Their air of light virtuosity softens painful ideas (gout, old age, the Napoleonic ravaging of Italy), and these ideas in turn subdue the comedy inherent in this kind of rhyme to a sort of wistful good humor. The result, of course, is no longer an instance of mere sprezzatura; such a touching effect, however, could not have been attained except by cultivation of technique.

As we see from this poem, the sense of occasion in eighteenth-century verse extends right into daily life. Where we send greeting cards, eighteenth-century people composed a song or an epigram. *Thraliana* abounds in such productions, the work not only of Piozzi but also of her friends. In writing them one performed not as a professional poet (whatever one's gifts) but simply as a sensitive human being prepared to perceive every experience as some kind of occasion and to honor it accordingly. No event is too trivial or meaningless or unpoetical to go unmarked by verse. The fall of an ash tree at Offley Park in 1760 elicits from Hester a long commemorative poem in which the death of the tree is made to correspond with the death of its mistress, her uncle's first wife; a visit to Leasowes, the estate of the poet William Shenstone, she marks by writing verses to the memory of Shenstone in imitation of his manner; the launching in 1785 of an air balloon prompts a sonnet; she makes lines for the opening of a newly repaired church; the death of a relative's horse calls forth an epitaph, and that of a dog evokes an elegy.[11]

Not only events, but things and places receive their due; they are dignified, and moralized, by inscriptions. Sundials were favorite places for such verses, for, like clocks, they evoked very clear moral meanings. When her husband planted a weeping willow next to their sundial one November, Piozzi could not resist the invitation to symbolize such an interesting juxtaposition:

Mark how the Weeping Willow stands
　　Near the recording Stone;
It seems to blame our Idle Hands
　　And Mourn the Moments flown.

Thus Conscience holds the fancy fast,
　　With Fears too oft affected;
Pretending to lament the past,
　　The present still neglected.

Yet shall this swift-improving Plant
　　With spring her Leaves resume;
Nor let the Example She can grant
　　Depend on Winter's Gloom:

Loiter no more then near the Tree,
　　Nor on the Dial gaze;
If but an Hour is given to thee
　　Act right while yet it stays.

In several ways this piece perfectly typifies eighteenth-century poetry, both minor and major. It is attached to an occasion and a place;
the reader is presumed there on the spot, looking at the objects the
verses point to. Further, the lines make no pretense to be original.
They are meant to be monitory, not revelatory. They but set forth
the implications that any morally alert observer of the scene would
be expected to draw; their chief symbols are presumed to speak a
universal language. Again, the poem exhibits what James Sutherland has called a "ratiocinative manner."[12] That is, its action consists
of reasoning, of making explicit analogies and deriving appropriate
conclusions from them; it has the air of a syllogism. And finally, it is
directed at the reader with the aim of ethically affecting him. He is
asked to remember the shortness of life, and to act accordingly.

Poetic Affinities

In the only other extended comment on her poetry to date, Piozzi
has been censured for narrowness of taste. Pope, it is alleged, "remained the most conspicuous influence on her verse." Pope certainly

was an influence; in her "Essay on Man" we have seen her both appropriate and resist him. That poem, however, is the climax of her relations with Pope. Thereafter, as a poet although not as a reader, she is essentially finished with him. One exception, a poem brought to light by Clifford, is occasionally cited as her best piece and submitted in evidence of her supposed lifelong enthrallment to Pope. In 1788 she began (but apparently did not finish) a satire in the manner of Pope's *Epistle to Dr. Arbuthnot.* Its immediate object was John Wolcot, who under the name Peter Pindar wrote lampoons on public figures including her, but she retaliates also against other detractors:

> Each full:filled Enemy, each Traytor Friend,
> Recounts his Pow'rs to hurt and to Offend;
> And skill'd of Wit and Sense to stop the Growth,
> One churns the Venom, and one spits the Froth.
> Now Pigmy Coleman speeds his feeble Dart,
> Now merry Boswell—hopes it in her heart;
> Baretti begs the *Murderous Style* to guide,
> And pliant Burney bows from Side to Side.[13]

She is trying for Pope's large anger and devastating portraiture; in some lines, such as the last, she achieves it. The very fact that the poem is unfinished, however, suggests that Pope's way was no longer fundamentally her own. This is not a typical Piozzi poem.

For Pope was but one of many influences on her; her taste, like the taste of her contemporaries, is eclectic. She at various times professes admiration of William Cowper, James Beattie, Thomson, John Hawkesworth, and Soame Jenyns (even, once, pointedly setting Jenyns above Pope: "Pope never crack'd the Kernel of Life, & tasted with more poignancy the Bitter Core—than did Soame Jenyns in those pungent Verses," *The Modern Fine Lady*). In her practice she is chameleonlike, trying different manners as different models impinge upon her. We thus hear echoes variously of William Collins, of Spenser, of Milton as we have seen; a whole strain of her verse, as we have also seen, derives from Swift (and ultimately, through him, from Samuel Butler); no sooner had Macpherson's *Fingal* been published than she was imitating it. An "Ode to a Robin Redbreast" (1763) was remarked by Johnson to be "much in Lord Lyttelton's Style. a good one [he added, smiling]—for a *Lady*." A political fable called "A Tale for the Times" (1778) she wrote in a "wild irregular Measure" that might be mistaken for an attempt at Pindaric

Ode, save that she says she "learnt it in Vanbrugh's Esop," a stage comedy.[14]

Another appreciable strain in Piozzi derives not from Literature at all but from popular literature. In this she again resembles Swift, but she derives from popular forms directly, not through him. A set of political verses takes the form and manner of a child's alphabet— "*A* was an Alderman, factious and proud" (1769). A tub-thumping performance against the French revolutionaries (1794) was written, she says, as "a Parody or Imitation" of John Newbery's *Chapter of Kings*, a rhymed succession of English monarchs intended to teach children history. This piece, eerily suggestive of Peter Weiss's *Marat/Sade*, accumulates gritty power through its nine stanzas, each ending with the same refrain; it is in fact a dance of death, or mock celebration of that Grim Reaper the newly invented guillotine:

> Now Hebert who hunted his King to Death,
> Resigns at the Scaffold his guilty Breath;
> And the Wretches who joyn'd to accuse the Queen
> Have all bow'd their Necks at the Guillotine.
> > For with all their Pother
> > Of this, that and t'other
> They all lose their Heads in their turn.[15]

Popular literature is the mode of her most famous and popular poem. To illustrate the proposition that people cling more stubbornly and irrationally to life the more aged and decayed they are she tells a tale of Farmer Dobson, to whom Death promises three warnings before his final summons. When Death at last visits him Dobson indignantly denies having been warned, but the ensuing dialogue compels him to learn that he has been warned indeed:

> I know, cries Death, that at the best,
> I seldom am a welcome guest;
> But don't be captious, friend, at least:
> I little thought you'd still be able
> To stump about your farm and stable;
> Your years have run to a great length,
> I wish you joy tho' of your strength.
> > Hold, says the Farmer, not so fast,
> > I have been lame these four years past.
> And no great wonder, Death replies,

However you still keep your eyes,
And sure to see one's loves and friends,
For legs and arms would make amends.
   Perhaps, says Dobson, so it might,
But latterly I've lost my sight.
   This is a shocking story, faith,
Yet there's some comfort still, says Death;
Each strives your sadness to amuse,
I warrant you hear all the news.
   There's none, cries he, and if there were,
I'm grown so deaf I could not hear.
   Nay then, the spectre stern rejoin'd,
These are unjustifiable yearnings;
If you are lame, and deaf, and blind,
   You've had your three sufficient Warnings.
So come along, no more we'll part,
He said, and touch'd him with his dart.

The popularity of this piece is easy to understand. For one thing its topic, the propensity of human nature strenuously to misinterpret its real condition, is the prime topic of eighteenth-century satire. Again, the age loved sermons and moral admonitions, whether straight or comic. Finally, the poem's meter is nearly irresistible. All in all it is a rare kind of tour de force, a composition by a learned writer that has the air of being a folk tale—complete with the archetypal folk number, three, and in Farmer Dobson an archetypal folk character, the would-be sharp dealer who talks himself into defeat. It is something of a shock to find that the poem's opening couplet, "The tree of deepest root is found / Least willing still to quit the ground," came to her from Euripides by way of Louis Racine, one smells so little Literature anywhere in this piece.[16] That the poem was ever supposed Johnson's ought perhaps to be taken as a compliment to him, however misplaced; he could not have written it.

Her real poetic relations with Johnson are both well known and badly understood. Well known are the relatively insignificant Boethius translations done with him and her translations from his Latin. Their fame gives the misleading impression that in poetry she was simply his apprentice. Not sufficiently understood is the actual impact of his imagination on hers, its effect on her romanticism. Ignorance here stems from the fact that the principal relevant document—and for better or worse, her most ambitious poem—has never been published. We may approach this troubled ground by way of her translations, of which the better known is her rendering of Johnson's "In Theatro" (1771), first printed in *Anecdotes*. In it she departs from Johnson's Latin, most importantly by addressing her version unmistakably to Johnson himself. This makes it at once a compliment and rebuke to him—and makes him a type of Milton's *Il Penseroso*, the poet-magus of "the lonely tower." Little accustomed though we may be to regarding Johnson as a link in the chain that runs from Milton's Solitary through Wordsworth's and Shelley's to Yeats's, Thrale perceives him as that kind of figure. He is out of place in a theater, for he is superior to common life.

> When threescore years have chill'd thee quite,
> Still can theatric scenes delight?
> Ill suits this place with learned wight,
>   May Bates or Coulson cry.
> The scholar's pride can Brent disarm?
> His heart can soft Guadagni warm?
> Or scenes with sweet delusion charm
>   The climacteric eye?
> The social club, the lonely tower,
> Far better suit thy midnight hour;
> Let each according to his power
>   In worth or wisdom shine!
> And while play pleases idle boys,
> And wanton mirth fond youth employs,
> To fix the soul, and free from toys,
>   That useful task be thine.[17]

Her version of Johnson's lines to Dr. Lawrence written when his eye was inflamed hews closer to the original, being a more deliberate attempt to emulate his style. Its first line, "Condemn'd to shun bright Sol's reviving ray," echoes the first line of Johnson's "On the Death of Dr. Robert Levet," "Condemn'd to hope's delusive mine"; in both cases the powerful and thoroughly Johnsonian word is "condemn'd." Later Piozzi picks up images from his *Dictionary* preface:

> Others, all glowing with Promethean fire,
> Strain their strong pow'rs to search and to enquire;

Hunt parent Nature to her last recess,
Force her retreats, and rend her sacred dress.

This recalls Johnson's defeated ambition, described in the preface, to "enter and ransack" "the obscure recesses of northern learning" and "to pierce deep into every science." This ambition is an instance of the doomed Promethean or Faustian quest that is central to Johnson's imagination. For Johnson, as Piozzi understood, was a romantic, even a fierce romantic in the mode of Shelley's *Alastor*. "To rest below his own aim is incident to every one whose fancy is active, and whose views are comprehensive," Johnson laments, again in the preface, "nor is any man satisfied with himself because he has done much, but because he can conceive little."[18] That is, only little minds can be satisfied; great ones always strain at the limits of possibility. Johnson, however, was a romantic who fought his own romanticism tooth and nail, insisting that every imaginative ambition must be defeated in reality and that "every one whose fancy is active" must, exactly, submit to "*rest* below his own aim." In a sense, the whole of Johnson's literary effort is devoted to compelling our acquiescence in this necessary defeat.

Among his contributions to Anna Williams's *Miscellanies*, and thus written at the time when he and Mrs. Thrale were new friends, is a female version of *Rasselas* called "The Fountains: A Fairy Tale." Its heroine, Floretta, is granted the power not only of having her wishes but of retracting them, too; to realize a wish she drinks at one fountain, and to retract it drinks at another. Everything she wishes for—beauty, a faithful lover, independence of spirit, wealth, genius— she eventually repents of, in the manner of *The Vanity of Human Wishes*; everything, that is, but genius, with which she cannot bear to part even though it renders her unable to endure the visits and chitchat that constitute a woman's daily life, sets her at odds with her companions, and makes her "an enemy to society." (A telling phrase; Johnson understood the position of women very well.) Floretta next wishes immortality; however, it is granted to her in exactly the same way that it is to the Struldbruggs in *Gulliver's Travels*. Finally, therefore, she asks for death and is released "to the course of Nature." This is Johnson's characteristic antiromance of defeated ambition, and it would be that regardless of Floretta's sex. For a woman reader, however, her sex gives it an extra poignance. Hester always identified with Floretta, believing that Johnson had modeled the character on her. In one of her supposed letters to him, dated 1782, she hints resentment of his doing so. "The newspapers would spoil my few comforts . . . if they could; but you tell me that's only because I have the reputation . . . of being a *wit* forsooth: and you remember *poor Floretta* who was teized into wishing away her spirit, her beauty, her fortune, and at last even her life, never could bear the bitter water which was to have washed away her wit; which she resolved to keep with all its consequences."[19] Hester writes as if Johnson had ascribed her troubles to her wit, implying that she had only herself to blame for them.

This is the bitter meaning that Piozzi takes from "The Fountains" in her own version of it, a dramatic poem called "The Two Fountains" (1790). If she wrote a major poem "The Two Fountains" is it—unfortunately, for her conception was confused and her execution is, at best, spotty. In her own comments on the poem she seems not to understand what she is doing. "I am writing for the Stage a Dramatic Trifle from poor Dr Johnson's Floretta: will it be liked I wonder?" She hopes the distinctions of the piece will be its "pleasing Sentiments & neat Expression; supported by Morality, & decorated with Showy Scenes," but also wonders uneasily, "Is that good Taste or bad?"[20] For many reasons it is impossible to imagine "The Two Fountains" surviving even one stage performance. Its expression is hardly "neat"; it does indeed offer "Showy Scenes," but they are irrelevant to the real issues in it; and the morality that ostensibly supports it is in fact its death. These comments are so consistently off the mark that they may be suspected of willful blindness. Piozzi perhaps did not wish to understand what she was really doing in "The Two Fountains," for what she was doing was too painful, rebellious, and dangerous. She was telling her own story, albeit slantwise.

The poem assumes the premise of Johnson's tale and dwells on Floretta's wish for a faithful lover. In its trappings and incidentals it is much more overtly romantic than Johnson, having a thirteenth-century setting, knights, ladies, fairies, and one or two quite fine fairy songs in the mode of *A Midsummer Night's Dream*. (Bishop Percy, after reading "The Two Fountains," declared "You have catered here for my Tooth exactly" and swore the fairies were "the best since Shakespeare's.") At the outset Floretta is consciously a being apart, and everything is done to mark her alienation from her fellows. Her birth has been "outlandish," or foreign; she has been bred "in a distant Climate"; she was "born an Orphan," her father having died.

Like a later romantic poet, the Shelley of "Mont Blanc," she has seen the Alps, and they have taught her to scorn lesser imaginings: "Had you but seen them Friend! These petty Scars / Rough to your present Sight would seem as nothing." The friend to whom she speaks is Gunhilda, a loyal, timid, "feminine" woman who makes most of her appearances being passively carried around by strong men; Floretta, by contrast, is fearless. Also, she is known to court solitude, to wander in the woods; she does this to visit Lilinet, her fairy godmother and the keeper of the fountains. She is on such an errand at the poem's opening, her quest this time being for "a Lover to my Taste . . . Unlike these Lords by which I live surrounded / Rude and unletter'd as their Vassal Hinds." She is about to reveal her secret to Gunhilda when an alarm of bandits is raised; Gunhilda urges flight, but Floretta stays, knowing herself invulnerable:

> Their Fears affect not me: where Fancy reigns
> She reigns despotic, and Reality
> Hov'ring aloof, hangs o'er the sightless Confines
> Of her wide Empire. My most strange Connexion
> With preternatural Beings steels my Heart
> Against all common Passions—Fear or Love.[21]

Thus does she "muse"—to adapt a line from "Mont Blanc"—"on [her] own separate fantasy." Later, contemplating the happy marriage of another character in the poem, Floretta disdains it in language that is startlingly Shelleyan:

> She now seems Happy;—Vulgar Nature *is* so;
> Refinement only, preying on herself
> Finds the wide Pool of Life oer laid with Scum,
> And terms Tranquillity—Stagnation.

These strong lines, by far the strongest in the poem, are the most deliberately romantic that Hester ever wrote. Their romanticism is that of the remorselessly impatient Poet in *Alastor*, whose heart is also steeled "against all common Passions" and who, in his pursuit of transcendence, may well be said to find "the wide Pool of Life oer laid with Scum." (The pool is in fact a central Shelleyan image.) Putting them into the mouth of Floretta, Piozzi in effect appropriates them to herself, and that they fit her is clear from the very fact of their strength. We thus come momentarily face to face with a Hester Piozzi who might have been, a poet of fierce romantic solipsism, even

a demonic poet in Yeats's antisocial sense of the demonic. For that is
the whole point about Floretta. She is antisocial, or rather not social-
ized; she lives not by female decorum but by her own sublimely arrogant fantasy. That is why she is strong. We do, once in a while, encounter this haughty, remorseless version of Hester Piozzi elsewhere:
in her wonderfully egotistical reply, when asked by Fanny Burney (a
Gunhilda figure) if she had ever been in love—"with myself . . . &
most passionately"; or again, in a late letter to her nephew, where she
reflects on broken friendships in terms surprisingly cold for a lonely
widow of seventy-two. "When Connections are once broken, 'tis a
foolish Thing to splice and mend; They never can (at least with *me*)
unite again as before. Life is not long enough for *Darning* torne
Friendships. . . . A new Dress can be better *depended* upon."[22] We observe here also her utter scorn of the "feminine" arts, darning, thrift,
and even peacemaking.

The ostensible aim of "The Two Fountains," however, like the
real aim of Johnson's tale, is to discredit this strong posture, and
Floretta is not allowed to hold it. It is genuinely dangerous, of course,
as well as strong. (Even Shelley does not exactly recommend *Alastor*
for our imitation.) The denouement of her poem shows us one of its
dangers, and in doing so takes us back almost thirty years in Hester's
life, to the family romance of Offley Park. For the man whom Floretta prepares to choose as the "Lover to [her] Taste" turns out to
be her stepfather, her mother's second husband; her wishes have,
indeed "against all common Passions," led her straight to incest.
(We will remember that Hester wrote of her father that she alone
"could please his very particular Temper.") Meanwhile the King of
the Fairies, Oberon, has learned of Floretta's fairy "Connexion" and
resolves to put an end to it as an irregular practice that allows her
altogether too much power. In the 1810 text Oberon here explicitly
plays the part of Johnson; he quotes *The Vanity of Human Wishes.*
Ostensibly Floretta, like Johnson's Floretta, is any mortal regardless
of sex. De facto, however, she is a woman, and her fate is a woman's
fate: she must surrender her freedom, give up the man of her choice
(he is married off to Gunhilda—a fine stroke of unconscious irony),
and marry a man she does not want. Oberon therefore also plays the
part of Mrs. Salusbury and even, in a way, of Henry Thrale. In effect,
he is a compound of them and Johnson, and ultimately a figure of
patriarchal authority itself: "Tyrant of Faery:Land," Lilinet significantly calls him. His function is to crop Floretta's imagination and

make a "responsible" adult woman of her. Floretta is accordingly brought to heel, accepts her loss like the dutiful daughter Hester had been in 1763, and utterly renounces her romanticism:

> I've led . . .
> A Life of much Indulgence: Solitude
> Has been my Choice; and thence arising—Scruples
> Combin'd with Visionary Phantasms
> Have oft perplex'd my Peace:—That Folly's over;
> 'Tis Time at length to muse no more; but live:
> Quit for Reality the Realm of Shadows,
> And step with Confidence from Truth to Truth.
> > Social Duty best can bind,
> > To its proper Path the Mind;
> > Wildest Wishes must comply,
> > Bound by Duty's vigorous Tye.

Even her renunciation speech is still strong, but the jingle at the end is a most lame and impotent conclusion. It lies on the same dead level with Hester Salusbury's lame letter to an aunt announcing her dreaded forthcoming nuptials: "His [Thrale's] real & grateful Regard for Her [Mrs. Salusbury] is no small proof of His Understanding—nor ought lightly to be esteem'd by me. I somehow can add no more."[23]

The condition of being a strong writer is attained by selfishness, the uncompromising demand that one's wishes be granted. Floretta's "choice," and Hester's in 1763, both produce, as they must, weak writing. They are, of course, the choice characteristically imposed on women, the enforced preference of duty to wishes. Virginia Woolf wrote therefore, with perfect logic, that before women can write they must "kill" the internalized feminine ideal, "the Angel in the House."[24] They must cease to be "obedient" and "good" and self-sacrificing. Piozzi had it in her to be a greater poet than she was— certainly she was no Gunhilda, even at her weakest—and she might have become one had she enjoyed the kind of support that women like George Eliot and Woolf enjoyed, the support of men who did not insist on Duty first. Her misfortune was to be beset instead by Thrale and Johnson; and Johnson, with his massive ratification of imaginative self-denial, perhaps represented the greater of the two misfortunes. This at least is suggested by "The Two Fountains," a poem that deserves, for the sake of the heart mysteries it touches on, to be better than it is.

Unlike Floretta, however, Piozzi never perfectly renounced her romanticism. Like Johnson himself, she went on struggling with it. Every one of her serious longer poems after middle life is a romantic poem of some sort. At Naples in 1786 she is moved to write "Irregular Stanzas," as Shelley was thirty-two years later. They open with an invocation of Parthenope, the Siren, "whose magic force" half seduces Wisdom itself, continue, in the mode not of Shelley but of Milton's *L'Allegro*, with a catalogue of the various imaginative pleasures presented by the earthly paradise of Naples, and close by repudiating them all in the name of Eternity:

> Let us who view the varying scene,
> And tread th' instructive paths between,
> See famish'd Time his fav'rite sons devour,
> Fix'd for an age—then swallow'd in an hour;
> . . . .
> Till, spite of pleasure, fear, or pain,
> Eternity's firm coast we gain,
> Whence looking back with alter'd eye,
> These fleeting phantoms we'll descry,
> And find alike the song and theme
> Was but—an empty, airy dream.[25]

It is certainly within the purview of some kinds of romanticism to repudiate the earthly paradise in favor of eternity, but when one repudiates "the song" as well, one repudiates poetry and imagination themselves.

The programmatic (and unconvincing) reversal that ends the stanzas at Naples is common enough in Piozzi's romantic poems, but at times it gives place to a more genuine vacillation that accommodates something from each side of her temperament. In 1795 she went into pastoral retreat, settling among the squirarchy of northern Wales, and her letters thereafter are full of praise for the landscapes one could see from her estate, Brynbella. But they also repeatedly ask for the London news, and she took care to spend several months of the year at Bath. This division is neatly enacted by a pair of poems (1804) celebrating the joys of sea-bathing at Prestatyn. The first is serious, and it essays description of "savage Nature's wild Sublime":

> Where Rocks in dreary Grandeur rise
> Whose hanging Summits throw
> A Mass of Shadow from the Skies
> Upon the Main below.

But although inanimate nature at Prestatyn is sublime, human nature there is repulsive. The peasantry, "by Squallid Poverty deprest," "untaught & slow / Lye torpid in their Clay." These repulsions notwithstanding, however, she closes in favor of "rude" Prestatyn; it is the place to which she will withdraw whenever "Society again . . . Shall twist me in her sev'n-fold Chain." The companion poem repeats these themes and vacillations in the idiom of comedy, if not of downright slapstick:

> She who thro Dirt and Wet can wade
> Without or Clog or Patten,
> May share the Fate of many a Maid
> That lives at poor Prestatyn.

By its style alone, this poem mocks the romanticism of the first. Its sentiments, pragmatically considered, are the same, but its language is loudly that of quotidian society—"Bond Street Beaux" and "Belles in Silk and Sattin."[26]

Perhaps because Piozzi is habituated as a poet to denying the power of imagination, she turns out in some few instances to be an impressively moving poet of old age. Among her strongest achievements in verse is an old-age poem, "A Winter in Wales" (1807). It is recognizably a romantic crisis lyric in the mode of Coleridge's "Dejection." Harold Bloom has proposed that these lyrics move through three stages. "These are: first, an initial vision of loss or crisis, centering on a question of renewal or imaginative survival; second, a despairing or reductive answer to the question, in which the mind's power, however great, seems inadequate to overcome the obstacles both of language and of the universe of death, of outer sense; third, a more hopeful or at least ongoing answer, however qualified by recognitions of continuing loss."[27] This describes truly what happens in "A Winter in Wales." As the poem opens we find her, at sixty-six, "condemn[ed]" (that Johnsonian word again) by "Destiny . . . in fading Life / To sing the Sorrows of a fading Year." It is a gloomy poem:

> Now cold Caducity—or call it Age
> With chilling Palsy blasts each wither'd Bough;

> While its last Leaf—torne by the Tempests Rage
> Leaps undelighted o'er the frozen Snow.

"Caducity" means tendency to decline or transitoriness and so applies to the departing year; it is also, however, a genteel word for old age, and so applies equally to the poet. Her rejection of it in favor of the plain word betokens grim determination not to prettify; she is going to see things just as they really and bitterly are. This is the world of objects beheld by a mind of winter. "Undelighted" also applies both ways. Applied to the leaf, it is the ghostliest of pathetic fallacies, for it is literally true. Applied to the poet, it is the perfect understatement for the withered muse who looks about her and sees nothing but the image of her own barrenness:

> Round the wide Range far as my Sight extends,
> No cultur'd Plains or verdant Trees I trace,
> But the sad Muse o'er the pale Prospect bends
> To pore upon dull Nature's dying Face.

She turns now from this "universe of death" to the universe of dead language, Thomson's and Cowper's language. With stirring wonder, she remembers that they had managed to make poetry of winter, to call dead Nature into imaginative life, and she salutes their achievement: "Various the Roads Ye took to well-earn'd Fame / And various were Your Gifts—Ye Mighty Dead!" But Thomson and Cowper are dead themselves now, and their might has become only their imitators' weakness: "Of us Your feeble Followers but the Shame, / Whilst with unequal Steps your Paths we tread." What now happens is an exceptional moment, in Piozzi's or perhaps in any poetry. It could only be a moment of old age, for no young poet could bear to submit to it. By virtue of its subject matter "A Winter in Wales" is necessarily in competition with Thomson's *Winter*. In that competition she has just acknowledged herself beaten. Now, as if in sheer weariness of spirit, she brushes aside the defeat.

> Blest be your Labours all! could less beguile
> The Melancholy Season? could less chear
> Our Hearts? or move a Momentary Smile
> In Days like these, to Land & Sea severe?

This is as much as to say that the labors of all the dead poets are, in the end, barely less dead than Nature itself. They can raise only, and nothing less than they can raise even, a momentary smile in this wintry beholder. This said, they slip out of her consciousness and cease to matter. They have made no difference.

She goes back to contemplating the scene, which still tells "the same sad Winter's Tale," and hears the local clock chime, "a Cold, unechoing, suffocated Sound." One thing alone recalls her from this imaginative all-but-death:

> And look what's left of my paternal Oaks,
>   That bore their old time-honourd Heads so high;
> Sad Victims to the Winds unpitying Strokes,
>   In scatter'd Fragments mid the Forest lie.

"To-morrow's dawn," she knows, "Shall see them drag'd disgracefully away / Pil'd in short Pieces near some Peasants Shed." But this extra humiliation, in a way more personal to her now even than her defeat as a poet, proves to be her "Best Consolation":

> 'Twas to warm the Poor
> Perhaps Heav'n struck our disappointed Pride
> Best Disposition of Superfluous Store,
>   When modest Want is by such Stores supplied.[28]

This is a version of her characteristic palinode, but subtler and more convincing. Weary, in chill old age, of the imaginative need that has been starving anyway, she is better able to humble herself to acknowledge the everyday needs of social duty. At its end her poem does conquer Thomson and Cowper, by the quietly radical solution of apparently conquering the need to write poems.

This would seem to be an absolute dead end for poetry, yet from time to time she can still make poems out of it. In 1812, at Prestatyn, imaginative need stirs again, in imagery predictive of Arnold's "Dover Beach":

> The Moon shines full, The Seas retire
>   And mock my following Sight;
> Restless I gaze with vain Desire,
> Till anxious Thoughts my Voice inspire,
>   To wake the Silent Night.

The full moon hardly needs comment; it is one of the prime images of high romanticism right up through Yeats's Phase 15 in *A Vision*.

The retiring sea, although it sounds proleptic of Arnold's retreating "Sea of Faith," has deeper affinities with Wordsworth's "Immortality Ode":

> Hence in a season of calm weather
> Though inland far we be,
> Our Souls have sight of that immortal sea
> Which brought us hither,
> Can in a moment travel thither,
> And see the Children sport upon the shore,
> And hear the mighty waters rolling evermore.

If Piozzi read Wordsworth she left, to my knowledge, no record of it, yet her poem is strongly Wordsworthian, as if she had read the "Immortality Ode" and were unhappily determined to refute it. The "immortal" sea to which Wordsworth "can in a moment travel" is, to her, refractory; it will not come back at her call.

> Then quickly turn, receding Tide!
> Once more my heart to cheer;
> As by thy Silvery Billows' Side,
> I once a bright'ning Gleam descried,
> That check'd my falling Tear.

The gleam also is Wordsworth's, "the visionary gleam" of childhood that has fled, even from him, but that has been compensated, for him, by the mature poetic imagination. In her poem the gleam does not return, and the sea tells her that it is lost forever:

> "Those Gleams no longer come or go,
> Cry Voices from the Main;
> Cease to rely on Empty Show,
> For Human Life's full:swelling Flow
> Can ne'er return again."

All that the sea offers her is the compensation (somewhat factitiously managed here, as at the end of her stanzas at Naples) of an Anchor, symbol of Faith in the Christian Apocalypse: "'Let Faith once fix it on the Strand, / Far Distant Prospects you'll command / Beyond this rising Moon.'" Most of the last verse rings false, but its initial phrase does go some way towards satisfying the yearning with which the poem began:

> Mansions of Peace! whilst toiling We
> Behold our Channels dry;
> Think but on *Those*; an Ebbing Sea,
> Or burning World by Heav'n's Decree
> Will scarcely prompt a Sigh."[29]

This poem does give us pretty much the last gasp of Piozzi's romanticism. Thereafter her serious poems take up the promise of Christian redemption in more traditional terms, anticipating her death and resurrection with some impatience. By 1810 she felt very old and out of date, and seemed to herself to be only marking time. In one poem of that year she addresses to her heart the irritable question, "Why maintain this doubtful Strife? / Forfeit once to Sin and Death / Yield thy long:reluctant Breath." The last day of 1812 she marked by composing "Stanzas on Death"; in its vehement opening verse she would fling herself at him.

> Let it die! since die it must;
> Die and perish—Guilty Dust.
> Long has Death cried Come away,
> Long defrauded of his Prey;
> Soul! regret not *thou* The hour,
> 'Tis not *Thee* he can devour.

Always fond of imagining epitaphs for herself, she also wrote a three-verse rondeau to be thrown into the grave with her. Its mood is that of Ecclesiastes:

> Earth to Earth again is turn'd;
> Where's the Flame our Bosoms burn'd?
> Where the Wits? and where the Learn'd?
> Foes that scoff'd;—or Friends that mourn'd?
> Here remote, we rest InUrn'd,
> Earth to Earth again is turn'd![30]

Her last significant poem, from 1815, returns to the theme of her first significant poem, the 1758 "Moral Stanzas from Rousseau." Conceptually the later poem is little more than a rewrite of the earlier, although its technique is immensely more assured. In six short verses it recapitulates the life of man from birth to death, dwelling with particular bitterness on the intellectual pretensions by which humans would distinguish themselves.

Is it of Intellectual Powers
Which Time developes, Time devours;
Which Forty Years we may call ours,
    That Man is vain?
. . . .
For forty years she reigns at most,
Labour and Study pay the cost;
Just to be rais'd is all our boast
    Above the crowd:

Sickness then fills th' uneasy chair,
Sorrow succeeds, with Pain & Care,
While Faith just keeps us from despair,
    Wishing to die.

Till the Farce ends as it began;
Reason deserts the dying man,
And leaves—to encounter as he can
    Eternity.

"What a World it is!" she writes to Mrs. Pennington in the letter
which holds these verses, "& you & I, and he *all* proud of our Talents, if we would confess it—Fine folly!!"[31]

The Florence Miscellany

Aside from "The Three Warnings," the works on which Piozzi's poetical reputation in her own time lived—and, too early, died—were
her contributions to *The Florence Miscellany* (1785). They have, however, little to do with her actual achievement in poetry. Of the sev-
enty-nine poems in that collection only nine are by her; of them,
seven are trifles and two, albeit more ambitious, are not very good.
One is the poem "To Wm. Parsons Esqr.," quoted in chapter 2; the
other is a translation of a pretentious "Hymn of Calliope" from
an epic poem in praise of British arms and freedom, *Gibilterra Salvata* by Ippolito Pindemonte. The remaining seventy poems are the
work chiefly of the three Englishmen Piozzi met in Florence, Robert
Merry, Parsons, and Bertie Greatheed. In their intentions they are
quite unlike the pieces she contributed. Like her, Merry, Parsons, and
Greatheed were enthusiasts of Italian literature; however, they were

also, unlike her, inclined to political activism in behalf of Italian liberation from Austria. In the *Miscellany* they were displaying sympathy with the Accademia della Crusca, the society for the cultivation of Italian letters that had just (1783) been suppressed by the Austrian grand duke of Tuscany. Most of their pieces aspire to high seriousness, and, in retrospect, the *Miscellany* looks like a proto-Shelleyan political gesture. The few who have read all of it have found it at least moderately impressive; some have argued that Merry's poems influenced Coleridge, Keats, and Byron.[32] Yet whatever importance *The Florence Miscellany* had for the history of romantic poetry or Italian politics, for Hester Piozzi it proved ultimately a cause of insult and grief, and for her readers it has been a red herring.

From the first, she did not take the *Miscellany* seriously. To her it was a jeu d'esprit, a delightful reawakening but not an ambition. "I have been playing the baby, and writing nonsense to divert our English friends here, who do the same thing themselves, and swear they will print the collection. . . . Mr. Parsons and Mr. Merry are exceedingly clever, so is Mr. Greatheed, and we have no critics to maul us, so we laugh in peace." When the book was printed the men asked her to write a preface. There, too, she maintains it was all for fun: "we wrote [the verses] to divert ourselves, and to say kind things of each other; we collected them that our reciprocal expressions of kindness might not be lost, and we printed them because we had no reason to be ashamed of our mutual partiality." This is sufficiently at odds with the *Miscellany*'s real character to raise the question, Is it meant to deceive, or was she herself deceived? The Austrian censorship required secrecy and deception; the book was privately printed—and therefore, she was later to insist, not really published—and blanks were left on some pages, to be filled by slips that were still more privately printed. It has been suggested, not much to the credit of her intelligence, that the men duped her into writing a preface that they knew would be innocuous; yet in later years at least, she understood that there had been danger of offending "the Inquisitorial Courts of Italy."[33]

She sent copies to friends at home, one of whom gave his to a London newspaper. Soon all her pieces were in the papers, and she became known as Merry's literary colleague—understandably, given the ways of newspaper chitchat. Just at the time when her poems were thus appearing, Merry himself, back in London and writing under the name "Della Crusca," was conducting in the same newspapers a particularly fatuous verse correspondence with one "Anna Matilda." Anna Matilda was Hannah Cowley the popular playwright, but until that became known some people thought she was Piozzi. During the later 1780s Merry enjoyed considerable celebrity both as an avant-garde poet and as a political radical; after 1789 he was one of the noisier friends of the French Revolution. By then Piozzi no longer esteemed him. Of his upwardly mobile marriage in 1791 she wrote in disgust, "Della Crusca has married a Woman of elegant Person & Address, & who will bring him perhaps 500£ o'year with an unblemished Character. . . . The husband meantime will congratulate himself charmingly on his *own Superiority*—no small Pleasure to some Minds;—and the World will always be on *his* Side in every Dispute, tho' he had neither Character *nor* Fortune when they met." Merry's politics, of course, raised enemies, who attacked his poems as well. One of them was the feisty, not to say savage, satirist, translator of Juvenal, and Tory, William Gifford. In *The Baviad* (1791), and again in *The Maeviad* (1795), both of which went through several editions, Gifford seized on Merry, on the newspaper excerpts from the *Miscellany* (the whole *Miscellany* he later confessed to never having read), on the name "Della Crusca," and on all Merry's associates real or reputed, including of course Piozzi, and subjected them to a thorough roasting. To Gifford more than to any other single person belongs the dubious credit of sinking Piozzi's reputation in verse. He made "Della Cruscan" a term of utter contempt, and far into the nineteenth century the name of everyone associated with the *Miscellany* continued to be tainted by it. Witness the editor of *Bentley's* in 1850: "Touching all matters of poetry, Mrs. Piozzi was mixed up with too tainted a school to be able to judge rightly. What could be hoped, under any circumstances, from a Della Cruscan?"[34]

Piozzi once met Gifford across a dinner table; her revenge on him, she says, was to charm him into courtly good humor. Nevertheless, his satire wounded her deeply. As late as 1814 the memory of it embittered a summing up of her literary career that she wrote for her nephew Piozzi:

> I have suffer'd enough for other People's Literary Faults, (if Faults they were;) from fine M.ʳ Giffard who attributes to me many Lines written by Parsons, & some by Greatheed, but never *publish'd*; so not by any Means amenable to Censure from Readers or Writers, if Justice or Mercy ever came into a

Critic's Mind. . . . Your utter *Aversion* to Literature would be
much increased if you knew half *les Tracasseries des Auteurs*; &
my *Affection* for it, must surely have been very great at first—
or how could I have borne the Insults of unprovoked Enemies
as I have done?[35]

A Candle-Light Picture

Anecdotes of Johnson

A transition from an author's books to his conversation, is too often like an entrance into a large city, after a distant prospect. Remotely, we see nothing but spires of temples, and turrets of palaces, and imagine it the residence of splendor, grandeur, and magnificence; but, when we have passed the gates, we find it perplexed with narrow passages, disgraced with despicable cottages, embarrassed with obstructions, and clouded with smoke.

Most of the very very great Men are odious.[1]

THE CANONICAL Johnson friendship is the one with Boswell. It has the force of a myth. Like Sherlock Holmes and Watson, the Johnson and Boswell of the *Life* exemplify that undemonstrative but rocklike loyalty between unequal men which has always been dear to the Anglo-American male heart. We see them strolling up a perpetual High Street, as in Rowlandson's cartoon, and forget that the actual time they spent together during twenty-one years amounted only to 425 days. The friendship of Johnson and Hester Thrale enjoys no such fame, in part, no doubt, because our culture affords no archetypes of male-female friendship to which it can be assimilated. Nevertheless, we can name very few people—perhaps only one person, Johnson's wife—who ever knew Johnson as well as Mrs. Thrale did. "Uniformly great is the Mind of that incomparable Mortal," she once burst out in *Thraliana*, "& well does he contradict the Maxim of Rochefoucault, that no Man is a Hero to his Valet de Chambre.—Johnson is more a Hero to me than to any one—& I have been more to him for Intimacy, than ever was any Man's Valet de Chambre."[2] If knowledge of the subject were alone sufficient to make a book, her *Anecdotes of Johnson* would enjoy the primacy, and Boswell's *Life* would take a distant second place. That their positions are reversed is in part a testimony to Boswell's superior literary skill. Whatever its value as biography (and it has been excoriated, as a biography, by no less eminent a Johnson scholar than Donald J. Greene), the *Life* is undoubtedly a great *book*. It consistently has a degree of esthetic finish and mythmaking power to which *Anecdotes* attains but fitfully. This said, it should be recognized that the *Life* and *Anecdotes* have different ambitions and different centers of gravity. Boswell's vision of Johnson is fundamentally comic; his physical distance from Johnson probably helped him achieve his comic vision. Hester's intense closeness to Johnson made that kind of detachment impossible. Where Boswell is able to relish Johnson as a genial father, not without a certain genial pooh-poohing of him as well, Hester must struggle with eighteen years' accumulated resentment of him. Her portrait is dark, as she knows: "a . . . *candle-light* picture . . . where every thing falls in dark shadow except the face, the index of the mind; but even that is seen unfavourably, and with a paleness beyond what nature gave it."[3] The mood of *Anecdotes* is far more purgatorial than comic; its mode is not comedy but melodrama, and it is often quite uncomfortable to read. Yet, although it is artistically inferior to the *Life*, emotionally, in its different way, *Anecdotes* is very nearly as strong. Boswell's *Tour* excepted, it is immeasurably stronger than any of the other first-generation books about Johnson and stronger than all but a handful of subsequent books about him. As interpretation of Johnson it is pretty clearly superior to Boswell, largely because it mounts resistance to him at points where Boswell cheerfully embraces or blandly steps aside.

The matrix of *Anecdotes* was the Thrale-Johnson friendship, and a review of it will be our prelude. That Piozzi has been remembered altogether too well as an episode in Johnson's life is one of the themes of the present book; from our point of view, it is Johnson who figures as an episode in her life. He was, however, an episode of immense consequence. Their friendship thus claims as much attention on her side as on his, not only as the matter of *Anecdotes* and *Letters* but also for its very great, if troubled, humanity.

"My Mistress"/"Father"

We have no cultural archetype of male-female friendship; instead we have an archetype—variously tormented, passionate, or leering—of male-female "intimacy." When they see Mrs. Thrale's statement that "I have been more to him for Intimacy, than ever was any Man's Valet de Chambre," twentieth-century eyes are apt to open wide. Katharine Balderston's did, and in 1949 she put forth what has been called, in the language of the gossip column, a "bombshell suggestion": that Johnson's attachment to Hester was sexual and sadomasochistic. Although Balderston's argument does not really sustain scrutiny, the facts that she marshaled naturally excited inquiries into the nature of Johnson's neurosis and Hester's conduct as the "confidential friend" of his health.[4] They are, first, a padlock described in the sale catalogue of Piozzi's library (1823) as "Johnson's padlock, committed to my care in 1768"; second, an entry in Johnson's diary for April 1771, "De pedicis et manicis insana cogitatio" ("Insane thought about foot-fetters and manacles"); third, a letter written by Johnson to Mrs. Thrale, in French, while he was at Streatham with her during May 1773 when her mother was dying, in which he pleads for rules to govern his behavior, hints that she may lock him in his room, reproaches her for having "condemned me to so many reiterated solicitations that the memory of them is horrible," and hopes that she will continue him in "the servitude which you so well know how to render happy"; and fourth, several entries in *Thraliana* in 1779. Besides the one quoted above, there is another in which Johnson is reported to say that "a Woman has *such* power between the Ages of twenty five and forty five, that She may tye a man to a post and whip him if She will," and to which Hester adds a note, "This he knew of him self was *literally* and *strictly* true I am sure"; and there is an exclamation, "How many Times has this great, this formidable Doctor Johnson kissed my hand, ay & my foot too upon his knees! Strange Connections there are in this odd World!" To this also she adds a note: "a dreadful & little suspected Reason for *ours* God knows—but the Fetters & Padlocks will tell Posterity the Truth."[5]

What all of this does tell is not so easy to construe as it at first appears to the reader steeped in rumors of Krafft-Ebing. In their historical context the details are not necessarily of a piece. Thus the most shocking single item, the padlock, in the eighteenth century was far more likely to resonate of insanity than of sexual kinks; the customary treatment of the insane was confinement with chains. It suggests that in 1768 Johnson's lifelong dread of insanity so overwhelmed him that he actually took practical precautions. In committing this equipment to Mrs. Thrale, he was entrusting himself to her custody in preference to risking the scandal and brutality of a public asylum. His diary thought about foot-fetters and manacles appears to run parallel with the real padlock. This episode, and the obsessive dread that gave rise to it, are probably alone the "secret" referred to several times in *Thraliana* and are almost certainly the object of Mrs. Thrale's remark that "the Fetters & Padlocks will tell Posterity the Truth." In *Anecdotes* all of this is reduced to a generality, although an accurate one: "Mr. Johnson's . . . over-anxious care to retain without blemish the perfect sanity of his mind, contributed much to disturb it. He had studied medicine diligently in all its branches; but had given particular attention to the diseases of the imagination, which he watched in himself with a solicitude destructive of his own peace, and intolerable to those he trusted."[6] Other passages in *Thraliana* should be read in the context of Mrs. Thrale's disposition to heighten, melodramatize, and affect certainty when she is not, in fact, certain. Thus in her comment, "This he knew of him self was *literally* and *strictly* true I am sure," her "I am sure" almost rules out her having witnessed any such event, for she is apt to use it just when she is not sure.

The padlock, however, is suggestive of melodrama also—of Johnson's melodrama, not of hers. If we try to imagine the scene of his presenting it to her, we can hardly conceive of it as anything other than Johnson's dramatization, to an astonished audience, of his own pain. It is theatrical, even Byronic. (I do not mean, however, that it was "insincere.") So, in its different way, is his assertion of a woman's power over men and his kissing of hands and feet. All of this suggests a theatrical courtliness, and for Johnson's propensity to that there is plenty of evidence. There is his well known delight in flattering women—not only Hester but also Mrs. Montagu, Fanny Burney, and others besides. A lifelong reader of romances, Johnson delighted to flirt with the rhetoric of romance; in his letters to Mrs. Thrale he gives way to it with gusto. "I hope on Monday to be your slave in the morning, and Mrs. Smith's in the Evening, and then fall again to my true Mistress, and be the rest of the week, Madam, Your most obedient." With Hester he had a standing joke, or half joke and half fantasy, of casting himself in the role of Colin, the lovesick shepherd of

Rowe's "Colin's Complaint": "my mistress . . . laughs, and frisks, and frolicks it all the long day, and never thinks of poor Colin." He can do this sort of thing safely, of course, precisely because there is no real "romantic connection" between them. It is all flirting, and it is done with some admixture of irony, of which the purport seems to be, "See what a gallant fellow this ugly dog is! Who'd have thought it?" In this there is a certain defiance, an angry effort to overcome the impression Johnson presumed his appearance would make on women. More fundamentally, his theatrical courtliness appears to be a compensation for the enormous demands he was prone to make on them. W. J. Bate's interpretation of his French letter to Hester is surely correct: it is a demand for loving attention couched in terms of a theatrically abject humility that is always about to turn ironic. Hester was not the only woman on whom he made such demands. Soon after she became a Streatham regular, Fanny Burney too discovered that Johnson's flattery, overwhelmingly pleasing as it was, was also a prelude to demands: "Whenever he is below stairs he keeps me a prisoner, for he does not like I should quit the room a moment; if I rise he constantly calls out, 'Don't you go, little Burney!' "[7]

What Johnson demanded from women was mothering. One root of this need was simply that his life was pervaded by bodily and mental pain to degrees that most people fortunately do not experience. His pain disposed him to self-pity. Well aware of this disposition, Johnson usually showed it no mercy; hence his oft-expressed scorn of valetudinarians—" 'It is so *very* difficult (said he, always) for a sick man not to be a scoundrel' "—and his growling when he does indulge the pleasure of being nursed: "when one asked him gently, how he did?—'Ready to become a scoundrel, Madam (would commonly be the answer).' " In the presence of women, however, Johnson's self-pity was always in danger of erupting into open dramatization. Even a stranger could bring it out, as Helen Maria Williams did when on one of the few occasions she met him she asked how he was: "I am very ill indeed, Madam. I am very ill even when you are near me; what should I be were you at a distance." Writing to Hill Boothby, whom he loved and wished to marry, he exerts a shamelessly eloquent rhetoric of pathos: "If I turn my thoughts upon myself what do I perceive but a poor helpless being reduced by a blast of wind to weakness and misery." With Fanny Burney he once passed a whole dinnertime in melancholy silence, speaking only to repeat to her, "Ah! you little know how ill I am."[8] From this to the padlock scene is not a very long step. The request is still the same: "Take care of me; be my mother." The manner of making it is theatrical, portentous.

In Johnson Hester thus found herself possessed, as it were, of an extra child. This is not how she chooses to see it in *Thraliana*, and in *Anecdotes* she at most hints at it; the evidence is in their letters. In one, Johnson adjures Hester to "keep strictly to your character of governess." In her reply to his French letter (a reply that is a model of tact), she does just that: "farewell and be good; and do not quarrell with your Governess for not using the Rod enough." In another letter Johnson refers to the Thrale children as "my *brother* and *sisters*" (the emphases are his). In still another, written when his eye was inflamed and he could not see, Johnson verges on baby talk: "I have had a poor darkling week. . . . I wish you could fetch me on Wednesday. I long to be in my own room. Have you got your key? . . . I long to be under your care." And in another, Hester, expecting him home from Oxford, writes, "you will be just finishing your Visits, and return to the Iron Dominion of Your most Faithful & Obedient Servant." (The joke of this is partly Mutt and Jeff; Johnson was about three times her size.) From her replies we may infer that she humored Johnson's fantasy. "Affectionate and tender," "a diligent & active Friend" in truth as well as in her own self-description, Hester enjoyed mothering Johnson. In him she found another in a series of men—more exactly, of children-in-men—whom she "loved Spoiling." The series consists of her father, whose "very particular Temper" she "alone could please," probably Arthur Collier, Johnson, perhaps Gabriel Piozzi, certainly his nephew and her adopted son John Salusbury Piozzi, and William Augustus Conway, the actor whom she met at Bath very late in life. (It was to Conway that she avowed her love of spoiling: "Mr. Piozzi said I had spoiled my own Children, & was spoiling *his*. —my Reply was that I loved Spoiling People, & hated any one I could *not* Spoil;—Am I not *now* trying to Spoil dear Mr Conway?")[9]

In mothering Johnson, probably the most valuable service she did was to listen to him. He would confide to her what he would tell almost no one else—preeminently, his dread of going mad. She understood how intensely Johnson suffered from it, and she neither dismissed it nor attempted to reason him out of it. Instead, like a discreet psychoanalyst, she humored him. His recourse, she says in *Anecdotes*, when he "felt his fancy, or fancied he felt it, disordered . . . was to the study of arithmetic," and she tells of an occasion of this kind when, "knowing what subject he would like best to talk upon," she tactfully engaged him on a topic in number theory.[10] On other occasions, at his request she apparently went so far as to lock him in his room; this was customary procedure with children who had been naughty or were simply, for the time, in the way (as Johnson feared he was when he wrote the French letter). And, although throughout these years she was often not well herself, she nevertheless gave Johnson or at least saw to it that he got a great deal of bodily nursing.

It has sometimes been suggested (indeed, it was rumored with cheerful malice in their lifetimes) that Hester and Johnson were in love. That they loved each other is beyond doubt. Hester delighted in the knowledge that "nobody loves me as Johnson does . . . but then nobody has as much Soul to love one with"; and we have many other testimonies to his "most sincere and tender regard" for her. Anna Seward, who did not like Johnson, surmised that his affection for Mrs. Thrale "was composed of cupboard love, Platonic love, and vanity tickled . . . from morn to night by incessant homage," and that "*she* loved him for the literary consequence his residence at Streatham threw around her." The remark is true but reductive. Johnson also loved Hester for her qualities of mind and temper ("you have as much sense, and more wit," he once declared to her, "than any woman I know"), and for her conversation, which he described as "a stream of Sentiment—enlivened by Gaiety." In this esteem he was not alone, for Hester's conversation was admired throughout her life: "that bright wine of the intellects which has no lees," Seward herself called it in a memorable phrase. And while it is certain that Hester valued Johnson for the "literary consequence" he brought her (why should she not?), it is equally certain that she loved him for his character, his playfulness, and his ready companionship. In *Thraliana* we get a glimpse of a common occurrence, their doing chemistry together, and at Paris in 1775 when the rest of the family went one night to the theater she and Johnson stayed home, where "we criticized & talked & were happy in one another—he in huffing me, & I in being huff'd."[11]

Reviewing their friendship with respect to its benefits for Johnson, a psychoanalyst has gone so far as to claim that Hester's care cured him of his lifelong neurosis. Her own claim, in *Anecdotes*, is that her care kept him sane enough to write his last works. His effects on her are less easy to state, in part because they were equivocal and in after years she stated them negatively ("while Johnson lived . . . I *could* not turn Author"), and in part because, to anyone who takes the view that her career was only a parody of his, they seem so obvious. On the positive side, we have seen how important Johnson had been to her in 1765. He had redeemed her from the damage done by Henry Thrale's cool indifference to her intellect, going far towards restoring a pattern that seems to have been necessary to her self-esteem, a pattern in which she plays the precocious favorite and cynosure of older men's attention. One paradigm of Johnson, then, was her father; she once apostrophizes him as "Friend, Father, Guardian, Confident!" Another paradigm, of course, was Collier, like Johnson a man of impressive intellect whose admiration of Hester's mind had warmed to love of her. The intellect of Johnson was still greater—she once said that she felt for him "the same respect and veneration as for a Pascal"—and his admiration not less. The effect of such admiration can only have been good; it must have contributed powerfully to allay her fear of incompetence, to convince her that her mental performances could be valued at the highest level. This is the meaning of her assertion that while Johnson lived she could not turn author; she could not, she says, because "whatever I wrote would have been attributed to *him*." At the same time, it must be said that even Johnson's admiration was not entirely unequivocal. Its expression was often stagy and hyperbolical, and it was sometimes negatived by characteristically male reservations. One of Hester's poems, he says, is "very pretty," and its style "a good one . . . for a *Lady*";[12] he asserts that she has "more wit," not than any person, but "than any woman I know." Still, without this admiration, however equivocal, Hester might not have written at all after 1763. In this sense it may be true that she owed her career to Johnson.

Unquestionably theirs deserves remembrance among the great friendships. To suppose, however, that it was embittered only by Hester's decision to marry Piozzi is to discover (as Johnson liked to say) very little acquaintance with life. For in fact it was shot through with tensions, and was bound to be, given their temperaments and sexes. In the first place Johnson, always prone to anger at his suspected self-indulgence (although also, often enough, quite unconscious of his real self-indulgence), accepted with little grace the affection Hester gave him. He also, not surprisingly, over sixteen years came to take it for granted, and Hester was more than commonly touchy about having her affection taken for granted; if one whom she has obliged, she says of herself, "does not express the Sense of Obligation" she is "soon disgusted." Again, Johnson's natural temper was arrogant and fierce. He struggled all his life against it, sometimes declaring with touching desperation that he was really "the civillest creature in nature," insisting that his famous outbursts were misunderstood, and perpetually urging to others the importance of learning to "be pleased." In the daily life of Streatham, however, he often relapsed. Fanny Burney was but one of many who found "astonishing" "the freedom with which Dr. Johnson condemns whatever he disapproves . . . ; and the strength of words he uses would, to most people, be intolerable." Burney took as evidence of Hester's "sweetness of disposition" that, "far from making a point of vindicating herself, she generally receives his admonitions with the most respectful silence." It was surely an angry silence as well. Frances Reynolds recalls with indignation an episode of this kind: "One Day at her own Table, before a large company, he spoke so very roughly to her, that every person present was surprised how she could bear it so placidly; and on the Ladies withdrawing, one of them express'd great astonishment how Dr. Johnson could speak in such harsh terms to her! But to this she said no more than 'Oh! Dear good man!' "[13]

She was not always so forbearing. Burney reports a dialogue in which Hester expostulates with Johnson about his rudeness: "Your compliments, sir, are made seldom, but . . . they have an elegance unequalled; but then when you are angry, who dares make speeches so bitter and so cruel?" Johnson defends himself ("I never do it but when I am insufferably vexed"), and Hester persists: "Yes, sir; but you suffer things to vex you, that nobody else would vex at. I am sure I have had my share of scolding from you!" Johnson's reply, one regrets to say, is a bit of stonewalling: "It is true, you have; but you have borne it like an angel, and you have been the better for it." Thus the dialogue goes on, to Burney's increasing nervousness. Hester mildly but firmly urges her side, Johnson maintains his, and at last she is moved to a remark now famous among Johnsonians: that when Johnson had testily asked why she lavished praise on everyone she met, she had answered, "Why I'll tell you, sir, . . . when I am with you, and Mr. Thrale, and Queeny, I am obliged to be civil for four!" "There was a cutter for you!" remarks Burney.[14]

Johnson so well knew himself to be difficult and petulant that he made it a prime tenet of his writings that one cannot dismiss a moral teaching merely because its author fails to live up to it; he feared that his good influence as a writer would be disgraced by his conduct as a man. Hester, however, lived with the man, not the writer. Although she could sincerely declare that he was "more a Hero to me than to any one," as the years passed she also found him increasingly hard to endure. At the end of her 1774 Welsh diary, when she has to face the prospect of going home to Southwark she explodes in rage: "I must be shut up in that odious Dungeon, where nobody will come near me; the Children are to be sick for want of Air, & I am never to see a face but M.ʳ Johnson's—Oh what a Life that is? and how truly do I abhor it!" His demands on her energy exhausted her; there is her well-known complaint in *Anecdotes* that he insisted she sit up to make tea for him hours beyond bedtime and belabored her with "vehement lamentations and piercing reproofs" if she moved to retire. Nor did he much reciprocate the daily sympathies she gave to him. Worn out by the 1780 election and disposed to a little self-pity of her own, Hester complains in *Thraliana* that her health is "hurt . . . radically & seriously. . . . I will however say nothing about it . . . Mʳ Johnson who thinks no body poor till they want a Dinner, or sick till they want breath, would only suppose I was calling for Attention, & shewing Consequence by bringing Physicians about me." In the 1779 dialogues on her own death Hester puts into the mouth of Mrs. Montagu a remark whose acid humor sufficiently expresses her own weariness: Johnson, says Montagu, "has had a Loss you'll allow— Mrs. Thrale, among her other Qualifications, had prodigious strong Nerves—and that's an admirable Quality for a Friend of Dr. Johnson's."[15]

Finally, although Hester sincerely venerated Johnson as her mentor, it is clear that by 1781 she had had enough of being a pupil. She was forty years old and feeling older; it was time, as she wrote in a passage we have seen before, to "rise to the Rank of a human Being conscious of its own power to discern Good from Ill." Her attachment to Piozzi is significant in its being the first time in her life that she sought out a man of her own age, and the very fact that he was her social inferior may well have helped to make him attractive: how pleasant to love a man of whom one did not have to be in awe! For of Johnson, intimacy and "governess" notwithstanding, one did have to be in awe; he would have it no other way. "He always wished to retain authority," she remembers in *Anecdotes*, "and leave his company impressed with the idea, that it was his to teach in this world, and theirs to learn." In her poem on the Streatham portraits, Hester attempts to present a balanced estimate of Johnson. The lines that leap out, however, are those expressing her resentment of his arrogance:

> To his Comrades contemptuous, we see him look down,
> On their Wit & their Worth with a general Frown:
> While from Science proud Tree the rich Fruit he receives,
> Who could shake the whole Trunk, while they turn'd a few
>   leaves;
> The inflammable Temper—the positive Tongue,
> Too conscious of right for endurance of Wrong;
> We suffer from Johnson—contented to find,
> That some notice we gain from so noble a Mind;
> And pardon our hurts, since so often we've found,
> The Balm of Instruction pour'd into the Wound.[16]

This, written in January 1781, is essentially the Johnson of *Anecdotes*, and the experience of him is purgatorial. (She printed these lines in *Anecdotes*, recognizing their fitness.)

During Thrale's last illness, when Thrale is projecting an impossible trip to Italy, Hester is moved to contemplate Johnson with bitter fury: "& who must go with us on this Expedition? Mr Johnson! he will indeed be the only happy Person of the party: he values nothing under heaven but his own Mind, which is a Spark *from* Heaven; & *that* will be invigorated by the addition of new Ideas—if Mr Thrale dies on the Road, Johnson will console himself by learning *how it is* to travel with a Corpse—& after all, such Reasoning is the true Philosophy—one's heart is a mere Incumbrance—Would I could leave mine behind." This, no doubt, is "not fair" to Johnson (although the charge that he regards life with epicurean detachment is not so very wrong, either). Right or wrong, however, she is sick of his intellectual ascendancy, and she is also envious of what she construes as his imaginative solipsism, his lofty freedom from the world of bedpans and feces and sickroom linen where she has been breaking her heart for sixteen years. Her anger is double. She is angry simply as a woman who feels used, and used up; she is angry also as a reawakening writer (she has recently published her first stage piece, her second piece under her own name) who needs to shake off his heavy tutorial presence. In after years she remembered "the venerating solicitude which hung heavily over my whole soul whilst connected with Doctor Johnson," and we have noticed her feeling of having been "swallowed up and lost" in Johnson's mind.[17] By 1781 Hester needed to divorce herself personally from Johnson, and as a writer she was beginning the same kind of quarrel with him that she had conducted with Pope some twenty years earlier.

True, in divorcing Johnson Hester did not act with as much candor as we like to see in people we respect. It is also true, however, that Johnson responded in precisely his worst manner. Suspecting her of withdrawal, he gave way first to petulance—there were repulsive scenes at Brighton in the fall of 1782—and then fell back on pleas for pity and stabbing reproaches, reproaches made all the more stabbing by their masterful eloquence. Among them is the famous, and still deeply moving, letter written after his stroke in 1783, in which he sits down "in no cheerful solitude to write a narrative which would once have affected you with tenderness and sorrow, but which you will perhaps pass over now with the careless glance of frigid indifference." He tells his story, and returns to pathos: "I have loved you with virtuous affection; I have honoured you with sincere esteem. Let not all our endearment be forgotten, but let me have in this great distress your pity and your prayers. You see I yet turn to you with my complaints as a settled and unalienable friend; do not, do not drive me from you, for I have not deserved either neglect or hatred." Suspecting his rhetoric of selfishness, Johnson adds, "I am almost ashamed of this querulous letter, but now it is written, let it go." That Piozzi published this letter is no small tribute to her honesty. It is not hard to understand why posterity, possessed of such a document, should have condemned her seeming cruelty to Johnson. Nevertheless, the best known treatment of this episode, Boswell's in the *Life*, does not stand up to the facts. Based on utter ignorance of the situation and composed almost wholly of hostile innuendo, it must be thrown out as worthless. As it happens, another Boswell sentence produced in quite another context suits this one rather well: "Such is the weakness and imperfection of human nature, that it will not bear to be too closely examined in any character."[18]

The Truth and Artistry of Anecdote

Readers who know *Anecdotes* only as it figures in the *Life* know it as one of those other books about Johnson that Boswell seems always to be correcting. His corrections are not confined to specific matters.

Throughout the *Life* there is a tendency to depreciate Piozzi's decency, probity, and truthfulness. Today we know that by 1790 Boswell had come to hate her and that he set out methodically to demolish her.[19] His motives were partly those incident to all authorial rivalries; he had long known that she too was likely to write about Johnson, and her edition of Johnson's letters had especially frightened and depressed him. Partly also they arose from a sincere feeling of injured honor. By denying his report in the *Tour* that she could not read Mrs. Montagu, Piozzi had impugned Boswell's own truthfulness. Nor can his treatment of her be ascribed solely to revenge, for Boswell, unlike Piozzi, was a reverent sentimentalist of Literature and Great Men, and he really did believe that her presentation of Johnson was unfair.

Judged simply as a lawyer's brief, Boswell's treatment of her is masterly. It did more to sink Piozzi's general reputation, probably, than any other circumstance. (It so influenced the eminent nineteenth-century Johnsonian, G. B. Hill, that he peppered his edition of *Anecdotes* with snide footnotes against her.) Yet the truth is that Boswell's attack is largely a feat of legerdemain. His corrections of Piozzi are more showy than numerous; his very frequent concurrences with her are almost all silent. Something much nearer his real estimate of her book may be seen in an exchange of letters with Edmond Malone, his ally in the writing of the *Life*. "I have read Mrs. Piozzi's book twice through," writes Malone; "there is a great deal of good stuff in it." To this Boswell replies, in part, "she is a little artful impudent malignant Devil. . . . The Book however has a great deal of valuable memorabilia, which prove themselves genuine." In the *Life* his main charge is that she distills into one small volume all the occasional and forgivable ascerbities of Johnson's behavior during twenty years. Here Boswell is saying no more than Piozzi herself admits: "When I relate these various instances of contemptuous behaviour . . . I am aware that those who will now have heard little of Mr. Johnson will here cry out against his pride and his severity; yet I have been as careful as I could to tell them, that all he did was gentle, if all he said was rough."[20] This disclaimer does not convince, for the emotional drag of *Anecdotes* is always towards Johnson's pride and severity. No doubt the *Life*, for all its own lopsidedness, is better balanced (it is, after all, about ten times the size of *Anecdotes* and that much more comprehensive), but it is also frequently shallow and euphemistic. The consequence, as most twentieth-century Johnsonians have understood, is that if Piozzi needs to be corrected by Boswell, Boswell needs as much to be corrected by Piozzi.

This remains true despite the fact that in writing *Anecdotes* she introduced into it a large number of what scholars would call "historical inaccuracies." That is, she departed from her original documents. In the climate of Boswellian legal-mindedness, it has been rather too easy to regard her changes as tokens of indifference to truth. ("Her code of truth is not severe," wrote the same scholar who dismissed her as "feather-headed."[21]) In fact, the situation is more complicated than that, and in order to estimate the significance of her changes we need to notice, first, the circumstances in which she wrote, and second, the form in which she cast her remarks on Johnson, the anecdote itself.

Compositionally, *Anecdotes* is the fruit both of long consideration and last-minute haste. In about 1768 Hester began a "table book" of Johnsoniana, now mostly lost. The contents of that book were entered in *Thraliana* in 1777. This account, the basis of *Anecdotes*, is clearly a trial run for such a book, if not quite its first draft. It elaborates the 1768 original and closes with a formal "character" of Johnson of the type that conventionally closed an eighteenth-century biography. (This character, which she says Johnson himself read and approved, is retained in *Anecdotes* almost verbatim.) In Italy, upon hearing of Johnson's death, Piozzi began to meditate the uses of this material. Her first thought was to write a biography, but for that she felt unready. Next she adopted a memoir-plus-letters scheme like William Mason's memoir of Gray (in *The Poems of Mr. Gray*); this would have yielded a two- or three-volume book to which the memoir would serve as a preface. On this plan she began writing, and she proposed it to the London publisher Cadell. Having left her trove of Johnson's letters in London, she intended to work up the memoir at leisure and publish after returning to England; but Cadell, with an eye to the mushrooming Johnson market, urged haste and offered to send her the letters. To that she would not consent, and, perhaps fearing to alienate him—it was her first experience of dealing with a publisher—she proposed a compromise: "If you will have the Anecdotes and print them first . . . I am willing to double my diligence, and we may publish the two other volumes when I get back."[22]

Many discrepancies between *Anecdotes* and its *Thraliana* basis are surely results of this decision. The *Thraliana* account, long enough to make a preface, was not long enough to make an independent volume. When she speaks of doubling her diligence she means writing faster to meet Cadell's timetable, but in practice it must also have meant writing more. Comparison of *Anecdotes* with *Thraliana* shows a gradual increase in the disparities between them: the later pages of *Anecdotes* contain proportionally more material that has no parallel in *Thraliana*, and of the material that does have *Thraliana* parallels more has been amplified. There are even instances in which Piozzi assigns to Johnson anecdotes whose counterparts in *Thraliana* have nothing whatever to do with him. From a scholar's point of view these changes are egregious. From an esthetic point of view (a point of view which Piozzi herself would probably not have admitted), they are unfortunate because the imported anecdotes are not as good as the genuine articles.

Thus, through these genetic accidents, *Anecdotes* is not the book that Piozzi meant to write, and it may in some respects be inferior to that book. It would not in any case, however, have been different in kind, and its kind is one that historical scholars, who are sometimes lamentably literal-minded, tend to misunderstand. Its kind is the anecdote. Everyone knows what the anecdote is: it is a tellable story. It is what the sociolinguist William Labov has called "natural narrative." The reason why scholars tend to misunderstand anecdote is that they think of it as "natural" in the sense of "innocent of verbal artifice." Labov has shown, however, what people who tell and enjoy anecdotes know already, that natural narratives are formally patterned, may be highly ornamented, and are held by their hearers to standards of significance. They must be "tellable," that is, worth telling for reasons above the merely practical. They are, in short, a literary form. In the later eighteenth century this was all perfectly understood; that period is the greatest era of anecdote in English literature, a fact attested by the popularity—and size—of compilations like William Seward's *Anecdotes of some Distinguished Persons* (five volumes, 1795–97) and John Nichols's *Literary Anecdotes of the Eighteenth Century* (six volumes, 1812). Noting in *Thraliana* the huge sum that Boswell was rumored to have made by the *Life*, Piozzi herself comments disgustedly, "the World is surely not in its Dotage alone, but its Anec*dotage*."[23]

Anecdotes are about people, and the ultimate ground of their tellability in the eighteenth century was the conviction that, as James Beattie put it, "human affairs and human feelings are universally interesting." One who acts explicitly on this premise is the diarist Thomas Campbell: "as I love to speculatise upon human nature," he writes one day, "I cannot help setting down . . . an anecdote I heared . . . from my fellow-traveller G——." He sets it down, and concludes, "What a creature is man!"[24] Here anecdote is made to exemplify an ethical truth, to enact an ethically significant moment of human character. This is precisely the use of it that Johnson urges in *Rambler* 60, where he asserts that to be of value a biography must often pass over the showy outside of a man's career and take us instead into the recesses of private life—that is, into anecdote as defined in his *Dictionary* (1773): "a biographical incident; a minute passage of private life." Biography must be anecdotal, he continues, so that we may see how a man comported himself not as a general or a statesman or a writer but as a human being like ourselves. Considered thus, as a story whose significance is typical, not merely individual, anecdote becomes a species of semifiction; it differs from history in the same way that Aristotle says poetry does, by tending "to express the universal." Accordingly, the truth value of anecdote cannot be quite the sort demanded by scholarly historians. Accuracy with respect to circumstantial detail is not what it seeks; rather, it seeks the essential gesture.

Many of the changes Piozzi introduced between *Thraliana* and *Anecdotes* are designed precisely for this effect. She wanted a more concentrated, more "typical," more "universal," and more dramatic Johnson than her record supplied. Perhaps her finest single change is the one she made in rendering Johnson's sentiments concerning treatment of the poor. In *Thraliana* they are given this way:

> But to return to his Notions concerning the Poor; he really loved them as nobody else does—with a Desire they should be happy—What signifies says somebody giving Money to common Beggars? they lay it out only in Gin or Tobacco—and why should they not says our D^r why should every body else find Pleasure necessary to their Existence and deny the poor every possible Avenue to it?—Gin & Tobacco are the only Pleasures in their Power,—let them have the Enjoyments within their reach without Reproach.

In *Anecdotes* this is first braced by a penetrating generalization, then rendered eloquent by the addition of a sentence lifted (in part) from quite another context in *Thraliana*.

Severity towards the poor was, in Dr. Johnson's opinion (as is visible in his Life of Addison particularly) an undoubted and constant attendant or consequence upon whiggism; and he was not contented with giving them relief, he wished to add also indulgence. He loved the poor as I never yet saw any one else do, with an earnest desire to make them happy.—What signifies, says some one, giving halfpence to common beggars? they only lay it out in gin or tobacco. "And why should they be denied such sweeteners of their existence (says Johnson)? it is surely very savage to refuse them every possible avenue to pleasure, reckoned too coarse for our own acceptance."

The fairly colorless speech in *Thraliana* has been stylistically heightened and its ethical point sharpened. But the best is to come. Piozzi turns back several pages in *Thraliana* and takes a sentence out of a different Johnson speech on a different topic, fitting it into this new context so naturally that one can hardly believe it ever belonged to another: *"Life is a pill which none of us can bear to swallow without gilding*; yet for the poor we delight in stripping it still barer, and are not ashamed to shew even visible displeasure, if ever the bitter taste is taken from their mouths."[25] If this is not what Johnson on any one occasion actually said, it is precisely what we want him to have said. It satisfies us both in itself, for its bitter force, and as a representation of "the Author of the *Rambler*."

Almost as satisfying in the same way is a change that by scholars' standards is merely reprehensible. In *Anecdotes* Piozzi correctly gives Johnson's sentiments about the making of vows, in these terms: "Much of his eloquence, and much of his logic have I heard him use to prevent men from making vows on trivial occasions; and when he saw a person oddly perplexed about a slight difficulty, 'Let the man alone (he would say), and torment him no more about it; there is a vow in the case I am convinced; but is it not very strange that people should be neither afraid nor ashamed of bringing in God Almighty thus at every turn between themselves and their dinner?'" We accept these for Johnson's sentiments because we find similar utterances in the *Life*, in his diaries, and elsewhere. Yet not one of the words attributed to Johnson in this particular passage was uttered by him in its *Thraliana* originals.[26] The phrase, "making vows on trivial occasions" comes from one of Hester's own observations. The first part of Johnson's supposed speech ("Let the man alone . . . I am convinced") is apparently pure invention, and the second part, with the phrase that makes it memorable, was spoken not by Johnson but by a nameless clergyman in an anecdote told to Hester by another friend. From these disparate and (as Boswell would say) "inauthentic" tiles, Piozzi fashions an emblematically truthful mosaic. The sentiments are true to Johnson, though perhaps the words never left his mouth, and they reach an epigrammatically satisfying climax. This is an achievement similar to Johnson's own in his "reporting" of Parliamentary debates. Supplied with little more than the names of the speakers and the sides they took, he composed speeches that would both represent their positions and afford the oratorial satisfactions that one wishes from, but never hears in, the real speeches of politicians.

These examples may serve to suggest that Piozzi's departures from her original versions are not slovenliness but artistry. The point wants stressing, for in *Anecdotes* there are indeed signs of authorial embarrassment which could be taken for slovenliness by the Boswell-ized reader. Cognate with Piozzi's indecision as to the form of the book and her capitulation to Cadell's demand for speed was a severe attack of authorial anxiety. Confronted with the task of writing her first book, she fell deeply into disclaiming her own competence and authority. Thus she permits herself to apologize for not (of all things!) having known Johnson better, she apologizes for not having more to tell, she doubts that she will ever again write for publica-tion, and she tries to turn her supposed literary debility into a virtue, truthfulness—"To endeavour at adorning, or adding, or softening, or meliorating such anecdotes, by any tricks my inexperienced pen could play, would be weakness indeed."[27] This last claim looks like a mode of deceit when it is actually a plea for toleration by a frightened author.

Her uncertainty as to the form she wanted also marks the book. At first it promises to be a sort of biography-with-digressions, but soon the digressions choke the biography. Were the book intended comically we would probably call it "Shandean" and find grave ex-cuses for its disorder, but it is not intended comically, and the reader with even a touch of a formalist critic in him will feel duly scandal-ized. Such a reader was Horace Walpole, whose withering remarks in a letter to Horace Mann are the second most famous attack on *Anecdotes*: "Two days ago appeared Madam Piozzi's anecdotes of Dr. Johnson—I am lamentably disappointed—in her, I mean . . . I had conceived a favourable opinion of her capacity—but this new book is

wretched—a high-varnished preface to a heap of rubbish in a very
vulgar style, and too void of method even for such a farrago."[28]
"Even for such a farrago" implies, at least, that collections of anecdotes were not held to high standards of structural integrity. The
virtue of anecdote is to be sought in the individual specimens, not the
arrangement of the total. Moreover, looseness of structure (to give it
a kind name) is a trait *Anecdotes* shares with many an eighteenth-
century classic, even though most paper over their cracks more plausibly. Boswell's *Tour*, for one, combines a travel journal with anecdotes of Johnson to what is ultimately somewhat odd effect, and the
disproportion of the *Life*, in which Johnson's career from 1709 to
1763 figures as little more than a preface to Boswell's own journal
about Johnson, is not merely notorious but also grotesque. Moreover,
it has had a far more damaging effect on posterity's idea of Johnson
than anything in *Anecdotes*.

Revising Johnson

Despite Boswell's campaign against it, *Anecdotes* quickly became a canonical text about Johnson; it looms large in the first extended life of
Johnson that is not a personal memoir—Robert Anderson's, a life
which already has the appearance of a standard modern biography
in that it synthesizes the accounts of Boswell, Hawkins, Arthur Murphy, and Piozzi and treats them all as equally authoritative. Then
began, with Macaulay's ineffable review of Croker's Boswell (1831),
the phenomenon that Bertrand Bronson called "the Double Tradition of Dr. Johnson." A "folk-Johnson" extracted out of Boswell
largely displaced all other knowledge of Johnson, even of his writings. In resistance to this caricature, twentieth-century commentators
sought to recover Johnson the writer. A monument of their effort is
J. W. Krutch's 1944 biography, the first to make use of the then
recently published Boswell papers and *Thraliana*, and in many ways
the paradigm for all subsequent interpretation of Johnson. Here
Anecdotes resumes its place as a major witness, a place it has kept ever
since.

Roughly, the two Johnsons correspond to the antithetical emotional drives of his two primal commentators. Both Boswell and
Piozzi are themselves revisionists, using Johnson according to their
needs. Boswell needs an embodiment of massive Authority, both to

reverence as an example and to tease; Piozzi needs a latent romantic at war with his own romanticism—a figure that she can both identify and quarrel with, and a figure so obviously tormented and tormenting that her break with him will be pardoned. In veering away from the Boswell-derived folk Johnson, then, modern interpretation could be said only to have preferred Piozzi's antithetical revision of him. This would be a simplification, yet there is truth in it. On some topics it is now traditional to find Piozzi rather than Boswell satisfying: she gives us more usable hints. Among these topics are Johnson's boyhood relations with his parents and several tendencies in his temperament especially illuminating for his ethics and politics.

In writing of Johnson's boyhood Piozzi had the obvious advantage over all his other commentators of having been a mother. She knew what children are like. The stories she tells are emotionally pregnant and highly characteristic. Moreover, they tally with Johnson's own autobiographical fragment unearthed in 1805. Perhaps the first thing today's reader will notice about them is their entire freedom from sentimentality. They are, in fact, at times startlingly "Freudian."

> The two brothers [Sam and Nathaniel] did not . . . much delight in each other's company, being always rivals for the mother's fondness. . . .

> The trick which most parents play with their children, that of shewing off their newly-acquired accomplishments, disgusted Mr. Johnson beyond expression; he had been treated so himself, he said, till he absolutely loathed his father's caresses, because he knew they were sure to precede some unpleasant display of his early abilities; and he used, when neighbours came o'visiting, to run up a tree that he might not be found and exhibited. . . .

> "Poor people's children, dear Lady (said he) never respect them: I did not respect my own mother, though I loved her: and one day, when in anger she called me a puppy, I asked her if she knew what they called a puppy's mother."[29]

Without these stories the interpretive power of every modern biography of Johnson would be diminished, and a psychobiography such as George Irwin's *Samuel Johnson: A Personality in Conflict* could hardly have been written.

Today's readers are so accustomed to seeing stories like these in biographies, and Johnsonians are so accustomed to these particular stories, that we do not stop to think how original it was for Piozzi to tell them in the first place. Five years before Boswell's *Life* and independently of his published *Tour*, she is here practicing the very method of seemingly unfiltered, candid-shot detail that Boswell is usually credited with inventing. If this claim seems exaggerated, we need only recall that the initial scandalous success of *Anecdotes* was of precisely the same kind, and arose from the same causes, as those of the *Tour* and the *Life*. Readers were shocked because all three works appeared to give the most indecently "raw" data about Johnson. The public of the 1780s saw no distinction, in this respect, between Bozzy and Piozzi, a fact attested by the journalistic joke of rhyming their names. In Peter Pindar's ludicrous "Bozzy and Piozzi, a Town Eclogue" (1786), both writers are made to reproach each other with those of their anecdotes that were thought most undignified or defamatory. Among them, sure enough, we find one of Piozzi's anecdotes of Johnson's boyhood: "*Who*, madd'ning with an anecdotic itch, / Declar'd that Johnson call'd his mother *b-tch*?"[30] Until *Anecdotes* no biographer had declared it; to declare it was to fly in the face of eighteenth-century biographical decorum.

As a general model for this unsentimental candor, Piozzi had Johnson's own *Lives of the Poets*, but as a particular precedent for the startlingly forthright details of his childhood she appears to have taken Rousseau's *Confessions* (books 1–6, 1782), in which Rousseau self-consciously lays bare his own unsavory boyhood conduct. "Why Sir," she makes herself say to Johnson apropos one of his recollections, "how like is all this to Jean Jacques Rousseau!" This is an act of inspired resistance to Johnson, whose hatred and distrust of Rousseau's principles (absence of principle, he would have said) were intense. In *Thraliana* she was fond of drawing parallels between Johnson's sentiments and Rousseau's, and she says she made Johnson acknowledge them.[31] That she admitted few of these parallels explicitly into *Anecdotes* is something of a loss, but what she did instead is more striking. In writing of Johnson's boyhood on the model of Rousseau's she brings into view the psychological, pre-Freudian Johnson who is, we now know, really there to see (he is present, for instance, in many *Rambler* essays) but who has hardly any place in Boswell's innocent vision. She is also doing something for which she has never been given credit: an avant-garde experiment in English biography. The credit for biographical innovation has traditionally gone all to Boswell.

The greatest value of *Anecdotes* is not, however, biographical; it is far less a biography than an extended character sketch. In *Thraliana* Hester enjoyed exercising herself in the brief character; we have noticed her characters of her father, herself, and Dr. Collier. The skill that she brought to characterizing Johnson was considerable, and many of her insights have been found so appropriate that we cannot do without them. Such an insight is her exceptional understanding of Johnson's feelings about the poor. Her eloquent comment on them, discussed above, affords a powerful corrective to the stock notion, derived from Boswell, that Johnson was an ossified Tory in the sense in which "Tory" has been understood during the past 150 years: a mere defender of upperclass interests and privileges. Its impact on modern writing about Johnson has been profound, and may be indicated by noting that Bertrand Bronson, in his seminal essay "The Double Tradition of Dr. Johnson," does not quote but rather remembers it. Johnson, he writes, "thought that the mass of the common people was in very little . . . danger from over-abundance of material delights, and always protested at their being denied any innocent sweeteners of a bitter existence."[32] Bronson had so assimilated the Piozzi-Johnson phrasing that his reminiscence of it appears half conscious. He does not cite *Anecdotes*.

It was not only Johnson's professed attitude towards the poor that Piozzi appreciated. She also discerned his fundamental identification with them and his latent anger at the comfortable middle classes—at, precisely, people like herself and Henry Thrale. She discerned it because she had suffered it. Two of her most potent anecdotes, painful to read because they cut so close to the bone, consist of Johnson's rebukes to her own unconscious snobbery. This is one of them:

> I was saying to a friend one day, that I did not like goose; one smells it so while it is roasting, said I: "But you, Madam (replies the Doctor), have been at all times a fortunate woman, having always had your hunger so forestalled by indulgence, that you never experienced the delight of smelling your dinner beforehand." Which pleasure, answered I pertly, is to be enjoyed in perfection by such as have the happiness to pass through Porridge-Island of a morning. "Come, come (says he

gravely), let's have no sneering at what is serious to so many: hundreds of your fellow-creatures, dear Lady, turn another way, that they may not be tempted by the luxuries of Por-ridge-Island to wish for gratification they are not able to ob-tain: you are certainly not better than all of *them*; give God thanks that you are happier."

This is the Johnson who wrote the devastating review of Soame Jenyns's fatuous attempt to justify poverty as being on the whole a good thing. Elsewhere Piozzi reiterates that "he loved the lower ranks of humanity with a real affection," and she adds: "though his talents and learning kept him always in the sphere of upper life, yet he never lost sight of the time when he and they shared pain and pleasure in common." To such remarks as these the modern under-standing of Johnson's social psychology is profoundly indebted. J. W. Krutch's superb observation that Johnson reminded himself of re-ality by reminding himself and other people of hardships, Donald Greene's perception that Johnson needed to draw his strength from "the world of small, ordinary, suffering, inarticulate people," and W. J. Bate's understanding of Johnson's "temptations toward reverse snobbery"—these either derive largely from or concur with Piozzi's portrait in *Anecdotes*.[33]

Still stronger is her treatment of Johnson's general ethics. Per-haps no other writer has so succinctly stated the main ethical inten-tion of his work. His precepts, she says, "tended towards the disper-sion of romantic ideas, and were chiefly intended to promote the cultivation of 'That which before thee lies in daily life.'" The quota-tion is from Adam's reply to Raphael in *Paradise Lost* (8.193); Adam has just been reproved for a latently Satanic (Faustian, Promethean, romantic) demand to know more than his nature permits. The quo-tation locates Johnson precisely in the ethical tradition we have out-lined in chapter 2, a tradition in which both he and Piozzi belong passionately if not wholeheartedly. It is a tradition of skepticism, and thus of resistance to imaginative extremes of all sorts, whether ro-mantic, religious, or philosophical. Attuned, however, to the deep currents in Johnson as well as to his overt positions, Piozzi sees that he could not rest in skepticism. Such was the fierceness of his tem-perament that he had to push skepticism itself to an extreme, be-coming a fanatic of skeptical reductivism. This is the tenor of her penetrating and ultimately satirical comment on "his favourite hypothesis," often quoted today as a commentary on chapter 32 of *Rasselas*, the chapter in which Imlac discourses on the meaning of the pyramids.

> The vacuity of life had at some early period of his life struck so forcibly on the mind of Mr. Johnson, that it became by repeated impression his favourite hypothesis, and the general tenor of his reasonings commonly ended there, wherever they might begin. Such things therefore as other philosophers often attribute to various and contradictory causes, appeared to him uniform enough; all was done to fill up the time, upon this principle. I used to tell him, that it was like the Clown's answer in All's well that ends well, of "Oh Lord, Sir!" for that it suited every occasion. One man, for example, was profligate and wild, . . . followed the girls, or sat still at the gaming-table. "Why, life must be filled up (says Johnson), and the man who is not capable of intellectual pleasures must content himself with such as his senses can afford." Another was a hoarder: "Why, a fellow must do something; and what so easy to a narrow mind as hoarding halfpence till they turn into sixpences."[34]

Usually when this is quoted as gloss on Johnson the middle sentence ("I used to tell him . . .") is omitted. That is exactly the sentence, however, in which Piozzi registers her critique. By insinuating that his hypothesis is monomaniacal, she points up how madly far into skepticism Johnson has gone. *Hypothesis* itself is an irony-charged word, especially in this context; it carries resonances of Swift's satires on intellectual crankery, and it thus suggests that Johnson has failed, in his frenzy of intellectual pride, to look skeptically enough at his own thought. This is not only strong exposition but also powerful criticism of Johnson, criticism that most, even of his modern commentators, have not been able to assimilate. Among them perhaps only W. J. Bate has had the courage and sagacity to confront as Piozzi does the strain of psychological reductivism in Johnson's thinking.[35] Johnson does indeed reduce all motives of human effort to the cravings of egoism or boredom, and among his authentic precursors, as Piozzi understands, are the hateful reductivist philosophers Hobbes and Bernard Mandeville.

We come now to a node of Piozzi's quarrel with Johnson, to the place in *Anecdotes* where she most tellingly expounds and resists him, and to a vantage point for observing the strategies of her own literary warfare. One of Hester's longstanding resentments, voiced frequently in *Thraliana* as well as in *Anecdotes*, was of Johnson's over-scrupulous refusals to affect concern he was not absolutely sure he felt. With them went refusals to accept other people's expressions of concern at face value. In her life with him she endured these as daily refusals to be civil, as manglings of etiquette, aggravated by Johnson's infuriating assertions to the effect that civility was a system of cant and that he alone, in being surly, was being honest. "Canter indeed he was none," she writes in *Thraliana* in 1780; "he would forget to ask people after their Relation's Welfare, & say in excuse that he knew they did not care, for why should they? every body had as much as they could do in this World to care for themselves; & no Leisure to *think* of their Neighbour's Distresses, however they might take Delight in *talking* of them."[36] In *Anecdotes* she envisions this behavior as a demonic puritanism whose antecedents are Mandeville and La Rochefoucauld. To appreciate what that signifies, we need a brief excursus.

Ever since its publication (1714), Mandeville's *Fable of the Bees* had been universally denounced for its mocking demonstration that Christian virtue and the ordinary customs of modern civilization are strictly incompatible. Very few books published in the eighteenth century were felt to be so scandalous and were so thoroughly unpopular. What galled readers was its thesis that "private vices," or "luxury," although contrary to Christian ethics are socially necessary, and that in strict truth no civilized society could afford to be Christian. Hence the *Fable* was received variously as an encouragement to vice and as a showing-up of everyone who both professed Christianity and lived a normal social life. Piozzi herself remarks of Mandeville's argument that he "strips Men naked to make them pious," meaning that his idea of virtue is inhumanly purgatorial. She sees no practical difference between Mandeville and his seeming antithesis William Law, author of the rigidly fundamentalist *Serious Call to a Devout and Holy Life*. They are equally extremists, and "each splits upon the same Rock too, for failing to define Luxury or Temperance, they both leave their Readers uninform'd whether any thing but Acorns & Water are allowable to people of strict Virtue, which Mandeville holds to be perpetual Self denial." (In this she concurs with Adam Smith, one of Johnson's nemeses, who detected "the great fallacy of Dr. Mandeville's book." The fallacy is "to represent every passion as wholly vicious, which is so in any degree and in any direction.") Mandeville is guilty of a reductive and inhuman ethical rigorism. Yet there was a side of Piozzi that confessed his force and even found him attractive. She speaks of his "coarse Truths," admitting their validity on an abstract, superhuman plane; more, she admires the wit and brilliance of the *Fable*, declaring (through the mouth of Una in her 1791 dialogues) that it "is a Work of wonderful Research, & vigorous Ability." She also sees in it "an admirable Antidote against *Shaftburism*," that is, against the liberal optimism which she believes has sapped Christianity's foundations. In *British Synonymy*, however, her considered verdict is against all ethical rigorists. Were we to be persuaded by them, "we must despair of pleasing God"; theirs is a counsel of moral suicide. Therefore, "whilst, as authors, we must ever esteem such men, and, as people of vigorous and powerful minds, we must for ever respect them, let us never take for teachers people, who, as our blessed Master expresses it, bind heavy burthens on the shoulders of others— and grievous to be borne—but they themselves will not move them with one of their fingers."[37]

Remembering Johnson's various assertions in defense of human weakness and his charming ingenuity in finding excuses for the bad behavior of people like Richard Savage, we might not be inclined to class him among those teachers. But Johnson's ethical practice is inconsistent; he could argue passionately both ways. If humane flexibility is one Johnsonian standard, then it is the standard by which Piozzi calls him to account for his departures from it. In *Anecdotes* she takes care to demonstrate his unofficial ethical alliance with Mandeville and with the equally raspish analyst of human depravity, La Rochefoucauld. "The natural depravity of mankind and remains of original sin were so fixed in Mr. Johnson's opinion, that he was indeed a most acute observer of their effects; and used to say sometimes, half in jest half in earnest, that they were the remains of his old tutor Mandeville's instructions. As a book however, he took care always loudly to condemn the Fable of the Bees." And now her own protest, in which many years of accumulated rage are crystalized:

> Few things indeed which pass well enough with others would do with him: he had been a great reader of Mandeville, and was ever on the watch to spy out those stains of original corruption, so easily discovered by a penetrating observer even in the purest minds. I mentioned an event, which if it had hap-

pened would greatly have injured Mr. Thrale and his family—
—and then dear Sir, said I, how sorry you would have been! "I
hope (replied he after a long pause)—I should have been *very*
sorry;——but remember Rochefoucault's maxim" ["In the
misfortunes of our friends we always find something that does
not displease us"].——I would rather (answered I) remember
Prior's verses, and ask,

> What need of books these truths to tell,
> Which folks perceive that cannot spell?
> And must we spectacles apply,
> To see what hurts our naked eye?

Will *any* body's mind bear this eternal microscope that you
place upon your own so?

She is right. Johnson had indeed read Mandeville, and avowed to
Boswell that "he opened my views into real life very much." Piozzi
implies, rather, that what he taught Johnson was a posture of excessive demand on life, a posture in some respects saintly but also
intolerable in its constant nosing-out of human falseness. Johnson
drives virtue to its apocalyptic limit. By opposing to this the more
conventional, more moderate ethic expressed here in the words of
Matthew Prior, Piozzi demonstrates again the extremity of Johnson's
stance. His Mandevillian "microscope," however admirable theoreti-
cally, pragmatically is inhuman. So disturbing is this insight that most
of Johnson's modern commentators have sidestepped it; again, only
Bate has been able to embrace it and build it into a larger understanding of Johnson's mind.[38]

Her use of Prior against Johnson, we may pause to note, is not
fortuitous; it is a calculated and cunning tour de force. She liked
Prior's verse, Johnson despised it, and they had disputed its merits,
as we learn from Boswell. The lines with which she opposes Johnson
are from Prior's *Alma*, a poem of which Johnson, in his *Life of Prior*,
speaks dismissively: "His greater pieces are only tissues of common
thoughts."[39] In *Anecdotes* Piozzi is having the last word, and having
it with great effect. This must be the only instance in all of Johnsonian commentary of a Johnson position's being called to account and
found wanting by the standard of so much lesser a mind as Prior.
Moreover, that Prior is a lesser mind is very much part of the point.
Piozzi, of course, knew that he is; she is using him exactly as a mouthpiece of the sane and ordinary—of, indeed, "common thoughts." He

is shorthand for "that which before thee lies in daily life." For all that Johnson, as she says, "intended to promote the cultivation of 'that which before thee lies in daily life,'" he could not himself, she is also saying, condescend to do it. He is too wise, too truth-obsessed, too proud, too much the Great Man, too much the destroying demon.

Contemplating this theme, Piozzi is moved to reflect on the community's relation to its great writers: "It is easy to observe, that the justice of such sentences made them offensive; but . . . I hope that the reason our hearts rebelled . . . against his severity, was chiefly because it came from a living mouth." Unbearable in person, the great writer becomes acceptable when removed to a distance from us by the book: "Books were invented to take off the odium of immediate superiority, and soften the rigour of duties prescribed by the teachers . . . of human kind—setting at least those who are acknowledged wiser than ourselves at a distance." Books blunt the edge of competitiveness, lessening its damage to our self-esteem; they are socially endurable. Yet, for that very reason books also fade from our minds: "When we recollect however, that for this very reason *they* are seldom consulted and little obeyed, how much cause shall his contemporaries have to rejoice that their living Johnson forced them to feel the reproofs due to vice and folly—while Seneca and Tillotson were no longer able to make impression—except on our shelves."[40] This is Piozzi's own vacillation between Prior and Mandeville, or between daily life and the prophetic truth which overturns and lays waste. In her own temperament as in Johnson's there was a strain of prophecy, to which in later years she gave rein.

Clearly, a great strength of her commentary is the cunning with which Piozzi relates Johnson to other writers. Especially shrewd is her treatment of the troubled relation in which Johnson felt himself to stand towards Swift. It is far superior to Boswell's puzzled regret that Johnson appeared to have so little respect for his predecessor. Overtly she concurs with Boswell, although with the difference that she can state a reason: "Though no man perhaps made such rough replies as Dr. Johnson, yet nobody had a more just aversion to general satire; he always hated and censured Swift for his unprovoked bitterness against the professors of medicine." Later she returns to the topic: "He . . . for the most part professed himself to feel directly contrary to Dr. Swift, 'who (says he) hates the world, though he loves John and Robert, and certain individuals.'" Johnson, on the contrary, "said always, 'that the world was well constructed, but that the particular people disgraced the elegance and beauty of the general fabric.' " Her phrasing, however, suggests by the patness of its reversals that the distinction Johnson ostentatiously makes between himself and Swift is a distinction without a difference. What, indeed, is the difference between despising the world and despising the people it contains? A little later still, one of her most flattening anecdotes lets out the secret, and does it by means of literary allusion:

> Mr. Johnson did not like any one who said they were happy, or who said any one else was so. "It is all *cant* (he would cry), the dog knows he is miserable all the time." A friend . . . told him . . . notwithstanding, that his wife's sister was *really* happy, and called upon the lady to confirm his assertion. . . . "If your sister-in-law is really the contented being she professes herself Sir [said Johnson], her life gives the lie to every research of humanity; for she is happy without health, without beauty, without money, and without understanding." This story he told me himself; and when I expressed something of the horror I felt, "The same stupidity (said he) which prompted her to extol felicity she never felt, hindered her from feeling what shocks you on repetition. I tell you, the woman is ugly, and sickly, and foolish, and poor; and would it not make a man hang himself to hear such a creature say, it was happy?"

The language given to Johnson in the last sentence smacks of Gulliver's language at the end of book 4 of *Gulliver's Travels*: "But, when I behold a Lump of Deformity, and Diseases both in Body and Mind, smitten with *Pride*, it immediately breaks all the Measures of my Patience." Probably Johnson never said these words; they are Piozzi's way of dramatizing the likeness she observes between his temperament and Swift's. It was a likeness perceived by another discerning woman, too. In the Hebrides, Johnson regaled his hostess Lady McLeod with a curt dissertation on human depravity; her muttered comment, Boswell tells us, was "This is worse than Swift."[41] Johnsonians today recognize in Johnson the affinity with Swift that seems to have made Johnson himself so uneasy, perhaps because he perceived in Swift's unrelenting, all-but-Gulliverian demands on experience the danger into which his own temperament could easily lead him, that he had to resist it by belittling Swift's achievement.

In sum, the Johnson we understand today is in important respects more the Johnson that Piozzi gives us than the one we find in

Boswell. It is even tempting to suggest that had Boswell never written we might have known Johnson better from the beginning, for the light Piozzi sheds on him, although less brilliant than Boswell's, is often shed upon more relevant places. The needs that actuated Boswell were often idiosyncratic and remote from anything that Johnson normally said or did; who but Boswell would have had to make Johnson into a sanction for "high feudal ideas" of family and baronial rights? As a writer, Boswell has no natural quarrel with Johnson; therefore he never comes to grips with Johnson's writings. He merely admires them sentimentally. Piozzi, never a sentimentalist of Johnson or of anything else (she is much too fierce for that), resembles Johnson both in temperament and in her acquired literary behavior. Like Johnson she is a literary fighter, and she wins her fights by many of the same means. The means are revisionary, and their fundamental strategy is reversal. Thus, for instance, if Johnson repudiates Swift, Piozzi reattaches Swift to him, undoing his repudiation. If Johnson is a greater mind than Matthew Prior, Piozzi so stations both of them that Johnson's greatness shall appear to be a liability and Prior's littleness health. If Johnson takes care "loudly to condemn" *The Fable of the Bees*, Piozzi demonstrates that he is a Mandevillian at heart. If Johnson's precepts urge "the dispersion of romantic ideas," Piozzi shows him to be a fanatic in need of his own counsel. If Johnson inculcates a wise skepticism regarding human motives, Piozzi insinuates that he is too little skeptical of his own skepticism.

In some of this we observe that she tries Johnson by his own professed standards and finds that he does not meet them. This is a technique that she practices also with other writers whom she is resisting: with Pope, whose avowed ambition was "correctness" and whom, accordingly, she often finds insufficiently correct ("Swift is infinitely neater, and more attentive," she remarks on one occasion); with Burke, who demands that political doctrines take account of human need and whom she will find insufficiently ad hominem. Another of her strategies is to play one writer against another: Louis Racine against Pope, Swift against Pope, even Soame Jenyns against Pope; Mandeville against Shaftesbury; Tom Paine against Burke, as we shall see; Prior against Johnson. In all of this she behaves very much like Johnson himself, one of the fiercest revisionists who ever wrote. Revisionism is virtually the ruling technique of his *Lives of the Poets*, in which, for instance, Milton is powerfully deployed against

Milton and Swift against Swift.⁴² In a word, *Anecdotes* is a deeply Johnsonian book, Johnsonian in its procedural dynamics, and the strength of its commentary derives from those dynamics. To these passions and their triumphs Boswell is pretty much a stranger.

"With Much Violence"

The best of Johnson's earliest commentators all found in him the makings of drama. Boswell's *Life* is not just comic, it is displaced stage comedy. The *Tour*, written in the same manner, Boswell himself calls "this dramatick sketch." Boswell was not the only one in whom the figure of Johnson inspired theatrical effects; Sir Joshua Reynolds composed Johnsonian dialogues, and Fanny Burney in her *Diary* dramatizes Johnson at times as well as Boswell does. So too Mrs. Thrale, in the first of her dialogues upon her own death, in which Johnson is made to stand out as a brooding giant among frivolous nonentities like William Weller Pepys: "(*Very loud*) Nay but give me leave—I did not interrupt you. —No Man I say has a Right to obtrude unpleasing Images on my Mind, nor force me for his Pleasure upon making ungrateful Comparisons between my past & present State of Existence. Would you declaim upon the happiness of sound Health to Beauclerc? Would you talk to your Friend (*sneeringly*) Keppel of the twenty seventh of July?"⁴³ Granted that Boswell, Burney, and Thrale were all frustrated or would-be writers for the stage who found in Johnson an object for the exercise of their talents, still Johnson's own self-dramatization must have been compelling to inspire such uniformity of practice in rendering him.

In *Anecdotes* Piozzi does not use stage dialogue, although she sometimes uses stage directions, such as "(hesitating a while)," to set up an effect. Yet her accounts, even when strictly narrative, often give the impression of drama, and specifically of melodrama. In this one there are the abrupt, enigmatic character of Johnson's first speech and the tormented emphasis of "*Do* not ask me": "One day when my son was going to school, and dear Dr. Johnson followed as far as the garden gate, praying for his salvation, in a voice which those who listened attentively, could hear plain enough, he said to me suddenly, 'Make your boy tell you his dreams: the first corruption that entered into my heart was communicated in a dream.' What was it, Sir? said I. '*Do* not ask me,' replied he with much violence, and walked away in apparent agitation. I never durst make any further enquiries."[44]

Indeed, if *Anecdotes* does not quite dramatize Johnson in the technical sense, it excels every other book about him in the degree to which it melodramatizes him. Inasmuch as melodrama is not an admired literary mode this may seem a perverse compliment; interpretively it would seem to promise disaster, since melodrama is antithetical to Johnson's whole literary effort. Yet interpretively, as we have seen, *Anecdotes* is powerful, and melodrama is emotionally right for it and unexpectedly persuasive.

The total effect of *Anecdotes* is its power to disturb; it was a shocker on its first appearance, and it can still make us wince. Its first readers ascribed their dismay to Piozzi's willingness to tell things improper in a memoir. Even before the book was finished, prudent Fanny Burney was wringing her hands in dread at the prospect of it: "What will she *not* say! . . . 'Tis an opportunity for imprudent anecdotes which might endanger indiscretion even in the most cautious & fearful;—She, therefore, *always in*cautious & fearless!—O with how little pleasure, & how much pain shall I ever see her Book!" Fanny knew her woman. If we judge by a standard of biographical decorum which says, as James Beattie did in criticizing Boswell's anecdotes, that "Johnson's faults were balanced by many and great virtues; and when that is the case, the virtues only should be remembered, and the faults entirely forgotten," then we will agree that Piozzi was remarkably tactless. Few memoirists are likely ever to write, for instance, this: "Dr. Lawrence told [Johnson] one day, that if he would come and beat him once a week he would bear it; but to hear his complaints was more than *man* could support. 'Twas therefore that he tried, I suppose, and in eighteen years contrived to weary the patience of a *woman*."[45]

This explosion, and other asperities in *Anecdotes*, erupt out of the feminist in Piozzi, who is here allowing herself to feel tired to death of what it has meant to her to be a woman. It has meant being an object of emotional importunity, being badgered, being always on call. Since most of Johnson's admirers (in print, at least) have been male, it is hardly surprising that such remarks have found no favor. They seem petulant only, and make it tempting to reduce *Anecdotes* to a sectarian document, "a more or less true impression of Johnson from a woman's point of view."[46] But "a woman's point of view" is, of course, intrinsically no more sectarian than a man's. It differs from a man's chiefly, in contexts like this one, by virtue of the fact that women have commonly felt obliged to absorb a good deal of male ill treatment. In daily life they experience combinations of intimacy and violence that men are less apt to visit upon each other, and with these they experience fear. Such, certainly, was Hester's experience with Johnson. After resentment, fear is the root emotion of *Anecdotes*; she was afraid of Johnson's latent violence and anguish, and she makes us feel these in him as does no other writer. She does it by melodrama.

We feel that to live familiarly with him must have been a perpetual walking on eggshells:

> [One] day, when he was ill, and exceedingly low-spirited, and persuaded that death was not far distant, I appeared before him in a dark-coloured gown, which his bad sight, and worse apprehensions, made him mistake for an iron-grey. "Why do you delight (said he) thus to thicken the gloom of misery that surrounds me? is it not here sufficient accumulation of horror without anticipated mourning?" This is not mourning Sir (said I), drawing the curtain, that the light might fall upon the silk, and shew it was a purple mixed with green. "Well, well (replied he, changing his voice), you little creatures should never wear those sort of clothes however; they are unsuitable in every way. What! have not all insects gay colours?"

This, she says in an acute phrase, is a specimen of Johnson's "temptation to sudden resentment." It was not the only demon in him. At many points in *Anecdotes* Johnson appears startlingly like (of all characters) Heathcliff in *Wuthering Heights*. There is the same countenance expressive of a soul in torment: "his eyes, though of a light-grey colour, were so wild, so piercing, and at times so fierce, that fear was I believe the first emotion in the hearts of all his beholders." There is the same capacity to turn a normal social occasion into a purgatory:

> Two gentlemen . . . dining with us at Streatham . . . when Elliot's brave defence of Gibraltar was a subject of common discourse, one of these men naturally enough begun some talk about . . . [cannon] balls thrown with surprising dexterity

and effect: which Dr. Johnson having listened some time to, "I would advise you, Sir (said he with a cold sneer), never to relate this story again; you really can scarce imagine how *very poor* a figure you make in the telling of it." Our guest . . . needed no more reproofs for the same folly; so if he ever did speak again, it was in a low voice to the friend who came with him.

There is the same savage verbal mockery of inferiors, in a nasty little scene between Johnson and his black servant Frank:

"What is the matter, child (says Dr. Johnson), that you leave Streatham to-day? *Art sick?*" He is jealous (whispered I). "Are you jealous of your wife, you stupid blockhead (cries out his master in another tone)?" The fellow hesitated; and, *To be sure Sir*, I *don't quite approve Sir*, was the stammering reply. "Why, what do they *do* to her, man? do the footmen kiss her?" No Sir, no!—Kiss my *wife Sir!*—*I hope not Sir*. "Why, what *do* they do to her, my lad?" Why nothing Sir, I'm sure Sir. "Why then go back directly and dance you dog, do; and let's hear no more of such empty lamentations."

This sounds very little like our notion of Johnson (and it has no counterpart in *Thraliana*); it could easily be an exchange between Heathcliff and his wretched boy Linton. More recognizably Johnsonian, but no less Heathcliffian, are Johnson's mysteriousness of manner ("the lofty consciousness of his own superiority . . . cast . . . an impenetrable veil over him when he said nothing"), his power to penetrate people's disguises ("he hated disguise, and nobody penetrated it so readily"), and his power of pathos, "which no one ever possessed in so eminent a degree" and by means of which he browbeat Hester into keeping late hours with him.[47]

Actually, Boswell's Johnson is just as unpredictable and aggressive as Piozzi's; it is from the *Life*, not *Anecdotes*, that posterity has derived its image of Johnson as "Ursa Major," prompt to knock down his conversation partners with the butt end of his gun. Boswell, however, valued Johnson's violence as an object of hero-worship. The attitude he takes towards it in the *Life* is adumbrated in his 1773 Hebrides journal. Here we learn that Boswell was perfectly aware of Johnson's irritability and its usual consequences: "I regretted that

Mr. Johnson did not practise the art of accommodating himself to different sorts of people. . . . But Mr. Johnson's forcible spirit and impetuosity of manner may be said to spare neither sex nor age. I have seen even Mrs. Thrale stunned." But although Boswell regrets this, he also frankly admires it: "But I have often maintained that it is better so. Pliability of address I take to be inconsistent with that majestic power which he has, and which produces such noble effects. . . . What though he presses down feeble beings in his course? They get up again like stalks of ripe grass."[48] In this singular, proto-Carlylian view, Johnson's petulance—of which he himself was ashamed—becomes an attribute of "power," and its "effects" are regarded as if they were esthetic objects. In the *Life* Boswell exerts his formidable skill to make them nothing less than things of beauty. Humanly speaking, this ambition is perverse.

Anecdotes is a much less beautiful but, I am suggesting, at bottom a more humane book. Piozzi makes us feel Johnson's purgatory, and the purgatories he created around him, as Boswell rarely does; she makes us feel, at moments, how it would really have been to live with such a man. Hugh Blair was one reader who felt it: "I should think it better to read him, and admire him at a distance like a stupendous object, than to have been too near him," Blair remarked after finishing *Anecdotes*. At the same time—and this is an effect unusual for melodrama—Piozzi makes us feel Johnson's human typicality. The man who dramatizes his pain, who resorts to "vehement lamentations and piercing reproofs"; the man whose "temptation to sudden resentment" is apt to unleash insults at the people he loves; the man who, reminded of a promise to write a charity letter, snaps, "When I have written my letter for Dick, I may hang myself, mayn't I?"—such a man is all too human. It has always been conventional among Johnson's biographers to imagine him as a representative man, albeit on a colossal scale. In him, writes Boswell, "the heterogeneous composition of human nature was remarkably exemplified." His life, writes W. J. Bate, "continues to hold attention because it is so close to general human experience in a wide variety of ways." In this his biographers have been his pupils, taking their cue from *Rambler* 60. *Anecdotes* partakes in this convention, and its portrait of Johnson is darker than most because Piozzi had experienced his overbearing humanity to a greater degree than anyone else who has ever written about him. But she also seems to have taken the cue of *Rambler* 14, one of Johnson's tacit apologies for his own bad behavior, in which he laments that "those who raise admiration by their books, disgust by their company."[49] The best part of every author, Johnson once cautioned an admirer, is to be found in his book, and he would have recognized with pain the theme that *Anecdotes* elaborates: Most of the very great men are odious.

FIVE

The Records of a Pure and Blameless Friendship

Johnson's and Piozzi's Letters

In this publication the republic of letters has received a valuable present, conveyed to them by the hands of a lady to whose genius, discrimination, and fertility of composition they have already been considerably indebted. Such, however, is the ingratitude, and such the caprice, of the readers of literary publications, that Mrs Piozzi has incurred from many a considerable degree of sarcasm and censure for a conduct that has merited nothing but applause.[1]

AT WORK ON *Anecdotes* in Italy, Piozzi wrote to a friend at home, "My book is in very pretty forwardness, but the letters I have in England are my best possessions." In her London bank vault and a trunk at Streatham she had over four hundred letters from Johnson to her and her family, approximately 25 percent of all the Johnson letters now known.[2] For about ten years she had been Johnson's principal correspondent, the one to whom he wrote not only most of his letters but also (although judgments on this have occasionally differed) his best letters. Her edition of them, *Letters to and from the Late Samuel Johnson*, is a landmark in the making of the Johnson canon, the first publication of a large mass of his correspondence. Like *Anecdotes* it made an immense stir, composed equally of dismay and delight. Its most passionate detractor was Joseph Baretti, Queeney's old tutor, whose virulent attack in three issues of the *European Magazine* impugns Hester's editing, her parenting, and her second marriage; this, with Boswell's, Walpole's, and Gifford's performances, completes the list of most famous savagings of her work. On the other hand, even before the publication of *Letters* Boswell himself predicted—with what queasy sensations we may imagine—that it would "be a rich addition to the Johnsonian Memorabilia." His ally Edmond Malone took home a copy, sat down to read, and was riveted: "I sat up till four o'clock reading away as hard as I could, and then my candle went out and I could read no more. . . . The letters are, I think, in general very pleasing. . . . I would not have one of them omitted."[3] Other admirers were William Cowper and, later, Jane Austen.

It is the common fate of editors that their work is superseded. Unlike *Anecdotes*, *Letters* has not stayed in print. It has been superseded twice: first by G. B. Hill's edition (1892) and then by R. W. Chapman's (1952), each of which gathers all of Johnson's letters. Of course, an editor whose work is superseded may yet be esteemed for it, as Johnson's editing of Shakespeare is still esteemed. Piozzi's editing of Johnson, although in fact estimable, has not yet recovered from the Boswell—and here, also the Baretti—stigma. From their innuendoes Hill learned to distrust her; obliged by the absence of manuscripts to use her texts in his edition, he nevertheless accused her of having forged parts of them. Obviously, in the absence of manuscripts with which to compare her texts this charge could only be speculative, and Chapman, who saw the manuscripts, found her not guilty. His edition, however, is naturally the one that students of Johnson now prefer. Although about fifty Johnson letters still exist for us only in Piozzi's texts, *Letters* itself is no longer in request.

And yet Piozzi's editing merits not just exoneration but praise, and *Letters* merits revival. She merits at least the minimum praise of having done first what others have since done better. More important, her editorial practice, like her biographical practice, was comparatively innovative. Not only did she produce generally accurate texts of Johnson's letters, but she contributed to bringing the personal letter itself into literary acceptance. Also, Johnson's letters to her stand out as a special part of his canon, and for purposes of enjoyment her edition is still the best form in which to read them. It has what Chapman's edition necessarily lacks, a unity of tone, design, and subject matter that raises it out of utilitarian scholarship and makes it literature. Its unity is, in part, a product of her editing. On all these grounds, the principles and practice of that editing deserve reconsideration.

From Letters to Literature

Editing texts is one of the central institutional activities of literature. To edit a hitherto unpublished text is to offer it for inclusion in the community's canon of literature—to claim that it holds interest for the community. In the eighteenth century the interest value (and therefore the literary status) of personal letters was still uncertain. Contemplating *Letters*, Fanny Burney had great misgivings: "improperly published," she calls it, and an "injury to [Johnson's] memory." Hannah More agreed: "They are such letters as ought to have been *written*, but ought never to have been *printed*. The imprudence of editors and executors is an additional reason why men of parts should be afraid to die." Both women voice the conservative position, the position taken by Thomas Sprat in his memoir of Abraham Cowley over a century earlier. "The truth is," writes Sprat, "the Letters that pass between particular Friends, if they are written as they ought to be, can scarce ever be fit to see the light." Such letters, Sprat reasons, "should have a . . . peculiar kind of Familiarity, which can only affect the humour of those to whom they were intended. The very same passages which make Writings of this Nature delightful amongst Friends will lose all manner of taste when they come to be read by those that are indifferent." The personal letter is by definition individual, particular, and local; it is tied to a specific occasion in one person's daily life. Literature, on the other hand, consists of those texts which the community accepts as having a high degree of *general* interest. The personal letter, then, no more merits printing than does the proverbial laundry list. This is exactly the criticism Piozzi anticipates in her mock review of *Letters*: "who can it benefit, or who can it please? to hear in one Letter that poor Mrs Salusbury has had a bad night, and that little Sophy's Head ach'd all Yesterday?"[4]

These views, of course, appear sharply at odds with the facts of publishing history. Eighteenth-century writing displays keen interest in letters, both in form and substance. Not only novels but travel books and other kinds of nonfiction employed epistolary form; epistolary form itself was the subject of manuals such as Richardson's *Familiar Letters on Important Occasions*. The actual letters of individuals—Swift, Pope, Chesterfield, Gray—had been warmly received by the public. The tendency of this interest, however, is towards the general, not the particular. Models of epistolary form are of obvious general interest, for they give instruction in the art and etiquette of letter writing. The letters of travelers, such as Lady Mary Wortley Montagu's letters from Turkey (1763), are of general interest for their subject matter; they are equivalent to essays on manners and narratives of journeys. A personal letter automatically becomes interesting if it conveys, or can be read as conveying, moral instruction; it then becomes a moral essay, detachable by virtue of its sentiments from the private accidents of its origin. The letters of Pope were esteemed in this way; Johnson, in his *Life of Pope*, suspects Pope of composing them expressly to be printed, with the design that the purity of their sentiments should enhance his public image. That is, Johnson perceives them as simply another part of Pope's literary effort.

Eighteenth-century editing of letters proceeds in accordance with the demand for general interest. By being printed, the private letter is being treated as literature; its matter or manner ought therefore to have literary value. William Mason justifies printing Gray's juvenile letters by the "hope that they may prompt [students] to emulate their elegant simplicity, and, of course, to study with more care the classic models from which it was derived. If they do this, I shall not be much concerned if graver readers think them unimportant or even trifling." Boswell prints Johnson's letter to Dr. Lawrence on the death of Mrs. Lawrence for its "admirable strain of sympathy and pious consolation"; he prints also a letter to a young clergyman "which contains valuable advice to Divines in general." It follows from this that all the characteristics of a letter that tie it to its original context, that are idiosyncratic or lacking in general import, are unworthy of print; one excludes or alters them. Mason omits from Gray's letters their stylistic eccentricities and their most intimate statements. Boswell declines to print some of Johnson's letters on the ground that they "would be improper to insert, as they are filled with unpleasing [medical] details." One also excises statements that might betray other people's privacy or hurt their reputations. On these grounds Boswell was obliged to change the text of one Johnson letter and to make omissions in others.[5]

Because in printing a letter one is adding it to its author's published canon, one has a responsibility to his reputation; one ought not to act contrary to his probable wishes or usual authorial practice. (This principle long survived the eighteenth century; it is urged by George Saintsbury as late as 1922.) In his omissions Mason emulates

Gray's own authorial fastidiousness, declining, for instance, to print a youthful translation from Tibullus because it exhibits inferior technical judgment and translating Gray's French into English because he doubts the French "would stand the test of polite criticism." Johnson himself, anticipating that one of his letters may be printed, entreats his correspondent "to revise it; there may, perhaps, be some negligencies."[6] Given these concerns, it goes without saying that no editor would have printed a letter with all its writer's peculiarities of punctuation and spelling; the printer would be trusted to normalize them, just as with any author's manuscript.

Piozzi treats Johnson's letters according to these principles. (In her editing she had the help of Samuel Lysons, a scholarly young man who was later appointed Keeper of the Records of the Tower of London. Chapman asserts that Lysons was "virtually the editor" of *Letters*, but this is a needless insult to Piozzi's competence. Her correspondence with Lysons during 1787 suggests that they worked jointly and that she had the final word.) Anticipating, like Mason, critical charges of triviality, she defends the letters on Johnsonian ethical grounds: "None but domestick and familiar events can be expected from a private correspondence; no reflexions but such as they excite can be found there; yet whoever turns away disgusted . . . will here be likely to lose some genuine pleasure, and some useful knowledge of what our heroick Milton was himself contented to respect, as *That which before thee lies in daily life*." In her standard of the admissible she is considerably more liberal than Mason. She printed the great majority of the letters she had; only ninety-two that are now known are not in her edition. These include Johnson's bizarre French letter, his first reply to her marriage announcement (a letter that does him no credit), some letters that mention people in possibly injurious ways, and many short notes without distinction of sentiment or style, all of them manifestly inferior to the letters she did print.[7] In her rejections Piozzi's literary judgment cannot be faulted.

"The letters," she states in her preface, ". . . remain just as he wrote them; and I did not like to mutilate such as contained either sallies of humour or precepts of morality, because they might be mingled with family affairs." It will be clear from the foregoing that they do not really remain "just as he wrote them." Besides concealing names she made occasional abridgements (fifty of the printed letters are known to be abridged), usually of postscripts or a single sentence but in one instance of fully half a letter, and in about a dozen letters she made verbal changes.[8] Unlike Boswell, who also abridged letters, she did not acknowledge her abridgements; hence we cannot tell whether her texts of letters now lost are complete. She sent to her printer the letters themselves, not copies (this too was common practice; Boswell did likewise), and she did not read proof against the originals (neither did Boswell). Thus for the actual line-by-line text of *Letters* we are indebted to a nameless typesetter. Whoever he was he did his job well, reading Johnson's crabbed hand with commendable accuracy. The result is by no means the editorial disgrace that it has been reputed to be. Her claim that the letters remain as Johnson wrote them is broadly if not literally true. *Letters* presents a good reading text, and a text that is far closer to what Johnson wrote than Mason's text of Gray is to what Gray wrote.

Usually her work has been defended, when at all, by appeal to the practice of her time. What she did badly, it has been argued, her contemporaries mostly did worse.[9] This, however, misses the point both of the practice itself and of her relation to it. Eighteenth-century editorial conduct makes perfectly good sense on its own premises. True, eighteenth-century editors do not give us what their authors wrote; they give us, rather, what they judge their authors would have printed. Mason's conservative judgment accords with Gray's general secretiveness and fastidiousness. Boswell, appealing to Johnson's published declarations in *Rambler* 60 and elsewhere that in a biography all should be told, accordingly produces texts that hew closely to what Johnson wrote. Piozzi also invokes Johnson's sanction: that is the import of her appeal to the reader not to "turn away disgusted" from "that which before thee lies in daily life." The real significance of her claim that "the letters remain just as he wrote them" is its highly Johnsonian flouting of decorum; it is the counterpart of her unsentimental anecdotes of Johnson's boyhood. Once again, she is engaged in the same innovating campaign as Boswell. The results scandalized many readers, who felt that trifling, subliterary documents were being obtruded on the public. Retrospectively, it is more accurate to say that Piozzi and Boswell were asking their public to enlarge its conception of literature. Obviously, in their campaign they succeeded. Between them they did canonize Johnson's letters; twenty years later Jane Austen was one who read them for literary enjoyment. In canonizing Johnson's letters, Piozzi contributed to canonizing the familiar letter itself. Her edition deserves honor as an act that changed the social conception of literature in England.

An account of the contents of *Letters* really belongs in a book about Johnson; moreover, his letters to Mrs. Thrale have been intelligently appraised by many readers. They are well characterized by one of his first biographers, Robert Anderson: "Some are grave, some gloomy, some pathetic, some sententious, and others are lively, literary, domestic, and descriptive. . . . We see him in health and in sickness, in solitude and in society, at home and abroad, and in all the petty business of life." Even if we accept Johnson's own judgment that "there is in them not much history of mind, or any thing else," we will certainly hold, with Thomas Seccombe, that each is "an epitome of the Johnson style, terse, dignified, full of linguistic energy."[10] There is, however, important "history of mind" in them. It was to Mrs. Thrale that Johnson wrote almost all his letters from Scotland during the 1773 journey; they amount to a diary of his encounter with the Hebrides and are the nucleus of his *Journey to the Western Islands of Scotland*. Seven years later, his letters to Mrs. Thrale provide our best register of Johnson's struggles with the *Lives of the Poets*: his day-to-day progress (and, often, lack of it), his pleasure when he does a poet well, his spells of boredom with the job, his impatience to be done, and his acute, tragic sense that being done will only throw him back on the emptiness of life.

Many of the letters represent Johnson in his best essayistic vein and are virtually extra numbers of the *Rambler*—such as this one, in which he reminds Hester of the antiquity of their friendship: "To those that have lived long together, every thing heard and every thing seen, recals some pleasure communicated, or some benefit conferred, some petty quarrel, or some slight endearment. . . . A friendship of twenty years is interwoven with the texture of life. A friend may be often found and lost, but an *old friend* never can be found, and Nature has provided that he cannot easily be lost." Their most persistent quality, however, is their sheer literariness; knowing intimately Hester's love of literature and completely at one with her in it, Johnson relaxes into every kind of literary allusion and play. He runs the gamut from the Latin classics to nursery rhymes; he parodies the jargon of newspaper politics and the cant of modern criticism ("Can you write such a letter as this? So miscellaneous, with such noble disdain of regularity; like Shakespeare's works, such graceful negligence of transition, like the ancient enthusiasts"); he writes a mordant little dissertation on the naive notion, "sounded by the knowing to the ignorant, and so echoed by the ignorant to the knowing," that in their intimate letters people bare their souls.[11]

Writing from Lichfield in 1767, where he has endured the boredom of his annual visit, Johnson thinks of coming home: "when I do come, I perhaps shall not be easily persuaded to pass again to the other side of Styx, to venture myself on the irremeable road. I long to see you." Johnson is thinking of the *Aeneid*, vi. 424, where the river Styx is called *irremeabilis unda*. This letter is number 4 of *Letters*. In number 354, the last, he remembers *irremeabilis unda* once more. He is urging Hester not to go to Italy, and he tells the story of Mary Queen of Scots: "When Queen Mary took the resolution of sheltering herself in England, the Archbishop of St. Andrew's, attempting to dissuade her, attended on her journey; and when they came to the irremeable stream that separated the two kingdoms, walked by her side into the water."[12]

The reader whose memory is long enough to hear in Johnson's last letter this echo of the first may be surprised by the symmetry. The symmetry is appropriate, for *Letters* as a whole displays a high degree of internal coherence, albeit in ways that are hard to specify. One way, the obvious one, is simply that 305 of the 354 letters are to Mrs. Thrale. Thus, in reading through them we seem to follow the whole progress of the friendship without interruption from its first complimentary flourishes through its maturity to its waning. In one of his letters Johnson calls their correspondence "the records of a pure and blameless friendship," and that is how *Letters* appears to the reader.[13] Here not only is Johnson at his best, but here also, we are tempted to say, is epistolary friendship itself at its most attractive. This heightened general appeal is just the effect aimed at by editing such as Piozzi's; to achieve it is the purpose of the principles she followed. Thus, in suppressing Johnson's first, violent response to her marriage announcement she acted not merely from self-interest and piety towards Johnson's memory but also from motives that must be judged esthetic; that letter strikes too jarring a tone. Johnson's second letter, number 354, breathes kindly resignation and makes a touchingly elegiac, and therefore far more artistically suitable, close to the correspondence. In a word, *Letters* is literature.

The Letters Composed for *Letters*

From Hester Thrale to Johnson, some 115 letters survive. In *Letters*, on the insistence of her publisher, she printed twenty-eight. These she treated very differently from Johnson's; she exercised her authorial rights over them so thoroughly that nearly all are new compositions. These letters never sent to Johnson are, on the whole, among her least attractive writings; they strike self-conscious postures. One of the things she elects to do in them is resent, once again, some of Johnson's more irritating sentiments. In *Anecdotes*, for instance, Johnson is said to have disdained conversation about "historical fact or general polity. . . . 'He never (as he expressed it) desired to hear of the *Punic war* while he lived: such conversation . . . carried one away from common life.'" In 1788 she allows herself the pleasure of rebuttal:

> So here's modern politicks in a letter from me; yes, and a touch of the *Punick war* too; for Mr.**** desired to consult with me . . . about his private affairs; and said how A—— and S—— had demanded their money, but he thought it imprudent to pay them *just now*, as cash ran low. Why that, Sir, said I, is the very reason you *should* pay them; and thereupon did I tell him how the old Romans were besieged by Brennus till famine had encouraged him to hope for their giving up . . . and how, to take all such hope away, they threw their last loaves over the wall . . . and made him believe they had bread enough within. And now, thinks I, Mr. Johnson says that history never is good to illustrate common life; but I say,
> When house and land are gone and spent,
> Then learning is most excellent.[14]

Although this letter prognosticates her later literary interests and does truly assert her taste, it is rhetorically so coy that one comes away from it disposed to agree with Johnson.

Two of the letters composed for *Letters* achieved celebrity of their own. One is supposed to have been written the day after the Thrales had attended a regatta on the Thames. "No indifferent specimen of her literary talents," it was called by one reviewer; "it is truly laughable and entertaining." It is an exercise on the Augustan, and specifically Johnsonian, axiom that man is a creature whose schemes of happiness are destined to ironic upset. Remembering a regatta she had attended in 1775, Piozzi in 1788 shapes it on the pattern of a chapter from *Rasselas*—probably chapter 6, in which the wings devised by the inventor do not keep him aloft but do, with saving irony, prevent him from drowning when he falls into a lake. On the day appointed for the regatta "a flag flying from some conspicuous steeple in Westminster gave notice of the approaching festival," and the ladies put on their best clothes. Despite ominous weather, "[we] set about being happy with all our might" and sought a barge from which to watch the entertainment. But a barge is not to be had, and they are constrained to jostle for places at a window, spoiling their head-dresses and seeing, withal, "scarce any thing" of the race. Instead they see only the other spectators—and this, the saving irony, turns out to be "the true wonder of the day": "they sat so thick upon the slating of Whitehall, that nobody could persuade me for a long while out of the notion that it was covered with black, till through a telescope we spied the *animals in motion*, like magnified mites in a bit of old cheese." Remains the hope of seeing the barges disembark at Ranelagh: "But the night came on; the wind roared; the rain fell; and the barges missing their way, many came up to the wrong stairs; the managers endeavoured to rectify the mistake, and drive them back . . . but the women were weary and wet, and . . . the procession was spoiled, and as to musick we heard none but screams of the frighted company as they were tossed about at the moment of getting to shore."[15]

Similar in its assumptions about human felicity is the second letter, addressed "to a gentleman on his marriage" and conceived, in the manner of Richardson, as a Letter of Advice. (Hester had written this letter, or a version of it, in 1773 to a young man in whose marriage she and Johnson had taken a kindly interest.) The problem she speaks to is that of attaining happiness in marriage—an ironic problem, of course, for the newly married man, enraptured by sexual fondness, cannot believe that he and his spouse will ever be bored by each other. "I see you smile," she writes accordingly, "at my wrongheaded kindness, and reflecting on the charms of your bride, cry out in a rapture, that you are happy enough without my rules. I know you are; but after one of the forty years, which I hope you will pass pleasingly together, are over, . . . rules for felicity may not be found unnecessary, however some of them may appear impracticable." The rules are studiously rational: Cultivate your wife's mind so that you may enjoy each other's company; do not treat her with suspicion; be civil to her on principle when you can no longer be so from fondness. They are also moderately feminist: "let your wife never be kept ignorant of your income, your expences, your friendships, or aversions . . . consider all concealment as a breach of fidelity." And again, "listen not to those sages who advise you always to scorn the counsel of a woman, and if you comply with her requests pronounce you to be wife-ridden." This is a prescription for companionate marriage on the Bluestocking model; it asserts that marriage is or ought to be the partnership of rational beings. It is good liberal doctrine. It is also, for perhaps the only time in Piozzi's career, discreetly trimmed in the manner of Hannah More by concessions to less liberal tradition, namely the tradition "that [a husband's] superiority should always be seen." (She adds, however, that it should "never [be] felt.")[16] The popularity of this letter is probably attributable to this judicious trimming.

It seems to have been Piozzi's destiny as a writer always to fall afoul of someone, however, and this time the blast came from radical feminism in the person of Mary Wollstonecraft. In the *Vindication of the Rights of Woman*, Wollstonecraft seizes upon this letter as an example of the truth that "women argue in the same track as men, and adopt the sentiments that brutalize them, with all the pertinacity of ignorance." The sentiments she means are contained essentially in one unfortunate Piozzi sentence which is intended to enforce the idea that women do not like to be neglected by their husbands. "All our attainments, all our arts, are employed to gain and keep the heart of man; and what mortification can exceed the disappointment, if the end be not obtained? There is no reproof however pointed, no punishment however severe, that a woman of spirit will not prefer to neglect; and if she can endure it without complaint, it only proves that she means to make herself amends by the attention of others for the slights of her husband." Alas, this sentence is the most personal in the letter; of Hester at least, as we have seen, it was too true that all her arts were employed to gain the heart of man. Perhaps Wollstonecraft sensed its sincerity; at any rate, she falls upon it with fury. "These are truly masculine sentiments. . . . Noble morality! . . . Whilst women avow, and act up to such opinions, their understandings . . . deserve the contempt . . . that men . . . have pointedly levelled at the female mind." Nor is this all. "Mrs. Piozzi, who often repeated by rote, what she did not understand, comes forward with Johnsonian periods."[17] It is painful to see a woman who professes to vindicate the rights of her sex abuse in the sneering language of a Gifford or a Walpole another woman who, after all, is engaged in exercising those rights. There was indeed, as Barbauld said, no band of union among literary women, any more than among men.

A Note on Piozzi's Later Correspondence

Between 1784 and 1821 Piozzi wrote at least two thousand letters. The total is large not because she was especially prolific (it comes to an average of one letter per week) but because she had many correspondents and was loyal to most of them until death, theirs or her own. Even if we leave out of account the letters she wrote as Mrs. Thrale—letters, for instance, to the Burney family—she remains one of the voluminous letter writers of her age, easily holding her own among figures like Johnson, Gray, Jane Austen, and Lady Mary Wortley Montagu. The edition of her letters now in preparation by Edward and Lillian Bloom, which will select less than half the total, will fill three or four volumes.

"I do not love to have my Letters shewn," wrote Mrs. Thrale in 1781, "they're often too airy, often too ostentatious—and always too full of familiar Allusions . . . to be Letters agreable in any Eyes but those of Friends." She adds, "tho' I die with Terror lest the Person to whom I write sh[d] show my Letters; yet I die with Vanity too, & make my Friends . . . happy in Opportunities of exposing me when my Frolick is over." Her "vanity" was encouraged by Johnson ("Never imagine that your letters are long; they are always too short for my curiosity") and by Fanny Burney ("your Letters . . . reflect nothing but credit upon your Head, Heart, & Disposition"), and it has been justified by posterity. Having contributed to institutionalizing the private letter as literature, Piozzi has justly enjoyed the benefits of its acceptance. Soon after her death her friends attempted to publish her letters; Sir John Salusbury, as usual, forbade them, but many letters nevertheless found their way into print. They are the one part of her work that has been consistently esteemed. "Her talk on paper, like her conversation, sparkled not infrequently with that bright wine of the intellect which has no lees," wrote Thomas Seccombe in 1910, and he predicted for Piozzi "a highly enviable place among the letter-writers of the last two centuries." The editor of a 1926 anthology of them agreed. "They produce . . . an atmosphere of repartee; a collo-quialism that provokes comment or reply; an abruptness in moving on to the next subject, as if they had been taken from dialogue. . . . The homely phrasing is often vivid and dramatic, destined to long outlive more sober statements."[18]

Like her notebooks, Piozzi's letters are alert, curious, and wide ranging. Her favorite topics are books, people, and politics; her comments on the first and last of these—on Scott and Byron and *Frankenstein*, on the dark intentions of the French Republic and Napoleon's rise and fall and the price of grain in north Wales—are moments in the history of English literary sensibility and documents of the middle-class British response to the French and Industrial Revolutions. However, their documentary aspect is the least of them. Like *Thraliana*, her letters both turn outward to the world and yet appropriate the world to themselves, making it their rhetorical playground. They are performances, and the world, nominally their subject matter, is more truly their instrument. Here is an example, a cogent-sounding observation about the state of Europe in 1797:

> 'Tis really not unworthy observation, how the vital part of every country has been struck at during the last ten years. Loyalty and love of their *Grand Monarque* was a characteristic of Parisian manners. *Their Sovereign has been executed.* Religion and the fine arts comforted the Italians for loss of liberty and of conquests. Their ceremonies are now insulted, their models of excellence taken forcibly away. Our English John . . . counted the treasures of the Bank and feared no ill while ships and money lasted. Our guineas are turned to paper, our fleets mutiny. . . .

The observation derives its cogency less from its analysis of Europe than from the artfulness of its design. "Every country" reduces to just three examples, which is not fortuitous; Piozzi is fond of threes. We notice also the neatness of the remark: the second, fourth, and sixth sentences are answered snipsnap by the third, fifth, and seventh. What we have is three pairs of striking antitheses, a witty Popean pattern. In commenting on Europe, Piozzi is exercising herself in ostentatious acuteness. (A sign of her literary narcissism is that in *Thraliana* we find either a trial version or a memorandum of this remark. She liked it so well that she also put it into *Retrospection*.)[19]

She called her letters "Pen & Ink Conversation," implying that they are innocent of premeditation. This, however, is the pretense of every eighteenth-century letter writer, even Pope. Penelope Pennington, writing after Piozzi's death, declared that "my dear, lost Friend possessed . . . in a wonderful degree" the talent of making her letters interesting; "however frequent, [they] never ran into commonplace, but were always novel." Their novelty results much less from their substance than their manner; they are almost entirely achievements of rhetoric. "My mind," she writes in 1811, "is worn as thin as an old sixpence, and shines, if it does shine, just as the old sixpence does, from mere beating out." Her rhetoric does shine, and it owes much of its brilliance to a cultivated audacity. Typical is a stabbing little anecdote intended to show the coldheartedness of society people in 1814. What makes it stabbing is the outrageous pun on *went off*: "Miles Peter Andrews, the rich and gay, sent out two hundred cards of invitation to see the festivities from his windows, verandah, &c., but Miles Peter Andrews (his friends say) *went off* before the fireworks; so his heir removed the body and received company *himself*." Or this mordant juxtaposition, which crystalizes in one casually authoritative sentence the main social truths about Bath: "Bath goes on as it used to do: now a coffin pushing you off the pavement, and now a bass-viol case." Reporting someone's death after an illness of sixteen weeks, she transforms gossip into grimly farcical bon mot: "Whatever door is opened for our departure, let us pray to God that it may not hang ajar . . . for sixteen weeks!" The absence of news itself can be her theme; she makes parody out of it. "The weeds of conversation weary me to death with 'Dear Ma'am,—I hope you caught no cold at the last party; Lord bless me! how hot the rooms were! Well! I do hate hot rooms above all living things.'"[20]

Pathos, melodrama, and farce are the modes of her letters; her topics are grist for those mills, and the result is often a powerful self-dramatization. Here the state of Europe again is her nominal subject, but what she is actually writing is personal elegy: "I remember Horton full well, the Seat of Lord Halifax; with whose Children my Childhood was past——but they are dead, & I am living; & those Maps that showed *us* the Kingdom of France, the Papacy of Rome, & the Republics of Genoa & Venice yet stick up against the old Wall perhaps——tho' Realms & Commonwealths are gone; & the good little Girls that used to learn their Lessons on them are gone too." Her response to the Peterloo Massacre in 1819 is to turn prophetess and utter Gothic fantasy: "The Times *do* exhibit a frightful Fore-Ground—a black and Cloudy Offskip: Figures dancing a la Ronde, and Folly jingling Bells to put them more and more out of Time." In still another letter, "a brawling Election" becomes a theater for wise-cracking; with casual egoism she admits as much. "What a brawling Election this has been! *My* best Joke was correcting the Motto worne on a Flag belonging to 14 associated *Taylors* who went to vote for some flourishing Fellow under Canopy of the Words Liberty & Independence—nay said I, let it be *Men & Measures*."[21]

In the art of letter writing Piozzi attained to high skill. Her authentic letters to Johnson are comparatively unformed, the work of a wife and mother whose domestic anxieties, as she sometimes reminds him, give her scant opportunity to compose. On her second marriage, as she settles down to leisure and literary work, she settles down also to cultivate epistolary composition. The difference appears quickly and at first is not pleasant. We may trace it in her openings. Here is the opening of a letter to Queeney written in August 1784: "My long & frequent Letters may convince my dearest Tit that I find Time to write, and I am sure it requires no Patience to read kind Letters." And here is its counterpart from another, written from Milan in February 1785: "My dearest Hester may be ever assured that my Inclination to write to her is always awakened by the Sight of the handwriting which I so dearly love to see." Whether the strain evident here be laid to Piozzi's first taste of Italy or to the uneasiness of her relations with Queeney, the stiffness of this letter reminds us that the art of letter writing is to hide art. Three and a half years later Piozzi has mastered that principle: "I wish my dear Mrs. Byron saw me with all my Papers for the *Book Stuff* and the People coming in every Moment, and the Dog flying at 'em, and Cecilia's Task to look over; and My sullen Maid with *Ma'am this Guinea won't pass*, and my husband crying Come, shut away this Work *do*, and write to dear Mrs. Byron."[22]

This is artful neglect of art. Her salutation, seemingly forgotten in haste, is simply embedded in the first sentence; the air of harried abruptness is secured by studiously thoughtless syntax; the paragraph even includes, as is proper, an explanation of her reason for writing. Twenty years later still Piozzi had learned the principle so well that she could afford to flout it. In 1810 we find her writing to her nephew, "a Letter, (say the Critics) should consist of Fact & Sentiment——so here is a little of both."[23] This is sprezzatura. In her later years letter writing was Piozzi's chief literary business; to the end of her life she conducted it with ever increasing authority.

SIX

Willing to Be Pleased

Observations and Reflections

In poetic texts, tropes are best understood as psychic defenses
. . . against the poems of the precursors. . . . They trope
or turn against anterior defenses, against previous or outworn
postures of the spirit.[1]

ELEVEN WEEKS after the publi-
cation of *Letters*, having found its reception satisfactory, Piozzi entered in *Thraliana* a decision that has an air of insouciance. "I will
write my Travels & publish them—why not? 'twill be difficult to content the Italians & the English but I'll try—& tis something to do."
She had begun to write her travels in 1784, upon leaving England;
this is no sudden impulse. Why, then, speak to herself as if it were?
The answer, surely, is "To allay anxiety." She is venturing into new
territory—new not only to her but to her sex, for in English travel
writing she appears to have had but two female predecessors, Lady
Mary Wortley Montagu (*Letters from Turkey*, 1763) and Anna Miller.
Miller's *Letters from Italy in the years 1770 and 1771* (1776) are much
concerned with painting, statuary, and connoisseurship; in her decision to "let loose . . . in this Journey the Fondness for Painting which
I was forced to suppress while Dᵣ Johnson lived with me," Piozzi was
perhaps following Miller's lead. Yet despite the successes of Montagu
and Miller, anxiety there must still be. Piozzi handles anxiety by belittling the effort that she is about to make; it will be only "something to
do," a sort of female pastime, not serious business. The author in her,
however, knew better. When she sat down to the task she worked with
speed and assurance, producing the first draft—the first revision,
that is, of her original journal—in exactly two months. That draft
runs to 521 large pages, which means that she wrote an average of 65

pages a week, a solid professional performance. (During these weeks she appears also to have been doing research in travel literature and checking her facts.) Equally professional is her unanxious objectivity about the book while she is writing it. "The Book I have really not *read* yet, only *written*," she explains to a friend who is innocent in the ways of authors; "I shall now read, correct & copy it over." She did so, preparing a newly revised draft during the autumn. Moreover, she appears to have done some fine tuning in proof.[2] *Observations and Reflections*, far from being the thoughtless jeu d'esprit suggested by her *Thraliana* entry, is probably her most deliberate performance.

Postures of Travel

Observations needed to be deliberate, for in writing a travel book she was entering a very crowded field and electing to compete with some of the foremost authors of her century. Among the writers whom she knew personally Boswell, Baretti, Charles Burney, and, of course, Johnson had all written travel books. Because the genre was so intensely cultivated, criticism of it, as Charles Batten has shown, had grown demanding and fastidious. One of the most severe critics was Johnson himself, both in his letters to Mrs. Thrale and in *Idler* 97 (1760), in which he asserts with scorn that most travel books have been worthless. "Of those who crowd the world with their itineraries, some have no other purpose than to describe the face of the country; those who . . . are curious to know what is done or suffered in distant countries, may be informed by one of these wanderers, that on a certain day he set out early with the caravan, and in the first hour's march saw . . . a hill covered with trees, then passed over a stream which ran northward with a swift course, but which is probably dry in the summer months." Johnson's demand is characteristically fierce and lofty: "He only is a useful traveller who brings home something . . . which may enable his readers to compare their condition with that of others, to improve it whenever it is worse, and whenever it is better to enjoy it."[3]

"Compare": Johnson enunciates the ideal of the genre. The travel book, like travel itself, was supposed to be educational. The traveler was conceived to be a sort of field worker in Lockian psychology, collecting sense impressions on which to exercise judgment and reflection. (The titles of eighteenth-century travel books, accordingly, often feature words like "observations," "remarks," and "reflections.") In behaving as a Lockian psychologist, however, the traveler was only doing in a wider and more distant arena what everyone else does at home, for everyone is a Lockian psychologist, even if only unwittingly. Travel, therefore, is much more than a pastime; it is training in the most fundamental of human actions, the use of one's faculties. To travel is to experience things, and to reflect upon one's travel is to ponder the meaning both of one's experience and of one's responses to it.[4]

As travel books proliferated and their ostensible subject matter became overfamiliar—all the books about Italy, for example, after Addison's *Remarks on Italy* (1705) mention most of the same places— their authors became more self-conscious about the travel book's latent subject matter, how one takes one's experience. "Readers," Piozzi noted in her own journal, ". . . grow wiser . . . & are aware of us; they know that one Traveller was in Pain, and another in Love when they made the Tour of Italy, and pick out their Intelligence of it accordingly." In *Observations* she repeats this remark, and adds that "Italy may be considered . . . as a sort of academy-figure set up for us all to draw from."[5] Not Italy but what we draw from Italy is the true subject of a travel book, at least of a sophisticated travel book like *Observations*. *Observations* is about the postures that one may adopt towards one's experiences. More specifically, it is about the postures that have been adopted by Piozzi's precursors.

Two of those postures are the "splenetic" traveler and the "philosophic" traveler. The first is irritable and hard to please, the second is penetrating and thoughtful, and both are skeptical. They are disinclined to believe what they hear and much inclined to draw dark, or at least dampening, inferences from what they see. They are also very, very English. They write in the shadow of that most imposing of all English travel books (no matter that it is fiction), *Gulliver's*. *Gulliver's Travels* imposes itself again and again on nonfiction travel writers, who often seem to be writing it anew even when they are apparently just describing the customs and manners of France and Italy: the splenetic and philosophic travelers reduce to the Swiftian traveler. On some topics this is patent. Here is Samuel Sharp, a well known splenetic traveler, writing from Italy in 1766. His topic is a favorite of English writers on Italy, the "pretended miracles" of "popish superstition."

We live in a quarter of the town called St *Lucia*, a Saint, as the legend informs us, who, in the persecution of the Christians, under *Dioclesian*, had her eyes torn out by the executioner; which circumstance has given her a great reputation for working miracles on every species of blindness. Her chapel is close to our house, and the day before yesterday was her anniversary. I attended the service both morning and afternoon, to see the method of cure. In the midst of the chapel is a paltry wooden image of her saintship, with a platter in her hand, containing the representation of two eyes. All the patients pass their hands over these eyes, and immediately rub their own, before the virtue exhales. There is also a small piece of bone set in silver . . . which they pretend to be a relick of the saint; this they kiss, which likewise operates miraculously; but I believe most of the patients take the advantage of both methods.[6]

From "the method of cure" on, this is *The Mechanical Operation of the Spirit*. Set in a travel context, it is Gulliver examining the absurd experiments at Lagado.

Another splenetic, and Swiftian, traveler is Smollett. He proclaims his posture early: "When I talk of the French nation, I must . . . except a great number of individuals, from the general censure. Though I have a hearty contempt for the ignorance, folly, and presumption which characterise the generality, I cannot but respect the talents of many great men, who have eminently distinguished themselves in every art and science." This is not Gulliver but Swift directly, in the famous letter to Pope (29 September 1725) that is customarily cited as a gloss on *Gulliver*: "I have ever hated all nations, professions, and communities, and all my love is toward individuals. . . . I hate and detest that animal called man, although I heartily love John, Peter, Thomas, and so forth. . . . Upon this great foundation of misanthropy . . . the whole building of my Travels is erected." Likewise the building of Smollett's *Travels*. The most astonishing single intrusion of *Gulliver* into Smollett occurs at Rome:

It is diverting to hear an Italian expatiate upon the greatness of modern Rome. He will tell you there are above three hundred palaces in the city; that there is scarce a Roman prince, whose revenue does not exceed two hundred thousand crowns; and that Rome produces . . . the most refined politicians in the universe. To one of them talking in this strain, I replied, that instead of three hundred palaces, the number did not exceed fourscore; that I had been informed . . . there were not six individuals in Rome who had so much as forty thousand crowns a year . . . and that to say their princes were so rich, and their politicians so refined, was, in effect, a severe satire upon them, for not employing their wealth and their talents for the advantage of their country. I asked why their cardinals and princes did not . . . encourage industrious people to settle and cultivate the Campania of Rome, which is a desert? why they did not raise a subscription to drain the marshes in the neighbourhood of the city, and thus meliorate the air. . . ? I demanded of him, why they did not . . . introduc[e] commerce and manufactures, and . . . giv[e] some consequence to their state, which was no more than a mite in the political scale of Europe? I expressed a desire to know. . . .[7]

This is Smollett-as-King-of-Brobdingnag, or as "my Master Houyhnhnm," putting to some poor local Gulliver the questions that expose his pitiable pretentions.

One more exhibit, this from the not very literary, indeed the frequently ungrammatical, Rev. William Cole, writing just for himself. He had gone eagerly to Paris in 1765, with a fantasy of settling in France. "I went there," he writes, "& was happily undeceived." He finds France and the French loathesome. In the course of writing his journal he has to pull himself back from digressions upon their loathesomeness, digressions of Gulliverian intensity. He is remembering, with a Swiftian rising gorge, the tables of animal organs set out for sale in all the streets of Paris: "It has been as much as I could do to forbear putting my Head out at the Coach Window many a Time in the Streets, the principal Streets of this Glory of the World, to bring up the Contents of my Stomach, when I have passed by so much Liver, Lights & other Offal, cut out in Slices & sold on small Tables in almost every Street . . . the monstrous black Sausages in great Guts, or Bladders, hanging by many of their Shop Windows; Quantities of Sheep's Heads boiled & partly dried, in Heaps on Stalls, are all such . . . sights, as would turn any other Stomach but that of a Frenchman." He recalls how "Monsieur le Parisien, & Madame la Parisienne with their Heads most elegantly *frisez* & *poudrez*, & their Tails bedaggled & full of Holes & all over Rags, cheapen, with a watery Mouth, some of these *bons Morceaux*"; indignantly, he suspects they would "turn up their Noses at . . . the Indelicacy of English Roast Beef." Finally he is seized by the close of book 4: "Poverty, Rags & a poor mean way of Living, are by no Means the proper Subjects of Ridicule, when unavoidable: but when Vanity, with a Contempt for the Manners of other People, are joyned to them, then surely there cannot be a more proper Subject to laugh at." To be exact, this is the penultimate paragraph of book 4, beginning, "My Reconcilement to the *Yahoo*-kind . . . might not be so difficult, if they would be content with those Vices and Follies only which Nature hath entitled them to," and continuing, "But, when I behold a Lump of Deformity . . . smitten with *Pride*, it immediately breaks all the Measures of my Patience."[8]

Johnson is supposed to have noticed disapprovingly, in 1778, "a strange turn in travellers to be displeased." Johnson himself was generally felt to have been one of those displeased travelers, and if "displeased" means skeptical the feeling is justified by his letters to Mrs. Thrale from Scotland and his diaries of his two tours with her. In considering *Observations* it is useful to bear in mind that Hester had traveled with Johnson and had not on the whole enjoyed traveling with him, in good part because he was apt to be overbearingly displeased. In 1774 she had wanted him to like Wales, her native country; he had not much liked it. At Bodvel, her birthplace, she walked through the rooms remembering her childhood; Johnson's remark was only, "This species of pleasure is always melancholy." At Paris in 1775 they tended to visit different places. At one place that they saw together Hester was impressed by the size of the rooms ("one was 50 foot long"), and Johnson was not ("The house has no very large room").[9] As we know, he also ridiculed her interest in paintings.

Johnson himself would have said that he was only a realistic traveler, one who tells the naked truth. "The use of travelling is to regulate imagination by reality, and instead of thinking how things may be, to see them as they are." How, then, are they, what is the reality that must regulate imagination, and what is the imagination that must be regulated? To Johnson, the imagination is pastoral-romantic. It is devoted to illusions of felicity and enjoyment. "You are perhaps imagining," he writes to Mrs. Thrale, that I am withdrawn from the gay and the busy world into regions of peace and pastoral felicity, and am enjoying the reliques of the golden age; that I am surveying nature's magnificence from a mountain, or remarking her minuter beauties on the flowery bank of a winding rivulet; that I am invigorating myself in the sunshine, or delighting my imagination with being hidden from the invasion of human evils and human passions in the darkness of a thicket.

But in reality,

here are mountains which I should once have climbed, but to climb steeps is now very laborious, and to descend them dangerous; and I am now content with knowing, that by scrambling up a rock, I shall only see other rocks, and a wider circuit of barren desolation. Of streams, we have here a sufficient number, but they murmur not upon pebbles, but upon rocks. . . . Of lawns and thickets, he must read that would know them, for here is little sun and no shade.

Reality is *laborious, dangerous,* and *barren.* Reality is disappointment. "You have often heard me complain of finding myself disappointed by books of travels; I am afraid travel itself will end likewise in disappointment." Reality is sameness. "One town, one country, is very like another: civilized nations have the same customs, and barbarous nations have the same nature." Reality is displeasure. "He that wanders about the world sees new forms of human misery." To "regulate imagination by reality" is to perceive not pebbles but rocks, a thoroughly Swiftian perceptual choice. And unquestionably it is a choice; even "barren desolation" *can* be perceived not as desolate but as exhilarating, and even Johnson can so perceive it when his guard is not up. "I am now looking on the sea," he also wrote to Mrs. Thrale, "from a house . . . in the isle of Skie. Little did I once think of seeing this region of obscurity. . . . I have now the pleasure of going where nobody goes, and seeing what nobody sees."[10]

Batten makes the useful observation that the travel writer's displeasure was conventionally accepted as a surety of his truthfulness. "The revelation of a melancholic temperament serves a clear literary function: it makes the traveler seem the kind of person whose descriptions should be trusted. . . . Most important, the spleen served as a sign of acute mental ability. . . . When France and Italy raise the ire of Smollett and Sharp, their misanthropic descriptions of foreign manners and customs show them to be travelers who are impervious to the seductive allure of outward appearances." It is tempting to re-clothe this statement in the vesture of Foucault and to say that in general, a discourse not of pleasure but of "disgust" constituted *le vrai* of English travel writing. "Disgust" is Smollett's word; the English, he writes, "are naturally . . . much subject to fits of disgust."[11] To be certifiably truthful and to be English—these are the same thing, to an English audience—one must be displeased. The discourse of displeasure is the discourse of penetration; the discourse of penetration is the discourse of satire; the discourse of satire is Swift. Thus it is that the splenetic and philosophic travelers become the Swiftian traveler, bursting out into *Gulliver* at almost predictable intervals.

A Journey from Satire to Romance

Swift, we have seen, was one of Piozzi's first-chosen precursors. Overtly, he seems to be one of the few male writers (perhaps Rousseau is the only other) with whom she has no quarrel. Her most conspicuous quarrel, in writing as in life, is with Johnson. In *Observations*, however, we behold her taking on not only Johnson again, but the entire posture of English "disgust," penetration, and satire. The specific precursor of *Observations* is a composite of Johnson (not his *Journey to the Western Islands* but his letters to her from Scotland—as well as *Rasselas* and, probably, Johnson himself as travel companion) and Smollett; in this composite figure she concentrates the posture of skeptical displeasure. That posture and her enmity to it are what *Observations* is finally about. The book has been praised for all sorts of trivial reasons—for the supposed liveliness and accuracy of its descriptions, for the sympathy (comparatively novel at that time) with which it depicts Italian life, for the charm of its author's personality. If these were indeed its strengths, *Observations* would be a forgettable book. Its true strength lies not in what it says about Italy but in its power to call in question the posture of displeasure. Its strength is revisionary. The attentive reader of *Observations* is so schooled by its revisings that he cannot again assume without question that pebbles are fantasy and rocks truth. *Observations* diminishes the power of ridicule and discloses the illusion in the stance of "wise disillusionment."

Unlike most of her other works it does not merely seek to revise her precursors, it succeeds in revising them. That is why it is her strongest work.

Observations is not novel in this revisionary aim; in its specific admiration of Italy and in its general resistance to satire it has precursors also. In the mode of rapturous exclamation ("not half but wholly divine Guercino," etc.) it is preceded by Anna Miller for one, in *Letters from Italy*. For the general posture of "good feeling" the theoretical precursor is Sterne's *Sentimental Journey*, which mounts an open attack on Smollett and all splenetic travelers under the name "Smelfungus." There is also Martin Sherlock, who in *Letters from an English Traveller* (1780) loves everything he sees, without distinction. I call Sterne a merely "theoretical" precursor because, however many imitators he spawned, Piozzi is not one of them; she writes as if *A Sentimental Journey* had never existed. (I presume that she read it but can find no evidence that she did; she did read and enjoy *Tristram Shandy*, but she seems fundamentally not interested in Sterne.) As for Sherlock, he is far below her powers; his book, written with all the bland fatuity of a modern tourist's puff, is precisely the sort of thing that justifies the belief that only dyspeptic writers tell the truth. The sensibility in *Observations*, by contrast, is the product of effort, and is a considerable rhetorical achievement.

To see that it is, however, we must make some effort ourselves. Unlike *Anecdotes*, in which the tensions are all on the surface and encourage superficial reading because other readings are too painful, *Observations* lends itself to superficial reading for the more common reason that it presents a placid and comfortable appearance. One superficial reading, then, will have it that the book records her wedding journey, during which, of course, she was happy; another, slightly less so, will say that she has now learned how to write a book. Neither gets at the action, which, to be sure, is largely covert. Let us approach it by indirection.

In Italy Piozzi kept a travel diary; she also made remarks in *Thraliana*. Moreover, years later, in various memoirs, she wrote other accounts of the journey. All these texts display a goodly share of her temperamental asperity and demonstrate that on this occasion, at least, she was quite as splenetic a traveler as Sharp, Smollett, and Johnson. At Milan, where she stayed several months, she was harassed by clergy who wished to convert her; "may Heaven set me & my Husband safe away from Bigotry & Infidelity," she prays. She is appalled by Italian morality: "All I ever heard, and much more than ever I heard concerning the depraved Morals & confined Ideas of Religion reigning in this Country, are terribly true. The *Cavalieri Serventi* [male companions to married women] are indispensible, and the whole Nation adapts itself with great Composure to a settled Scheme of Vice, a System of Adultery." She tries to resign herself to it all: "Well! these are the Vices of hot Countries—& as such let 'em pass, for I hate General and indiscriminate Satire." But then she thinks of how Italians talk and is revolted again: "the Intercalations of these People are more horrible than Xtian Ears can endure with Patience: Blood of God! Body of the Lord Jesus! Father of Christ! are the common Exclamations even of the Clergy." And she goes off into a paroxysm of fury—not Swiftian, to be sure, but Biblical fury: "*&* *Shall I not be revenged on such a Nation as this?* . . . but indeed Vengeance is coming on them with hasty Strides; I hope I shall have Time to view the Monuments of ancient & Modern Art before they are all destroyed by the Judgments of an incensed Creator, & then retire . . . untainted by their Crimes, to *Some* Corner of the Earth . . . where . . . Moral Virtue is not become ridiculous."[12]

All this is at Milan, in March 1785. More than a year later, returned to Milan from her tour through Venice, Florence, Rome, and Naples, she writes again in *Thraliana*. She has been "entertained extremely well upon the whole . . . and enriched with many new Ideas," but does she like Italy and the Italians any better? No. "I have been diverted with Folly, & shocked by Vice, pained by Incredulity, and sicken'd with silly Implicitness of Belief." Although she had quitted England in relief and anger, she has decided that England, after all, is the better place to live. "Our People do not run after each other with unbridled Licentiousness as the Venetians make no scruple of doing. . . . Our People of Fashion do not rob, nor our Robbers acknowledge themselves such without a Blush, like the Inhabitants of Milan or Ancona; our *Beckfords & Bickerstaffs* . . . do not keep their Male Mistresses in Triumph like the Roman Priests & Princes. This Italy is indeed a Sink of Sin . . . and the Italians grossness of Conversation is still *very* offensive & nauseous, tho' so long accustomed to it." More, she has, she feels, confirmed that Johnson's "Knowledge of the World" was "nearly intuitive," with only one exception: "that he never could perswade himself to think Mankind as wicked as I have since found them to be." In sum, her experience of Italy, as of June 1786, has been more Johnsonian than Johnson; it has been Swiftian.

And not just of Italy. In her travel diary we find this caustic note on Vienna: "Sherlock says he who leaves Vienna unsatisfied is his own Satirist—I shall save my Enemies & Critics some Trouble."[13] From this note we can gather not only that she is planning the travel book but that she is planning a splenetic travel book, one in which travel is disappointment.

Years later, annotating a copy of *Observations*, she remembers the horrors that it does not tell. In Milan Piozzi became so distrustful of his compatriots that when a box of chocolates arrived at their house one day he refused to touch them, fearing poison. They dreaded being robbed and murdered by their Italian servants, and to prevent it changed their servants frequently. She lived in fear of every abbot and bishop they met, lest she be browbeaten to convert. The servants at the Crocelle Inn, Naples, used the stair landing as a toilet. Elsewhere, rereading Thomson's *Summer*, she annotates line 282, "Nor undelightful is the ceaseless hum": "So truly undelightful is it in Italy . . . that no man goes 'musing through the *woods at noon*;' . . . one must be bitten to death by the gnats." All this is very much after Smollett, who also professes the utmost distrust of Italians (they are treacherous, vengeful, and "the most villainously rapacious" people "I ever knew"), who also is nauseated by "popish superstition" and its "spirit of religious fanaticism," who suffers nightly at foul inns, including one at Siena "that stunk like a privy," and who also declares it "impossible," in summer, "to keep the flies out of your mouth, nostrils, eyes, and ears."[14]

Piozzi had all the makings of a good hater and abundant material for a book that could have matched anyone's in intensity of loathing. She chose not to write it. She did not mention the servants' using the stairs as a toilet, she says in the same marginalia to *Observations*, because she did not wish to spoil her "Panegyric" on Naples. That is, she suppressed the nastiness for the purpose of showing enjoyment. On the face of it this sounds like mere censorship or euphemism. It even calls to mind a traditional myth about the female sensibility, the myth that the female sensibility is "delicate," "genteel," and "repressed," or, in short, that it shrinks from a "manly" confrontation with reality. Certainly the travel book that Piozzi did write represents a repression of the one she did not, and we need to inquire into the aim of that repression. The question is especially urgent in her case, for not only is her natural temper irritable ("warm even to Irascibility") but also resentment, as I have suggested, is her motive power in writing, and resentment is just the power from which this particular repression would seem to cut her off.

One purpose of suppressing the nasty is to vindicate her marriage choice. All her English friends and enemies knew—indeed, all of London society and a good part of the reading public knew—that the journey was her wedding journey, and it must be shown to have been a success so that her choice of Piozzi can be shown to have been right. The pleasure she represents herself as taking in Italy is her answer to the Gothic rumors of her having been "locked in a convent." She has another reason, also, for thus representing the journey, as she pointedly hints in her preface. Her book, she writes there, "shall serve as a vehicle for conveying expressions of particular kindness to those foreign individuals, whose tenderness softened the sorrows of absence, and who eagerly endeavoured by unmerited attentions to supply the loss of their company on whom nature and habit had given me stronger claims." Further, she hopes "to obtain from a humane and generous Public that shelter their protection best affords from the poisoned arrows of private malignity."[15] In all this she alludes to the hostile conduct of her daughters and such erstwhile friends as the Burneys; she is praying for a success that will shame them, and she intends to shame them herself by recording the tender attentions she received from foreigners in their stead. In a word, she wants revenge.

The spleen that she represses on one side, then, she looses on another; not Italy but England is its object. Her predecessors compare their experience to English norms and customarily "discover" what they always believed anyway, that England is better. A distinct theme of *Observations* is criticism of England; in this it resembles English travel books of the 1920s and 1930s far more than it resembles any of its precursors. No sooner is she arrived at Milan—in the book—than she is finding agreeable differences between *here* and an implied *there*: "Nothing . . . can exceed the agreeableness of a well-bred Italian's address when speaking to a lady . . . the politeness of a man of fashion *here* is *true* politeness." At the theater she finds the accommodations infinitely above those at London: "Can one wonder at the contempt shewn by foreigners when they see English women of fashion squeezed into holes lined with dirty torn red paper, and the walls of it covered with a wretched crimson stuff?" Remarking on that "settled Scheme of Vice" (as she had called it in 1785), cicisbeism or the system of male companions for married women, she contrives to turn even it into criticism of the English: "we will not send people to Milan to study delicacy or very refined morality to be sure; but were the crust of British affectation lifted off many a character at home, I know not whether better, that is *honester*, hearts would be found under it" than those at Milan.[16]

Stronger still, she converts "the Italians grossness of Conversation" (1786) into a triumph over English social anxiety. "In Italy . . . nobody dreams of cultivating conversation at all—*as an art*; or studies for any other than the natural reason, of informing or diverting themselves, without the most distant idea of gaining admiration, or shining in company, by the quantity of science they have accumulated in solitude." She drives this home with a keen thrust. "*Here* no man lies awake in the night for vexation that he missed recollecting the last line of a Latin epigram till the moment of application was lost." This is not euphemism in defense of the Italians; rather, it is assault upon the English. The English demonstrate good breeding, or class, by verbal performance, the excruciating ballet of conversational one-upsmanship so brilliantly and sickeningly documented in the *Life of Johnson*. They are a culture of verbal narcissists. First the creature and then the victim of that ballet, Piozzi is perfectly situated to expose it. She knows exactly what behavior to attack, understands its motives, and knows therefore how to wound. Speaking of Venetian ladies, she says that they must not be tried "by English rules," for they do not live like English ladies. At first the passage seems antifeminist, but it is more properly anti-English. "Here is no struggle for female education as with us, no resources in study . . . no necessity of reading, to supply without disgrace the evening's chat; no laughing at the card-table, or tittering in the corner if a *lapsus linguae* has produced a mistake, which malice never fails to record." And now the stinger: "A lady in Italy is *sure* of applause, so she takes little pains to obtain it."[17]

English travelers, beginning at least with Addison, assert that Italians "are stiff, ceremonious, and reserved." Piozzi seems to concur when she allows that "the Italians are not a laughing nation," but she at once turns the charge back upon the English. She does this by making *laughter* mean *ridicule*. "The Italians are not a laughing nation: were ridicule to step in among them, many innocent pleasures would soon be lost." One innocent pleasure is that of singing impromptu verses in company, and in England it would be killed by dread. "A man must have good courage in England, before he ventures at diverting a little company by such devices: while one would yawn, and one would whisper, a third would walk gravely out of the room."[18]

Allowing that Italians, unlike the English, enjoy no political liberty (another standing topic of English superiority), Piozzi retorts upon the English that they enjoy no social liberty; they "forge shackles for themselves, and lay the yoke heavy on society." By contrast, she declares feelingly, "it is a choice delight to live where the everlasting scourge held over London and Bath, of *what will they think?* and *what will they say?* has no existence," and where one need not pretend to be other than one is. If in Naples there are dungeons and arbitrary imprisonment, in England there is malicious nosiness and scandal. "I would be loath to see the spirit of producing every one's private affairs . . . before the public eye, spread into *this* country: No! let that humour be confined to Great Britain, where the . . . laws do protect, though the individuals insult one: but *here*, why the people would be miserable indeed, if to the oppression which may any hour be exercised over them by their prince, were likewise to be added the liberties taken perpetually in London by one's next door neighbour, of tearing forth every transaction, and publishing even every conjecture to one's disadvantage."[19] The concession of English liberty is sandwiched between the attacks on English gossip, and is perhaps further neutralized by "tearing forth," which sounds unpleasantly like disembowelment. Further, the protection of laws is abstract, but the "liberties taken perpetually" by one's neighbor are all too concrete. England is made to appear a nation of spies; it is an eighteenth-century version of *1984*.

In all of this, Piozzi's revenge on England is achieved by a rhetoric of reversal and overturning; fair is foul and foul fair. Ordinarily she manages this rhetoric without ostentation, so that it operates subliminally and by accretion. Once in a while, however, she allows herself the pleasure of doing it overtly, and then all the traditional postures of the English traveler emerge, in exquisitely revisionary form. Our text now is her arrival at Florence. Reading it, bear in mind that one great topic of misery for the splenetic traveler is foreign food, and that inns, for him, are always potential and usually actual scenes of suffering. For Smollett in particular, they are occasions for fulminating against Italian rapacity. Of course, the more "civilized" an inn is—i.e., the more like home—the better it is; it then becomes a scene of brief respite from the general horror. Bear in mind also that up to this point in her journey Piozzi has had almost nothing but praise for the food she has met with—a matter on which she has all along been quietly revising her precursors. She comes then to Florence, late at night, tired but cheerful, for they are going, she hears, to an English inn:

> and many of the last miles were passed very pleasantly by my maid and myself, in anticipating the comforts we should receive by finding ourselves among our own country folks . . . and by once more eating, sleeping, &c. *all in the English way,* as her phrase is. Accordingly, here are small low beds again, soft and clean, and down pillows; here are currant tarts, which the Italians scorn to touch, but which we are happy and delighted to pay not ten but twenty times their value for, because a currant tart is so much *in the English way:* and here are beans and bacon in a climate where it is impossible that bacon should be either wholesome or agreeable; and one eats infinitely worse than one did at Milan, Venice, or Bologna: and infinitely dearer too; but that makes it still more completely *in the English way.*

It is Smollett, or the splenetic English traveler generally, turned inside out on almost every detail. The effect is so revisionary as to be prophetic. This passage prophesies English writing of 150 years later, in which the Englishman abroad is all too likely to be treated as a fatuous tourist who will go to any length to remind himself of home, and in which "home" equates with bad food. Piozzi's spoiled bacon foretastes of the nauseous stuffs consumed by characters in George Orwell.[20]

The repression from which Piozzi wrote *Observations* is partly a redirection of feeling, not its denial, and is well recompensed by the revenge it gives her. Nevertheless her revenge, however sweet, comes at some cost: Attacking the English, she necessarily attacks also the Englishwoman in herself. (Welshwoman, actually; she always so calls herself, and thus holds herself slightly apart from the English—a difference that no doubt made it easier to attack them.) This cost becomes apparent as soon as we recall her own verbal narcissism and its triumphs in conversation, her own "struggle for female education," her own "resources in study . . . to supply . . . the evening's chat," her own "tittering" in *Thraliana* at every *lapsus linguae* she has heard and never failed maliciously to record, her own pains to obtain applause. Attacking English ridicule, she turns against her own satirical temperament, a temperament so satirical that even Johnson suffered from it ("You care for nothing says he, so you can crack your Joke"[21]). Her spleen against England in *Observations* is important, but its expression is only occasional; fundamentally *Observations* is written against spleen and therefore against her own spleen, both personal and literary.

This repression cannot have been easy, for spleen is virtually the social signifier of *intelligence*. We recall Batten's remark: "The revelation of a melancholic temperament . . . makes the traveler seem the kind of person whose descriptions should be trusted. . . . The spleen served as a sign of acute mental ability." Batten cites medical lore, but for our purposes spleen has less to do with medicine than with social psychology. Eighteenth-century English people in "good society" claim status by refusing to be pleased; this signifies discernment. Refusal to be pleased is precisely the object of Piozzi's criticism in *Observations*; for instance, she writes that the willingness of Italians to laugh "at the same joke for months and months together, is perhaps less despicable to a thinking mind, than the affectation of weariness and disgust, where probably it is not felt at all." The English, she charges, affect sullenness: "a gay heart often lurks under a clouded countenance, put on to deceive spectators into a notion of his philosophy who wears it." In *Anecdotes* Piozzi had reported Johnson's censure of just such a person: "Delicacy [i.e., true delicacy] does not surely consist . . . in impossibility to be pleased." This is a genuine Johnson sentiment, yet the man who uttered it is the same man who is sure that travel will end in disappointment and who says in his pride that there is nothing new to see. Johnson's greatest personal struggle was against his own fierce refusal to be pleased.[22] He won that struggle finally, if at all, only on his deathbed; in his writing it is never won for long.

On the strength of *Observations* we may hazard the theory that Johnson could not permit himself to be pleased because to be pleased would mean surrendering a prime signifier of intellect—and Johnson, as we know, had spent his whole life fighting his way by his intellect. In *Observations*, I shall now argue, Piozzi carries to a far fuller conclusion than Johnson could the program implied by "Delicacy does not surely consist in impossibility to be pleased." She does for herself and her reader what Johnson could not consistently do: she finds a rhetoric of pleasure which subdues the rhetoric of spleen and yet retains intelligent perception. She overcomes her own interior Swiftian-Johnsonian satirist and reverses the terms of Johnson's letter to her from Scotland, quoted earlier, so that they almost read, "You are perhaps imagining that by scrambling up a rock I shall only see other rocks, and a wider circuit of barren desolation; but in reality, I am withdrawn from the invasion of your imagined evils into regions of peace and pastoral felicity, which are not around me, but in me."

Her achievement is the more convincing because it is won gradually, in the course of the book and therefore seemingly in the course of the journey. This itself is a revisionary move. Smollett, in his *Travels*, begins his tour of Italy with gladness: "I felt an enthusiastic ardor to tread that very classical ground which had been the scene of so many great atchievements"; but his journey's end is dominated by a nightmarish march—on foot, his coach having broken—through mud and darkness from Perugia to Florence. *Observations*, per contra, opens with a tedious channel crossing and a dismal Johnsonian reflection: "Of all pleasure, I see much may be destroyed by eagerness of anticipation." The sight of sunrise and sunset at sea has disappointed her, "and if the sun itself cannot satisfy the cravings of a thirsty imagination, let it at least convince us that nothing on this side Heaven can satisfy them, and *set our affections* accordingly."[23] This, at the very outset, is the weary wisdom of that other central eighteenth-century travel book, *Rasselas*.

Paris, when she gets there, gives her no delight; she is inclined to be critical, but an accidental reading of Madame Boccage's *Lettres sur l'Angleterre* checks her. Madame Boccage, she says, "had more opportunities than I for observation, not less quickness of discernment surely. . . . Yet, how was she deceived in many points!" If a European traveler may be wrong about England, an English traveler may be wrong about Europe. On this principle of mere justice, Piozzi resolves to "tell nothing that I did not *see*." What she sees, however, as she works her way south, is disappointing enough to certify her competence in spleen. "Every town that should adorn these lovely plains . . . exhibits, upon a nearer approach, misery"; a traveler "requires . . . some days experience to convince him that the squallid scenes of wretchedness and dirt in which he is obliged to pass the night, will prove more than equivalent to the pleasures he has enjoyed in the day-time. . . . He who should fix his residence in France, lives like Sir Gawaine . . . whose wife was bound by an enchantment, that obliged her at evening to lay down the various beauties which had charmed admiring multitudes all day, and become an object of odium and disgust."[24]

The last of these sentences is sufficiently Johnsonian to establish his tonality, from which she now swerves by way of Johnson's own cry against displeasure. She reflects that she does not wish to be a "troublesome fellow-traveller" to her husband; "how little do those ladies consult their own interest, who make impatience of petty inconveniences their best supplement for conversation!—fancy themselves more important as less contented; and imagine all delicacy to consist in the difficulty of being pleased!" A few more pages bring her to the Alps, a plausible topic, even for a splenetic traveler, on which to effect the reversal that she has been preparing. "Surely the immediate sensation conveyed to the mind by the sight of such tremendous appearances must be in every traveller the same, a sensation of fulness never experienced before, a satisfaction that there is something great to be seen on earth—some object capable of contenting even fancy." These terms are chosen with care. They too are Johnsonian, and they represent the utmost limit of Johnsonian sublimity. In the *Lives of the Poets* Johnson employs them in praise of the highest poetical achievements, the Alps of poetry. Milton, he writes of *Paradise Lost*, "never fails to fill the imagination." The Johnsonian mind is always "hungry" and in quest of fullness, but as *Rasselas* is written to demonstrate, it can never find objects capable of filling it for long; the "hunger of imagination . . . preys incessantly upon life."[25] From this unsatisfiable condition of mind one could infer the Christian doctrine that the mind's true object is not earth but eternity; Johnson does so infer at the close of *The Vanity of Human Wishes*, and Piozzi so infers at the opening of *Observations*. One could also infer, however, that the mind goes hungry because it will not deign to feed itself with what earth offers; its hunger is fastidious rejection, or refusal to be pleased. Contemplating the Alps, Piozzi is so far at one with Johnson, that is with the occasional and transient Johnsonian admission of a satisfying object, which is as far as Johnson will go. The Alps are so stationed in her book, however, as to undo the first inference—they *can* "satisfy the cravings of a thirsty imagination," so something "on this side Heaven can satisfy them." The second inference remains possible as Italy lies all before her.

The following pages have an indefinite character suitable to the openness she has achieved. The first town in Italy is Novalesa, "where the hollow sound of a heavy dashing torrent that has accompanied us hitherto, first grows faint, and the ideas of common life catch hold of one again." Here are Smollettian insects and dirt, but because she is writing in the present tense impressions come and go, and nothing is forejudged. The next town is a nullity, but the one after that affords "an admirable dinner." They now enter the avenue to Turin, "most magnificently planted, and drawn in a wide straight line" that reminds her of St. James's Park in London. After twelve miles it grows "dull." Still, "the town to which this long approach conveys one does not disgrace its entrance." She approves the elegant symmetry of Turin, finding in it "a soft repose for the eye, wearied" by the heights and depths of Alpine sublimity. The next sentence shifts to a confirmatory past tense, a prolepsis of secured pleasure, and its mood is sudden rapture. "Model of elegance, exact Turin! where Italian hospitality first consoled, and Italian arts first repaid, the fatigues of my journey: . . . how shall I consent to quit this lovely city? where . . . every pleasure which politeness can invent, and kindness can bestow, was held out for my acceptance." So strong is this proleptic delight that it can subsume even that nastiness, the "smells" of a public privy. They "poison all one's pleasure," she says, but not for long; they are no sooner mentioned than forgotten, in the "splendour" of a royal palace. She is moving toward the mode of romance, and she now secures it by an irony not of disappointment but of innocence. "I go about like Stephano and his ignorant companions, who longed for all the glistering furniture of Prospero's cell in the Tempest, while those who know the place better are vindicated in crying, '*Let it alone, thou fool, it is but trash*.'"[26] This is the inverse of Johnsonian irony, for instead of discovering disappointment it prophesies still greater pleasure.

It is one of the glories of Piozzi's rhetoric in *Observations* that she makes no move in haste. Revising Johnson is a huge job and is not to be done by mere fiat. So, although she is moving into the mode of romance she takes care to authenticate it by remaining open to reservations. On the road from Turin to Genoa she writes a passage prefigurative of Keats's "Ode to Autumn": "The prospect from St. Salvadore's hill derives new beauties from the yellow autumn; and exhibits such glowing proofs of opulence and fertility, as words can with difficulty communicate." But she adds, in Johnsonian fashion, "The animals, however, do not seem benefited in proportion to the apparent riches of the country." In Johnson, *however* and *but* signify, typically, that hunger of imagination that can never be satisfied because it can always find some abatement to pleasure; they are skeptical conjunctions. They so signify in Smollett, also, and can be illustrated by Smollett's treatment of the falls at Terni. These falls, writes Smollett, *would* be sublime, *if only*: "Such a body of water rushing down the mountain; the smoak, vapour, and thick white mist which it raises; the double rainbow which these particles continually exhibit while the sun shines; the deafening sound of the cataract; the vicinity of a great number of other stupendous rocks and precipices, with the dashing, boiling, and foaming of the two rivers below, produce altogether an object of tremendous sublimity." They *do* produce it, says his verb, and one would think that would be that. But no: "*yet* great part of its effect is lost, for want of a proper point of view, from which it might be contemplated."[27] They would be sublime, if only we could stand somewhere to see them; but we can't, and are disappointed.

In Johnson again, less typically, *but* can also be compensatory; it is so in chapter 6 of *Rasselas*, where the flying-machine projector's wings are useless to him in air but preserve his life when he falls into the lake. Johnson's compensatory *but* aligns with his counsel to be pleased. In *Observations* Piozzi is writing against the skeptical *but*, and her weapon is frequently the compensatory *but*. She employs it, for instance, on the traditionally troubled question of Italian diet. Noting, as many other English had noted with contempt, the Italian fondness for small birds, she gives praise that appears extorted: "it must be confessed that they dress them incomparably." Then she enters the appropriate, and very English, reservation: no mutton. "The sheep here are all lean and dirty-looking, few in number too." But this converts to a virtue: "but the better the soil the worse the mutton we know, and here is no land to throw away, where every inch turns to profit in the olive-yards, vines, or something of much higher value than letting out to feed sheep."[28] Her *but* is a *but* against *buts*, and against mutton, and against the imaginative poverty of demanding mutton in the midst of other plenty.

Her first long stay is Milan, where she will settle for some months. It is time therefore to decide on what principle she will conduct her observations of Italian life. This is not merely a question of what to see and what to ignore, but a question of ethics. She ponders it in the language of *Anecdotes*. First she recalls Johnson's injunction, which she had there given in the words of Milton. "*I* ought to learn that which before us lies in daily life, if proper use were made of my demi-naturalization." But there is a difficulty in this, as she candidly avows: "surely if there was much wrong [in the daily life of Italy], I would not tell it of those who seem inclined to find all right in me; nor can I think that a fame for minute observation, and skill to discern folly with a microscopic eye, is in any wise able to compensate for the corrosions of conscience, where such discoveries have been attained by breach of confidence, and treachery towards . . . unsuspecting innocence of conduct."[29] By itself, this repudiation of Johnson's "microscopic eye" could damage her credentials for truthfulness, credentials which it is imperative that she maintain. It does not ultimately damage them, for she has already begun to sap his skeptical posture by convincing reversals and because she will employ those reversals again and again throughout her book; moreover, her argument always has far less to do with Italy as such than with how one perceives experience. One can make Johnson's perceptual choice, but, she is saying here, it carries a high price. Its price is corroded conscience, the sin of rejecting one's fellow creatures, the refusal of festivity—in a word, surliness.

Her own contrary choice has to be shown to be undeluded, however. She proceeds to subject it to a classical test for an English traveler, monks. To the English writer, a monk is a sluggard at best, a closet villain at worst, and an apparatus for Gothic fiction. At Milan Piozzi is invited to see a theatrical performance by the monks of St. Victor, and it is pretty foul: "the comic part . . . was intolerably gross; the jokes coarse, and incapable of diverting any but babies, or men who, by a kind of intellectual privation, contrive to perpetuate babyhood, in the vain hope of preserving innocence." It is worse than coarse, it is obscene and possibly pederastic; the boy sopranos playing the female parts "blush[ed] for shame . . . while the company, most of them grave ecclesiastics, applauded with rapturous delight." Moreover, "this dull buffoonery" goes on till one in the morning. A Smollettian disaster, in short, from which no good could be expected, and which appears to confirm English lore about monks, Italian sexual nastiness, and Roman Catholic hypocrisy, all at once. The irony, a saving irony, is that these monks have human faces, in fact Welsh faces, and they are pleasing to look at. "Pleasure, when it does come, always bursts up in an unexpected place; I derived much from observing in the faces of these cheerful friars, that intelligent shrewdness and arch penetration so visible in the countenances of our Welch farmers."[30]

"In an unexpected place": Skeptical irony trades on the fiction that we never expect disappointment, but its form, as in *Rasselas*, becomes highly predictable. The open irony of *Observations* tropes against skeptical irony by having it that we do expect disappointment—we are wise, having been well instructed by Johnson—and are surprised into pleasure. The most daring single coup of this sort Piozzi performs at Venice. The place is well chosen for two reasons. First, it is far enough into her book to have been prepared. Second, Venice itself is not, by convention, an unexpected place for pleasure; the first view of Venice is an occasion for enthusiasm even in Samuel Sharp, a traveler otherwise impervious to joy. On her first view of Venice Piozzi is as warm as Sharp, and in subsequent pages she is more pleased than he is, until she comes to the Rialto. There she turns peevish: The Rialto is dirty. In fact all of Venice is dirty, and it stinks, and the skeptic in her begins to stir. She wants to know whether it is true, the rumor that Venetian gondoliers sing bits of Tasso and Ariosto while they row; she doubts it, and goes on to criticize their vanity and self-importance. Now the surprise. She is in her room, writing these remarks (for *Observations* preserves the form of a diary): "But hark! while I am writing this peevish reflection in my room, I hear some voices under my window answering each other upon the Grand Canal. It is, it *is* the gondolieri sure enough; they are at this moment singing to an odd sort of tune, but in no unmusical manner, the flight of Erminia from Tasso's Jerusalem." Thus startled by the truth—or by what, at least, she has heard—she exclaims, "This wonderful city realizes the most romantic ideas ever formed of it."[31]

As she penetrates farther into Italy she establishes the mode of romance with increasing firmness. At Florence we begin to hear, in rich detail, of flowers: "wallflowers perfuming every street, and even every passage; while pinks and single carnations grow beside them . . . and from the tops of houses, where you least expect it, an aromatic flavour . . . is diffused." Leaving Florence, she is fearfully mindful of "tremendous tales" by English travelers "of terrible roads and wicked postillions, and ladies labouring through the mire on foot" (this is Smollett's tale, specifically). But the road she takes is no terror: it passes "thick hedges . . . loaded with uncultivated fruits; the wild grape, raspberry, and azaroli, inviting to every sense, and promising every joy." And it conducts her to the little republic of Lucca, where the climate resembles that of the Golden Age and "where no man has been murdered during the life or memory of any of its peaceful inhabitants."[32]

There are, to be sure, vicious gnats at Florence, and vipers and scorpions at Lucca, and at Pisa spiders; the Bagni di Pisa provide a splendid exercise in traditional antipastoral in the Johnson mode. There, delighted by the baths, "I . . . begged my husband not to hurry us to Rome, but take the house we lived in for a longer term, as I would now play the English housewife in Italy I said; and accordingly began calling the chickens and ducks under my window, tasted the new wine as it ran purple from the cask, caressed the meek oxen that drew it to our door; and felt sensations so unaffectedly pastoral, that nothing in romance ever exceeded my felicity." This is so explicit that it begs to be deflated. Accordingly, a page later, "my fairy dream of fantastic delight seems fading away apace": Mr. Piozzi has come down with some local sickness, no doctor is at hand, and the peasants are gouging the price of lemons. The last stroke hits when, changing her husband's bedding, she rips the mattress and finds it *"all alive* with creatures wholly unknown to me." Three nights later comes a thunderstorm, "such as no dweller in more northern latitudes can form an idea of," and even a small earthquake. The next morning they pack their coach and leave.[33] This Johnsonian episode does not work to Johnsonian effect, however, for she has passed out of Johnson's mode and recalls it here only for what we might call authenticity. She has passed through flowers, has entered the garden, and the vermin there—the scorpions and spiders of antipastoral—merely confirm its reality.

Perhaps not at once. I have said that a glory of her rhetoric is that she does nothing in haste; *Observations* establishes itself with great deliberateness, for all the surface vivacity of its diction. From Pisa she moves to Sienna, "through the sweetest country in the world," a country of vineyards. Now comes a short series of reversals: "I have eaten too many of these delicious grapes however, and it is now my turn to be sick—No wonder, I know few who would resist a like temptation, especially as the inn afforded but a sorry dinner, whilst every hedge provided so noble a dessert." This is a beautiful stroke, for the indoor dinner of nominal civilization *can* be bad when the outdoors of a real Eden compensates it. She immediately follows this with something even outrageously Edenic. There are no insects at Sienna, "only *lizards*, lovely creatures!" who sun themselves at the foot of every tree. "Lovely" is not ironic; they are light green and scarlet. Moreover these lizards are said—and the tales, she hears, "are strictly true"—to be friends to man; she reports "an odd anecdote" of a young farmer who, going on an errand to his mistress, took a nap under a tree and there would have been bitten by a snake "had not a friendly lizard waked, and given him warning of the danger." Well! Although Sienna is as lovely as its lizards she prudently does not linger there, but takes us on to Rome, and to more authenticating dismalness. En route they sleep at Radicofani, atop an extinct volcano, where nothing is to be seen but black rock, the very antithesis of Eden. Then the Roman Campagna, agreed by every traveler, and by her, to be a waste place—but she adds her now characteristic saving *but*: "The present sovereign is mending matters as fast as he can, we hear."[34]

Writing up Rome itself is an inevitable problem, the place is so central to eighteenth-century English high culture. "Of Trajan and Antonine's Pillars what can one say?" She divides the task, writing of Rome both on her way south and again on her way north, but this question overhangs all of the twelve pages or so that she gives to antiquities and galleries there, not the best pages in her book. Her best page on Rome is Gulliverian, and recalls the various sufferings of Gulliver among outlandish peoples.

> The Roman ladies cannot endure perfumes, and faint away even at an artificial rose. I went but once among them, when Memmo the Venetian ambassador did me the honour to introduce me. . . , but the conversation was soon over, not so my shame; when I perceived all the company shrink from me very oddly, and stop their noses with rue, which a servant brought to their assistance on open salvers. I was by this time more like to faint away than they—from confusion and distress; my kind protector informed me of the cause; said I had some grains of marechale powder in my hair perhaps, and led me out of the assembly; to which no intreaties could prevail on me ever to return, or make further attempts to associate with a delicacy so very susceptible of offence.

What makes this delicacy the more outlandish is that, to her nose, the city itself reeks; every arch and vestibule in it is used as a privy. "The Roman nobles are not disgusted with *all sorts* of scents it is plain; these are not what we should call perfumes indeed, but certainly *odori*." Yet, as at Turin, these impressions are banished by others. Her last visit is to the Villa Borghese: "But the vases in this Borghese villa! the tables! the walls! the cameos stuck in the walls! the frames of the doors, all agate, porphyry, onyx, or verd antique! the enormous riches contained in every chamber, actually takes away my breath and leaves me stunned."[35]

Her journey's apogee is Naples, her description of which she later called a "Panegyric." Her arrival there is more properly melodrama: it is two in the morning, in the midst of a fierce thunderstorm and an eruption of Vesuvius. She is no sooner in her room at the Crocelle, however, than these terrors become delightful. Her room, "a noble apartment," "commands a complete view of the mountain," and does so "at exactly the distance one would chuse to observe it from"; with such a spectacle before one's eye, who needs sleep and supper? She resumes the mode of romance now with another prolepsis: "Such were my first impressions of this wonderful metropolis, of which I had been always reading summer descriptions, and had regarded somehow as an Hesperian garden, an earthly paradise."[36]

As yet, she realizes as she writes them, these expectations have not been met; daily experience, however, confirms them. There is the climate, for one, so mild in January that the lazaroni "like to sleep out of doors" and throw off most of their clothes. They are even, she suggests, freed of Adam's curse, work, since for all she can see they pass their time playing on the beach or sauntering the streets. The sight of "whole boars, kids and small calves . . . with all their skins on," hanging in "every third shop," a sight which had nauseated poor William Cole in Paris, to Piozzi signifies "abundance." Here also "are the most excellent, the most incomparable fish I ever eat; red mullets, large as our maycril, and of singularly high flavour; besides the calamaro, or ink-fish, a dainty worthy of imperial luxury;" and here, on 20 January, are "almond and even apple trees in blossom," "all the hedges in blow as you drive towards Pozzuoli, and a snow of white May-flowers clustering round Virgil's tomb." She mounts Vesuvius, now quiet, and proceeds to pastoralize even it by noting that villagers live at its foot and grow oranges there; never mind that she also burns her fingers picking a piece of sulphur. While she is at Naples the Queen of Naples gives birth, and "all resolve to be happy, and to rejoice in the felicity of a prince that loves them"; there follow a great feast and a carnival. The only sadness is that she must depart. "My stay has been always much shorter than I wished it, in every great town of Italy; but *here!* where numberless wonders strike the sense without fatiguing it, I do feel double pleasure; and among all the new ideas I have acquired since England lessened to my sight upon the sea, those gained at Naples will be the last to quit me."[37]

So begins the journey back. At Rome this time she visits churches and religious sites, and these lead, of course, to a topic she has until now kept relatively out of sight, the "pretended miracles of popish superstition." Her posture throughout the book has been to trope against skepticism without, however, actually avowing credulity; "I am not," she asserts, "naturally credulous." At Rome, then, she is shown "the spot where it is supposed St. Paul suffered decapitation," and the guide points to three fountains nearby "which were said to have burst from the ground at the moment of his martyrization." Her language, we see, is carefully noncommittal. On such a topic the approved mode is irony and scoffing. This she supplies, but in the mouth of "a Dutch gentleman in company, and a steady Calvinist," who "loudly ridiculed the tradition, called it an idle tale, and triumphantly expressed his certain *conviction*, that such an event *could not possibly* have ever taken place." Because to an English reader a Dutchman is proverbially stupid and a Calvinist proverbially fanatical, this is as much as to say that the approved irony and scoffing are both stupid and fanatical. "To this assertion," she goes on with exquisite ironic tact, "no reply was made"; skepticism is here a social *faux pas*, to be overlooked if possible.[38]

The company, including the Dutchman, drive home together, and as they drive they chat. He rambles into "a long Rousseau-like tale of a lady he once knew" and her extravagantly romantic conduct involving love, honor, and self-denial, those well-known staples of sentimental fiction. It is Piozzi's turn to be skeptical. "Seeing some marks of disbelief in my countenance, he begun observing, in an altered tone of voice, that *common* and *vulgar* minds might hold such events to be out of possibility, and such sentiments to be out of nature." Again she says nothing, and reserves for her book this crushingly Johnsonian retort: "it was more likely nature should have been permitted to deviate in favour of Paul the apostle of Jesus Christ, than of a fat inhabitant of North Zealand, no way distinguished from the mass of mankind." This is sufficiently ad hominem, but then the question itself is ad hominem, for it has much less to do with the truth or falsehood of miracles and relics than with the good or ill temper with which we treat our fellow men. "He who at the moment a dead martyr's robe is shewn him, begs grace of God to follow that great example, is certainly doing no harm," and "no one has a right to ridicule the love of what once belonged to a favourite character, who has ever felt attachment to a dead friend's snuff-box."[39] This is exactly the conclusion we should expect from one who has been teaching herself, through some 290 pages, how to "be pleased."

From Rome Piozzi takes what appears to have been Smollett's road, for it goes by Terni, and "the mountains after Terni grow steep and difficult." Here had begun Smollett's nightmare, and here, sure enough, Piozzi's coach breaks down. But this accident yields, instead of horror, pleasure: "being tied together only with ropes, we cannot hurry through a country most delightful of all others to be detained in." From here on, good humor hardly forsakes her; it is the reversal of Smollett again, whose humor at this stage of his journey is exceptionally foul. She comes to Loretto, a place notorious in English travel books for its *Santa Casa*, the supposed house of the Blessed Virgin. On this topic much ingenious irony has been expended, from Swift to Dr. John Moore in *A View of Society and Manners in Italy* (1781). The Santa Casa, according to canonical legend, was moved to Loretto from the Holy Land by angels. Moore describes the journey:

> A blaze of celestial light, and a concert of divine music, accompanied it during the whole journey; besides, when the angels, to rest themselves, set it down in a little wood near the road, all the trees of the forest bowed their heads to the ground, and continued in that respectful posture as long as the Sacred Chapel remained among them. But, not having been entertained with suitable respect at the castle above mentioned, the same indefatigable angels carried it over the sea, and placed it in a field belonging to a noble lady, called Lauretta, from whom the Chapel takes its name. This field happened unfortunately to be frequented at that time by highwaymen and murderers: A circumstance with which the angels undoubtedly were not acquainted when they placed it there. After they were better informed, they removed it to the top of a hill.[40]

And so on; it is amusing. Piozzi's treatment, however, simply (and quietly) devastates this irony. She does not retell the tale, knowing that it is well known. Instead she has "a learned ecclesiastic" at Rome deflate it himself, by his own judicious but respectful skepticism. "There is no need," he had told her when she had informed him that she would visit Loretto, "to caution a native of your island against credulity; but pray do not believe that we are ourselves satisfied with the tale you will read there." He himself details the reasons for disbelieving it, and in the face of such urbanity satire such as Moore's appears merely sophomoric. For the rest, Piozzi is free to speak of what is really true about Loretto. It is really an object of veneration; it is really a treasure house of immense riches, the collected offerings of Catholic Europe; its very name is really respected even by the Turks. "Why then should the place be to any order of thinking beings a just object of insult or mockery?" Her final comment applies to much more than Loretto; it could be the motto to her book. "As there is always infinite falsehood in the world, so there is always wonderful care, however ill applied, to avoid being duped; a terror which hangs heavily over weak minds in particular, and frights them as far from truth on the one side, as credulity tempts them away from it on the other."[41]

By this point romance has virtually banished irony. Her broken coach itself becomes the vehicle of romance, for "it drew us slowly through so sweet a country. The medlar blossoms adorn the hedges with their blanche roses; the hawthorn bushes . . . perfume them; and the roads"—another quietly outrageous Edenic detail—"little travelled, do not torment one with the dust as in England." She revisits Venice and returns slowly to Milan. Then, at the end of summer, they take a vacation-within-a-vacation, a "Villeggiatura at the Borromaean palace, situated in the middle of Lago Maggiore, on the island so truly termed Isola Bella." This place is Eden overtly, or rather its very near displacement, the Happy Valley of *Rasselas*:

> The palace is constructed as if to realise Johnson's ideas in his Prince of Abyssinia: the garden consists of ten terraces; the walls of which are completely covered with orange, lemon, and cedrati trees, whose glowing colours and whose fragrant scent are easily discerned at a considerable distance, and the perfume . . . reaches as far as to the opposite shore. . . . Every thing one sees, and every thing one hears, and every thing one tastes, brings to one's mind the fortunate islands and the golden age. . . . It is the garden however more than the palace which deserves description. He who has the care of it was

born upon the island, and never strayed further than four miles, he tells me, from the borders of his master's lake. Sure he must think the fall of man a fable: *he* lives in Eden still.[42]

The pull of the entire book has been towards this recovery of the Happy Valley, here purged of Johnsonian disappointment and made new. The singular beauty of the last sentence, "Sure he must think the fall of man a fable: *he* lives in Eden still," carries its own conviction, and it enforces on us the realization that *Observations* is by much her greatest poem. It is a poem convincingly in the mode of Milton at his most humanist, his celebration of innocent human sensuality in book 4 of *Paradise Lost,* and in the mode also of two later poems, descendants of this strain in Milton, Keats's "Ode to Autumn" and Stevens's "Sunday Morning." Piozzi's own ode at Naples, which it contains, and which as we have noticed is an exercise in the apocalyptic romanticism that rejects the things of this world, is clearly a mere excrescence. In teaching herself to be pleased Piozzi has turned herself, at least for the purposes of this book, into a Keatsian-Stevensian secular humanist. She has done so by overturning *Rasselas* and banishing Johnson from his own Happy Valley, a triumph of revisionary strength.

Her book, of course, cannot end here; she has to come home. This means departure from Eden, an experience that, in the context she has established, cannot repeat that of Rasselas but could repeat that of Adam and Eve in Johnson's own precursor work, *Paradise Lost.* It does, but not in grief. Milton's Adam is instructed before they go in the ways by which Providence shall turn their evil to good, and is promised "a Paradise within thee, happier far" than the one they leave behind. In learning how to be pleased rather than disappointed, Piozzi has been possessing herself of that Paradise within.

On her way out of Italy towards Austria she stops at Verona, another Eden, and there moralizes her book: "I never saw people live so pleasingly together as these do; the women apparently delighting in each other's company, without mean rivalry, or envy of those accomplishments which are commonly bestowed by heaven with diversity enough for all to have their share. The world surely affords room for every body's talents, would every body that possessed them but think so; and were malice and affectation once completely banished from cultivated society, *Verona* might be found in many places perhaps." Although she adds that at present Verona seems to exist only at Verona, she has successfully envisioned a possible condition of mind, an interior peaceable kingdom. Earlier she had remarked in passing that "every place produces amusement when one is willing to be pleased."[43] That casual statement, in itself a cliché, points to the same condition of mind; and having experienced the strenuous, albeit quiet, rhetoric of *Observations*, we understand that "willing to be pleased" is an act, not a mere passive disposition.

From this peak of vision the remainder of the book descends gradually, through sixty pages of Austria and Germany. We are not to imagine that her good humor remains perfectly unruffled throughout them, any more than it has throughout Italy; indeed, still reversing her predecessors, we find her liking things less as she gets nearer to England. Berlin and Potsdam bore her, and Westphalia is a hog sty. None of this much matters, or it matters only to confirm the authenticity of what does matter, that she has substituted romance for irony without sacrifice of intelligence, and in so doing has rectified the programmatic skepticism of her precursors in life and writing. The position she ends with, in fact, is not far from Johnson's conceptually, but it is very far from him emotionally. "What I have learned from the Italians is a maxim more valuable than all my stock of connoisseurship: *Che c'e in tutto il suo bene, e il suo male*—that *there is much of evil and of good in every thing*." "The life of a traveller," she adds, "evinces the truth of that position perhaps more than any other."[44] If the travel book is an exercise in unillusioned discrimination, a reality test, the strength of *Observations* is its power to convince us that in her great precursors the test has been rigged by a dark illusion, the illusion of being disillusioned.

SEVEN

An Intruder on the Rights of Men
Piozzi as Arbiter of Style and as Stylist

Erudition, ARROGANT *of her own just claims, . . . looks . . .*
with somewhat like unmerited disdain upon the writer of this little
book, and asks how long the sprightly *lady has fancied herself*
initiated among the Gnosticks, while Error marks her pages and
Ignorance guides her pen.

Through the construction of cartoon figures like Sheridan's Mrs.
Malaprop and Fielding's Mrs. Slipslop . . . they implied that
language itself was almost literally alien to the female tongue. In
the mouths of women, vocabulary loses meaning, sentences
dissolve, literary messages are distorted or destroyed.[1]

THE HIGH POINT of Piozzi's lit-
erary career was 1789. The generally warm reception of *Observations*
confirmed her celebrity; for about ten years she figured among the
most fashionable writers. The books that earned this reputation
she had produced with great rapidity and apparent ease; a little
more than four years had brought them all into being. It was to be
five years, however, before she would publish their successor, *British
Synonymy*, and two and a half years before she would even decide to
write it. What was she doing during those two and a half years?

It appears that she was experiencing troubles that sometimes
attend success, compounded by a setback to her plans and aggra-
vated by her sex. Her career plan in 1789 did not provide for *British
Synonymy*. Rather, it called for a play. Having sent the manuscript of
Observations to the printer on 5 February, she declares her intention:
"If all goes well this Time, I'll have a Stroke at the Stage another
Year." This ambition harks back ten years, to May 1779 when she
had meditated writing a comedy, and it accords with her taste for

writing dramatic prologues and epilogues. In 1789 her friends included Sarah Siddons and John Kemble, manager of Drury Lane Theatre; with their sponsorship she might reasonably expect to get a play produced. Later in February she notes the first idea for "The Two Fountains"; by the end of the year, or the first of 1790, she is writing it. By July Kemble had read it and not been impressed, and she is angry at him; he did not definitely reject the piece, however, until December 1791. In the spring of 1792 Thomas Percy read "The Two Fountains" and advised her to print it ("'tis too good for the Stage"). This she refused to do, giving as her reason that "then the Managers would get it up directly, & save my Benefit Nights by my own hasty Folly."[2] Her reason is logical only on the supposition that Kemble indeed wanted the play and was waiting to get it cheaply; she seems to suspect him of chicanery. By refusing to print she is putting a high value on the piece (managers generally paid more for new plays than booksellers did); she is also, however, avoiding the risk of its failure. The episode is indicative of a certain paranoia that beset her, and it is not the only such episode.

A few days before *Observations* was published she set out on a journey through Scotland that was to last six months. As usual, she kept a tour journal. Even though she did not go to the Hebrides, comparisons with Johnson's tour were inevitable, and she kept herself well minded of them by reading his *Journey* as she traveled. ("'Tis one of his first Rate Performances," she wrote to a friend, "I look it over now every day.") Back home at the end of the year, she thinks about the implications of writing a second travel book. "When People press me to write my *Tour of our own Island* in good Time! they say it to ensnare me: was I to act according to such Advice I should deservedly lose the little Fame I have already acquired." She will not let herself be maneuvered into such an open competition with Johnson. This caution is prudent; it is also, however, profoundly distrustful of her friends ("they say it to ensnare me"). She continues, "How false the Creatures all are!!! but I *know* them." She remembers that "when a Baby I was always the Dupe to my Playfellows," declares that her friends "have always played the same Game with *me* whatever my Name or Place was," and goes into an orgy of self-righteous wrath at them: "Those who have aim'd at shortening my Life, lowering my Reputation or emptying my Purse, have had the constant Torment of seeing my Health stronger, my Fame fairer, and my Pockets fuller than almost anybody's else. So shall it ever happen to those who seek not their own Justification; *the Lord will avenge the Cause of the Simple, & put down the despitefulness of the proud.*" That such an outburst should be provoked by the innocuous suggestion of writing her Scotch tour is astonishing. She must have been tempted by the idea. (Her journal is fully written in the manner of her European journals. In Scotland she had been received flatteringly as the antithesis to Johnson, one who would give a friendly account of the country.)[3] Her conviction that the attempt would ruin her career, however, evinces not just suspicion of her friends but, much more, suspicion of her own success. She seems not to believe in it; she suspects that she is being duped, put up to be made a fool.

Distrust of one's own success is hardly an unhappiness peculiar to women, then or now, but for a woman writer it would certainly have been aggravated by the prevailing mythology that a pen is not "an Instrument for *Ladies* to manage." That mythology would whisper in the ear of any lady who did manage it that there must be some mistake, that either she is duping the public or the public is duping her. The "bumblebee" account of Piozzi's literary career is just a particular instance of the general dogma that women cannot really be writers. According to this dogma, a success by a woman writer must be a qualified success and must be attributed to causes other than her own ability. The success of *Anecdotes* and *Letters* could be (and frequently has been) attributed not to her but to her subject, Johnson, and that attribution makes *Observations* in effect her first book. Considered this way, her anxiety in 1789–91 can be likened to the first-novel syndrome that we know so well today: Do I really have it? and What do I do next? During those two years she was casting about for answers to these questions.

Her first plan was to write for the stage, and here, for the only time, she parted company with her talent. For all its thematic interest and occasional poetic force, "The Two Fountains" is simply inconceivable on the stage; it is a dramatic poem, not a play, and to offer it to Kemble at all was a mistake. Equally inconceivable, although for different reasons, is a comedy, "The Adventurer," which she perhaps wrote at the same time.[4] Its dialogue is spirited and witty, as one would expect from her 1779 dialogues; its plot is a woeful disappointment. Act 1 postulates an intrigue in which the hero, Ferdinand, appears suspiciously intimate with the wife of his landlord, Reinwell, a situation which Reinwell is too preoccupied by money worries to notice. At the same time, Ferdinand is the object of Lady

Rental's romantic interest. During the act other characters, Sir Malabar Spleenwort, Captain Bustler, and Mr. Triplet, encounter Ferdinand, are startled to see him, and remember him from India, the Navy, and other dubious places; it looks as if he has a shady past, although he steadily professes the utmost virtue and integrity. This knot, pleasant enough albeit trivial, is vapidly unraveled in act 2. Someone announces that Ferdinand is really Mrs. Reinwell's long-lost brother, so that their seeming romance proves to have been mere family affection and Ferdinand is free to marry Lady Rental, and for no discernible reason Sir Malabar decides to award Reinwell a post in India, which saves him from bankruptcy. Such is "The Adventurer." One would not wish to see it produced.

More substantial, albeit still unsatisfactory, are the six dialogues between Una and Duessa composed in the spring of 1791. Their mode is not theatrical but, ultimately, Platonic, and their more recent precursors are works like Shaftesbury's *The Moralists* (1709) and Joseph Spence's *Crito* (1752). The speakers are true to their namesakes in *The Faery Queene*: Una utters truth, Duessa specious falsehood. They hold forth in Thomson's "Castle of Indolence," to an audience who sleep, loaf, or otherwise ignore them. This inattention is a comment on people's indifference to questions of truth and falsehood, and also Piozzi's deprecation of the dialogues themselves—a sadly accurate deprecation, for the dialogues do not sustain attention. They touch a variety of topics, some stale, such as the relative merits of poetry and painting, others newly current, such as liberty of the press, Negro emancipation, and democratic politics, but they develop none. This is regrettable, for at moments they are trenchant. Piozzi finished them in July 1791 and laid them aside, giving as her reason that "Mr Piozzi won't let me print it, for fear of making Enemies, & such Stuff." A more likely reason is that she distrusted their success. She might have remembered William Mason's remark in his memoir of Gray: "This ridicule on the Platonic way of dialogue (as it was aimed to be, tho' nothing less resembles it) is, in my opinion, admirable. Lord Shaftsbury was the first who brought it into vogue, and Mr. Spence . . . the last who practised it. As it has now been laid aside some years, we may hope, for the sake of true taste, that this frippery mode of composition will never come into fashion again."[5]

The most animated parts of "Una" are those that deal with politics; as we shall see later, it was as a political writer that she finally regrouped her forces. "Una" is a move towards that regrouping. So is

British Synonymy, although it was not conceived that way. It was conceived, in December 1791, in rather casual terms: "The Synonymes François makes a pretty Book; perhaps an English one on the same plan might be useful, I have half a mind to try my skill for the purpose." By the following spring she was at work on it, but only as her "other Project." Her first project was "a little Poem something like More's female seducers [i.e., fable 15 of Edward Moore's *Fables for the Female Sex*] about Love Avarice & Ambition, how they ran a Race to divert Duessa when She had driven Truth from the Earth."[6] A poem employing Love, Avarice and Ambition as leading characters recalls her early fable "Imagination's Search after Happiness," a poem thematically similar to Johnson's "Fountains," in which Hester Salusbury had bid farewell to her literary aspirations. These hints seem to speak of difficulty, of a turning back on herself. In "The Two Fountains" Hester had turned back to tell her own story—a story of loss, which she chose to tell at the time of her success. Floretta possesses imaginative strength and is punished for it. Having, in *Observations*, attained to imaginative strength, Hester proceeded in "The Two Fountains" to punish herself for it. Clearly the moral is that imaginative strength is wrong for a woman. We may speculate that the "little Poem something like More's female seducers" was designed as another such reminder by the fifth-columnist or self-saboteur within her. From now on, we shall be hearing more from the self-saboteur.

That particular poem, however, seems not to have been written. Instead she wrote *British Synonymy*, almost, it would appear, as a *faute de mieux*, and with some trepidation. This is how she conceived it: "My other Project is a two Volume Book of *Synonymes* in English, like what the Abbé Girard has done in French, for the use of Foreigners, and other Children of six feet high: such a Business well manag'd would be useful, but I have not depth of Literature to do it as one ought.—a good parlour-Window Book is however quite within *my* Compass."[7] We see at once the source of her hesitation: "I have not depth of Literature to do it as one ought." She had extensive literature; we must not take her at her word. She did not, of course, have a file of illustrative quotations such as Johnson used for his *Dictionary*, but she unquestionably could have collected one—indeed she could have used Johnson's in the *Dictionary*, had she been willing to be indebted to his work.

Her hesitation had to do not with her actual but with her felt qualifications for the task. She is venturing into a genre dominated by men as no other genre in which she had written, not even poetry and the travel book, had been. In this genre, where language itself is the subject matter and the writer's authority over language the paramount issue, the woman writer must perforce suffer more than usual anxiety as to her competence. We have seen that Piozzi was openly greeted by one review of her work as a "usurper," and a usurper is, of course, one who lacks a legitimate title. The next woman to write in this genre, Elizabeth Jane Whately almost sixty years later, although highly competent herself nevertheless concealed her sex behind her father's name, publishing her *Selection of English Synonyms* as if it were his work.[8] Piozzi was uncommonly competent to undertake *British Synonymy*, but she was able to undertake it only by persuading herself that it would be altogether a "woman's book," a book for "children" and the parlor window. This was also the ploy by which she allowed herself to write *Retrospection*, her other large-scale incursion into male letters, and in both cases the ploy exacts a high price. By its means she does get them written, but at the cost of not taking them seriously enough herself to make them as good as they could be, and of inviting her readers not to take them as seriously as they deserve to be taken.

"The Choice of Phrases"

All of this, even the parlor window, she unhappily puts into the preface to *British Synonymy*. "If . . . to the selection of words in conversation and elegant colloquial language a book may give assistance, the Author, with that deference she so justly owes a generous public, modestly offers her's; persuaded that, while men teach to write with propriety, a woman may at worst be qualified—through long practice—to direct the choice of phrases in familiar talk." The "long practice" to which she somewhat acidly alludes is probably the practice of correcting her children's speech, a matter in which she was punctilious. She continues, promising not what her book will do but what it will not do. It will not attempt to teach grammar: "Such excellence were in truth superfluous to a work like this, intended chiefly for a parlour window, and acknowledging itself unworthy of a place upon a library shelf." It will not attempt "studied definitions of every quality coming under consideration," for "although the final cause of definition is to fix the true and adequate meaning of words or terms, without knowledge of which we stir not a step in logic; yet *here* we must not suffer ourselves to be so detained, as synonymy has more to do with elegance than truth." In consideration of her not encroaching on these disciplines, or even on "truth," she hopes that the critics "will not over strictly examine, or with much severity censure my weak attempt"; her ambition is only to "dispel a doubt, or clear up a difficulty to foreigners, who can alone be supposed to know less of the matter than myself."[9]

In this ballet of apology and deprecation the reviewers played their appointed parts. The *European Magazine* had feared, from "the known erudition of Mrs. Piozzi, her close acquaintance with the most celebrated literati of the age, the former productions of her pen, and particularly the subject of her present publication," that *British Synonymy* would be "a work strictly and completely philological." Fortunately, a perusal of her preface "agreeably dispelled" that apprehension: "These sentiments are modest and becoming." The *British Critic* found himself entirely seduced:

> To a book so modestly announced, and so modestly prefaced as this is, by a lady, it would be very wrong to bring the solemnity of a metaphysic brow, and to strain her definitions on the rack of logic. . . .
>
> Our fair critic calls her book, "a work intended chiefly for a parlour window;" which we think it but justice to interpret thus, that she has aspired to make it rather entertaining than profound, rather convenient for colloquial reference, than a grave and philosophical production, directed to the . . . improvement of our language. In this light, therefore, we shall consider it, and shall very easily prove . . . that it is in truth a very entertaining book.[10]

The Critical Review alone refused to play. Not to be ungallant, it allowed that a work like *British Synonymy* seems "not ill adapted to the powers of a sprightly and cultivated female." Although such a work, coming from a woman author, would of course lack "a little in depth of erudition," still it would yield a short catalogue of feminine virtues: "a certain felicity of phrase; a sort of tact in the delicate gradations of sentiment, and a kind of instinctive quickness, in sorting and arranging the nicer shades of ideas and semi-tints of expressions." Having thus, in his own estimation, approved himself a friend to lady writers, the reviewer is "sorry to say that little of this is perceivable" in *British Synonymy*. He proceeds to censure severely its style, its methods of discriminating words, and its sentiments. The final judgment, however, was the *British Critic*'s again, in an end-of-the-year summary. *British Synonymy*, it declared, is "the best, if not the first, imitation of the Abbe Girard's celebrated work on Synonymous Words."[11] With this we may turn to consider the actual place of Piozzi's "parlor-window" book in the history of synonymy-writing, a history in which it enjoys genuine priority and which it contributed to shape, by setting examples both of what and what not to do.

Its acknowledged precursor is Gabriel Girard's *La Justesse de la langue françoise* (1718), revised as *Synonymes françois, leurs différentes significations, et le choix qu'il en faut faire pour parler avec justesse* (1736, and thirty subsequent editions to 1806). Girard's is apparently the first dictionary of its kind in a modern language. By the standard of *Webster's Dictionary of Synonyms* it looks meager; its 1741 edition, in 339 entries, discriminates only about 900 words. In 1766 an English imitation appeared: John Trusler, *The Difference, between Words, esteemed Synonymous, in the English Language; And, the Proper Choice of them determined: Together with, So much of Abbé Girard's Treatise, on this Subject, as would agree, with our Mode of Expression. Useful to all, who would, either, write or speak, with Propriety, and, Elegance*. In 371 entries, Trusler discriminates 889 words. Piozzi never mentions him, but it is hard to believe her unaware of his work, which went to a second edition only nine years before she began her own. Hers, the second in English, manifestly surpasses both his and Girard's in one respect: it discriminates more words, 1180 in 315 entries. After *British Synonymy* (which itself enjoyed a reprint in 1804) came the flood: in 1805 William Perry's *Synonymous, Etymological, and Pronouncing English Dictionary*, in 1806 James Leslie's *Dictionary of the Synonymous Words and Technical Terms in the English Language*, in 1813 William Taylor's *English Synonyms Discriminated*, in 1816 George Crabb's *English Synonymes Explained* (the first really popular synonymy book, in print through numerous revisions as late as 1945), in 1846 George Graham's *English Synonyms Classified and Explained*, in 1851 Elizabeth Whately's *Selection of English Synonyms*, in 1852 Roget's *Thesaurus of English Words and Phrases*, and a number of later nineteenth-century dictionaries leading at last to *Webster's* (1942).

These dictionaries do not all attempt the same thing; some, like Roget's, are not synonymy books at all, but "word-finders." The professed synonymy books themselves vary in the scope of their subject—they do not even agree in their ideas of what a synonym is—and in their procedures. In them we confront not a series of straight-line transmissions but a knot of competitors, each seeking to define and claim the field, each sometimes copying, sometimes reviling, and sometimes ignoring his precursors. The ancestor of them all, Girard, took as his point of departure the French Academy's *Dictionary*. Logically, synonymy is a branch of lexicography; the discriminator of words, whether of synonyms or near-synonyms, is engaged in determining meanings. Moreover, one can hardly begin the task without an existing vocabulary, a word list. For Girard to turn to the French *Dictionary* was therefore appropriate—indeed, inevitable. The counterpart for an English synonymist was Johnson's *Dictionary*, and we would expect the first English emulator of Girard to use it. He did not. Trusler, by temperament an eccentric and by trade a miscellaneous writer, simply translated Girard's book, which is a very different thing indeed from composing an English synonymy. Rightfully, Trusler's performance ought to be expelled from the canon. The first genuinely English synonymy—the first that, although written "on the same plan" as Girard's does not consist largely of translation—is Piozzi's.

Alas, she did not permit herself to capitalize on her priority, or even to perceive the opportunity it gave her. She appears to have acted on the idea that whatever was good enough for Girard would be good enough for her. Thus Girard, despite his boast of originality and his claims for the importance of the subject, nowhere states how he decided what words to discriminate, on what principle he selected his vocabulary, and neither does Piozzi. From occasional mentions in the body of her book we gather that she consulted Johnson, but when she cites the *Dictionary* (as she does in her entries for *Affection*, *Blaze*, and *to have Rather*) she does so only to disagree with it; she makes no use at all of its illustrative quotations. (Systematic use of Johnson was thus reserved for her immediate successor, Perry, who, however, did it badly.) Indeed, it was while she was working on *British Synonymy* that she wrote the letter we have previously noticed: "I would not accept help from Doctor Johnson . . . or I should not have waited for his Death before I commenced Authour." Her conduct squares with these sentiments, unfortunately. She is so busy setting herself apart from Johnson that she does not think of appropriating him—a case of self-defeating rebelliousness, of which she understood the psychology perfectly well when she found it in someone else. In *Observations* she had remarked of Rubens, "I know not why he has so fallen below himself in the Madonna's character; perhaps not imitating Tintoret's lovely Virgin in Paradise, he has done worse for fear of being servile."[12]

True, her anxiety that her work not be taken for Johnson's proved justified when a rumor arose that the best parts of *British Synonymy* had been pilfered from a manuscript he allegedly left her. (Unforgivably, this canard is repeated by Roget's biographer.)[13] Had she, then, professedly and systematically employed the *Dictionary* she might well have been told that none of her work was her own. Still, in a task of this nature to ignore the accepted authority is to impair one's own and to settle for less. In her choice of words she stays clear of Johnson, but she cheerfully takes them from friends (the letter to Queeney just quoted is a letter requesting a list of words) and, in the end, from Girard. *British Synonymy* is not another translation of *Synonymes françois*, but a good share of its vocabulary is transposed from Girard's, with the unhappy effect that it seems to put itself after all into competition with the inferior, fundamentally inept work of Trusler. It comes off looking merely better than Trusler, when it ought to look what it really is, the first native English synonymy book.

Even without questions of authorial rivalry the selection of words to discriminate would have been troubling enough. Piozzi professes to treat only colloquial words—those used in conversation, not in writing—and to intend aid to foreigners. The first stipulation would provide, at best, only a rough test of inclusion: it would tend to admit plain words and to exclude learned and technical terms. *British Synonymy* adheres to this test well enough to make its occasional lapses conspicuous (*Durability* and *Duration,* philosophically used, *Socinianism, Lozenge, Parallelogram, Necromancy, Primordial substance, Exergue, Imprese*). The same test might also admit some slang (e.g., *Quack, Quits, Even*), but one is at a loss to explain why it passes the argot of highwaymen (*Cole, Ready rino, Chink, Corianders*—all low slang for *Money*).

These bits of verbal grotesquerie equally defy her second stipulation; except in stage comedy, it is hard to conceive that a genteel Italian, such as Gabriel Piozzi or the various dukes and marquesses who visited the Piozzis, would ever be in danger of saying *Ready rino* for *Money*. (This, however, is a matter to which we shall return.) To suit the needs of foreigners, one would have to proceed either entirely empirically, collecting words that they do actually confuse, or by judgment, collecting those words which are confusable, especially those that are susceptible to confusion by false analogy with words in other languages. Piozzi did some of both. She was attentive to misusage, whether by children or foreigners, and between the one and the other had been correcting mistakes for nearly thirty years. For instance:

> Count Mannucci has written me a very long and very kind Letter on the *Change of my Existence*! he mentions you with grateful Tenderness, & says in his Foreigners English, that he recollects *your last Embracements with a sweet Commotion.*

And:

> I fancy Madam D'Arblaye lives much with foreigners. She talks of *demanding* and *according* in a way English people never talk; and of *descending* to breakfast, and says one sister aided another to rise, or lye down, as English people never do. We say *ask*, and *grant*, and *help*, and *go down stairs*, you know; the other words are French.

And again, of her linguistically less alert fellow citizens:

> What faults in Conversation for want of a little Turn to Etymology! People talk for example of a bright Capacity nothing so common? yet the Allusion is borrowed from a Vessel— wide or narrow if you will, capacious or not capacious, but what nonsense is a *bright* or a *dull* Capacity![14]

The second of these, at least, is a clear instance of confusion by false analogy. French *demander* leads falsely to English *demand*, its true English equivalent being *ask*; for the French-speaking visitor, then, *demand* and *ask* should be discriminated. (As it happens, *British Synonymy* treats neither *demand* nor *ask*.) Not all of them, however, have to do with synonymy; *embracements* has to do with correct termination, and *bright* and *dull* capacity with propriety of metaphor. They are items appropriate not for a dictionary of synonyms but for a work such as Fowler's *Modern English Usage*. Insofar as such items appear in *British Synonymy*—and they appear frequently in it—they dilute its usefulness as a synonymy book, although of course they also broaden its purview. In truth, *British Synonymy* is an ancestor both of *Webster's Dictionary of Synonyms* and of *Modern English Usage*.

Once the words have been selected, on whatever principle, their meanings must by some method be discriminated. In this part of the work *British Synonymy* has been singled out as a paradigm, albeit a negative one; in their review of their precursors' achievements, the authors of *Webster's* respectfully dissent from "the Piozzi method." What that method is, and how far it is in fact her own, may be suggested by a series of parallel entries from Girard, Piozzi, and *Webster's*.

> *Abandonner* se dit des choses & des personnes. *Délaisser* ne se dit que des personnes.
> Nous *abandonnons* les choses dont nous n'avons pas soin. Nous *délaissons* les malheureux à qui nous ne donnons aucun secours.
> On se sert plus communément du mot d'*abandonner* que de celui de *délaisser*. Le premier est également bien employé à l'actif & au passif. Le dernier a meilleure grace au participe qu'à ses autres modes; & il a par lui seul une énergie d'universalité, qu'on ne donne au premier qu'en y joignant quelque terme qui la marque précisément. Ainsi l'on dit, c'est un pauvre *délaissé*, il est généralement *abandonné* de tout le monde. . . .
> Souvent nos parens nous *abandonnent* plûtôt que nos amis. Dieu permet quelquefois que les hommes nous délaissent pour nous obliger à avoir recours à lui.

Familiar talk tells us in half an hour—That a man FORSAKES his mistress, ABANDONS all hope of regaining her lost esteem, RELINQUISHES his pretensions in favour of another; GIVES UP a place of trust he held under the government, DESERTS his party, LEAVES his parents in affliction, and QUITS the kingdom for ever. . . . 'Tis a well-received colloquial phrase to say, You LEAVE London for the country. Telling us you QUIT it seems to convey a notion of your going suddenly to the Continent.—That any one DESERTS it can scarcely be said with propriety, unless at a time of pestilence or tumults of a dangerous nature, when we observe that the capital is DESERTED. . . . That you GIVE UP London looks as if you meant in future to reside upon your own estate in the country . . . while to RELINQUISH a town life seems as if something was required to make the sentence complete—as we RELINQUISH the joys of society for the tranquil sweets of solitude. . . . To FORSAKE London would be a foppish expression; and to say we were going to ABANDON it, as if it could scarce subsist without us, would set people o'laughing. The participles from these verbs evince the various acceptations of their principals.—That fellow is GIVEN UP to every vice, is an expression popular and common; but when we speak of him as ABANDONED of all virtue . . . the phrase approaches to solemnity, and is at least expressive of the man's total ruin even in this transitory world.

Abandon, in its strictest use, implies surrender of control or possession and, frequently, the knowledge that the thing abandoned is left to the mercy of someone or something else. "The ghost of grandeur that lingers between the walls of *abandoned* haciendas in New Mexico" (*M. Austin*). . . . *Desert*, in precise usage, commonly implies previous occupation, companionship, or guardianship, and often connotes desolation; in its narrower sense . . . it emphasizes violation of one's duty as guardian or protector, and extreme culpability. "He that takes the forlorn hope in an attack, is often *deserted* by those that should support him" (*Scott*).[15]

Girard describes conditions of usage (*abandonner* may be said both of things and persons, *délaisser* of persons only; *abandonner* may be either active or passive) and frequency of usage (*abandonner* is more commonly used than *délaisser*); he attempts to specify a word's force; and he gives ideal instances of its use, some of them having a decidedly moralistic tinge ("Dieu permet quelquefois . . ."). *Webster's* specifies implications and cites actual instances of use. The "Piozzi method," of which this entry is an especially full blown example, consists largely of stringing together ideal instances like Girard's; it is the Girard method, really. The weakness of the method is that it leaves most of the work of inference to the reader. (Does a man forsake only mistresses, or can he also forsake other people? Why does he *forsake* her, but *leave* his parents?) On closer inspection, we see that Piozzi does discriminate conditions of use (one *deserts* London only in times of crisis), implications (*give up* London implies an intention to settle in, rather than to visit, the country), and degrees of force (*abandoned of all virtue* "approaches to solemnity"). One wishes that she did so more explicitly. No lexicographic method, however, is watertight, as Johnson well knew, and while we are in the business of criticizing we may notice that *Webster's* is also vulnerable. The quotation from M. Austin, although it says *abandoned*, could as well have said *deserted* on the ground that *desert* "commonly implies previous occupation"; if *desert* "often connotes desolation," so, in Austin, does *abandon*.

In fact one can collect numerous instances of felicitous discriminations in *British Synonymy*, as good as any other dictionary could supply. Here is one, on *Amiable, Lovely, Charming, Fascinating*: "the first of these appear[s] to *deserve* our love, the next to *claim* it, the third to *steal* it from us as by magic; the last of all to *draw*, and to *detain* it, by a half invisible, yet wholly resistless power." *Webster's* on *charm* is only more wordy, not more substantial: "In its commonest use, *charm* implies a power to evoke or attract admiration, but it usually heightens that implication by retaining the suggestion of casting a spell over the senses or, far more often, over the mind." Or this, in which Piozzi does write definitions: "In serious talk, GOODNESS seems generally to mean patience . . . or gentle forbearance more than any higher quality; while VIRTUE appears to imply active beneficence, or heroick greatness displayed in some deed worthy of being recorded.—MORAL RECTITUDE refers us to settled principles and long-tried conduct,—whilst RIGHTEOUSNESS is scarce a conversation word." Or finally, a more complicated case: "Whatever is woven may be TORN, whatever is brittle or fragile we can easily BREAK; the hardest substances will SPLIT, if gunpowder be applied . . . for that purpose. Jealousy will SEPARATE with violence the closest friendships; and the spirit of party rage DIVIDE the nearest ties of blood. Flesh is LACERATED by a thousand accidents; but irruptions from a volcano REND even mountains asunder."[16] Here she mixes the bases of discrimination, analyzing sometimes in terms of the substance being acted on and sometimes in terms of comparative intensity. *Rend* is more violent than *tear*, yet one can rend as well as tear cloth. In ordinary usage, however, to speak of *rend*ing one's clothes would be to speak biblically or poetically, and thus inappropriately. For practical purposes her initial distinction of *tear* and *break* is admirable, and it is also impressively succinct.

"Synonymy," she writes in her preface, "has more to do with elegance than truth." This claim is at least disputable; her own concern, however, is more with elegance than truth, and *British Synonymy* is as much a manual of linguistic etiquette as it is a dictionary of synonymy. Many of its entries are better understood if we think of them as prefiguring not *Webster's Dictionary of Synonyms* but *Modern English Usage*. Like Fowler, and like Johnson—in fact, like most Englishmen—Piozzi is keen in the faith that one's language tells one's class. "Nothing is so certain a brand of beggary in our country as coarse and vulgar language." She means not simply cockneyisms but habits of discourse: "the most awkward and vulgar people commonly describe by causes, while eloquent and polite speakers are careful to avoid such grossness; choosing rather to dwell upon the adjuncts of the thing described." Her aim, like Fowler's, is to inculcate habits of "polite" usage, the kind of speech that evinces unaffected good breeding and smacks of no particular occupation, not even the occupation of being well bred. "Good breeding," she explains, "consists in the art of banishing . . . pedantry. . . . Indeed the pedantry of a drawing-room is no less offensive than that of a college, or an army coffee-house, or a merchant's compting-house;—all are tedious and disgraceful, and should be swept away."[17]

All this is very much in the mode of Fowler, even to the imaging of linguistic malpractice as dust or debris ("swept away"). The enemies of good breeding, the sources of pedantry, are exactly the same for Piozzi as they are for Fowler: newspaper writing and literary fad, the latter traceable, often, to contemptible emulation of the French. Here is an entry from *British Synonymy* that collocates several enemies, offering also their genealogy, a move favored by Fowler as well.

> CIRCUMSTANCES are only those adventitious minutiae which *surround* a fact, as a glance upon the etymology will soon convince us. You cannot accuse a man of murder without knowledge of the CIRCUMSTANCES . . . for there is no knowing how any action stands *relatively*, till the CIRCUMSTANCES to which it *relates* have been examined. All this is well. Commercial phraseology however, extending the influence of this substantive, pronounces a man rich or poor according to his CIRCUMSTANCES. Nor is this *very* wrong, because opulence will attract agreeable APPENDANTS round a person, who is now by a strained metaphor said to be in *easy circumstances*—a silly adjective for those who know not that they use it because the French have a way of calling competence *les coudes franches*, easy-elbowed;—able to move in short,—contrasted against *genée*. Our news-paper dialect meantime improving this perverseness into downright absurdity, tells us that the minister

is unlikely to hold his post *under* the present CIRCUM-
STANCES—a phrase very difficult to comprehend—since however he may be said to lie *under* heavy censure as *under* the rod
. . . a man cannot lie *under* CIRCUMSTANCES, because they
are sure to stand *around* him, . . . for so their very name
implies.

(Ironically, Fowler himself defends "under the circumstances" as
"neither illogical nor of recent invention," and censures objections to
it as "puerile.")[18]

"Silly," "absurdity," "puerile": these words put us in the domain
of satire, or at least of ridicule. Readers of *Modern English Usage* soon
discover that Fowler is adept at both and loves them dearly. Here, for
instance, is Fowler on "Didacticism":

Men, especially, are as much possessed by the didactic impulse
as women by the maternal instinct. Some of them work it off
ex officio upon their children or pupils or parishioners or legis-
lative colleagues, if they are blest with any of these; others are
reduced to seizing casual opportunities, & practise upon their
associates in speech or upon the world in print. The Anglo-
Indian who has discovered that the suttee he read of as a boy
is called *sati* by those who know it best is not content to keep
so important a piece of knowledge to himself; he must have
the rest of us call it *sati*, like the Hindoos (ah, no—Hindus) &
himself.

Fowler is not, observe, speaking of the word *didacticism* but decrying
the practice; his entry is a little essay on it, embellished by a tiny
Theophrastian character (several of them, in fact; there are also "the
orientalist" and "literary critics") and concluded by the moral, which
is: "Seriously, our learned persons & possessors of special information should not, when they are writing for the general public, presume to improve the accepted vocabulary."[19] The idea is to shame
them out of their bad conduct; the writer of an etiquette book, if
he takes his etiquette seriously, must be prepared to perform as a
satirist.

Although Piozzi entertained reservations about the moral right-
ness of satire, in *British Synonymy* she permits herself to joke at that
traditional figure of fun, the foreign visitor who hasn't got his English in order. "A Roman or Florentine naturally catches at a Latin

derivation; an inhabitant of Dresden or Berlin at a Saxon or Dutch etymology:—the first tells you he DEVIATED exceedingly from the right path between Warwick and Kennelworth. . . ; a Prussian will say that he SWERFED." "An intelligent nobleman from the Continent asked me . . . where that Mr. *Londini* lived, that made so many and so good musical instruments, particularly the piano e fortes, which always bore his name in front."[20] Mistakes like these are staples of stage comedy; denied the theater, Piozzi infuses its spirit into *British Synonymy*.

In Fowler's condemnation of didacticism, not simply a verbal practice but a moral principle is at issue; this becomes clear as soon as we ask *why* one should not "presume to improve the accepted vocabulary." Linguistic practice and ethical conduct are, rightly or wrongly, linked by long tradition. Girard, we noticed, illustrates the meaning of *délaisser* by a sentence intended also to put us in mind of God's mysterious providence. Johnson, we are told, took care to admit into his *Dictionary* no author whose words might tend to corrupt the reader's principles. George Crabb, Piozzi's fourth successor in synonymy, made explicit the rationale of this customary association: "A writer whose business it was to mark the nice shades of distinction between words closely allied, could not do justice to his subject without entering into all the relations of society, and showing, from the acknowledged sense of many moral and religious terms, what has been the general sense of mankind on many of the most important questions which have agitated the world." Her Victorian successor Richard Trench, in his lectures *On the Study of Words* earnestly agrees: "with every impoverishing and debasing of personal or national life there goes hand in hand a corresponding impoverishment and debasement of language."[21] All of this may defy current canons of lexicography, but the tradition has persisted for all that: its strength in the twentieth century is evidenced by Orwell's "Politics and the English Language."

British Synonymy belongs squarely in this tradition, being every bit as much a book about ethics as a book about language. Many of its entries are about the things named by the words, not the words themselves; they are short essays and characters. The entry on *Bravery, Valour, Fearlessness, Fortitude, Intrepidity, and Courage* consists of ideal instances of each; *Blameless* is illustrated by Socrates and Sir Thomas More, *Guiltless* by Louis XVI; *Luxury* and *Religion* inspire full-blown Theophrastian characters. Her best piece of this kind is surely her character of the Officious Friend, who

> crams your sick children with cake, advises immediate inocula-
> tion, and fetches in the surgeon himself, that the business may
> not be delayed—who hurries people into marriage before the
> settlements are drawn, advising them not to put off their hap-
> piness, but steal a wedding while the old folks are consulting,
> &c.—who proclaims a bankruptcy which might have been pre-
> vented, and gives you notice to save what you have in his
> hands, by taking up goods instead of cash—who, in his zeal
> for the reconciliation of his two best friends, traps them into a
> sudden meeting, shuts them into a room together before their
> resentment is cooled, crying *Now* kiss and be friends, you hon-
> est dogs, *do*; and stands amazed to hear in an hour's time that
> they have cut each other's throat. These men deserve a
> rougher appellation than TROUBLESOME.[22]

From general ethics to particular politics is but a short step. As Johnson could not resist the occasional political barb in his *Dictionary*, so in *British Synonymy* Piozzi takes every opportunity, and invents oth-ers, of attacking the French Revolution. For doing so she was chas-tised by some reviewers, but once again we may observe that she was not alone in the practice. "The great French Revolution has made also its contributions to the French language," writes Archbishop Trench darkly, some sixty years later; "and these contributions char-acteristic enough. We know much of that event, when we know that among other words it gave birth to these, 'incivisme,' 'sansculotte,' 'noyade,' 'guillotine.' "[23] Fowler, who nowhere explicitly takes sides, nevertheless draws such multitudes of bad examples from political speech or reportage that his book gives a very dim view of English political life between the wars.

British Synonymy is thus at once much more and something less than its title and preface announce. As a language book it is con-cerned more with propriety than with truth; yet it is also concerned at least as much with things as with words, and with proper conduct as with correct usage. These concerns impair its usefulness as a dic-tionary of synonyms; on the other hand, they make it eminently readable, something that can hardly be said of a dictionary of syn-onyms. In its professed purpose it has too little connection with

Johnson's *Dictionary*; in its actual performance it often calls to mind the *Idler*. Nowhere, to my knowledge, does Piozzi avow an ambition of essay writing, but a large number of the 315 entries that make up *British Synonymy* are in truth short essays on topics suggested by their words. *Beautiful* and *Beauty* yield, naturally, essays on esthetics; *Cold, Chill, Bleak* might be called "A Comparison of Italian, German and English Weather"; *Durability and Duration* is an exercise in philosophy; *Hunting, Coursing; Shooting, Setting* is really "The Delights of Rural Sports." *Identity and Sameness* is a satire on philosophical skepticism, *Large, Big, Bulky, Great* a discourse on animal-breeding. *Ludicrous* and its synonyms is better titled "A Comparison of Shakespeare and Jonson, with Remarks on James Beattie's Account of Humour; Concluding with an Elegy on Garrick." *Melody, Harmony, Musick* is really "Italian and German Music Critically Compared." *Name* is a short dissertation on comparative philology, *Soil, Earth, Ground* another in geology. *Symbol, Type, Emblem* elicits an essay in biblical typology. *Vale, Valley, Dale, Dingle, Dell* and *Wood, Forest, Grove* are travel-pieces; *Malice, Maliciousness, Malignity* and *Wayward, Froward, Perverse* offer advice on child-rearing. There are also many (too many) essays on "The Position of Affairs in France at the Present Time." Nowhere outside of *Thraliana* do we find in one place so many of Piozzi's sentiments on such a variety of subjects.

She once called *British Synonymy* a "Book of Knowledge,"[24] a phrase that suggests an encyclopedia. In Piozzi's literary behavior there is a predilection for the encyclopedic form, the *omnium-gatherum*; some years later she attempted a repeat performance of *British Synonymy*, a dictionary of proper names called "Lyford Redivivus." But *British Synonymy* is not really an encyclopedia; it touches many topics, it exhausts none, and it is always personal rather than magisterial. It is an essay book in the form of a dictionary, and its successors include not only Webster and Fowler but also Charles Lamb.

"I Rattle *on Purpose*"

Contemplating *British Synonymy*, William Gifford professed himself "thunderstruck" by the huge disparity between its ambition to teach English usage and its author's stylistic credentials. "To execute" such a work, he declared, "required a rare combination of talents, among the least of which may be numbered, neatness of style . . . and Mrs.

P—— brought to the task, a jargon long since become proverbial for its vulgarity." About her reputation he was accurate. From the beginning, Piozzi's readers complained bitterly of her style. The best remembered complaints are Horace Walpole's; until his death, Walpole avidly read—and avidly criticized—everything she published. His remarks on *Anecdotes* ("a heap of rubbish in a very vulgar style") we have already noticed. Of *Observations* he wrote, "It was said that Addison might have written his [travels] without going out of England. By the excessive vulgarisms so plentiful in these volumes, one might suppose the writer had never stirred out of the parish of St. Giles." By "vulgarisms" Walpole meant such locutions as "though" and "so" and "I trow"; "if," he wrote indignantly to Mary Berry, "you could wade through two octavos of Dame Piozzi's *though's* and *so's*, and *I trow's*, and cannot listen to seven volumes of Scheherezade's narrations, I will sue for a divorce *in foro Parnassi*." Anna Seward, who admired Piozzi, could not understand how she could publish a book "in wh. while she frequently displays a *power* of commanding the most beautiful style imaginable, she sullies almost every page with inelegant & unscholarlike *dids*, & *dos*, & *thoughs*, & *toos*, producing those *hard angles* in sound, that stop-short, & jerking abruptness in the close of sentences, wh. are fatal to *grace*, & *flow* of style."[25]

Seward's objections may be supplemented from a review of *Observations* in the *European Magazine*. The reviewer complained that Piozzi's "affectation of an easy, playful, and familiar stile . . . betrayed her into the frequent use of such mean and vacant terms as '*to be sure*,' '*sweet creature*,' '*lovely theatre*,' '*though*,' '*vastly*,' '*exactly*,' '*so*,' '*charming*,' '*dear, dear*,' and many others of the like nature with which the work abounds." These complaints do not proceed only from late eighteenth-century ideas of stylistic decorum, for they have been repeated in the nineteenth and twentieth centuries. A reviewer in 1861 lamented that Piozzi "seems perpetually to have run herself out of breath." Reviewing *Thraliana* in 1942, Frederick Pottle and Charles Bennett opined that "her prattling prose, tripping from anecdote to allusion and again to anecdote, speedily becomes wearisome."[26]

There is also another, quite different strain of comment on Piozzi's style, which is, however, not less hostile. "The style of our authoress is peculiarly strong, perhaps a little Johnsonian." This, in a 1798 memoir of her, is the neutral form of the comment. An instance of its hostile form occurs in Wollstonecraft, in the attack we have noticed in chapter 5: "Mrs. Piozzi, who often repeated by rote, what she did not understand, comes forward with Johnsonian periods." Reviewers of *Retrospection* were prompt to accuse that work both of "chit-chat language" and of pretentious stylistic elevation, "a tissue of affectation, inversion, and obscurity."[27] These two strains of comment together would suggest a writer who contrives to err in both extremes, the familiar and the lofty.

Alternatively, we might suspect these double criticisms as signals of a double bind, the double bind made famous by Robin Lakoff in *Language and Woman's Place.* Although the critics do not flag them as such, the Piozzian stylistic traits to which they chiefly object are all traits of the speech habits that Lakoff identifies as "women's language." Many of them appear among Lakoff's specimens of that language—for example, adjectives such as *adorable, charming, sweet, lovely,* and *divine,* and the substitution of "an equative like *so* for absolute superlatives (like *very, really, utterly*)." Three of Lakoff's "female" adjectives occur in the *European Magazine*'s list of "mean and vacant terms" in *Observations,* and so does *so.* Lakoff's inventory includes also "the use of hedges of various kinds . . . words that convey the sense that the speaker is uncertain about what he (or she) is saying, or cannot vouch for the accuracy of the statement"; examples are " 'I guess' and 'I think' prefacing declarations or 'I wonder' prefacing questions, which themselves are hedges on the speech-acts of saying and asking." These hedges do indeed abound in Piozzi's writing ("I trow" and "to be sure" would count among them), and they do give it an air of nervous uncertainty. Lakoff's analysis of the social significance of women's language also appears appropriate to Piozzi's case. The language represents, indeed enacts, the comparative social powerlessness of its speakers. Having little actual control of the world, women learn to assert little control of it in their speech. Their language denies them "the means of expressing [themselves] strongly" and encourages "expressions that suggest triviality in subject matter and uncertainty about it." What women can do is act ladylike, which means talking like a lady. Doing so, however, entangles them in the famous double bind: If a woman "refuses to talk like a lady, she is ridiculed . . . as unfeminine; if she does [talk like a lady] . . ., she is ridiculed as unable to think clearly, unable to take part in a serious discussion."[28]

Lakoff's argument is not unimpeachable: it is grounded on "introspection" rather than a large fund of data, and it purports to describe oral speech, not writing. An altogether different kind of analysis has been performed and urged by Mary Hiatt in *The Way Women Write*. To ascertain the truth of distinctions stereotypically made between men's and women's styles, Hiatt subjected to computer analysis random samples from fifty books by men and fifty books by women. Her findings often contradict Lakoff's; of the words flagged as "female" by Lakoff, only *lovely* is borne out by her samples.[29]

These divergences suggest caution. Hiatt's sample is not eighteenth-century; at the same time, in the eighteenth century Lakoff's "so very," at least, is not peculiar to women writers: it is used by the overbearingly male writer Joseph Baretti ("The church . . . is so very dark, that you cannot see at one glance all the fine things in it"). Also, a stylistic trait of *Retrospection* that was particularly censured is the dropping of the definite article—e.g., "It was he who threw the beautiful bridge over Danube." "Why not," one reviewer complained, "over *the* Danube." This usage does not seem to be a peculiarity of female style; the writer who most conspicuously employs it is Gerard Manley Hopkins. Nor did the reviewer ridicule it explicitly as female; he resented it as affectation, a departure from English idiom. However, it is also true that affectation was a common charge against women writers, and *Retrospection* was derided by the same reviewer as a "piece of female patch-work" and a display of "female vanity." There probably existed as much lore about female style in the eighteenth century as in the twentieth. (Piozzi herself approvingly quotes Johnson on the subject: "Dear Doctor Johnson always said you know that there was a *sex* in style as in everything else.")[30] Whether that lore was as wide of the lexical and syntactical facts as Hiatt claims of its latter-day versions only a study like hers can tell.

As a social fact the double bind did exist, and it was understood in very much the terms in which Lakoff states it. "If she refuses to talk like a lady, she is ridiculed . . . as unfeminine" can be paralleled from conduct books for young ladies which urge, precisely, that a lady talk like a lady or be considered unfeminine. Dr. John Gregory, in *A Father's Legacy to His Daughters*, puts it with almost Machiavellian candor: "Be even cautious in displaying your good sense. It will be thought you assume a superiority over the rest of the company.—But if you happen to have any learning, keep it a profound secret, especially from the men, who generally look with a jealous and malignant eye on a woman of great parts, and a cultivated understanding." In an obituary of Piozzi, her friend Penelope Pennington commended Piozzi's erudition and her prudent concealment of it: "wisely considering the line usually prescribed in such pursuits to her sex, she made no display of scholarship." Edward Mangin remembered likewise that "she frequently assumed a childish style, to avoid . . . being thought laborious and pedantic"; and to be "pedantic" would mean, in the words of James Boaden, "to resign . . . much of her *proper* charm, that graceful modesty, which retires from even praise itself."[31] "Feminine" means modest, charming, and intellectually submissive in manner, if not in substance.

"If," on the other hand, "she does [talk like a lady] . . . , she is ridiculed as unable to . . . take part in a serious discussion" finds its parallel in the very fact that women were not thought capable of success in "manly" literature. It is represented by all the lore about "the errors of a female pen." Female "chattering" itself becomes evidence of female "incompetence." It is therefore hard to believe that the complaints of Piozzi's style—the ones that advert to its "chattery" aspect—are not indeed covert impugnments of her competence, their implied burden being that she "writes just like a woman."

Whatever may be the actual lexical and syntactical markers of women's writing in the eighteenth century, these social pressures exist, they are felt by the women who write, and they must by some means be surmounted or eluded. One of Hiatt's findings is highly relevant here: the women writers in her sample "are as a group more aware of rhetoric than the men; they are more aware of effect than the men." It is at least reasonable to assume the same of their eighteenth-century forebears; at any rate, in no case should we assume blank innocence of rhetoric. Whatever Piozzi does as a stylist, we should regard it as deliberate strategy. Indeed, she tells us so herself: "I have a great deal more Prudence than People suspect me for; they think I act by Chance, while I am doing nothing in the World unintentionally: and have never . . . uttered a Word to Husband, or Child; or Servant or Friend without being very careful & attentive what it should be. Often have I spoken what I have repented after, but that was want of *Judgment*—not of *Meaning* . . . when I err, tis because I make a false Conclusion, not because I make no Conclusion at all. When I rattle, I rattle *on purpose*."[32] We need not agree that a choice is wise to see that it is a choice, or declare a strategy successful to see that it is a strategy.

Piozzi's stylistic maneuvers are to be regarded, then, as artful responses to a difficult—in fact, an impossible—situation. The fundamental choice confronting her, a choice that no male writer had to face, was whether to write as a woman or a man. This was not simply a question of whether to take a pseudonym; taking a pseudonym was only the extreme form of choosing to write as a man. Hannah More thus disguised her sex when she wrote politics under the name Will Chip, but even in *Strictures on the Modern System of Female Education*, written in her own name, she disguises herself stylistically. "Among the real improvements of modern times, and they are not a few, it is to be feared that the growth of filial obedience cannot be included. Who can forbear observing and regretting . . . that not only sons but daughters have adopted something of that spirit of independence, and disdain of control, which characterise the times?" More is careful and moderate; we note the syntactical parallels ("observing and regretting"), the concessions ("and they are not a few"), the tempered assertions ("it is to be feared that . . . ," "something of"). It goes on like this for two volumes, a calm, plain, unimpassioned voice. Also a disembodied voice, for the style calls attention to everything but the writer: Not "I fear" but "it is to be feared"; not "I cannot forbear" but "Who can forbear." When More writes "we" (as in "we cannot *cheat* children into learning or *play* them into knowledge") she means not herself but all of us, here all of us who have authority over children.[33] When she speaks of women she does so in exactly the same way that she speaks of children, as objects out there.

In her rhetoric More contrives to identify so entirely with institutional authority—the Parent, the Family, and especially Christianity—that she simply disappears into it, to reemerge as its Voice. In her statements, or rather in Its statements, she herself seems never to be implicated, and thus she can deprecate "a female Polemic" without seeming to deprecate herself. This is a rhetorical triumph undoubtedly, a neutering operation by which, without pretending to be a man, she nevertheless ceases to be a woman. It translated into a career triumph also; further, it gave her a certain freedom to promulgate cautiously feminist sentiments. The cost of this rhetoric, however, is not hard to reckon. In shedding her sex More shed also her human presence; one cannot feel a person behind this voice.

Piozzi, too, was attracted to the balanced, judicious style of "manly" writing—specifically, to the style of Johnson. In Johnson, she remarked, "I think is found at last, ye true Standard of English Prose." Although she has never to my knowledge been credited with any success in this style, she could in fact handle it powerfully. "He who feels more pain than he can possibly suppose his due in the beginning of life, will be apt to sweeten the middle part of it with vicious pleasures: he who lives by chance gets no habits of oeconomy, and he who has been dipt deeply in distress, is dipt as in the Stygian waters; his sensibility is seared, and its pores closed; when he hears of sorrow he says to himself, '*Graviora tulli*—I have suffer'd worse than this;' and then turns his head away in hopes of better entertainment."[34] This comment on the character of Charles II is impressively Johnsonian—and also simply impressive—in its blend of charity and unsparing judgment, and in the authoritative largeness of view that makes that blend possible. The sentence is launched in a thoroughly Johnsonian way, with a sonorous "He who . . . ," and is urged along, as Johnson's often are, by variations on its opening phrase. Not Johnsonian but distinctly Piozzian are the gestural image at its end ("turns his head away") and the quietly withering "entertainment." If we want to find fault, we will complain of "Stygian" as too stiffly mythological (albeit suitable to the sense) and may reject the Latin as pretentious (although it does dignify, and so adds to the charity side of the balance).

Certainly Piozzi was able to write in the "manly" style, and to do so with greater feeling than More did. Yet its very attractions were also necessarily its liabilities. Because it is Johnson's style it can give her shelter, conferring authority on her; but because everyone knows it is Johnson's style it can never be her own no matter how well she manages it. If it is commended for strength, the strength is attributed to Johnson ("the style of our authoress is peculiarly strong, perhaps a little Johnsonian"); if it is perceived as Johnson's, she can be ridiculed as his parrot ("Mrs. Piozzi, who often repeated by rote, what she did not understand, comes forward with Johnsonian periods"). The Johnson style, much as she loves it, can only be a danger to her.

She is on stronger ground in a different male style, one to which she is at least equally attracted, which is genuinely congenial to her, and which also provides a partial solution to the double bind. Against the presumption of female incompetence it is possible to counterattack by converting one's presumed incompetence into a rough-and-ready virtue. "We country folks," Piozzi declares in a letter to a friend, "are well inclined to think that style is like hay; that which gives most trouble and takes most time in making, is sure to be the worst."[35] This maneuver has a tradition from which to draw strength, the tradition of the plainspoken Englishman who scorns the frills of

pretentious elegance. Its great exemplars are Butler ("All a rhetorician's rules / Teach nothing but to name his tools"), Swift ("Proper
words in proper places make the true definition of a style"), and, in
the twentieth century, George Orwell. Piozzi's deliberate rusticities
("we country folks") are securely at home in this mode, which thrives
on blunt, homely images, from Swift's barnyard imagery through Orwell's famous kitchen-plumbing image for stylistic pretentiousness,
"tea leaves blocking a sink."

It is in this mode that she writes to her daughter, a very genteel
young lady, "Well! Hope is a sweet soft Passion; mild & nourishing
like Milk, but like Milk too, when *long kept* it turns sour on the Stom-
ack, and is the hardest of all things to *bring up again.*" This is rather
clearly Swiftian, and it is matched by occasional forays in her published writings. In *British Synonymy*, ridiculing people who attempt in
the spirit of modern liberalism to keep their minds free of prejudices, she executes a decidedly Swiftian turn on the idea of the *tabula
rasa*: "that some PREVAILING opinions should keep rule in a man's
head is necessary: he will . . . become an unsteady character . . . if
from fear of prejudices he keeps his mind like a carte blanche, for
any fool to write what he pleases on; or like a shop-keeper's dirty
slate with a sponge tied to it, ready to wipe out one set of notions at
any time, for the more convenient insertion of another set." The
defiantly plain, downright style serves Piozzi well on several occasions. It is the style of "The Three Warnings," and in *Anecdotes* it is
the means by which she is able to make Johnson's talk sound like
Johnson: "he observed of a Scotch lady, 'that she resembled a dead
nettle; were she alive (said he), she would sting.'" The difficulty of
this style, however, for a woman writer—or speaker—in her time and
place is that it is not ladylike, as Piozzi knows too well. That is one
reason why she likes it, especially in writing to other women. Thus
she teases her timid friend Penelope Pennington: "What . . . gives me
most Disturbance, is a Disposition to burst out into sudden *Sweats*, we
must call them so; because the *dainty* Word is quite inadequate to my
dripping Hair, & wet Pocket:handkerchiefs after wiping my Face."[36]
A lady, of course, does not say "sweats."

For most public purposes, then, the two male styles that attracted
Piozzi would be ambiguous in their effects. One opened her to accusations of parroting, the other invited charges of coarseness. There
remained Hannah More's triumph of impersonality, but Piozzi was
temperamentally unable—and unwilling—to rise to such entire sup-

pression of self. She always identifies herself as a woman and does not wish to unsex herself. She would not unsex herself even as a white lie, to see a painting; she was proud of women's successes, as women, in literature; and in any case, she was much too egotistical to believe that she could not win audiences by doing what everyone said she did best, being a witty woman.

In her general stylistic behavior, then, Piozzi presents herself forthrightly, even emphatically, as a woman; with her usual daring, she takes all the risks. In *Retrospection* she "talks like a lady" (Lakoff's phrase again) whenever, instead of citing a source, she writes, "I quote from memory alone . . . the rest have slipt my recollection, and I know not where to find them," and "'tis said by some writer, I forget who," and "I first did read this story at a bookstall many years ago."[37] Moves like these were indeed in accord with "the line usually prescribed . . . to her sex" (Pennington's phrase); in them Piozzi affirms her femininity at the obvious cost of her authority. In doing so she is playing for the second-order reward that commonly accrued to femininity and that has certainly accrued to her, the reward of being doted upon as charming. (It is likely that every male commentator who has doted on her in this way has in that moment of doting reincarnated her uncle, Sir Thomas Salusbury. An unnerving thought— but also, it must be confessed, a testimony to her considerable success as a feminine stylist.) This reward, of course, becomes a punishment as soon as anyone invokes the first-order standards of male discourse. We then hear not of her charm, but, contemptuously, of her "prattling prose."

Here, we may say, the stakes were not worth the risk. Yet Piozzi was a canny writer and knew what she was about. She seems to have worked on the premise that a woman's language ought to be as acceptable as a man's, and she aimed to play to its strengths even while she also begged indulgence for its supposed weaknesses. Her general solution to the problem of the double bind, therefore, is to write in the mode of drawing-room conversation. In the drawing room (at least, in the drawing rooms of Mrs. Thrale and Mrs. Montagu and Mrs. Ord and Mrs. Vesey) women's language stood on its strongest ground: women were allowed eminence in the graces of conversation, and Hester had experienced admiration for her conversation again and again. Sir William Pepys, a Streatham regular, is supposed to have declared in 1825 that "he had never met any human being who possessed the talent of conversation to such a degree" as Mrs.

Thrale, and this appears to have been a truly representative opinion.[38] (When we think of the company Pepys kept at Streatham, it is also extraordinarily high praise.)

If we turn back to the descriptions of Piozzi's style with which we started—the *so*'s, *though*'s, *too*'s, and so forth—we at once perceive that they are traits of conversation and that in conversation they are, by and large, quite at home. *So*, for instance; mentioned by Lakoff among the female markers, it is actually better analyzed by Fowler, who also states its danger: "The appealing *so*. The type is *Cricket is so uncertain.* The speaker has a conviction borne in upon him, & in stating it appeals, with his *so*, to general experience to confirm him; it means *as you*, or *as we all, know.* A natural use, but more suitable for conversation, where the responsive nod of confirmation can be awaited, than for most kinds of writing. In print . . . it has a certain air of silliness." Like Lakoff, Fowler also identifies the usage as "feminine."[39]

Fowler's analysis of *so* can stand as a satisfactory description of Piozzi's conversational mode in general. In this mode she does appeal to the reader for confirmation, just as if the reader were a conversational partner in the room with her. Another of her favorite words is therefore *we*; it too treats the reader as her companion in experience and ally in sentiment. In itself her *we* has the same import as Hannah More's ("we cannot *cheat* children into learning"); indeed, it has the same import as Pope's ("'Tis with our Judgements as our Watches, none / Goes just alike") or Johnson's ("we are perpetually moralists, but we are geometricians only by chance"). Its presumption is that author and reader belong to the same community regardless of their sex. Piozzi could reasonably assume that the conversational mode should appeal to the common ground of eighteenth-century discourse, the ground on which men and women stand shoulder to shoulder in their common humanity (despite their sexual difference) just as they can sit and converse together in the same room.

On this reasoning, the same traits that mark her style as female equally mark it as intimate, social, friendly; she should therefore be received not as a female who is attempting to crash the community but rather as a member of the community who happens to be female. In short, what works in the drawing room ought also to work in the world of letters. The reasoning is further supported by the fact that the drawing rooms she had known were pretty nearly coextensive with the world of letters; they were staffed by the same people. The conversational mode thus aims at the same result, authority on equal footing with men, as Hannah More's sexless impersonality. Where More, however, is willing to barter away her sex, Piozzi is not. Her stylistic conduct asserts that she is female even while it also asserts that her being female should not matter.

It is consistent with this posture that she responds to hostile reviews of her two last books with the hurt puzzlement of one who feels betrayed by an ally. "So these Democratic Reviewers are ten thousand Times kinder to me than is the British Critic: on whose Civilities I thought the High Church Principles of the Book [*British Synonymy*] had a sort of Claim."[40] This is reasonable on the premise that being an ideological comrade is more important than being male or female. Her reviewers, however, were far more alert to her sex than to her public spirit; where she intended community, they heard "chitchat."

Retrospection was particularly roughly treated on this ground. The style of *Anecdotes* could be tolerated as the "casual escapes of a female pen"; the style of *Observations* could be endured as characteristic of a travel journal; the style of *British Synonymy* could be excused—at least by Piozzi herself—on the premise that *British Synonymy* professes only to teach the style of conversation. With *Retrospection*, however, written after (and against) the massively polished histories of Hume and Gibbon, her stylistic familiarities were perceived as flagrant and unforgiveable. In it she herself professed to address the many, not the learned few; *Retrospection* was ostensibly designed to engage the interest of readers who would probably never have the nerve to tackle Hume or Gibbon, and it was to bring them in on the side of church and state. Reviewers apparently understood this— one of them described it as "history . . . reduced to light reading for boarding school misses, and loungers at a watering place"—and they scorned it precisely for having that purpose, that audience, and that manner.[41] In the end her solution did not work, for all its theoretical merit. She did not get herself accepted as a member of the literary community who happens to be female; rather, she was perceived as inept and shameless, a purveyor of female jargon in male places. The conversational mode was utterly remote from *le vrai* of contemporary historical discourse; *Retrospection* consigned its author to the position of a complete outsider.

She aggravated the offense, moreover, by displays of learning. Pennington's praise of her for "wisely considering the line usually prescribed in such pursuits to her sex" is not, in fact, accurate. Her books, especially her later books, display considerable quantities of biblical and philological lore. Also, a distinct trait of her style is a penchant for similes drawn from the natural sciences. Sometimes they are extraordinarily elaborate:

> The nobles indeed were losing power apace in Spain, . . . for able as the statesmen were . . . they saw not, what the lower orders seemed as if beginning instinctively to perceive, how in this new plantation, modern monarchs grew not like the ancient agaric, which, although spongy, and drawing all nutrition to itself, was salutary in medicine, and capable of giving light to the wand'ring traveller, who recognized the old majestic oak by its *igniarius*. Whilst these [modern] princes, clinging like Peziza to a half dead stick, that quickly ruins its weak supporter, mean insects, nourished by such a process, devour soon the swelling fungus's contents, and leave it at last an empty skin or puffshell.

In a footnote to the first of these sentences she cites the Dutch chemist Boerhaave; in a note to the second, Linnaeus. She can be still more pedantic and technical than this, however: "The conquerors could not . . . conquer the world and keep it: metals once separated from their ores, may defy chemistry herself to make them any more amalgamate; the arsenical particles completely *roasted out*—oil, earth spirit and salt, maintain their several stations, but never can be made cohere again." And, more concisely, "Enthusiasm acting upon ignorance, produced a flame as when the chymist pours his aromatick oil on nitrous acid: the burst will not be hinder'd *even by vacuum*."[42]

Actually, in this ostentation Piozzi is only exaggerating a trait of late eighteenth-century prose style; chemical imagery appears often in the writing of her contemporaries, male and female alike. In *British Synonymy* Piozzi herself condemns the practice: "A . . . wise writer having SAGACITY to discern how necessary it is to make coarse minds comprehend and approve his tenets, will show great JUDGMENT in forbearing all allusion to sciences they cannot comprehend, because such lights only dazzle, and do not illustrate." Her precepts about style are always in favor of plainness and simplicity. "For Historical, Political or Moral Truth, the plainest Diction is the best. . . . Information is clouded by Multiplicity of Ideas however elegantly expressed."[43] Her practice, however, when she goes into her "learned" mode is quite another matter.

Its effect has been tellingly characterized by Joan Klingel as "metaphysical," that is, suggestive of the metaphysical poets. During most of the eighteenth century, as we know so well from Johnson's *Life of Cowley*, the metaphysical poets were out of fashion. In *British Synonymy* Piozzi complains of Cowley just as Johnson does: "none but instructed readers can find amusement" from him, for his "common practice is to illustrate a thing not very plain, by another still more obscure and recondite."[44] It need hardly be emphasized that this is just what Piozzi herself is doing when she "illustrates" the difference between ancient and modern monarchs by comparing them to agaric and fungus, or likens the effect of religious zeal on the masses to that of aromatic oil on nitrous acid. Such comparisons are indeed the stock in trade of the lesser metaphysicals (and of the greater also, in their many lesser moments). Equally metaphysical is the combination of such comparisons and such allusions with a style prevailingly familiar, even intimate. The contradictions, the paradoxes even, of Piozzi's mature style are therefore of a type that we have learned to recognize even if her first readers had not. We can describe them, in the terminology offered by Northrop Frye, as throwbacks to the "modal grandparent," to the metaphysical poets and to their contemporaries in prose, practitioners of "the Senecan amble" such as Robert Burton.

We can describe them also as throw-aheads, to the laboriously learned yet intimate and conversational prose of Coleridge. Piozzi drew her prime rhetorical strategy in the first instance from Bluestocking conversation, and the distinguishing feature of that conversation—the feature for which it was notorious, even—was learnedness. To admit learned talk into mixed company was its very purpose. Piozzi adopted it as the main mode of her writing for the same purpose, so that she might write learnedly to a mixed company. At the same time—such is the very fine line that she drew for herself to follow—she depended on the informality of conversation to secure her from critical accusations of arrogance and outright invasion of "manly" literature. The conversational mode pretends not to compete directly with the mode of male scholarship; rather, it pretends to comment upon, interpret, and broker the results of that scholarship to others less instructed. This is the declared strategy of *Retrospection*, and it explains such awkward statements as "on my epitome indeed, scholars will scarcely be induced to look . . . I . . . guide such only as have just curiosity enough . . . to try for a glimpse of *Retrospection*."[45]

Piozzi adopted this strategy as a technique of literary survival. Ultimately it failed her, but in it, as in other things, she can once again be seen as a forerunner, this time of the characteristic nineteenth-century stance of author towards reader. To mention Coleridge in this connection is to remember that Coleridge lectured, and then to remember that the lecture is a primary mode of nineteenth-century nonfiction discourse. In the lecture, of course, a speaker faces an audience in the same room and speaks more or less spontaneously. His speech is marked therefore by indicators of face-to-face intimacy, of his presence as a person. It is marked also by the turns, abruptions, and interpolations of spontaneous talk. The lecturer is learned, of course, but is not characteristically performing as a scholar; rather, he is performing as a commentator, interpreter, and exhibitor of his impressions. Although his discourse is informal—that is, not studied—it may rise to moments of eloquence and oratory. I am describing, let us say, Coleridge's lectures on Shakespeare and Milton. I am also describing the Piozzian conversational mode in its fullest flower, as it is found in *Retrospection*. Piozzi herself was not able to make this mode work as she wished it to, yet it is entirely characteristic of her that in seeking a strong use of "women's language" she happened upon a stance that later writers would adopt with more success. Her position as a woman writer drove her to be resourceful, and her resources, we can now recognize, were those of the great nineteenth-century prose stylists.

EIGHT

Our Bounden Duty
Political Writings and *Retrospection*

But what have women to do in society? I may be asked, but to
loiter with easy grace. . . . They might . . . study politics, and
settle their benevolence on the broadest basis; for the reading of
history will scarcely be more useful than the perusal of romances,
if . . . the character of the times, the political improvements, arts,
&c. be not observed.[1]

IN POLITICS as in poetry, Hester
Piozzi exerted herself both early and late. Her very first publications,
those pseudonymous letters "about a Bridge, an Exhibition, or any
such bauble," were political in taking public controversies for their
subjects, and one of the tastes she learned from Arthur Collier was a
taste for "Whig & Tory." It was not, of course, an appropriate taste
for a woman. Hester learned to dissemble hers, assuring other people (even as she raised the subject with them) that she understood
not "a syllable of it" and talked "without knowing an Atom of the
Business," and even convincing herself: "I am no Politician . . . nor
either think much or care much about publick Concerns."[2] The little
trickle of publications by which she amused herself, when she could,
during her first marriage are almost all political; they are also all
unsigned or pseudonymous. And they are all squibs, tending to suggest by their manner that politics is silly stuff for silly people; from
them one could not predict that their author would rise to the deadly
serious fervor of *Retrospection*.

Retrospection is a far more impressive work than it has ever been
supposed. It is the product of an astute political intelligence of the
type that Wollstonecraft recommended: its purview is exactly "the
character of the times, the political improvements, arts, &c." It is
a work of great daring in every way. As a world history, it is epic

in scope; it competes at the highest level of "manly" letters, where even the men are few. Not surprisingly, it appears to be the first world history ever written by an English woman. Piozzi's only female predecessor in the multivolume history is Catharine Macaulay, whose eight-volume *History of England, from the Accession of James I to that of the Brunswick Line* (1763–83) has been as neglected as *Retrospection* and with less reason. Piozzi knew of Macaulay chiefly as a notorious republican, and regarded her as a fitting mate for John Wilkes. Her own history is written on principles antithetical to Macaulay's. Those principles are royalist and conservative, but it will not do to assimilate them, as her biographer does, to the politics of twentieth-century "Red scares."[3] Piozzi's politics are more interesting and humane than that, as a fresh survey of them will show.

The Sentiments of a Church-of-England Woman

It may begin where she began, with her "first Essay as a Political Writer," "Albion Manor" (1762), in which she announces some fundamental loyalties and aversions. She is a warm supporter of the House of Hanover, revering the memories of George I ("a fine, hearty, handsome old Gentleman" who "loved his Tenants") and George II. She recalls the Revolution of 1689 in traditional terms, as a restoration of the ancient freedoms rudely invaded by James II. These sentiments, so central to eighteenth-century British politics as to be neither Whig nor Tory, are very little changed in *Retrospection* forty years later. There, for instance, she calls the Stuart uprising of 1745 a "foolish adventure," which it was; its failure "put an end to what was left of jacobitism among us, and the whole nation joined the grateful chorus *God save great George our King!*" Of George III, however, she is at first suspicious. In "Albion Manor" his first minister, Lord Bute, is accused of "bullying" the electorate: "Folks won't be trampled upon by Stewards," she warns. Bute, a stiff and tactless Scot, was generally resented; in *Retrospection* Piozzi still dislikes him, although now for the more accurate reasons that he could not command allegiance and his resignation from office against the king's wishes was a desertion of duty. Throughout the difficult 1760s and 1770s she thinks slightingly of George's ministers for their incapacity to govern. She is enraged by the conduct of the American War: the king, she writes disgustedly in 1778, is "despised at home, ridiculed abroad; insulted by the French, uncertain of Protection or Assistance from the English; his Colonies revolted & declared Independent by foreign Powers; his own Subjects on the point of Rebellion . . . Public Credit a Jest, and a National Bankruptcy talked on as necessary, & expected as irresistible." Like everyone else she feels the war economically, in high prices and falling income, and by January 1780 she wishes, as did most of the nation, that the king "would put an End to this destructive War." In *Retrospection* some of these attitudes have changed. George III is now an object of gushing affection. (In this she changed with the nation; his illness in 1788–89 had made him popular.) She resents the Americans for revolting but also treats their revolt, congruently with the thesis of her book, as historically fated, a part of the impending dissolution of Europe. Her disapproval of England's conduct towards the colonies still survives, however: Grenville's stamp tax, she says, was conceived "in [an] evil hour."[4]

Although her distaste for Bute happens to coincide with that of Wilkes and Churchill's antiministerial *North Briton* and her warning that "folks won't be trampled upon" seems to have an odor of "Wilkes and Liberty," she is steadily hostile to John Wilkes and his adherents. In a 1768 squib she ridicules as "Asses" the mobs that "huzza Mr. Wilkes" for his defiance of Lord Chief Justice Mansfield. In 1777 she met Wilkes and took instant dislike to him: "he professed himself a Lyar and an Infidel, and I see no Merit in being either." Twenty years later, in *Three Warnings to John Bull*, she returns to the charge: Wilkes was "a man, who openly professed infidelity; but whom our *foolish* fellows delighted to follow, because he taught them to cry Liberty; and our *cunning* fellows found out that he was an useful member of society, so long as he continued a thorn in the king's side." The thorn is not only Wilkes's irreligion, it is republicanism. Because in her political writing of the 1790s French republicanism is the archenemy that she will quite seriously identify with the Beast of Revelations, it is well to note that her sentiments are the same early as well as late and differ only in the tone of their expression. Thus she writes of Junius and another newspaper writer, in 1769: "*Junius* defending, with false Argument, a fallen Cause, and the *Friend to limited Monarchy* exerting his feeble Powers in Praise of Principles truly Republican, are Undertakings childish enough." In the election of 1774, again, she felt it necessary "to quiet the Minds of our Constituents who were run mad with Republican Frenzy, and had made choice of a half American Representative."[5]

"Our Constituents" reminds us that during fifteen years (1765–80) she engaged in periodic electioneering for Henry Thrale, helping him to garner votes against Wilkite opponents. In Parliament, Thrale is probably best described as one of the "country gentlemen": members who, not aspiring to high office, prided themselves on their independence and sat as judges of government, supporting when they conscientiously could and opposing when they felt they must. They regulated themselves by the "patriotic line of conduct," a commonsense middle course between extremes of obedience and opposition to government measures.[6] During most of the 1770s this meant supporting the government of Lord North, if only because, by contrast with the feeble and confused ministries of the 1760s, it was a government, and because it was under sporadic attack by Wilkite radicals. This was Johnson's line in his political pamphlets; it is also Mrs. Thrale's line, consistently. She is a friend to stable government, and she distrusts extremism on either side. She holds herself free to criticize, even severely, specific measures and ministers for being too harsh or too feeble, but she abhors radical criticism, she distrusts schemes of reform, and she despises a government which cannot govern.

One standard by which she judges events, and not only judges but feels them, is the ministry of the elder Pitt in the years 1759–60, the "Annus Mirabilis" of the Seven Years' War. She always remembers this as the Golden Age of the nation, as also of her own life—the years at Offley Park. From "Albion Manor" onward, Pitt is the standard by which his successors are found wanting. She opens *Three Warnings to John Bull* (1798) with a version of pastoral: "in the year 1760, when the great William Pitt . . . was minister to George II . . . there was no dispute in the House of Commons, except whether our success was owing to our unanimity, or our unanimity to our success. This was John Bull's happy time, his wedding day." In *Retrospection* Pitt is made into a figure of heroic romance: "Never man so enjoyed, never man so deserved a nation's confidence. . . . Every soldier, every sailor he employed, caught and communicated the patriot flame. . . . Riches likewise, upon the wings he wove, flew far and fetched in more."[7]

Fulsome as this may sound, it is not mere jingoism. Piozzi's vision of Pitt incorporates some of her principal desires of any government, and they are certainly humane desires. She expects a government to secure the material wellbeing of its subjects. The heroes of human history in *Retrospection* are those monarchs and ministers who study the public good—such as the emperor Hadrian, who, "being . . . persuaded that a sovereign was only made such for the people's good, began his reign by instantly forgiving the forty millions debt to government," and King Alfred, who "encouraged business" and secured property, and Edward III, who "left . . . some new coins invented, and a great advance . . . in woollen manufactures," and Louis XI, who, although personally unsavory, "certainly promoted general welfare" by establishing a postal system, building roads, and planting trees. In short, she wants a government to provide its subjects "opportunity of procuring knowledge and wealth, those great instruments of good to man."[8]

We observe that she conceives the public good in terms of commerce, manufactures, and property. On the social value of commerce Piozzi reads exactly like Adam Smith or Tom Paine. "In all my publications," writes Paine in the Second Part of *The Rights of Man*, "where the matter would admit, I have been an advocate for commerce, because I am a friend to its effects. It is a pacific system, operating to unite mankind by rendering nations, as well as individuals, useful to each other." Paine's boast could equally have been Piozzi's; in all her publications where the matter admits, she is a friend to the effects of commerce. "Let princes dispute, and soldiers reciprocally support their quarrels; but let the wealthy traders of every nation unite to pour the oil of commerce over the too agitated ocean of human life, and smooth down those asperities which obstruct fraternal concord." This is said in *Observations*; in *Retrospection* she asserts that it is by commerce that "arts, manufactures, and even science, live."[9]

There is one effect of commerce that she distrusts, and she states it also in *Observations*: "The principles of trade are formed in direct opposition to that spirit of subordination" that has hitherto characterized society. Here, as in *Retrospection*, she associates trade with "that state of openness and freedom to which Europe is hastening."[10] This, of course, is correct and penetrating. On this topic, the difference between Paine and the Piozzi of *Retrospection* is that she perceives this one effect as a disaster.

Her concern for subordination is fundamentally a concern for the British Constitution. She is here at one with characters as diverse as Swift, Hume, and George III. "The complex system of the 'mixed form of government,'" writes Namier, quoting Hume, "combined 'by skilful division of power' the best of the monarchy, aristocracy, and democracy; and it was viewed . . . with pride and satisfaction. . . . They relished its 'checks and controls', and the 'mutual watchfulness and jealousy' which its delicate balance demanded from all concerned; and they cherished a constitution which safeguarded their rights and freedoms when 'in almost every other nation of Europe' public liberty was 'extremely upon the decline.'" Likewise Piozzi, giving in *John Bull* what in 1798 she takes to be a necessary reminder: "that admirable form of government which in itself unites the perfections of every other form: where King, Lords, and Commons, subsist in one another, by one another, through one another. . . . Our blockheads have . . . been disputing which of these three should have the preeminence, and that is the sure way to ruin all." In *British Synonymy*, under the entry *Prerogative and Privilege*, she enunciates the standard constitutional position on the rights of the people: "to the *people* have been granted valuable PRIVILEGES, which 'tis their interest and duty to keep from violation by continuing to deserve, and studying to maintain them." Confronted with anything that smacks of invasion of these privileges, she bristles; in *Observations* she is pleased to write that "my republican spirit . . . boiled up" at the impositions of French customs officials.[11]

In truth, the one thing that she dreads more than republicanism is despotism, a prospect which the regency crisis of 1788–89 seems to her to threaten: "Fox, Burke, Sheridan, all The Opposition People want an unlimited Regent:—how unconstitutional! how dreadful!" She can better tolerate "a settled Republick; how unconstitutional is *that* too, but far less dangerous—anything but Despotism for God's Sake." In 1791, when flurries of pro-French and radical polemic are driving the second Pitt's government towards repressive legislation, Piozzi has Una declare emphatically for liberty of the press, against Duessa's wheedling question whether its "retrenchment" is not "necessary": "to diminish either its Liberty or Influence would be dreadful. . . . He is the healthiest Man who can do most, and suffer most, without being made very sick, and that is the best governed Nation that can allow great Liberty without being in Danger of losing the Balance." To this Duessa retorts, mockingly, "You are now then an arguer for Freedom!" Una replies, "I ever was. . . . Without Freedom there would be no Government—confusion, Oppression[,] Anarchy would make this . . . World a Chaos; while their new Doctrine of the rights of Men might be propagated where it first was broach'd, among the Hunters of wild Beasts, scarcely more savage than their mad Pursuers."[12] This is a shorthand version of standard theory from Locke to Burke. Where there is no freedom there is no government properly so called, there is only the oppression of the weak by the strong; and where there is no government there is no freedom, there is only the "natural right" of any organism to bare survival, a right it may at any moment lose to a stronger organism.

For beliefs so generally held as these it is hardly necessary to find a source. Still, one fountain of Piozzi's politics, as of so much else in her work, is surely Swift: *The Sentiments of a Church-of-England Man*, with its emphasis on stability, unanimity, and moderation, and its contempt of disputes about "Ceremonies" and "meer speculative Points." "Do not the Generality of *Whigs* and *Tories* among us, profess to agree in the same *Fundamentals*; their Loyalty to the Queen, their Abjuration of the *Pretender*, the Settlement of the Crown in the *Protestant* Line; and a *Revolution Principle?*" It is for the blessings of unanimity that Piozzi extols the memory of the first Pitt; it is in the spirit of balance that she calls herself "a Tory in the Church, and a Whig in the State." The British Constitution, as the title of Swift's pamphlet reminds us, includes the Anglican Church; church and state are so intimately connected "that I think, whoever is an Enemy to *either*, must of necessity be so to *both*." This is a fundamental point also of Piozzi's political writing. In Italy, reconfirming herself in Anglicanism, she does so in Swiftian language: "I have always been partial to *Peter* as elder Brother . . . but I shall now be a follower of dear *Martin* as much from preference as from being born and educated where his Heaven-dictated Reformation is the established Church." As a profession of faith—"The Sentiments of a Church-of-England Woman," as it were—she writes the tractate designed "to shew the Necessity of that Union between Religion & Morality, which Bigots [i.e. Roman Catholics] & Skepticks [i.e. "infidels"] are alike diligent to destroy."[13]

In the 1790s, however, as the Catholic Church is extirpated in France, Piozzi exhorts all Christians of whatever sect to join against the common enemy, anticlericalism: "Whenever a Church falls, the State which neglects to maintain its venerable dignity . . . and meanly tries to starve its true ally, deserves the distresses which soon will fall upon it, and join in mutual ruin what ought to have been connected in happiness and power. For as the State punishes deviation from the rule of right as *crimes* only, not as sins; it stands in need of assistance from the Church to correct sinful actions which are overlooked by the civil tribunal, though highly pernicious to society."[14] The necessary alliance of church and state is a theme also of *Retrospection*, in which she treats the Roman Church, in pointed rebuke to her anticlerical predecessors Hume and Gibbon, with the most tender respect.

Such, then, in outline, are Piozzi's general politics. From early to late they are the mainstream politics of her class, place, and age, except that in the matter of commerce they are on the progressive side. In her later—that is, her chief—political writing their expression is far more severe, strident, and polemical than in her early pieces, but in this too she is representative, and is responding to extraordinary events. It was her sorrow to live on into interesting times, having grown up in dull ones, and to experience stupifying shocks to everything she took for granted as most stable in the world. In *Thraliana* and her letters she faithfully registers them all. To read through her entries is to behold an eighteenth-century sensibility awakening to horrors of a twentieth-century kind. In 1789 she can still consider the doings across the Channel as "Bustle." Four years later this is no longer possible. News of the execution of Marie Antoinette tears from her a cry of grief and rage: "*No, No. No. No.* And will not the Lord be avenged of such a Nation as that?" They continue to come in, stories of a kind all too familiar to us, but in her experience utterly new and unexampled. The massacre stories: "A private Letter from Nantes says that the victorious Republicans in the Vendèe took 400 Women—chiefly Ladies—and 400 Priests last Week; when tying them together in *Pairs*, a Lady & a Clergyman—*Stark Naked*—they threw them into the Loire." The refugee stories: "My Daughters tell me that the little Sheds about St. George's Fields are full of Emigrée French dying of actual Want. . . . Poor Things! they expire quietly now, & say nothing; but Stirring up Oatmeal & Cold Water together, live on *that* while they can get it—and then—perish. Countesses, & Children of high Quality in France, thus lost . . . how very poignant the Reflexion!" The uncovery of assassination plots: "a Scheme to kill George the Third by an Air Gun, or some say an Arrow—some say a Poysoned Dart—Lord God! how dreadful is this!" Add to these the abolition, in France, not only of the Church but of the very calendar ("They have abolished Sunday now. . . . In that frantic Nation *chaos is come again*");[15] the French invasion of Europe, and the subsequent revolutionizing of almost all the European states; the threat, more or less continuous from 1794 through 1806, of a French invasion of England; all the domestic miseries resulting from unprecedented wartime inflation aggravated by bad harvests and food shortages; and the constant dread of their potential consequence, which Piozzi was prompt to discern and of which she experienced some rumblings in her own neighborhood—an uprising of the English peasantry itself.

To these provocations she responds in two manners: with coolheaded and impressively steady assessments, and with apocalyptic passion. She can write of the times as of a Gothic horror: "The Times . . . are signally aweful; & I verily think that Daemons are roaming about among us, with enlarged Permission both to tempt & terrify." Feeling thus, she prays against perhaps the greatest temptation, rage: "God preserve us! even from our own bad Passions; he only can: *mine* are sometimes ready to run away with me now, for Welsh Blood heats . . . till it boyls again." She can also discipline her passion into the service of understanding, as when she explains that, confronted with such times, old whigs like herself must turn tories: "even PRINCIPLE itself must a little yield to the times. . . . Tillotson and Russell, were they now living, would be high churchmen and tories; for, though firm in a just persuasion that unlimited power in either church or state is dangerous to man's free will . . . they would in times like these, when democratic rage produces the same evils, combined with a thousand more, . . . throw the weight of their influence into the opposite scale—preserving . . . authority from being trampled on, nobility from being despised, all ranks of subordination broken, and even the just rewards of industry plundered."[16]

This is a good account of her own political conduct in the 1790s, and no apology for it was necessary; she yielded less of principle than many others did—conspicuously less than William Pitt the Younger, who in about five years went from proposing Parliamentary reform to promulgating the infamous laws against sedition. Never as liberal in theory as Pitt had been, she was rarely as illiberal in practice as he became. Her humanity, and a lively sense of the small wrongs of life, forbade it. "I have had an Antipathy to compulsive Measures public & private," she once wrote, "ever since My Mother told me that She was severely whipped once o' Year because She would not eat *Melon* when a Child—& Why should one human Creature compel another human Creature to eat *Melon?*" In this homely sentence resides a world of humane political morality. By and large, she held true to it. After giving Pitt's legislation a three-year trial she sensibly concluded, "this Bill against Seditious Meetings is ill-contrived—it will irritate the People I'm afraid, without restraining them." She wants not enforced but voluntary loyalty. She is pragmatic enough to appreciate accordingly the value of a loyalist riot, like the one at Birmingham in 1791: "One Loyal Riot is worth twenty legal Punishments."[17]

In turbulent times one does not expect loyal members of the propertied class to show much sympathy towards the mob. Be it said to Piozzi's honor, then, that in her fiercest opposition to democracy she does not forget that a nation must somehow provide for the wellbeing of all its members. She took most seriously her social obligation as a landowner, distributing food to "my own Poor" around Denbigh, inviting them to dinners on festival days, and even, it appears, arranging for the elementary education of their children. Her motive in this is pragmatic as well as charitable. She understood that a nation's health depends upon the diffusion of its riches, and that scarcity must bring upheaval. Watching ominous weather in June 1792, she writes, "our Opulence keeps People here from fomenting that general Spirit of Insurrection, that pervades all the neighbouring Nations—but if Famine should make an Attack, *our* Savageness would soon break forth." In the middle 1790s famine did attack, and she notes its inroads with fear and concern. An especially bad year was 1795. In January "the Distress upon the poorer Sort in ev'ry Town & County" was "frightful & alarming"; "Handbills too of an inflammatory Nature posted on our Church Doors at Streatham . . . *demanding*, not *requesting* Relief for the lower Orders—terrifie one." At Denbigh, in April, there was a riot, and "every Day brings anonymous Letters . . . threatening the Gentlemen & Clergy." In July "there have been immense Subscriptions for ye Poor again, yet they complain bitterly—& Cakes are distributed with Mottoes in them, inviting the people . . . to rise."[18]

Despite these terrors, her resentment is not of the poor but of the government which seems indifferent to their misery and its threatened consequences. In May 1799, expecting another famine, she fumes at Pitt: "What will become of us? Mr Pitt cares not—he has a Majority in ye House . . . for carrying on ye War." Indeed, she fumes even at the "fine People" and at "you *Towns ffolk*," her friends of her own class: "Oh little do you *Towns ffolk* know how prejudicial is this Weather to Country Farmers Labourers &c. . . . *My* honest Neighbours have but just barely *Bread* in the *strictest* Sense. . . . When the Gardiner came Yesterday scratching his head & saying There would be no *wallFruit* this year, I could hardly answer him civilly, but I *did* say for Gods Sake think about the Hay & Corn, and hang the fine People & their WallFruit. The Produce of whole Meadows may be seen swimming down our overflooded River . . . this Moment, and carrying with it the Subsistence of Hundreds of Innocents." After five years' experience of famine she is morally and pragmatically enraged by the neglect of the poor. "*Why* are the Poor so little attended to I wonder, & their wants so ill supplied. . . . If Justice & Generosity are both dead amongst us, & Humanity to be found only in Kotsbue's Plays or Godwin's Novels; Common Prudence should suggest a Consideration for the Poor in Days so dangerous, when they have Teachers innumerable to acquaint them of their own Strength & Capacity . . . to help themselves."[19]

Obviously these are sentiments of self-interest, but of a self-interest that is also far-sighted and ennobled by humane passion. In that passion she is capable even of entertaining the raw vision of class warfare that animated the radicals. In a *Thraliana* passage written for posterity she contemplates with outrage the combination of inflated prices for staple foods and strangely low ones for "Dainties," and she asks what inference can be drawn from it. Her angry answer is, "the Increase of Luxury & ruin of the Poor—when every thing is made smooth to the *Rich*, & every thing made rough to *them*: when Articles of Voluptuous Enjoyment are grown Plenty, & the Necessaries of Life are grown scarce: What Inference would you have her make?"[20]

To read through Piozzi's political remarks from the 1790s is to encounter again and again sharable sentiments emphatically expressed. Her moral sympathies are never dogmatic, never morbid, and rarely parochial; they are simple, healthy, and direct. In *Retrospection*, for instance, we read that "the greatest miracle, in my mind, which ever came within our common eye" is the doubling of England's population between 1377 and 1487, and we are caught up short. She thinks people are a good thing! She is glad to see them increase and multiply; she is sorry to see them sicken and die. Her heroes and heroines are those who promote human life—Lady Mary Wortley Montagu, for one, who introduced smallpox inoculation into England and thereby "saved . . . numberless valuable members to society." Also in *Retrospection* we read her honest outrage at the Spanish mistreatment of native Americans, and we realize that it does not proceed from a glamorous abstraction; she is not an "anti-colonialist," she simply hates torture, fraud, and theft. Neither is she a pacifist, but she very much prefers peace to war. In this she is, by her own account, characteristically female. "Female politicians," she writes in *British Synonymy*, "confide in negociation. Elizabeth of England, Isabella of Spain, hated war, and took every possible method to avoid it; while Queen Anne's natural ardour to conclude the peace of Utrecht cost her almost her life." But if there must be war—and in 1798, against France, there must, in the interest of national survival—she believes in sacrificing private convenience to public good. "The cries of individuals" against Pitt's wartime taxation, she writes in *John Bull*, are "selfishness." Moreover, she defends Pitt's graduated income tax in terms that are refreshing—and rare—for the generosity of their public spirit. She defends it precisely for bearing hardest on those who, like herself, can best afford to pay it: "Care has been taken not to touch the poor; the richest men bear the heaviest burdens."[21]

All of this betokens a sensibility remarkably untainted by cant, and that is all the more impressive because the 1790s offered many kinds of cant to be tainted by. For a conservative, perhaps the two most seductive were the cant of "the decline of virtue" and "the purity of past times." In the first of these, indeed, she is disposed to wallow: *John Bull* proposes, among other measures, "AN IMMEDIATE AMENDMENT IN OUR MANNERS," and in private Piozzi grumbles often against the depravity of the times. Yet she also, at least in the early 1790s, resists this line. In "Una & Duessa" it is Duessa who plays the "croaking" role; to her fashionable hand wringing Una replies, "Morality . . . was *never* found in such a State as good Men wish it was, and I desire . . . but that it decays more in England than in France Spain or Italy I utterly deny—and that there is no less now in Great Britain than there was two or three Centuries ago, I willingly opine. I know not how to define Cant if such Complainings may not be called so."[22]

This argument is set forth again in *British Synonymy*, where its target is that particularly vicious cant, the misty-eyed sentimentalizing of the feudal past. Piozzi will have none of it. What we really see in every dungeon and drawbridge, she declares, is a proof of our ancestors' fears and loathings. They had no other way "to restrain hard-mouthed passion and licentious wantonness . . . while ignorance kept their vassals half unconscious of the indignities they submitted to, and the wife of a peasant was secured from the desires of his patron only by her deformity or his forbearance." In *Retrospection* she is willing to allow that chivalry once had a social use *faute de mieux*: "when laws afford no protection the military *must* take up domestick quarrels, or still more dreadful scenes, and cruelties inspired by revenge will follow." But for the persistence of knight-errantry into an age when laws began to govern, and for all the pretty stuff of tournaments and jousts, she has only the utmost contempt: it was "absurd and poisonous mischief."[23]

There is another kind of cant also, to which not conservatives but wits and writers—and those who would be thought wits and writers—are vulnerable: the cant of "wit" itself. Piozzi tended to identify it as the vice of elegant freethinkers like Gibbon, and of their parlor admirers who do so much to set the intellectual tone for the reading and writing class. It is the cant of theorizing about things instead of feeling them, discussing things instead of believing and acting on them—the cant of being clever about things. Piozzi was, of course, tempted to join in, to be clever, to win applause; throughout life she did her share of this, and more than her share.

However, she also understood the power of this cant to vitiate the moral sympathies. In *British Synonymy* she declares against the practice, made fashionable by Shaftesbury, of putting beliefs to the test of ridicule, "that manner of proof [as Shaftesbury defines it] by which we discern whatever is liable to just raillery in any subject." Her position, rather, is that ridicule is "odious and terrifying." The fashion of ridicule, she perceives, leads to "contempt of good faith and pristine ideas of honour," and ends in the moral "bankruptcy" of the individual. So also of social institutions, which owe their authority in large part to opinion, that is, to habitual sentiments of respect, and which therefore decay when opinion turns against them. One of the themes of *Retrospection* is that in modern times "whiggism" has undermined the authority of institutions, and by whiggism she means, *inter alia*, the Shaftesburian free play of wit: "Freedom became the universal theme, and freedom in opinion pervading church and state, laughed at old rules, and pointing out absurdities in parents, guardians, kings and governors, lessened authority in every hand that was accustomed to hold it." To many of us, who are hardened habitual Shaftesburians, this will seem only humorless. Yet it is well occasionally to remember that on some subjects being humorless is a virtue, and Piozzi is a useful monitor. "The People who find or make a Jest out of Blasphemy, Treason, Rape & Adultery; are merrier than I."[24]

She was not content merely to censure other people's misplaced wittiness; she curbed her own as well. We have the pleasure of watching her do so on the subject of Negro emancipation. When she first thinks about it, in 1788, she scorns it as a fad. "The Ladies now wear the Figure of a Negro in Wedgwoods Ware round their Necks, the Inscription . . . Am I not a Man & a Brother? So The great Heiresses in the next Generation will perhaps be . . . perswaded by their Patriotic Mothers to find the African Blackamoors equally fit for a *Man & a Husband.*" This is nasty enough and not very witty, either. But it is not where she stays. She returns to the topic three years later, putting these very words into the mouth of her "croaking" alter ego, Duessa, so that Una may reprove them. Una's reproof is simple and unequivocal: The slave trade is "a publick Sin" and virtue demands its abolition, whatever the consequences. Thereafter, in public, Piozzi speaks emphatically for the right side. "When the human soul . . . is SET FREE from all corporeal temptations . . . how will theirs rejoice that have from pure motives, from honest and generous principles, contributed towards EMANCIPATING the Blacks, and DELIVERING them FROM SLAVERY!"[25] Her refusal to settle for an easy racist ridicule, her insistence on reforming her own sentiments, witness to the honesty and strength of her moral principles. For there is still another kind of cant, the cant of "independent judgment," which would rather be wrong than be in vogue, even when the vogue happens to be right—and especially when it is favored by people one dislikes, such as Catharine Macaulay. From this cant also she keeps free.

She was an astute observer of events as well as a moral one. Much of her passing commentary consists of predictions and prophecies. The prophecies we must take up later; here we can notice how sound her predictions could be. In her earliest remark on the French Revolution she betrays no hostility to it; the French, she notes in November 1788, are "beginning" to rid themselves of "Despotism." By 1 May 1789 she is becoming skeptical: "they will not know how to use" liberty, she suspects. One week after Bastille Day she predicts the eventual outcome: "I do believe that less than ten years will scarcely suffice to quiet the storm . . . in France; that the present sovereign will have much to suffer; but that . . . the French will have fatigued themselves with their own violent exertions . . . by the year 1800, [that] Louis Charles shall receive the voluntary homage of his adoring subjects, and . . . shall lead them where he pleases—*mais toujours à la victoire.*" Change Louis Charles to Napoleon, and she is correct to the very date. On 19 September 1797 she notes in *Thra-*

liana that "Buonaparte may make himself Emperor"; this is two years
before his coup d'état and almost seven before he took the name
itself. In September 1796 she predicts that the Holy Roman Empire
and the Papacy will cease to exist as of 1800; by 1801 the Papal States
had become virtually French possessions and the Pope a French prisoner, and the Empire officially died in 1806. In July 1797, contemplating peace negotiations about to be opened between England and
France, she writes apprehensively, "Lord Malmesbury's Journey puts
People in Spirits, & nobody loves Croakers; so I dare not say how
very—very Ill I think of public Prospects. Here is no Peace coming—
All Mankind is preparing for Battle." She is right; in September the
talks collapsed and France resumed belligerence.[26]

A model of prudent skepticism is her analysis of the Peace of
Amiens. She sees from the first that it won't work. To begin with,
it will leave France encumbered with an immense army that has
learned to live off conquest and must conquer in order to live:
France will see "her own hungry & desperate Plunderers come home
clamorous for Rewards they never can receive, & Food which the
neglected Lands could not produce for them." Indeed, the animating
principle of Napoleon's rule was to distract attention from want at
home by conquest abroad, and Piozzi correctly suspects that France
cannot afford peace. Neither can the rest of Europe tolerate it on
French terms, for those terms grossly violate the principle on which
European diplomacy has been conducted for more than a century,
the principle of the balance of power by which European sovereigns
have long been accustomed to guarantee one another's sovereignty.
She makes the point by alluding to Louis XIV, whose schemes of
conquest brought this principle into play in the first place: "A Peace
which leaves unresisted France Mistress of more Territory than was
ever hoped for by her proudest Monarch in his proudest day;—
which annihilates before her Grasp, Principalities & Powers . . . can
not be viewed without horror." She is convinced that "there will
be no lasting Quiet for Europe" until the French monarchy is re-
stored.[27] On all these points she was right. The Peace of Amiens
lasted just over a year (1802–3), during which Napoleon made it
plain that he meant to go on annexing territory and the English
government found his designs impossible to live with; Europe did
not obtain "lasting Quiet" until the Congress of Vienna settled a king
in France in 1815.

Properly pessimistic here, she is optimistic, and prescient, when she writes on 1 June 1808: "I think the World's Drama will soon be over. . . . Spain resists Buonaparte's Aggression in desperate Earnest; now let us see if he can conquer a Great Nation against its will. . . . for my own Part I say No."[28] This, written before the opening of the Peninsular Campaign, deserves to be called prophetic. The savage resistance of the Spanish population in the years after 1808 made it possible to bring an English army onto the continent, and Napoleon's last act did indeed begin in Spain.

"Those Who Cannot Fight Must Write . . ."

In 1810 Piozzi recollected that "the year 1778 turned every body into Politicians—& I wanted but little *turning*." She is twelve years early as to the date. In 1778 she was, to be sure, decrying the American war and printing political squibs in the newspapers, but she was also professing herself "no Politician" and flirting with Johnson's dictum that "public affairs vex no man." Even the French Revolution, for all her astute predictions about it, she did not at first take very seriously; in January 1790 she wrote, "I am sick of the French Politicks, and wish the Discourse at an end."[29] Then, in November, she read Burke's *Reflections*, just published. Not the revolution naked, but Burke's discourse on it, turned Piozzi into a politician, and determined her public role for the rest of her writing career. *Reflections* came at a good time, for in 1790, as we have observed, she was at a critical point in her career: almost, but not quite, finished with Johnson, she was uncertain where to turn next. She had established as her authorial stance the swerve from a male precursor; she required a new male precursor from whom to swerve, a new inspiration and a new quarrel. Burke supplied both.

This is suggested by entries in *Thraliana*. The first registers something close to pure ecstasy, a sort of biblical alleluia, on encountering the *Reflections*: "How finely does Burke beat them down under his feet!" This surely is the moment of inspiration, the moment when the ephebe elects the precursor. Within days, it is followed by a resolve: "I would now be glad to fight these Infidels to the last drop of the Ink Bottle, and shew their Followers at least that all Learning is against them." Two weeks after this we find her beginning to execute the characteristic swerve, the same that she had performed with Pope and then with Johnson: "I am told Burke's Book is dying already, my heart felt it was Mortal." She likens it to the brief brilliance of fireworks: "'Tis the work of a wonderful Genius. . . . Could Fireworks continue longer, what an Art would their Construction be considered! but the *Splendour* is *transient*, & the *Scaffolding mean*." In her Streatham years she had thought Burke a great voice but a dubious character; "splendid meanness" is the theme of her verse about him in "The Streatham Portraits":

> See Burke's bright Intelligence beam from his Face,
> To his Language give Splendor—his Action give Grace;
> Let us list to the Learning that Tongue can display,
> Let it steal all Reflexion, all Reason away;
> Lest home to his House we the Patriot pursue,
> Where Scenes of another Sort rise to our View;
> Where Meanness usurps sage œconomy's Look,
> And Humour cracks Jokes out of Ribaldry's Book;
> Till no longer in Silence, Confession can lurk,
> That from Chaos and Cobwebs could spring even Burke.[30]

When she says that Burke's book is dying she refers to the barrage of hostile reviews and counterblasts it received. Among them was Paine's *Rights of Man*, published in March 1791. Piozzi read it, and in April she began "Una & Duessa." There we find her constructing an argument against Paine, an argument intended to defend not Burke but what Burke defends—the upper classes of society and social hierarchy itself. Her argument resembles nothing in *Reflections*, being at once destitute of Burke's rhetorical nobility and entirely free of his proclivity to sentimental fustian. Her argument is simple, pragmatic, and openly bourgeois; in manner it is much closer to Paine than to Burke. It addresses itself to the nouveau riches, and to all who hope ever to be of that class. "Trade means at last to end but in Gentility . . . no Man risques Money in Commerce but with Intent sometime to realize it in Land. . . . The rich retir'd Trader who hopes Distinction for himself and Title for his Sons . . . forms one respectable Class of Men whose Ardour in Commercial Matters would abate, had he not that excitement." Social leveling is "ill calculated sure to please the English, whose Prosperity depends so much on the Commercial order of Mankind:—for who would trade but to gain Money? & what is Money good for, but to buy Establishment?" This strikes at Paine by means of Paine's own bourgeois faith in commerce; it is another Piozzian reversal. (Paine himself, explaining in the second part of *The Rights of Man* how to redistribute wealth, ends up admitting that "it would be impolitic to set bounds to property acquired by industry.")[31] She also strikes at Burke, simply by being too raw for him; her argument might be said to tear the decent drapery from his politics and to reveal their naked, shivering class nature. At the same time, however, it is practical Burke in that it addresses people and circumstances, not abstract principles detached from their human relations. It aims to carry that Burkean imperative into action.

Piozzi aims, in fact, to carry the Burkean imperative farther than Burke does himself. This is the posture of doing the precursor one better, or of doing for him what he cannot do, and it is the posture that she explicitly adopts in the spring of 1792. "We want . . . a Monitor," she decides then, and Burke is not it, for although "Mr Burke has not been wanting in Attention" (an astonishing dismissal, but, of course, for her purposes the required one), "more still is necessary; and in a courser, a more popular Style of writing." Burke has failed, in short, because he has not been sufficiently "coarse" and "popular"—he has misjudged his audience. Not that Piozzi has lost her relish of his eloquence; in 1796 she is still extolling the "Constellated Radiance" of his rhetoric. But for practical purposes, to serve the concrete needs of the day which she now takes to be her own literary mission and the only mission that the times demand, Burke's radiance is precisely not what is wanted. In 1800 she puts the case this way, retrospectively: "Steady fortitude has power to restrain those whom no logick can convince, no rhetorick persuade. Mr. Burke's eloquence . . . did no good. The pen which taught how 'unobtrusive virtue, exciting no astonishment, kindling no emulation, extorting no praise, is still most difficult and most sublime,' *strengthened* those eyes which *his* book did but *dazzle*."[32] What the times require is virtue, not esthetic display.

This is a highly pertinent criticism of Burke; it suggests that his writing is actually more about stylistic narcissism than about real people. It is the criticism leveled against him by Mary Wollstonecraft (in her *Vindication of the Rights of Man*) and Paine. "He is not affected by the reality of distress touching his heart, but by the showy resemblage of it striking his imagination. He pities the plumage, but forgets the dying bird." A very pointed, albeit tacit, rebuke to just this strain in Burke may be seen in *Retrospection*, when Piozzi comes to consider Marie Antoinette. In *Reflections* that hapless queen is made an occasion for Burke's most egregious eloquence: "It is now sixteen or seventeen years since I saw the queen of France, then the dauphiness, at Versailles; and surely never lighted on this orb, which she hardly seemed to touch, a more delightful vision. I saw her just above the horizon, decorating and cheering the elevated sphere she just began to move in,—glittering like the morning-star, full of life, and splendor, and joy." Breathtakingly beautiful, of course, but also a piece of shameless myth making. Like chivalry, of which, in fact, it is a specimen, Piozzi will have none of it. Her account might almost have been written by Tom Paine himself: "The conduct observed by her when on the throne of France, made mankind stare indeed, but not *admire*. . . . Parental tenderness itself recoiled from sight of her portrait taken to Vienna; and conjugal passion, although carried to a half-despicable, half-criminal uxoriousness, felt momentary disgust at the bankruptcies, still more perhaps at the blasphemies brought on by her incessant frolicks; among which gaming, though least offensive to relate, was possibly most dangerous to endure."[33] It is not that Burke is tender-, and Piozzi hard-hearted; we have seen her response to the execution of Marie Antoinette. It is rather that Burke is thinking of his own grandiloquence and that she is thinking of the real effects of real actions by real people. *Retrospection* is every bit as monarchist a work as the *Reflections*, but Piozzi is telling the truth even when the truth makes against her. She is pointedly being the more honest rhetorician.

Incited by Burke, then, but characteristically swerving from him, Piozzi conceives her mission as a political writer in the most concrete possible way. She becomes a propagandist, a Tom Paine of the status quo. "Those who cannot fight must write for their country," she exhorts the readers of *John Bull*, and, with impressive public spirit, she follows her own urging. She writes patriotic songs for distribution at taverns and other places—songs like this one, at the time of the Great Mutiny (1797): "Ye British Seamen list to me / And scorn the Democratic Tree, / They'll hang you on't, not make you free." She turns *British Synonymy*, begun before she had altogether decided on this mission, into a vehicle of political catechism ("I am only afraid the title may prove a millstone round its neck: no one will think of looking for Politics in a volume entitled *British Synonymy*"). Hearing that "the parts of Tom Payne's Book most easy to comprehend, have been all translated into Welch, and are supposed to do no small Mischief among the low People hereabouts," she commissions a Welsh transla-

tion of "Hannah More's Antidotes," *Village Politics* (1793). To stiffen
national resistance to a French invasion, she translates and prints a
letter from her husband's brother in Venice, detailing the ravages
of the French army there and warning against seduction by democratic sympathizers: "Venice was not conquered!—she was seduced,
deceived, betrayed—by empty sounds. . . . The fatal words *Liberty*
and *Equality*, not the French Arms or Courage, were *our* ruin."[34]

Against another invasion threat she writes a short "Address to
the Females of Great Britain," exhorting them to act rationally, to
stand by their menfolk, and to make themselves useful. And against
still another she translates a pamphlet, the *Tableau Spéculatif de l'Europe* (1798), by Charles François Dumouriez, quondam general of the
French Republic and later one of its royalist opponents. His purpose
was to exhort Europe to combine against France by predicting the
hideous consequences of a republican triumph; hers is to alarm to a
proper sense of their danger the ladies and gentlemen of her own
class, whom she takes to be fatuously confident that no harm can
befall them.

> Dumouriez saw at Distance . . . what we are suffering *now*: his
> Book was read & thrown aside—his fearful Predictions disre-
> garded all; but in six Years Europe beholds them verified: Let
> us look over them again & see what can be done to avoid the
> fatal Termination of his Prophecies. . . . It is to *us* that Coxe
> applies when he relates . . . poor Switzerland's Defence &
> Death:—predicted by Dumouriez in this Volume—It is to *us*
> . . . that I tell the . . . Tale of the Italian Cardinals who when
> the bold Destroyer [Napoleon] was advanced no further than
> the South of France exclaimed—Oh never fear, Our Moun-
> tains will protect us—but when the Alps were pass'd—their
> Word was—Oh never mind—The Saints will save us. Of
> Mountains . . . *we* have but *few*—of Saints still fewer—yet every
> day hears Englishmen & Women crying confidently All will be
> well, our Fleets will save Great Britain. If we live on, to see a
> Camp of Frenchmen entrenched upon Newmarket Hill in
> Sussex——Will not the Ladies at Brighthelmston say—All is
> well yet, S.ʳ James[']s Volunteers will save dear Bond Street.

Finally, her motive even in starting the study of Hebrew was patriotic; she had heard that "the Illiterate and Itinerant Preachers of
Methodism up & down, *all* study Hebrew, to torment the clergy."[35]

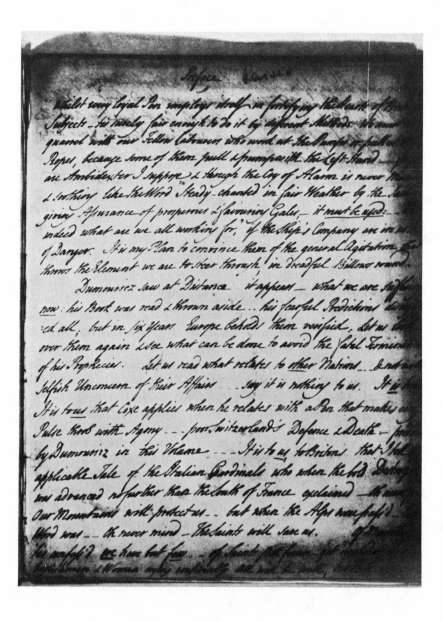

Hester Lynch Piozzi, "Preface" to Dumouriez, *Tableau*
(Ry. 641, f1r) reproduced by courtesy of
The John Rylands University Library of Manchester.

About these activities several comments may be made. The first is that they are not so much a literary production as a war effort, undertaken in a spirit of self-effacement. "It was meet, right, and our bounden duty, to oppose their principles and practice," Piozzi says of the propaganda campaign against the democrats, and she says it, significantly, in the language of the Anglican catechism. Self-effacement means the sacrifice of authorial egoism. Not one of these performances, including *John Bull*, is signed with her own name. In private she takes an egotistical interest in their success, as when, pretending ignorance of its author, she asks Penelope Pennington, "Have you seen my Three Warnings made Political Use of in a new Pamphlet?" And she is rueful in comparing her own effort with William Cobbett's *Porcupine Gazette*: "Peter Porcupine has done more service than any of us—My Three Warnings to John Bull was inefficacious enough I believe, The intent only was good."[36] This is disappointed egoism certainly, but it is still egoism subordinated to the aim of public service.

For a woman writer that aim could not have quite the same significance as for a male writer; the sacrifice of egoism was precisely the virtue (or the "virtue") to which women of her class were being called. Remembering this, we can turn back to Piozzi's criticism of Burke in *Retrospection*. "The pen which taught how 'unobtrusive virtue . . . is still most difficult and most sublime'" was a female pen, Hannah More's, and it urged upon everyone the "female" virtue of self-effacement. Piozzi's swerve from Burke, then, is almost explicitly a female swerve: a swerve from the peacock egoism of male authorship, from "dazzle," to selfless utilitarianism, or nurture.

As an act of public spirit, this authorial self-abnegation deserves more respect than any commentator on her has hitherto given it. As a career move, it is obviously more ambiguous. To undertake pamphleteering in England in the 1790s was to fling oneself into an ocean, and to pamphleteer in the ad hoc and ad hominem fashion of *John Bull* was to court a short life and a long oblivion. A recent anatomist of the pamphlet literature produced between July 1789 and December 1793 provides material for estimating the place and probable fate of Piozzi's pamphlet. During those four and a half years perhaps 1,400 titles were printed, an average of not much less than one a day. In political tendency, conservative pamphlets outnumbered reformist pamphlets by about two to one; *John Bull* ran, therefore, among the large majority of a crowded field. It probably did not run in more than 1,000 copies, and more likely in half that number. Like the great majority of such pamphlets (at least 80 percent), it did not reach a second edition. Clifford opines that *John Bull* went "practically unnoticed," yet, given these numbers, there is no ground for supposing it less noticed than eight out of every ten of its fellows.[37] The effects of that entire literature must be estimated not in the individual but in the gross, and even then probably the most one can say is that the entire propaganda effort of the loyalist majority *may* have contributed to avert revolution in England.

All of this is to say that the consequence of authorial self-effacement is, precisely, effacement: the drop of water gets lost in the ocean. Yet that loss is not necessarily failure, except by a standard that defines success as the imposition of one's ego on rival minds, or the assertion of self over others. This is, of course, the standard assumed by almost all writers, literary critics, and literary historians in our culture (including Piozzi herself most of the time), and it probably has much to do with the ideology of male competition and aggressiveness. By this standard, Piozzi was a failure as a pamphleteer because she was not Edmund Burke and *John Bull* was not *Reflections*. As we have seen, however, in this phase of her work she herself repudiated this standard in favor of a female one. She thought of herself not as seeking glory, but as contributing to a collective effort and cooperating with her fellow pamphleteers—some of whose writings, indeed, she urges the reader of *John Bull* to get by heart.

One further fact about the mass of pamphleteers deserves to be mentioned, a highly ironic one in the context of this discussion. Of 464 identified authors, "fewer than twenty" were women: "Political polemic was a masculine metier," Pendleton concludes.[38] Among those fewer than twenty female authors was Mary Wollstonecraft. Piozzi, never the explicit feminist that Wollstonecraft was, once again is behaving like a feminist de facto in undertaking to pamphleteer at all; she is asserting, as it were, the female right to propaganda. Once again also, she is asserting it in her characteristic way, by acting as if there were no important differences between herself and the men.

After all this, it may be asked what sort of piece *John Bull* is. It is tight, neat, and efficient, organized sermonlike, around three topics which are the *Three Warnings* of its title: "An Unanimous Spirit of assisting Government, A just and manly Regard for our established Religion, And an immediate Amendment in our manners." These are the virtues to which, by various arguments, it exhorts its readers. The arguments are simple, short, and liberally spiced with ad hominem appeals—no theory mongering here, nor grandiloquent Burkean metaphors. Here is the principal argument in behalf of loyalty to government: "This [the British] government . . . must be obeyed—and to this government . . . resistance is rebellion. For limited monarchy we know, limited aristocracy we understand, and limited democracy we saw lately in Switzerland: but *limited government* is a contradiction in terms. Without power to enforce obedience . . . there is no government; and place the sceptre of authority where you will, it must be obeyed." This is a short version of Johnson's chief argument in *Taxation No Tyranny* and is directed not against the doctrine that all sovereignty resides in the people but against the grumpy disposition to resist government merely because it is government. She would shake them out of their grumpiness with blunt logic. Also, she has no compunction about appeals to fear and loathing. She retells the Abbé Barruel's Gothic tales of the French National Assembly ("where [Satan's] hierophants in horrid cells howl the dark orgies of their mystic union"), and she deplores the fall of women's necklines in terms that are meant to be, and are, disgusting: "the fat oilman's slippery daughter, and the dry salter's lean and shrivelled wife, alike exposed their unregarded nakedness to the men's eye."[39]

To women of her own class she directs a feminist appeal. Neither *John Bull* nor her "Address to the Females of Great Britain" is a feminist tract, yet in them Piozzi employs feminist arguments for her own antiradical purposes, and she does so in some measure of agreement with the radicals whom she opposes. Thus one strain in Wollstonecraft's feminism is utter contempt of "ladies": "Women . . . all want to be ladies. Which is simply to have nothing to do, but listlessly to go they scarcely care where, for they cannot tell what." We have observed Piozzi mocking "the Ladies at Brighthelmston" ("All is well yet, S.ᵗ James[']s Volunteers will save dear Bond Street"). In Wollstonecraft the standard by which ladies are mocked is a standard of rational, adult competence that calls on women to surrender their pedestaled babyhood. Piozzi, in her "Address to the Females," summons women to assume their share in the national defense and asserts they can no longer take shelter in babyhood and "feminine graces": "The Days are past when one Moiety of your Species affected to treat the other Moiety with a peculiarity of Manner expressing half Admiration and half Contempt. Every Statue now stands

without its Pedestal, so that its true Size can no longer be mistaken.
. . . Nobody hinders [women] from being wise or strong, Learned or
brave; nor does any one . . . pretend to like them better for being
weak, ignorant or pusillanimous. You are therefore . . . called upon,
to act rationally, & steadily: & to maintain that Place among reasonable Beings we have so often heard you urge a Claim to."[40] This is
quite Wollstonecraftian, but we observe a tinge of challenge in it, as if
Wollstonecraft herself were the one being addressed and were being
dared to act up to her own demands ("maintain that Place . . . we
have so often heard you urge a Claim to"). Feminists are challenged,
in effect, to prove their title by acting with patriotic responsibility.

In *John Bull* Piozzi challenges them again, this time to wake up to
the implications of their republican slogans. She does this by throwing their feminism back in their faces. Wollstonecraft had written
that the conventionally feminine woman is submissive only because
she has no social power to resist; she "smil[es] under the lash at which
[she] dare not snarl." Piozzi, glancing at this image, declares that were
the republicans to succeed, women would indeed be powerless to resist oppression: "When these new Doctrines, levelling all Distinction,
shall confer power upon *corporeal* advantages alone; and leave the
dispensation of what shall then be left to dispense—in rough and
brutal hands," women may expect to "sink . . . into mere toys of pleasure for the men; and crouch, with counterfeited smiles, for bread,
to souls beneath their own."[41] In thus turning on Wollstonecraft
Piozzi turns not on feminism itself but on the political radicalism
(whether serious or fashionable) of its proponents.

The Revisionary Eye of *Retrospection*

In January 1791, on her birthday, still tingling from her encounter
with Burke, Piozzi meditates her own name. "That Hester is a Word
signifying *Secret* we all know: but I have some Notion there was a
great and curious Mystery couched under the Name of the patriotic
jewess who through her Beauty's Influence saved her Countrymen's
Lives from the Decree of Ahasuerus." She teases the word etymologi-
cally and concludes that "the Secret then consisted perhaps in the
very *Name*."[42] The secret of this meditation consists in Piozzi's calling
to mind her biblical namesake, a woman who had saved her people.
She had begun her swerve from Burke before this; here it looks as if

she is seeking to displace him with a female precursor. Who should it be? Hardly Helen Maria Williams, whose *Letters from France* she has also just been reading; Williams, although her friend and admirer, is also a friend and admirer of the French Revolution. Hardly Wollstonecraft either, and not Catharine Macaulay. In *Retrospection* she will reject Burke out of the mouth of Hannah More, but by then Piozzi had fashioned the role in which to write that book, and in 1791 More had not yet published her great polemics. The role that Piozzi fashioned is biblical; *Retrospection* might be said to be the Book of Hester.

Hitherto we have contemplated Piozzi the pragmatic politician. That person is certainly evident in *Retrospection*, but so, to a much greater degree than in any other of her works, is Hester the prophet. In conjoining politics and the Bible—in construing the one through the other—she behaves much less like Burke or Paine than like Blake, like the author of *Antichrist in the French Convention*, and like millenarian radicals such as Burke's nemesis Richard Price. Piozzi correctly identifies this mode as Protestant, and "chiefly" low Church; one would expect her, therefore, to be wary of it, as she is of the Methodists. Not so. She was, as Baretti once remarked, "very fond of her Bible"; moreover, she insists on taking the Bible as literally true, down to the last word: "Surely to doubt *one Word* of the Sacred Scriptures, is no other than a direct *Sin against the Holy Ghost.*"[43] Of greater relevance to her romanticism is the fact that the Biblical books to which she most often recurs are the "Miltonic" ones, the Old Testament and the Apocalypse; we have seen that the apocalyptic close is a trait of her romantic poems. Her romanticism, then, like Milton's and Blake's, is in the line of biblical prophecy and apocalypse. This is the line of *Retrospection*. *Retrospection* is a work of vision, the substance of its vision being European history understood prophetically.

As *Retrospection* is by much her most ambitious, possibly her most original, and assuredly her least understood work, we may pay it the respect of tracing its beginnings. On 1 May 1789 she writes in *Thraliana*: "The Emperor's Death will make a great Bustle in Europe, & there is enough already. The French struggling to obtain . . . Liberty. . . ; The Rage for emancipating Negro Slaves, & the Number of Jews lately baptized into Protestant Churches; The expected Comet, and the propagation of the Gospel in so many newly-discover'd Countries, make one think the end of the World approaches." This might seem conventional hyperbole, but it is not. She is in serious earnest. She goes on, "especially as we are now close upon the Year 1800. which leaves only two Centuries more, and the third Division of Time is completed—2000 Years from the Creation to the Deluge, 2000 from the Flood to the Coming of Jesus Christ—and 2000 more from his Crucifixion to his second Appearance in Glory preceded by a flaming World."[44] "The third Division of Time" is the subject of *Retrospection*, the first two divisions being premised. In this entry she is not planning it or any other book, yet much of *Retrospection* is already here. Besides the biblical time scheme there is the immense range of events; there are also the two sensibilities, hardly compatible with each other—the one that says "Bustle," and the one that foretells the end of the world.

In her subsequent remarks on events, millenarian anticipations have as much part as mere intelligent predictions. Here is one from February 1793: "They [the French] have bred a Riot at Rome . . . where one of their vile Democratic Agents being killed, they threaten that old City with Fire & Sword—Will *my* Explanation come true? will their Anarchy end in a *Decemvirate*, to make out the *Ten horns* [she is thinking of Rev. 17:16] which hate the Whore, & hurt her, & eat her Flesh, & utterly burn her with Fire?" She concludes, chillingly, "it looks promising enough to be sure." Regarding a report that the planet Mercury had been seen at noonday, she declares, "[There] are indeed Signs in the Sun, & in the Moon & in the *Stars*: not Emblematical alone, or figurative; but litteral & true. I am convinced the World's End is approaching." She goes to work to prove it out of Scripture and demonstrates expertise at biblical exegesis, as here, with Zech. 4, Jer. 51:25, and Rev. 13: "altho' these Texts agree literally with Babylon, I have an Idea that they agree typically and figuratively with what is now called the *Mountain* par Eminence, or French Convention consisting at one Time of *666* people—the exact Number of the Beast." In the spring of 1794 we find her meditating on the Providential significance of things, in another remark pregnant with *Retrospection*: "It is very surprizing that a Revolution such as the late one in France should produce Imitation in lieu of Antipathy . . . for no one is benefited by it: yet so are the Scriptures fulfilled without Man's Concurrence somehow, without his Observance, and in Defiance to that *immediate Interest* which for the last Century has been the acknowledged Idol of Humankind."[45]

Some of this enters into *British Synonymy*, although it does not find a home there. She ventures to intimate the Millennium: "the present strange state of things around one presents perpetual temptation to imagine some approaching change. Great events have marked every two thousand years from the beginning." This she takes back again lest she be ridiculed, but at the close of the work she cannot resist turning apocalyptic once more. The words she is distinguishing are *Zone, Girdle, Circuit, Boundary,* and *Limit. Boundary* and *Limit* easily suggest moral ideas; she passes at once to denunciation of "those writers who encourage the present race of political madmen in their frenzy" and quotes, from a pamphlet by Anna Laetitia Barbauld, a passage that is itself enthusiastically apocalyptic: " 'the minds of men are in movement from the Borysthenes to the Atlantic . . . what but an instant before seemed firm, and spread for many a league like a floor of solid marble, at once with a tremendous noise gives way. . . . The genius of philosophy is walking abroad.' " Barbauld writes this in radical fervor, not in dread. Piozzi pays it the compliment of calling it true, solemn, and sublime—but true, she means, in a very different sense. "A genius *is* abroad; the genius of anarchy, obscurity and barbarism." And she closes her book with the last lines of *The Dunciad,* thereby letting Pope do for her the counter-apocalyptic work that she really wants to do for herself but is at this point afraid to do.[46]

Early in 1795 she broaches the first explicit idea of *Retrospection,* in terms that are diffident enough: "I could make a pretty Book . . . to bring out on the last Days of 1799 or the first of 1800 . . . as *Anecdotes* of the late Century—not a History." It is still another year, however, before she resolves to write. "This Day [20 January 1796] I determined on a Project my Brain has been long hatching—that of getting a Book ready for Publication this Time five Years . . . containing a Summary of Events, & general Ideas of what has happened in the World. . . . I must make the Title of it RETROSPECTION." She worked for four and a half years, at times feeling vexed and intimidated by the greatness of the task but warming to it also, and coming to feel that *Retrospection* would be her best book. That feeling she confided to *Thraliana:* "I think 'tis worth 1000$^£$ I really *think it is.*" To others she made lighter claims, suggestive of "feminine" virtues. The book would be readable and pleasing: "*A fast and easy Goer,*" "Scholar's Work done by a Wit." She also braced herself for hostile reviews, and "in a merry humour" wrote one herself.[47] She knew too well what to expect. When the reviews appeared, they were savagely dismissive.

In *The Madwoman in the Attic* Gilbert and Gubar remark upon the "oddity" of much of the literature produced by women, the fact that a great deal of it does not "seem to 'fit' into any of those categories to which our literary historians have accustomed us." *Retrospection* is a signal instance of this phenomenon; its reviewers could make nothing of it. "How shall we characterize a work so perfectly singular?" exclaimed the *British Critic*. In forty-eight chapters totaling somewhat more than a thousand pages, *Retrospection* presents a summary chronicle of the eighteen centuries of the Christian era: the rise—and, latterly, the decline—of the Church, alterations in systems of government, and the progress of trade and civilization. Although it professes to take in the whole civilized world, it dwells in fact almost entirely on Europe and the Middle East and, within Europe, increasingly on England. It is not, and repeatedly declares it is not, a work of scholarship like Gibbon's, Hume's, and Mosheim's histories; rather, it is a distillation from these and other works. It is addressed not to scholars but to general readers ("we who are neither historians, nor inventors, but sober Christians, engaged in a mere *Retrospect* of past occurrences"), and also to "young readers."[48]

All of this seems simple enough; Clifford perceptively likened *Retrospection* to H. G. Wells's *Outline of History*. But *Retrospection* is not the prototype of twentieth-century popular history, for it was too quickly and completely forgotten to have such influence. Nor, despite resemblances to modern school textbooks—the chronicle format, emphasized in the chapter titles (e.g., "From Constantine to Theodosius, A.D. 400")—and despite her hope that it would be used in schools, can *Retrospection* be claimed as an ancestor of the school history text.[49] Her narration is not distinct enough to be freshly informative; it is allusive, and its effect is to remind one of what one has forgotten, not to convey information that one never had. Aggravating this effect is the style of the work: conversational but also complexly oratorial, intellectual ("witty"), and even poetic, it bears about the same relation to the style of Piozzi's earlier works as the style of, say, *The Ambassadors* bears to that of *The American*. Indeed, if Piozzi wrote a stylistic masterpiece, it is *Retrospection*; but it is hardly a "fast and easy Goer." Considered as a summary for the instruction of unlearned readers, *Retrospection* must be said to defeat its own purpose by being too learned. Considered as an attempt at learned history writing, it proclaims itself, again and again, a failure. Either way, reviewers felt perfectly justified in declaring it worthless.

Except for these rather limited purposes, *Retrospection* does not, however, read like a failure. Certainly it has dull and irritating pages, and one may reject its biblical premises. Yet to compare *Retrospection* itself with most of the little that has been said of it by subsequent commentators is to appreciate how tenuously critical rumor can connect with textual fact. Its first critics, however hostile, were at least speaking of what they had read, and in their very abuse of the book they evince a refracted comprehension of it. "A series of dreams by an old lady," wrote the *Critical Review*, identifying in one stroke two important points. *Retrospection* is less a history than a meditation upon history, a point in which it bears some resemblance to a more famous and not less eccentric work, Yeats's *A Vision*. And although *Retrospection* is not particularly visual in detail its cumulative effect is, as it were, processional, like a mural. This effect is not fortuitous. Describing the work to her nephew some years later, Piozzi likens it to "the Catalogue[s] of Pictures you see advertised so often," and in *Retrospection* itself she speaks of "these . . . little moving pictures of our show, these . . . *tableaux de nos petits ombres chinoises*," which makes it a diminutive ("female") analogue of history painting. The optical metaphor of its title in fact dominates the work. We are never allowed to forget (as one reviewer complained) that we are retrospectors and that *Retrospection* is not history but rather a looking back at history. Once she calls it "a convex glass" or diminishing mirror, suggesting Renaissance ethical mirrors such as *A Mirror for Magistrates*; the whole point of her optical metaphor, indeed, is ethical.[50]

The prose meditation as a genre is characterized by considerable ornateness of style (*A Vision* again, and also Sir Thomas Browne), and *Retrospection*'s reviewers were prompt to take note of its style. "Frequently, we have been inclined to suppose that the author had originally written her narrative in blank verse," says the *British Critic*, "and that it had afterwards been disjointed. . . . When Mrs. P. means to raise her style, she writes in tragic numbers." He illustrates by printing a sentence as blank verse, and so performs a useful critical service:

> But when th'unfeeling north pour'd forth her waste
> Inhabitants, and bid them roam for prey,

Regardless of the ruin left behind:
Onward they press'd in countless multitudes,
Unconscious shoals; as when old ocean half
Acquires solidity from life that stirs
Within.[51]

These are, to be exact, not tragic but Miltonic numbers. *Retrospection* includes the *disjecta membra* of epic poetry; this is one of its points of connection with Gibbon's *History* and the Gibbonian understanding of history writing as a species of epic. Blank verse is also the condition towards which oratorial prose tends; the prose meditation is itself a species of poem.

This prose-poem chronicle is powered by a biblical fundamentalist thesis that must have smelled disreputable to the liberal intellectuals even of 1800. It may be no more savory to readers here and now, yet we must examine it—more generally, we must examine Piozzi's attachment to the Bible—in order to appreciate a large part of what she is attempting in *Retrospection*. Her tenacious biblical literalism seems out of character, for her temperament was neither literal minded nor rigid; on the contrary, she tends to be skeptical, satirical, and rebellious. We have seen that her politics, on the whole, are generous rather than illiberal, and thus not the politics that we associate with religious fundamentalism.

We have also seen, however, again and again, that her literary posture is adversarial. As a young woman, translating Louis Racine, she attacks Pope on the ground of his supposed deism. In *Anecdotes* she stations Johnson in a posture of inhuman skepticism and herself in a posture of humane opposition to it. In *Observations* she does implicit battle with the satirical habits of male travel-writers, taking instead a stance of benevolent credulity. In *British Synonymy* she gets off shots at Locke, Hume, and Shaftesbury. In *John Bull* she attacks Paine, and in *Retrospection* she criticizes Burke. The pattern is one of continual resistance, not alone to a tradition of skepticism but to the republic of letters itself and the male writers who stand at its head.

Retrospection is her largest campaign against them, and its principal target is Gibbon: the biblical thesis is explicitly anti-Gibbonian. It consists of a move to make Gibbon's *History*, which is one of her prime sources, mean the opposite of what Gibbon intended it to mean.

Like Balaam, blessing where he meant to curse, that great historian's book is found of use to those who . . . are earnest to deduce the truth of prophecy from ancient story, as an adversary's testimonial can never be suspected. He has . . . given us many land-marks . . . whence our *retrospective* eye may see more clearly how religion and politicks have advanced . . . till they arrive at the place we now find them. He . . . asserts with equal sense and truth, that when contempt of the religion long established by law pervades a whole community, revolution cannot long be kept away. He tells from old times, what is completely verified by modern ones, that when the majority secretly loses strength . . . that state has suffered a most fatal symptom, and her destruction cannot be far off.[52]

What Gibbon writes of Roman paganism against burgeoning Christianity, Piozzi applies to modern Christianity against burgeoning irreligion; she makes Gibbon a monitor in behalf of the status quo.

In itself this is no great departure from the *History*: Gibbon's ethics are broadly conservative. What makes it adversarial is her assumption that Gibbon "meant to curse." She always resents Gibbon, and it is instructive to see what she resents him for. In *John Bull* he succeeds Wilkes as "our next promoter of the infidel scheme" who "contributed exceedingly to the sapping religious foundations"; also he is characterized as "finical" and fastidious. For her work on *Retrospection* she borrowed a set of the *History*, an expensive and elegant item: "You would laugh to see my Anguish about Mrs. Heaton's *beautiful Infidel Gibbon*," she writes her daughter, "lest a Spot of Ink should penetrate the Papers I have wrapped him in, and make him black on the *Outside*."[53] The resentment here is not more of Gibbon than of Mrs. Heaton and her like, the fashionable fastidious readers of fashionable books. It is resentment of literary trendiness. In *Retrospection* Gibbon figures as the representative of a literary establishment that Piozzi intends to flout. The Bible is her weapon, prophecy her authority, and the Apocalypse her revenge. What appears at first blush to be mere religious fundamentalism turns out on scrutiny to be something else as well: the protest of an outsider—in effect, a female protest.

A second prime source of *Retrospection* is Hume's *History of England*—she transcribes and summarizes it in dozens of details—and her treatment of Hume is like that of Gibbon, but less explicit. One has to trace it in the fabric of her work, where one finds continual skirmishes with him. A good place is her account of the Crusades, where she is skirmishing with Gibbon as well. Hume's judgment of the Crusades as a whole is short, simple, and contemptuous: "the most signal and most durable monument of human folly that has yet appeared in any age or nation." Gibbon's, less blunt and more tempered, is not ultimately kinder. Piozzi concurs with them in doubting the moral utility of the enterprise, albeit she does so in terms that constitute a tacit reproach to their presumed irreligion: she will not "much extend" herself "to prove, what in this day none will dispute, how men had better serve the Lord at home, obeying his precepts, and imitating his example; than by undertaking a tedious journey for the sake of seeing the place where his cross was first erected." She then, however, adhering to her programmatic sympathy with religious motives however manifested, makes an attempt at historical understanding: "Manners *must* in some measure change with times. There were then no scriptures publickly read and known, nor were the limits of duty ascertained as now, within the well-known precincts of the gospel." In short, why must the piety of the eleventh century act like that of the eighteenth? She cites as further explanation a wave of millenarian alarm at the close of the tenth century, which induced many people to "run to meet their Saviour where he suffered," an explanation which neither Hume nor Gibbon offers.[54]

As in larger matters of interpretation, so in small details. She is glad to catch Hume in the error of miscalling Pope Urban; where Gibbon doubts the reported number of crusaders, she reasserts it. Hume remarks, in scandal, that "women themselves, concealing their sex . . . attended the camp"; Piozzi corrects this to "pious women." One source for the history of the Crusades is the Princess Anna Comnena's life of her father, the emperor Alexius; from this comes the famous image of "Europe precipitating itself on Asia." Hume quotes this image without crediting Anna; Gibbon quotes it also, and derides her: "Instead of the simplicity of style and narrative which wins our belief, an elaborate affectation of rhetoric and science betrays, in every page, the vanity of a female author." Piozzi names Anna and bridles at Gibbon, setting "the natural sublimity of the princess" above his "French *tournure* [cast of style] and delicacy."[55]

As she perceives them, Hume and Gibbon are among the authors of the European crisis to which *Retrospection* is her response.

Her chief purpose in writing is to explain how we came to this pretty pass, the French Revolution, and how the Revolution fits into the scheme of things. In her explanation she distinguishes first and second causes, the second causes being those natural and human ones that modern "philosophical reasoners" (such as Hume and Gibbon) find "of course" and the first cause being the divine one that they ignore. The divine cause is simple. Humanity was allotted six thousand years from Creation to Redemption in three periods of two thousand years each; the third period is about to expire; in this scheme the French Revolution must be regarded as the preparation for Antichrist, who has lately appeared in the person of "Apollyon" Bonaparte, "the first who ever wore *as a name* the title of *Destroyer*." Second causes are to be traced *sub specie* this first cause. In this three-part division of time we will recognize the Augustinian division of history; a remote precursor of *Retrospection* is *The City of God*, which like it was evoked by a crisis, the Sack of Rome by the Goths. (Piozzi points up the connection herself when she describes modern philosophical skeptics as "a bold irruption of Vandal forces.") Piozzi would have assented fully to the Christian historiography of a more recent historian, the late Sir Herbert Butterfield, who is best known for his demolition of the "Whig myth" that history is progressive. The Christian historian, Butterfield wrote, is "a person under a certain kind of discipline for the purpose of examining the ways of Providence and the structure of the providential order"; "having in his religion the key to his conception of the whole human drama, he can safely embark on a detailed study of mundane events, if only to learn through their inter-connections the ways of Providence."[56] To show the ways of Providence, or as Piozzi says, "to deduce the truth of prophecy," is the program of *Retrospection*. We turn now to her analysis of the second causes, an analysis which holds some surprises.

She posits the traditional three forms of government, monarchy, aristocracy, and democracy; the third era of human history commenced at the height of the Roman Empire, which was the last universal monarchy, and has descended through aristocracy towards democracy. This descent, Providentially ordained, was effected through collisions of human purposes. She sums it up this way, looking back from the threshold of the eighteenth century: "We . . . have seen many attempts made by individual princes, proceeding from that hard baronial phalanx which broke down the Roman empire, (last of appointed monarchies) to synthetize the ruptured parts anew, and reign over those realms, which of right belonged to their fellows. To this end, we have observed each taking the same method of attainment, calling in help from the lower ranks to shake their highly-set competitors, yet never seeming to think they should themselves be shaken."[57]

The thesis exhibits a good measure of ironic beauty. Part of it inheres in her taking the view *sub specie aeternitatis*, in which what we customarily call the European monarchies are seen as so many petty baronies in contention with one another for a universal monarchy that is no longer obtainable. These baronies and their rulers descend from the Goths, who could shatter Rome but could not put it back together again. In her analysis of their "method of attainment" she treats Europe very much as if it were England or France writ large. The kings of England and France attained superiority over their baronial rivals—that is, consolidated the monarchies—by allying with the commons against the barons. In France, Louis XIV is a paradigm instance; in England, Edward III. In his reign, writes Piozzi, "Windsor's proud turrets now lifted their heads on high, and every thing evinced the progress of authority from barons independent of their sovereign, to a consolidated mass of king and commons, supporting royalty against the nobles of the land."[58]

In calling on the commons, however, the monarchs unwittingly called into being their own executioners. Piozzi is clear and definite as to how it happened: "The commons were obtaining wealth . . . and wealth . . . leads distantly and unsuspectedly to power." This is not a mere passing remark but a distinct theme of her book. Thus in England during the reign of Henry IV, "the commons . . . rose each moment in respectability: their agriculture improved, their sheep increased; corn was exported, wool was manufactured; and when they grew important, they found out they were *aggrieved*. A reader of history, from this hour will find the lower order ever restless, ever uneasy: they had tasted the tree of knowledge, and knew all their wants." The tree of knowledge is wealth, and where wealth leads, consciousness follows: "Princes to thwart each other, had for some time been calling up the mercantile order to depress nobility. Trade had increased their general importance, and now the demagogues drew on the commons to think that other forms of government existed, where *they* might rule without regard to ancestry." In the eighteenth century, with commerce triumphant, "it is not much amiss to observe how care for preservation of kingdoms or estates to issue male died off, with other old aristocratical ideas: since commerce had ploughed away many distinctions, and levelling each hill, exalted in proportion . . . *every valley.*" "What then remains?" she asks, and answers, "The reign of trade, of manufactures, arts, luxuries; the reign of knowledge, opulence, and consequently *power*; no more concentrated but all diffused . . . the reign then of democracy, *last* act of [the] political drama."[59]

Late in the work she contemplates the England of her own time, and we observe how sensitive she is to the reciprocity between things and thoughts. "Since the accession of [the] Brunswick house, a manifest change (improvement we must call it) with regard to civil society had taken place; and the last thirty years, from 1750 to 1780, made an almost miraculous alteration in London and country manners." She instances transportation and styles of dress, the beautification of London and improvements in painting and the mechanical arts, cotton and thread manufacture, new inventions, and lower prices; and side by side with these she instances the insubordination of children to parents and the frittering away of distinctions of rank. "Spinning jennies were contrived to hasten these productions, steam engines to facilitate rougher operations; machines imitated mortals to unhoped perfection, and men found out they were themselves machines. The *new* philosophy, as it was rightly called, pervaded all the meetings of the workmen even in country towns."[60]

Reading all of this, we may rub our eyes. The idea of historical process as an inexorable, ironic dialectic whose agents cannot foresee how their acts will ultimately destroy them; the firmly drawn rise of the bourgeoisie, who must of material necessity overthrow the monarchies that called them up; the clear perception that not only political power but even ideology has its material basis in commerce; the keen sense of relations between things and ideas ("machines imitated mortals . . . and men found out they were themselves machines"); the ambivalent estimation of material progress ("improvement we must call it," although it sweeps away the old society whose end she is also lamenting); and not least, of course, the conviction that history as it has hitherto been understood is nearing its end, and a democratic revolution is ushering in an apocalypse: All this, which we recognize as the substance of Marxian history writing, is a "series of dreams by an old lady" whose bare intellectual competence has by no means been taken for granted.

As a historiographer she has not only force but also integrity.

Although she loves the Reformation and is a born-again Protestant, she entertains no illusion that religion on earth is exempt from the same historical process that governs secular society. When she writes at one point that "commerce softens the mind of one man to receive the ideas of another," she is speaking explicitly of religious ideas. She writes in the conviction that "historians should recollect, whether rulers will or no, that when the church falls the state will not long remain behind"; accordingly, in her account of the fall of the state, the fall of the church runs parallel. That fall originates in the quarrels, during the Great Schism, of Urbanists and Clementines for papal supremacy: "tearing the ecclesiastical power in pieces, [they] tore likewise the veil which had till then concealed much misconduct. Disgraceful truths were told on both sides, and while the partizans of one pope *thought* they were only tormenting his rival—all aided in reality the sect of Wickliffe, which spared no pains in pulling out the black deformities of the *papal power*, regardless of any particular individual, and exposing them to open view." In the decrees of the fifteenth-century church councils that "they had power to depose popes who possessed in turn no power at all to reverse decrees of council," she perceives at once "a new doctrine, and dangerous in its nature to the essence of monarchick government." Without quite saying it, she implies that the Reformation was the natural ideology of capitalism (the famous Weber-Tawney thesis); she does indeed say that "Reformation and civilization . . . walked forward hand in hand," that the political freedom of the bourgeoisie was its natural attendant, and that by the seventeenth century "the passage was short and the transition easy, from no bishop to no king."[61]

These ingredients come together in the English Revolution of 1688, of which her analysis is remarkably unsentimental and sophisticated in its appreciation of causal complexity. It was, she writes, "a revolution formed and carried into effect by a large body of Protestant nobility, a church oppressed and struggling for existence; a country party rising in opulence and dignity every day: assisted by merchants and traders rich beyond even the . . . wishes of their fathers, and who of course desired stability to their enormous gains. To all these, learning, wit, and satire lent their combined forces, exalting the happiness of freedom, and free enquiry into every thing sacred and political, civil, natural and moral." As she construes it, the entire intellectual history of the ensuing century reflects the full tide of bourgeois power and the concomitant running amok of

Protestant ideology. In literature, there is bourgeois sentimentalizing of the lower orders: "as a lower order of mortals stept forward
into notice, *their* characters adorned the literature of the day. In
every novel, comedy, and letter, the pert, vivacious, faithful footman
shines: the Tom, Trim, Jeremy, of our English theatre." In ethics,
there is sentimental benevolism and noble savagery: "*Good* people
helped this work [the decline of Christian belief] forward too, more
than they would have wished, had its consequences been laid open to
them, by reproaching their Christian brothers everlastingly with the
superiority of savage virtues, till it has at length become the mode to
find out excellence in all *but* Christians." There is, finally, the total
repudiation of the institutional church in the name of philosophy
and reason: "a bold irruption of Vandal forces overwhelmed us, scoffers and tramplers—*complete Protestants*, as Mr. Gibbon blushes not to
style himself, *protesting* against every faith as folly."[62]

This, in outline, is Piozzi's account of how we came to grief, and
it is a powerful piece of historiography. To us, living after more than
a century of Marx-derived history writing, the story she tells must
sound thrice-told. That, however, in no way impeaches her achievement in telling it. Nor is it any impeachment to note that the elements of this story came to her from her precursors Gibbon and
Hume. From Gibbon, of course, she has the decline-and-fall paradigm. What she has from Hume is somewhat more complicated, and
to describe it we must briefly expound the tendency of his *History
of England*. Although his political sentiments are mainstream conservative—Piozzi often concurs with them tacitly, and even sometimes explicitly—in his historiography Hume subscribes to the "Whig
myth" of progress. His history traces the construction of the British
Constitution to its perfecting, the Revolution of 1688, and there it
stops. Hume is persuaded that England today enjoys "the most perfect and most accurate system of liberty that ever was found compatible with government"—a persuasion that could comfortably be
held in the 1750s, when Hume wrote.[63] This system of liberty developed, according to Hume, through the contentions of crown and
barons, in which the crown consolidated its position by allying with
the commons, an alliance by virtue of which the commons obtained
privileges.

Hume's story is thus the origin of Piozzi's—is, indeed, the same
story, but with two differences. One difference is that Hume conceives the rise of the commons in terms of legal and jurisdictional

powers, and Piozzi in terms of economic power; by our lights, she is the more modern historian. The second difference is that she, writing forty years later, utterly revises the values of the story by the light of its outcome, the French Revolution. Her history follows Hume's only to complete it, and, in completing, destroy it. Where Hume sees unequivocal progress, Piozzi perceives latent, and ironic, disaster. What Hume regards complacently as a perfected state, Piozzi reinterprets as a late stage in a process of decline. All this she does tacitly; explicitly she quarrels with Hume's anticlericalism. By identifying Hume as the irreligious opposition, however, she stations him among the "Vandal forces," the "scoffers and tramplers" thrown up by bourgeois hegemony. So stationed, in her scheme he implicitly appears as an ironic self-destructor, shortsightedly contributing to undermine the very building that he congratulates us on having completed. It is Hume that she censures when she writes that "historians should recollect . . . that when the church falls the state will not long remain behind." Written to demonstrate this position, *Retrospection* ultimately demonstrates the much stronger one that is familiar to us from Marx. She arrives at it by fighting Hume, much as Marx arrived at his by fighting Hegel. In the history of Piozzi's literary warfare this, her last, must be accounted her most impressive combat. The *History of England* is certainly a better history than *Retrospection*, but Piozzi's historiography exerts a stronger grip than Hume's.

Conceptually, then, *Retrospection* is a performance of which she had reason to be proud. One could argue plausibly that its debacle was entirely the making of the *Critical Review* ("a series of dreams by an old lady"): the *Critical's* attack seems to have been the one that scotched its sale and frightened her publisher from issuing a second edition. The consequence was that *Retrospection* became a scarce book; only 750 sets were printed, and of those only 516 were sold.[64] A book that is not easy to find and has been booed by the critics is not likely to be read, and rumor and ignorance do the rest.

Yet it is also true that Piozzi contributed to the debacle. She contributed to it in precisely the manner to which women writers were vulnerable, by doubting her own authority. *Retrospection* is shot through with disclaimers, apologies, and self-deprecations, all the unhappy postures that bedevil most of her work from *Anecdotes* on. There is a relation between these postures and the varying reception of her works; reflections on it will make a suitable epitaph both to

Retrospection and to her literary career. The relationship has to do with what we may call the perceived grounds of authority.

If we ask on what grounds *Anecdotes of Johnson* has been credited traditionally, the answer is, "She was Johnson's intimate." On that ground the book was bought, read, and credited by its first readers, and her disclaimers of competence in it were largely nullified by their knowledge that she had been Johnson's intimate. A memoir can be credited on that ground without its author's being obliged to demonstrate competence as an author. Much the same can be said of *Letters*; although with them the question of her editorial competence arose, still the letters had been written to her, they were unique documents, and she was known to possess the originals. One read her edition of them, at worst, *faute de mieux*.

With her travel book the grounds of credit begin to shift; the book must, to a greater extent, certify its own competence by making the approved kinds of moves, and with *Observations*, accordingly, we begin to hear sharp complaints of her style. Yet she can still be credited as an eyewitness, insofar as she talks of where she has been and what she has seen. With *British Synonymy* the question of competence takes center stage, and with *Retrospection* it is virtually all in all. To appear nervous, frightened, or unsure in these genres is to invite dismissal; it only confirms the male readers—who are the only ones who count, institutionally—in their assumption that a woman writer is a pert, vain, silly thing. Women have traditionally, to be sure, been allowed competence in matters of etiquette, and *British Synonymy* got by on its pretension only to adjust the etiquette of speech—and to address people much less competent even than women, namely foreigners.

For *Retrospection*, however, there could be no perceived extra-authorial ground of competence whatsoever. (Piozzi appears to have been aware of this fact; in her mock review of *Retrospection* she grounds her authority—inadequately, of course: that is part of the mock—on her having traveled in Europe.) Here the anxiety of authorship must be met head on, and the book itself must manifest its author's competence. *Retrospection*, alas, does not do that. Although a strong book, it declares itself a weak one. She researched it thoroughly (visitors to Brynbella during the late 1790s saw her in her study, surrounded by heaps of books), but then, with a sort of airy impudence, disdained to footnote. She catches out her sources in their errors, and neglects to correct her own. (There are a great many; the typesetting alone of *Retrospection* was atrocious.) She does not distinguish grain from chaff, and crowds her strong historical thesis with a considerable amount of crankery and trifling, another way of not taking herself seriously enough. She justly felt that *Retrospection* was her best book, and yet allowed herself to sabotage it in these and other ways. Thus disfigured, what should have been her masterpiece appeared instead as a monumental proof of "the errors of a female pen."

This relation between genre and the perceived ground of authority, as I have just sketched it, sounds very much like the traditional bumblebee account of Piozzi's career, the account according to which she was not really an author but only the friend of Johnson who stumbled into authorship with *Anecdotes* and spent the rest of her life proving that she was not an author. In fact, however, the bumblebee thesis itself is only a particular version of this relation, and this relation is the historical unhappiness of women writers. If, in the blunt phrase of Gilbert and Gubar, "a pen [is] a metaphorical penis,"[65] women are sexually incapable of writing; they have no authority. Whatever credit their work receives must be grounded on some extraneous authority, some accident of experience like knowing a great man, or some competence that women are socially allowed, such as etiquette. As an author every woman is a bumblebee, or was, and Piozzi's is an entirely representative case. The woman who demanded to be credited simply as an author did so at the hazard of having her presumed sexual incompetence driven home to her—and also of having to face directly her own fear of incompetence. *Retrospection* was Piozzi's principal attempt of this kind. It failed not because she was incompetent but because she could not overcome her fear of being incompetent. Its defeat is no disgrace to her and signifies much more than her own failure to surmount the emotional obstacles to success. Its defeat, rather, is a condemnation of the sexual politics of literature.

NINE

The Farce of Life
Piozzi's After-Career

*Yet poor old Dr. Harrington must be thought of; he will be seen
no more. Was it not pretty and affecting that they played his
fine sacred music so lately, and by dint of loud and reiterated
applause called him forward as he was retiring, to thank him
for their entertainment? He returned, bowed; went home,
sickened, and ———! This was a classical conclusion of his life
indeed; like the characters at the end of Terence's plays, who cry*
Valete omnes et plaudite!

*What signifies changing Character in the Close of Life?—let us
at least* superannuate *naturally—The Catastrophe should in
any wise be worthy of the* Farce.[1]

I T   W A S   N O T immediately appar-
ent to Piozzi that *Retrospection*'s debacle had ended her career. She
fought back against the reviewers, complained of her "Literary enemies," and, in some moods, even professed to find their abuse exhilarating: "beating [the book] forth and back *keeps it up*." To the end of
her life she remained loyal to *Retrospection*, evolving a myth that it
had been attacked only because of its printer's carelessness and correcting the typographical errors in every copy she could lay a hand
on. Although she was perfectly capable of attributing the public's
abuse of other women—Joanna Baillie, for instance—to sexual preju-
dice, she did not so interpret her own case. Rather, she adopted the
posture of intellectual alienation that we know so well from more
recent writers: "It is a grievous thing to Think how very little can be
done by *either* Talents or Literature. Piety & Business will effect in a
Month what the other Two could not perform in a Year"; "to *me* who
have always made my Pride & pleasure out of Literary Acquirements

it is particularly affecting." What proved to be her penultimate publication, an elegy on Elizabeth Carter written in 1806, is also obliquely an elegy on herself:

> Must Carter's Form fade from this changeful Scene
>   Unnotic'd by the busy Crouds below?
> And is there no Leaf left of dusky Green
>   To bind round ancient Learning's wither'd Brow?
>
> None:—where contend the rich the Bold the Young,
>   Wisdom's pale votarist unheeded dies;
> But memory's Daughters will repair such wrong
>   Tow'rd her who calld them from their native Skies.[2]

Overtly, she laments the foolish world's neglect of ancient wisdom. Perhaps, however, lines seven and eight may be construed as offering feminist compensation, "memory's Daughters" being taken for other intellectual women as well as for the Muses.

Actually, Piozzi did not "fade from this changeful Scene" altogether "unnotic'd by the busy Crouds below." In 1808 the playwright Lumley St. George Skeffington asked her for an epilogue to his play "The Mysterious Bride"; he had previously, in 1804, requested a prologue to a play called "Friends and Enemies," which appears not to have been produced. As late as 1817 the twenty-six-year-old Henry Hart Milman applied to her for an epilogue to his tragedy, *Fazio*. This request she refused; she had by then written her literary last will and testament. The event (or rather, nonevent) that decisively ended her career was her failure in 1815 to find a publisher for "Lyford Redivivus," an etymological dictionary of Christian names imitated from Edward Lyford's *True Interpretation and Etymology of Christian Names* (1655). This attempt was conceived in 1806—"silly Mrs Piozzi planning a new Book," she notes in *Thraliana* that September; the last entry in one draft is dated almost nine years later.[3] Yet "Lyford" is a short work, short and spiritless.

An otherwise sympathetic commentator has argued that Piozzi published only so long as her work met a favorable reception, that writing for her was just a way of pleasing people even as being precocious had been a way to please her elders. That Piozzi wrote for narcissistic rewards is no doubt true, yet every writer is moved by narcissism among other passions. In her essay, "Why I Write," Joan Didion frankly avows that motive. Didion likes the very words "why

I write," she says, because "the sound they share is this: I I I. . . . Writing is the act of saying *I*, of imposing oneself upon other people, of saying *listen to me*." That Piozzi withdrew her efforts once it became clear to her that the reward was no more to be had is, at worst, evidence that her narcissism was not strong enough to survive a total and jeering rejection. It had unquestionably been strong enough to thrive on acceptance. At the height of her career, in 1789, a male observer reported with some surprise (she was, after all, only a woman) that "she expects to talk and to be listened to."[4]

The pathos of her last twenty years, indeed, is precisely that she could not stop writing, although without practical hope of publication. Without writing, she was desperately bored: "I hate to leave my Mind—like my Portmanteau—empty of the *More* that it is capable of holding." "When I can do nothing else for Heat, or for ill Health, or for Ill humor, I can turn Epigrams—Embroidering a Butterfly won't do." Although the tone is self-congratulatory, the dilemma is classical: In an age when women are supposed to be satisfied with embroidering butterflies, an intellectual woman must go mad for lack of adequate employment. Simply on this principle Piozzi went on writing: *Thraliana*, carried on till March 1809; "Minced Meat for Pyes," a notebook begun about 1796 for *Retrospection* and carried on in a scrappy way for the next twenty-five years; a "New Common Place Book" begun in 1809, laid aside for five years, then carried on till 1820; a volume called "Piozziana" (1811–13) and another called "Scrap & Trifle Book" (1813–14), both of them, like the others, collections of anecdotes, bon mots, reading notes, verses, etymologies, and numerological speculations; and her pocket diaries, one of which (1816) became for a while a miniature notebook. She busied herself also with annotating books and making presentation copies to friends. More, she obsessed herself with her poems, copying most of the verses in *Thraliana* into a three-volume collection for her nephew ("Poems on several Occasions," 1810), selecting 59 of these, again, to copy out in a volume called "A Collection of Hester Lynch Piozzi's MSS Poetry" (c. 1810), and compiling yet another volume (c. 1818) of 223 poems, mostly not her own, in the manner of a poetical miscellany.[5]

These last two collections, painstakingly copied in her best scribal hand, are nothing less than manuscript books, "publications" for an audience of one, and they are pathetic testimony to her need to keep the pen moving. "I feel ashamed even of this empty Employ-

ment," she writes in the 1810 "Poems," "and at 70 Years of Age confess an Apology necessary for copying out Nonsense never worth
much regard." Closing the third volume of "Poems," she vows to de-
sist for good: "These are the last Dying Words of my Folly & Foolery
. . . for I do certainly mean to play the Fool no more." There follow
more poems, and then the same vow again: "Now here is really the
Muse's latest Spark—ere She drop into the Dark." But it is not the
latest spark. At the end of the "Scrap & Trifle Book," still addressing
Salusbury, she asserts, "'tis all over now"; but it is not all over, even
yet. From these vows one would gather that she was preparing to die.
In asserting her intention to die as a writer, they are complicatedly
bitter: writing is useless to her now except as relief from boredom,
but as that it is hardly different from embroidering butterflies; its
presumption of an audience where there is no audience upbraids her
with the solipsism of it; the fact that there is no audience enrages
her, and she turns her rage on herself, accusing herself of not being
worth an audience after all. This rage spills into the Preface to "Lyford Redivivus," where she writes, "I expect to be read *once* by every
one who has a Name, if it is but to look for his own"; and onto the
title page, which reads, painfully, "Lyford Redivivus or A Grandame's
Garrulity. By An old Woman."[6]

She survived not only her literary audience but her friends, enemies,
and associates, in alarming numbers. In a rereading of Boswell's *Life*
in 1808, when she came to the sentence "Dr. Goldsmith died April 4,
this year," she wrote next to it: "Alas! Alas! & now Johnson & Boswell
& Blair & Robertson & Garrick & Reynolds—& almost *all* the People
named in these Books add to the dead cold list." As early as 1799, still
identifying with Johnson's Floretta, she had begun to perceive herself as a survivor in an unhappy sense: "'tis a melancholy Thing—as
Floretta found it in Dr. Johnson's Tale—to outlive Lovers & Haters,
& Friends & Foes; & find ones' self surrounded by those with whom
one has no Ideas in common." Ten years later, reaching Lichfield on
her way from Brynbella to London, she notes in her diary, "ask'd for
old Acquaintance—all dead!!"[7]

Although she never lacked acquaintances and admirers, and
although she could imperiously brush aside the ruins of a friendship, her later years were made miserable by increasing isolation. It
started at home, with her daughters. Her relations with the eldest,
Queeney, have long been a topic of attack and defense, and of point-

less side-taking. Obviously Hester has proven much the more interesting person, and it may well be that Queeney resented her mother's continuing to be interesting long after she should, according to social propriety, have stepped aside in favor of the daughter. Queeney herself seems to have had her mother's capacity for bitter coldness without her contradicting impulsiveness and passion; when she was twelve her mother wrote of her, "There is something strangely perverse in Queeney's Temper. . . . 'Tis all one to this Girl if She is kiss'd or cuff'd She can but hate one and She does that naturally." Queeney, on her side, once expressed suspicion of her mother's "original and persevering dislike, and real hatred of us all from her hatred of our father." The second marriage precipitated a state of war between them; in 1787 Queeney attempted to take guardianship of her youngest sister, Cecilia, and thus commenced a series of ugly lawsuits between daughter and mother. For six years (1787–93) they did not speak to each other. Hester made overtures of peace, and when they were rejected wrapped herself in a mantle of righteousness: "When we heard at the beginning of the Winter that Miss Thrale was not well, I sent her a very Affectionate Letter; & received for Ans[r] an open Billett *with Thanks for obliging Enquiries.* How have I *provoked*! how have I *deserv'd* such Treatment."[8] There was a formal reconciliation in 1793, followed by another quarrel and lawsuit, this time (1796–97) over Cecilia's marriage. Another truce gave way to yet another suit, initiated by Queeney in 1800, over property claims stemming from Henry Thrale's will. And there was yet another, in 1811, over the upkeep of Streatham Park.

That Hester felt deeply hurt by these hostilities is beyond doubt, and it is hard to feel much sympathy with Queeney's part in them; at the same time, one may suppose that Queeney's belligerence was designed to put a dent in what might well have seemed to her Hester's infuriating complacency. For in Hester's various responses to it all there is a kind of buoyant egoism, the self-dramatization of the confirmed author for whose verbal mill everything is grist. Her letters to Queeney just before her marriage in 1784, when it is perfectly obvious that Queeney wants nothing to do with the business, display what can only be called sublime disregard of Queeney's feelings. Not only do they act as if there is no rift, but they sprinkle Italianisms into the wound—e.g., "I expect my Sposo tonight." From Florence, a year later, she professes innocent incomprehension of Queeney's distance, not without a little belletristic teasing: "Why do you my sweetest Girl, write so coldly and so queerly? . . . is it because I am married to Mr Piozzi? that Reason (as Shakespear says) *is somewhat musty*." She then describes the celebration of her wedding anniversary, listing the notables who heaped attentions on her, and continues in terms that make Queeney into the skeleton at the feast: "When *every* body then is thus goodnatured to me, when *every* body expresses a just sense of Mr Piozzi's Merit, and seeing his Value pays him a proper Respect— why should you be the only Person to stand out? the only Person not pleased to see your Mother happy, and well treated."[9]

In 1800, notified of Queeney's new lawsuit and at the same time much concerned with the condition of Europe, Hester dramatizes her plight to her confidante Penelope Pennington. She is not a wounded parent but rather a beleaguered state, like England: "It is exceedingly offensive to be forced into Submission to [Czar Paul's] Caprices—but I suppose George the 3:^{d} at close of Life will not find new Enemies a good Thing any more than poor H:L:P does; or will be able any better than H:L:P to find *Supplies* for a new Contest, which like hers *can* terminate in no Advantage, and will be attended with *certain* Loss abroad, Increase of Poverty & of course Illhumour at home." Six weeks later, informed that the suit has been withdrawn, she makes it an occasion of glorying in *British Synonymy*: "& now let's hear no more on't; and do not Sweet Soul! make me in Love with *Resentment*. for . . . 'tis an unpleasing Quality & productive of nothing but Evil. We must quote our own Book of Knowledge after all, and in the Article—Forgiveness . . . you read these Words—A *Wise* Man will make haste to forgive because Anger is a painful Sensation & he wishes to be rid on't. A *great* Man will pardon easily because he finds few things worthy his Resentment, and a *good* Man will never resent at All, knowing how much he has himself to be forgiven. I wrote to the Girls by yesterday's Post, exactly as if no such Transaction had past between us—so long live British Synonymy!"[10] A proud determination not to resent seems indeed to have been her policy toward Queeney. Throughout these years she kept writing to her, chatty, cheerful letters that often recount her literary plans and progress and that even manage to draw Queeney into them, at least to the extent of getting Queeney to send her books she needs. They are the triumph of egoism over experience, always contriving to deny Queeney's persistent aloofness.

A source of pain that could not be denied was Gabriel Piozzi's health. He had gout, a bad case; as attack succeeded attack, with annual and then more than annual regularity, leaving him each time more crippled and more ravaged, Hester's life became yearly more restricted. Her letters tell this story. In November 1791 he suffered an attack so crippling that he could not urinate without assistance. During a fit in December 1793, "for twenty hours he screamed like a Woman in labour. I did not know . . . that Gout could have been so bad." It progressed, and she had to relive the experience of watching baffled doctors stand helplessly around. In January 1798 she complains to Penelope Pennington of her "Domestic *Comforts*. On the 20th of *October* My poor Master went to Bed wth a raging Fit of Gout in Breast Side Back & Collar Bone—but soon fixing in one Heel & one Toe,—it *tore them open* into the most frightful *Ulcers* I or poor Mr. Moore ever did behold. There has the Gout gnawed & bitten for *12* entire Weeks—during wch Time has the truly wretched Patient suffered Torments inexpressible, & I believe rarely endured." His attacks become a staple of her news: "M^r. Piozzi has for some Days been confined w:^th Shrieking Pain." While they last she can do nothing, can go nowhere; frayed with anguish, she is also beset by boredom: "Write sometimes *do*, I see no Creature but M^r. Moore, & hear no Sound but Groans with this vile Gout." In the final weeks of his life Piozzi was in constant delirium, either from the pain or from the opiates against it. He died of gangrene from the ulcers, 26 March 1809. Hester was left stupified by grief: "My Head seems quite *stunned*." Four days later she closed *Thraliana*. "All is over; & my second Husbands Death is the last Thing recorded in my first husband's Present! Cruel Death!"[11]

In 1798 she and Piozzi had adopted his five-year-old nephew, John Salusbury Piozzi, and brought him to England to educate. He was to be their child, and, for her, the replacement of her favorite son, Harry. As Thrale had hoped great things from Harry, so now Hester hoped great things from Salusbury, as she called him: "*he must be a Scholar* & we will try hard to make him a very good one." This recalls the "Children's Book" and her delight in Harry's forwardness. She did try hard, too hard, and Salusbury proved refractory, a stubborn disappointment. She exhorts him to study: "*Your Uncle* has no Taste to see *you* Ignor[ant, and] he will be very angry if you do not Study hard . . . and let me beg of you not to give yourself the future Pain & Disgrace of being out of Countenance for want of Knowing the History of Greece Rome & England;—They are *Indispensable* to a Gentleman's appearance in proper Company:—so are the Classics, so is Heathen Mythology. a Lad who has not these old Stories in His head—may as well have *no Head*." He is not even a proper audience for her usual witty, allusive, joking letters, and she has to explain her jokes to him: "Can't you understand it yet Salusbury? . . . Learn to know Jest from Earnest: and do not be such a mere *Matter of Fact Fellow*, though I shall ever rejoyce in your Spirit of Virtue & Prudence." In this too her egoism flouts reality. The boy had come to her a stray, a refugee of the French invasion of Italy. His earliest experiences had been of slaughter; on his first sight of a butcher's stall in Bath, he was reminded of a basket of human heads he had seen at Brescia.[12]

Unpromising or not, after Gabriel Piozzi's death Salusbury was the only male whom Hester had left to love, and in the following years she turned on him a torrent of frustrated affection. Her letters to him, 472 between 1807 and 1821, are the most passionate and vulnerable she ever wrote. She pours out her need to be loved and responded to ("on *You* my Thread of temporal Existence is now suspended"); she worries about him; she writes constantly, is in agonies of expectation of his replies, and is excessively grateful when they come.[13] That is not often. For the same years, from him to her, only twenty-seven letters now exist; many of hers to him are annotated, "requires no reply."

In 1811 she sent him to Oxford, where he lasted a year "and Kept me in continual Terror lest the bad habits of the Place should ruin him, Body Soul and Purse." Then, to her relief, he decided to marry and settle down to gentleman farming. With characteristic lavishness she gave him Brynbella as a wedding present; as characteristically, she then resented his taking it. He went on taking, having apparently decided that his aunt was good for money if for nothing else. In this disposition she acquiesced; in one of her letters to him she even tries to make light verse about it:

> Farewell then; for here the Gazette shall conclude,
> And the Writer no more with such Nonsense intrude:
> For where no Tale's to tell, and no Money to grant,
> I suppose We may *hang* Your *Affectionate Aunt*.

In 1814, having given him most of her fortune, she settled in lodgings at Bath, comparatively destitute and feeling herself to be a broken woman. There is a savagely self-pitying entry in her pocket diary for August 1815: "*My Aunt*—with the *Boarding House* a new

Farce acted without much Applause even from her Nephew, by poor wretched H:L:P.—I think I shall really be driven quite down. Oh God forbid!"[14]

At Bath she met three young men who were in various ways to be important to her: Sir James Fellowes, a naval surgeon, for whom she wrote one of her autobiographies and whom she named her literary executor; the Rev. Edward Mangin, he who, after her death, wrote the first memoir of her; and William Augustus Conway, a not very successful actor for whom also she wrote an autobiography. To all of them she wrote frequent and striking letters. To read through those letters is to be swept up, even against one's better judgment, in an overwhelming self-dramatization. "HLP," as she now calls herself, is every bit as much a rhetorical personage as Byron's Childe Harold or Shaw's GBS. She is a creature of self-mockery and profound bitterness and self-pity: "poor wretched H:L:P," "hapless H:L:P," "poor old superannuated" HLP, and even, once, "the *little Bundle of black Rags* . . . at N°. 8 Gay Street."[15] She is also the Ancient of Days, or, as she likes to put it, one of "nous autres Octogenaires," and is privileged by virtue of extreme age to speak of herself in the third person (something like the regal *we*) and to regard her lifetime's experience as exemplary of the human or, sometimes, the female lot. Finally, she is the last living authority on Johnson, whom she now treats as a personal possession and mouthpiece for her own pronouncements.

No single letter shows all of this, although some come close— such as this one, which takes off from one of her favorite topics, being ready for death:

> Johnson said We lived in a besieged Town—all of us: and that we ought not slumber at our Posts as if the Enemy was retired from the Ground;—if so, how much more vigilant should *we* be? nous autres Octogenaires?—*Our* Slumbers must be like those of a Soldier sleeping on the Attack.
>
> Life is a Magic Lanthorn certainly, and I think more so to Women, than to Men: who often are placed very early in a Profession which they follow up regularly, & slide on;—Labitur et labetur almost unconsciously:—but We Females (myself for Example,) I pass'd the first 20 Years in my Father & Uncle's Houses, connected with their Friends, Dwelling:Places & Acquaintance; and fancying my*self at home* among them:—No such Thing. Marriage introduced me to A *new* Set of Figures

... another Marriage drove that Set of Figures quite away, and I began the World anew. . . . I did however fancy when Piozzi built me a beautiful House on the Estate & in the Country my Parents quit in my early Childhood——that I was got *home* again somehow tho' oddly; *quite* a Mistake was *that*. . . . *Bath* is my home.[16]

The air of bitter puzzlement and ironic self-correction is also part of HLP. In many ways the role is a weak, unhappy one, a reveling in defeat. Yet she plays it so completely that there is no arguing with her; HLP is a definite verbal achievement, a species of the egotistical sublime.

Fellowes and Conway had a special emotional value to her. They replaced ungrateful Salusbury in her maternal affections, as Salusbury had been intended to replace her dead son. To Conway she played a mother's part, counseling him in his effort to marry, applauding him on the stage. At the same time, she is overwhelmingly grateful to both men for attending to her, for responding to her performances as people of old had done. On this note she closes her autobiography for Fellowes in December 1815: "you make me an Egotist, & force me to remember Scenes and Ideas I never dreamed of communicating. —The less so—because finding my Fortune of late circumscribed in a Manner wholly new to me—no doubt remained of all Celebrity following my lost Power of entertaining Company—giving Parties &c. and my Heart prepared to shut itself quite up,—convinced there existed not a human Creature who cared one Atom for poor H:L:P.—now She had no longer Money to be robbed of." On the same note she ends her memoir for Conway almost four years later. Only here her bitterness against Salusbury is more explicit, and rises to such an ecstasy of pain that criticism falls back from it speechless. After his extortion of Brynbella from her (for such she now feels it to have been),

Retirement to Bath with my broken heart & Fortune was all I could wish or expect. . . . Well! no matter—one Day before I left [Brynbella], there was Talk how Love had always *Interest* annex'd to it; Nay then Said I—What is *my* Love for Salusbury? Oh replied Shephard [Salusbury's Oxford tutor], there is *Interest* there. M^rs. Piozzi . . . *could* not I am *sure exist* without *some* one, upon whom to energize her Affections. his Uncle is gone; and She is *much obliged* to Young Salusbury for being ready to her hand to pet & spoil—her Children will not suffer her to love Them, and with a coarse Laugh—what must She do when This Fellow throws her off—as *he soon will?*

Shephard was right enough; I sunk into a Stupor, worse far than all the Torments I had endur'd. . . . & such was *My* Case when *Your* Talents *rouzed*—*Your* offer'd Friendship *opened* my heart to Enjoyment. Without *You* Dulness, Darkness, Stagnation of every Faculty would have enveloped & extinguished all the Powers of hapless H:L:P.[17]

In this melodrama of abuse and rescue Conway is Perseus to her Andromeda. Reading it, one feels that the situation is not new to her; and it is not. In 1765 Johnson had been her Perseus, rescuing her from "stagnation of every faculty" following her marriage to Thrale. In 1785 she had credited William Parsons with reviving her "stagnant" imagination. Now Conway, for all that he figures to her as her newest child, figures also as the man whose admiration her intellect requires, the father-uncle-tutor to whom, once again, her performances are delightful.

Bereft of her public, alienated from her family, and deserted every year by some friend's death, Hester nevertheless found in Bath a new audience among the younger generation. To them she was not the celebrated author but rather a relic of the departed eighteenth century, and they came to her as to a tourist attraction. To Thomas Moore, who was taken to see her in 1819, she appeared radiant of legends: "a wonderful old lady; faces of other times seemed to crowd over her as she sat,—the Johnsons, Reynoldses, &c. &c.: though turned eighty, she has all the quickness and intelligence of a gay young woman." A woman visitor, some years before, had not been so easily impressed: "I stood for some time near Mrs. Piozzi that evening, but did not hear her make any observation that *any other person* would not have made. Her figure was little and animated, highly rouged, & dressed in rather a whimsical style . . . but when I afterwards met with her at Miss Maltby's, & sat next her for some time, I heard her conversation with much pleasure, indeed she seemed to wish to *please* far more than *astonish*, & this evening she looked very like what I supposed Mrs. Piozzi to be."[18]

"What I supposed Mrs. Piozzi to be": the legend was forming fast. She was being sent verses too, as in her youth at Offley Park, but now the topics are changed:

> How charming must have been those days
> When shone that intellectual blaze
> That Johnson, Reynolds, Burke supplied—
> Ere Murphy, Gray, or Goldsmith died!
>
> . . . .
>
> There lovely Thrale among them shone
> With charms peculiarly her own;
> Admired by all, by all confessed
> The fairest as the wittiest.

To all intents and purposes, this is already the nineteenth century's obituary on her. The living woman is no less pastoralized:

> Age & Time were softly stealing,
> All their darker lines concealing,
>   To Piozzi's cheerful home,
> But their artful plans defeated,
> Wit & Fancy firmly seated,
>   Guard with ease the favour'd dome.[19]

Although Piozzi enjoyed this attention she perceived its implications: both the legend and the "wonderful old lady" are figments of tourism. "That grave Mr. Lucas brought his Son here, that He might see the *first Woman in England*—forsooth. —So I am now grown one of the Curiosities of Bath it seems & *one of the Antiquities*." And again, after a visit to the sea at Weston: "*I* certainly liked it, and found Weston very agreeable, and 'tis the true Ton to say how the Place agreed with Mᵣˢ Piozzi—so it will now become the fashionable Retreat for Old Age & *Haggardism*."[20] Her own celebrity—farcical celebrity, as she perceives it—thus becomes a topic of HLP's irony; we can begin to imagine how she would have commented on the things written about her by her more gushing admirers.

Besides farcical irony there is also pathetic irony, the irony of the clown whose heart is breaking, who knows that his popularity depends upon his keeping up the show and knows also that he cannot keep it up for ever. Piozzi kept it up extraordinarily well, bringing her public life to a triumphant close on the night of her seventy-ninth birthday, when, in the assembly rooms at Bath, she threw a gala ball for over six hundred guests and led the dancing herself till early in the morning—an almost Roman act of lavishness, considering that she had hardly the money to pay for it and had to live the following year at sleepy little Penzance to make up the cost. The cost of keeping it up was not, however, just monetary. In an undated note to Mangin written when she was suffering toothache there is the utterly unironic cry, "pity me Dear Friends! for we are going to sit down 14 at Dinner this Day——& how I Shall amuse them God knows." She apprehended also that her repertory was growing thin; in another letter she speaks of her *"potted Stories."*[21] To judge from her late notebooks, she speaks truly; in them we often find stale bon mots introduced by the line, "When Johnson and Jack Wilkes were cracking jokes together," a line that alludes to the famous scene in Boswell's *Life*, not to anything in her own Johnson books, and in doing so displays a sad falling off of her own anecdotal skill.

Ideas of the theater fill her mind no less in late life than in early—indeed, more. Everything now is theater, and usually farce. Retailing to Mrs. Pennington a bit of gossip, she puts it onto the stage: "Doctor & Mrs Whalley seem to have been giving la Comedie gratis here while the Theatres were shut up. [They have been having domestic quarrels.] Incidents are certainly not wanting, and the Catastrophe kept quite out of Sight, as Bayes recommends [in *The Rehearsal*]; for purpose of elevating & surprizing." Commenting on the "frightful Catastrophe" of Princess Charlotte's death in childbirth, Piozzi concludes, "but the Farce of Life must go on till Death drops the Curtain—I suppose." She continues to amuse herself with politics, but they also are theater, both in their own right and for her. "We had an attempt at a meeting yesterday, but all proved abortive; so we make an address. 'Lord, Sir!' said I to Arch-deacon Thomas— 'why, England will be divided soon like the Hebrew alphabet—into *radicals* and *serviles*!' Oh, how that joke was applauded!" She is ashamed of herself, however, for continuing to care about making a hit. "Silly! at my age to hope for approbation! but 'even in our ashes live their wonted fires.'"[22]

Performance anxiety, the need to make a hit, was of course the daily experience of every genteel female, for whom, girl and woman, good breeding meant being constantly "on stage." Piozzi, having been on stage in this sense for some seventy-five years, was at last growing heartily sick of it. Here she is speaking about the writer Sophia Lee, now old and ill and unwilling to receive visitors: "Why should She let the People in to *visit* her . . . ? She knows they come for Curiosity— not from Affection; & I suppose her Means of doing good have been curtailed by Accident,—her Powers of pleasing by Infirmity & Age. Why should she then exhibit the *Skeleton* of Wit?—or Beauty if she ever possessed it?" Sophia's case is just her own; both are unbearably imposed on by the obligations of female decorum. "Is there no Time when one may be permitted to die in a Corner [after] arranging our little Matters for the Journey—Lord! I [shall have] to expire in a Curtsy & a Compliment, & request the Spe[ctators to] *honour* me with *their Commands*—to The next World." All the meanings of being on stage conjoin at last for her in one of her latest letters to Mrs. Pennington, where, in a typically compressed association of ideas, the style of genteel ladyhood (being "at home" to visitors) goes with her image of herself as a worn-out theatrical entertainer. Her "Comfort," she writes on 4 March 1821, "is that She is likely soon to escape the truly uneasy Sensation of out living Friends & Enemies——and standing alone upon the Stage of Life till hiss'd off for being able to furnish no further Amusement . . . . After having been *At Home* on the Boards like Mathews the Buffoon so many Silly Years."[23] A verdict on her own lifetime of performing and pleasing and being clever, this is also a bitter summary of what it has meant to her to be female.

This letter she wrote from Penzance. She had been ritually predicting her death for many years; this time her prediction proved true. On 10 March, traveling from Penzance back to Bath, she stopped for the night at Exeter and there took a fall as she was climbing into bed. The next day she pressed on, reaching Clifton and settling in lodgings there. In the fall she had hurt her leg, and she regarded the injury, with apparently placid satisfaction, as likely to be fatal. During the rest of March she visited and dined; in April, however, she began to grow weak. On 27 April she wrote her last diary entry. Her daughters were notified of her decline; when they arrived at Clifton on 1 May, she is reported to have said, theatrical to the end, "Now I shall die in state."[24] She died the following evening, 2 May 1821.

In what is surely her grandest diary entry, Piozzi in July 1820 forecast for herself a heroic, if controversial, after-fame. "At my Death the Battle about my Merits & no Merits, will be renewed over my

Memory. Friends wishing to save it—Foes contending for the Pleasure of throwing it to the Dogs like the Body of Patroclus in Homer." On hearing the news of her death, Fanny Burney d'Arblay, although estranged from her for thirty-six years, entered in her own diary a long and moving eulogy. The heart of it is a comparison of Piozzi with Madame de Staël.

> They had the same sort of highly superior intellect, the same
> depth of learning, the same general acquaintance with sci-
> ence, the same ardent love of literature, the same thirst for
> universal knowledge, and the same buoyant animal spirits,
> such as neither sickness, sorrow, nor even terror, could sub-
> due. Their conversation was equally luminous, from the
> sources of their own fertile minds, and from their splendid ac-
> quisitions from the works and acquirements of others. Both
> were zealous to serve, liberal to bestow, and graceful to oblige;
> and both were truly high-minded in prizing and praising
> whatever was admirable that came in their way. Neither of
> them was delicate nor polished, though each was flattering
> and caressing; but both had a fund inexhaustible of good hu-
> mour, and of sportive gaiety. . . . Both were kind, charitable,
> and munificent, and therefore beloved; both were sarcastic,
> careless, and daring, and therefore feared.[25]

The terms of this eulogy are indeed essentially heroic. They are such as might be used in eulogizing a great man: "Highly superior intellect," "ardent love of literature," "thirst for universal knowledge," "fertile mind," "splendid acquisitions," "beloved," "daring," "feared."

Not only are they essentially heroic, but they are also essentially true. One wonders what reputation Piozzi might have had if it had remained in the custody of writers like Burney—with the condition that such writers, unlike Burney, had had the courage to publish such assessments, and the further condition that the literary world would take them seriously. We may notice, for one thing, that there is not a word in this about Johnson, or about Streatham, or about hostessing, or even about the second marriage, even though Burney had lost Piozzi's friendship on its account. There is, rather, intelligent and high respect for Piozzi's abilities, ambitions, and power of enforcing herself. A literary culture consisting of writers like Burney—that is, of literary women—possessed of the courage to publish and fearing no belittlement would, of course, have been a rather more feminist literary culture than the one that did take custody of Piozzi's reputation. In such a culture Piozzi might well have been honored in just the way that she had prophesied in *Retrospection*—as one of the authentic foremothers who left to their posterity "works of acknowledged merit as remembrancers."

Certainly she must be honored as some kind of forerunner. She could speak of herself in terms as belated and sorrowful as those of any post-Miltonic male poet, lamenting with the worst of them that "I have not a Spark of Originality about me";[26] and yet it would be hard to name many among them of whom we can demonstrate so much priority as we can argue for her. If Bloom is right, it is the hopeless aspiration of every male writer to be, in effect, the first writer, and, of course, it is every male writer's curse to know that he is much nearer the end than the beginning. How refreshing to find this situation altogether reversed in Piozzi. She thinks herself destitute of originality, yet she stands at or near the beginning of almost everything she undertakes. Consider the list of her priorities, so far as they can be determined. She is the fifth or sixth memoirist of Johnson, the second really important one, and a fountainhead of modern interpretation of him. She is the first editor of Johnson's letters. In the course of being these, she is also an innovator in English biography and in the promotion of the personal letter to literary status; in both, she is one of the breakers of old decorums and the makers of new. She is apparently only the third Englishwoman to write a travel book. She is the acknowledged mother of English synonymy, the first writer of an English synonymy book that was not merely a translation of a foreign one. She is among the first to take up Mary Wollstonecraft's challenge to women that they might engage in politics. She is the second woman in England to write a large-scale work of history, and the first to attempt a world history. Every one of these works is flawed, even badly flawed, but every one of them is also strong. This is an astonishing achievement.

Some, although not all, of her priority is the effect of her being a female writer when females had as yet written little. This, however, is hardly a discount. Piozzi would have been no less a writer had she been male. She was as fiercely egotistical as almost any of her male counterparts, a natural fighter, and a revisionist who knew how to go for the jugular; had she been male, and therefore received the support of her literary culture, she would assuredly have made herself a formidable figure. She is a strong writer greatly malformed by her culture's sexual selections. Most of the authorial faults that have been attributed to her supposed "flightiness" or amateurism are properly effects of that malformation. They are compromises between the anxiety that bedeviled her, the whisperings from within that told her, every time she began a new book, that she could not really do it, and the counterwhisperings that allowed her to do it on condition that she not take it too seriously and invest too much in it. The second voice was the one that urged her to be "charming," and undoubtedly she listened much too often to it; not charm, but fierceness was her natural tendency. She heeded that voice, however, in order to silence the first; she sought strength, but often had to settle for charm in order to write at all; self-sabotage was the price she paid for authorship. In her last works especially, that price was fearfully high.

Nevertheless, we need not wish that she had been male. Had she been male she would have been heir to the sorrows of male influence, as Bloom calls them, the pressures of belatedness that in their own way malform male writers; she would have been but one more competitor, however strong, for their crowded and darkening space. If being female malformed her, it also made her a pioneer. She belongs to what might well be called the Heroic Age of the female literary subculture. Without support, against convention, she dared to claim for the female pen the major genres of writing, and this required not only more than ordinary courage but also resourcefulness and cunning.

Finally, when she prophesied that the women writers of her time would leave "remembrancers" to posterity she prophesied more truly of herself than of most of her sisters. *Anecdotes of Johnson, Observations and Reflections*, her letters, *Thraliana*, and some few of her poems have, in fact, stayed in the canon, and most of the writings of Montagu, Carter, Chapone, More, Barbauld, Seward, Macaulay, and other female contemporaries, whatever their merits, have not. In a literary history that respected the bare facts of canonic survival, Piozzi would be represented as what she has proved to be: by far the most considerable of the Bluestocking writers, and one of the most eminent women writers in England before Jane Austen.

Notes

In the notes the following abbreviations and short titles are used.

(J)B   (James) Boswell
BJRL   *Bulletin of the John Rylands Library*
Clifford   James L. Clifford, *Hester Lynch Piozzi (Mrs. Thrale)*.
    2d ed. Oxford: Clarendon Press, 1968.
EM   *The European Magazine* (London)
GM   *The Gentleman's Magazine*
(S)J   (Samuel) Johnson
LC   *The London Chronicle*
LSJ   *The Letters of Samuel Johnson, with Mrs. Thrale's Genuine
    Letters to Him*, ed. R. W. Chapman. 3 vols. Oxford:
    Clarendon Press, 1952. (Cited by letter number.)
HL(S)(T)P   Hester Lynch (Salusbury) (Thrale) Piozzi
PA   *The Public Advertiser* (London)
Piozzi 1762a, etc.   Published writings by Piozzi are cited by date of
    publication, and are so listed in Sources, pp. 287–89.
Piozzi MS H P, etc.   MS writings by Piozzi are cited by short titles and are
    so listed in sources, pp. 289–90.
QL   *The Queeney Letters*, ed. Marquis of Lansdowne.
    London: Cassell, 1934.
Ry. 533, etc.   MSS in the John Rylands Library, Manchester,
    England. (Quoted by permission.)
SJC   *The St. James's Chronicle* (London)
T   *Thraliana: The Diary of Mrs. Hester Lynch Thrale (Later
    Mrs. Piozzi), 1776–1809*, ed. Katharine C.
    Balderston. 2d ed. Oxford: Clarendon Press, 1951.
    (2 vols. paged continuously.)

PREFACE

1. Mangin, *Piozziana*, pp. 4–5; Broadley, *Dr. J and Mrs. T*, p. 77. See also
Lobban, *Dr. J's Mrs. T*, p. xxxi.
2. Piozzi MS N C P B, f12r.

CHAPTER ONE

1. Piozzi MS Mangin, 4 September 1819; Piozzi MS N C P B, f121v (November 1818).

2. *T*, pp. 321, 471, 127. John Salusbury's fragmentary novel is Ry. 655.8.

3. *T*, pp. 6, 288n.

4. Sir Robert Cotton to H. M. Salusbury, 9 November 1747 (in Clifford, p. 11); HLP to *The Monthly Mirror*, 17 June 1798 (in Bloom et al., "Portrait," p. 330); Piozzi MS Fellowes, pp. 5–6, 9; *T*, p. 751. For her earliest reading see Clifford, p. 9n, and *T*, p. 292. The "Dissertation" is Ry. 628.

5. Gordon, "Parable," pp. 31–32, 28.

6. *T*, pp. 288n, 487, 415.

7. Piozzi MS Fellowes, pp. 10–11; *T*, p. 296.

8. Piozzi 1861, 2:44; *T*, p. 16.

9. *T*, p. 322; Wilson to HLS, n.d. 1759 (in Myers, "Ironies," p. 62); Parker to HLS, 15 January n.y. (Ry. 536.23); Piozzi 1956, p. 156.

10. Boswell, *Life*, 1:494; Boswell, *Laird*, p. 69; Piozzi 1786, p. 134; Piozzi MS N C P B, f1r; Piozzi MS Conway. Her library catalogue is Ry. 612. She remembers *King John* in *T*, p. 766.

11. *T*, pp. 37, 63.

12. Piozzi MS Ry. 624, f3. For the date of this poem see Clifford, p. 28.

13. For the controversy see Pope, *Essay on Man*, pp. xv–xxii.

14. Piozzi MS Ry. 624, ff13r, 13v, 21v, 38v, 41r. Her note (f9r) asserts that Racine states Pope's principles in Pope's words, but he does not.

15. Piozzi MS Ry. 624, ff41v, 42r; *T*, p. 464. See also *T*, pp. 443, 455, 622, 900, 944, 1037n.

16. *T*, pp. 85–90.

17. Piozzi MS Ry. 646.11; Johnson, *Works*, 6:106.

18. *T*, pp. 17, 18–19. See Ry. 612.

19. *T*, p. 322; Piozzi 1762a; Piozzi 1762b; Piozzi MS H P, 1:46.

20. *T*, p. 492; Piozzi MS Fellowes, p. 16; Collier to HLS, 5 April 1763 (in Clifford, p. 40); *T*, p. 296.

21. Piozzi MS Fellowes, p. 18; *T*, pp. 303, 304.

22. Collier to HLS, n.d. and 17 April 1763 (in Clifford, pp. 42, 40).

23. Barker, *Screen*, pp. 79–80; Burgh, *Dignity*, p. 128; More, *Strictures*, 1:97–98; Wollstonecraft, *Rights of Woman*, p. 189; HLP, unidentified letter (in Newton, "Light-Blue," p. 190).

24. Piozzi 1763; Piozzi MS Fellowes, pp. 22, 24; *T*, pp. 307, 306, 308.

25. *T*, p. 355; Wollstonecraft, *Rights of Woman*, p. 155; Bloom, *Anxiety*, p. 24.

26. *T*, pp. 84–85.

27. *T*, p. 886.

28. Clifford, p. 53.

29. *T*, pp. 309–10.

30. Piozzi 1786, p. 102.

31. Burney, *Diary*, 1:53.

32. Campbell, *Diary*, pp. 61, 51; Burney, *Diary*, 1:92, 117, 113.

33. Piozzi 1977, p. 110; Piozzi MS Fellowes, p. 26; Piozzi 1861, 1:70 (HLT to John Perkins, 28 September 1773); *T*, p. 313.

34. Piozzi MS Conway; Piozzi MS Mangin, 13 November 1817; Piozzi 1977, p. 60.

35. Piozzi 1977, pp. 21, 49.

36. Piozzi 1977, pp. 110, 124; *LSJ* 415a; Piozzi 1910, pp. 160, 164, 168, 171–72. See Baretti, "Strictures," and Stone, *Marriage in England*, pp. 289–93.

37. Piozzi 1977, pp. 150, 152, 160, 163. Harry's death is attributed to "fulminating septicemia" or meningitis (p. 153).

38. *T*, pp. 1, 748. There were also Drummond's conversations with Ben Jonson (unpublished in her lifetime) and Joseph Spence's anecdotes of Pope, of which she saw a MS copy in 1780.

39. Burney's biographer, Roger Lonsdale, found in *T* "the most extensive objective account of his character which is available" (*Dr. Charles Burney*, p. 229).

40. *T*, pp. 1016, 858; HLP to Fellowes, May 1820 (in Bloom et al., "Portrait," p. 313); *T*, pp. 134, 28ff.

41. *T*, pp. 482, 339, 416, 492, 502, 53. See also pp. 375, 460, and xvi–xvii.

42. Piozzi MS Ry. 629.29a; Burney, *Diary*, 1:344. For Jerningham see *T*, pp. 438–39; for her rating system, pp. 330–31.

43. Piozzi 1932a, p. 102; Burney, *Diary*, 1:102.

44. *T*, p. 488.

45. Piozzi 1861, 2:302–3 (to Fellowes, 10 October 1815).

46. *T*, p. 452.

47. *T*, p. 531; Montagu to Elizabeth Carter, n.d. 1765 (in Myers, "Breaking Away").

48. *T*, pp. 544–45.

49. *LSJ* 969a, 970, 970.1a, 972.

50. *QL*, pp. 70, 85 (Burney to H. M. Thrale, ?September 1783, 21 February 1784); Rowson, *Charlotte Temple*, p. 60; Montagu to Elizabeth Vesey, [25] July 1784 (in Myers, "Breaking Away"); Piozzi 1850, p. 164 (20 January 1785). Johnson's letter is *LSJ* 972. For a characteristic sexual sneer see Pigott, *Female Jockey Club*, p. 171.

CHAPTER TWO

1. *Literary Memoirs*, 2:135, 139–40; Boaden, *Memoirs*, p. 2; Piozzi MS Ry. 590.445, 10 May 1820.

2. Wimsatt, "Images," pp. 363–65; *LC*, 28–30 March 1786; Spacks, "Scrapbook," p. 227. See Scott, *Bluestocking Ladies*, pp. 95–121.

3. Frye, *Anatomy*, p. 18.

4. Scott, *Advocate*, p. vii; *T*, p. 748. The bibliography is in preparation by Sarah English, Rebecca Gibson, and Judith Stanton. In a progress report Prof. English states, "it . . . seems clear that more British women were publishing during the eighteenth century than anyone has any idea of. Their work has simply been lost to modern scholarship" ("The Project Up till Now").

5. Finch, *Poems*, p. 100; *Critical Review* (1801), p. 28; *LC*, 28–30 March 1786.

6. Finch, *Poems*, pp. 4–5; Cowley, *Works*, 3:9; *T*, p. 704; Piozzi MS M M P, f33r. See Rogers, *Feminism*, pp. 97–103.

7. *Monthly Review*, pp. 241–43, 371; *T*, p. 905.

8. Raleigh, "J Without B," p. 49.

9. Piozzi MS Ry. 618, 1:f13v; Piozzi 1932b, pp. 203, 199; Piozzi 1785, p. 44; Piozzi 1932b, p. 206. Her prologue to *The Royal Suppliants* appeared in *GM*, 51 (1781):134.

10. Piozzi 1801, 2:118–19. See Hume, *History*, 4:306; her literary quarrel with Hume is treated below, pp. 247–49.

11. *T*, p. 445; Piozzi 1861, 2:44; *T*, p. 813n; HLP to H. M. Thrale, 22 August 1793 (in Clifford, p. 368); *Literary Memoirs*, 2:137.

12. Pigott, *Female Jockey Club*, pp. 172–73; *Literary Memoirs*, 2:140; Brownley, "Publishing Career."

13. Murphy, "Essay," p. 356; More to her sister, n.d. April 1786 (Roberts, *Memoirs*, 1:237). See *EM*, 10 (July 1786):5–6.

14. Piozzi MS Ry. 634, ff1, 20r. For her earnings see Clifford, pp. 264n, 295. The two popular letters are treated below, pp. 000–00; for American reprints see Clifford, p. 320n. Her epilogue to *The Regent* was printed: *LC* and *World*, 5 April 1788; also Greatheed, *The Regent* (London, 1788), pp. 74–75. Her prologue for Exmouth appeared in *LC*, 25–27 September 1788; her epilogue for Dover in *PA*, 16 February 1789. See also *T*, pp. 693, 722–23.

15. Pigott, *Female Jockey Club*, p. 172; Smith, *Sketch of a Tour*, 3:276–77. See Clifford, pp. 341–42.

16. *T*, p. 866n. The dictionary is *Literary Memoirs*; the magazine is *Monthly Mirror*. The Siddons epilogue appeared in *EM*, 31 (May 1797):343.

17. See Gilbert and Gubar, *Madwoman*, pp. 47–51.

18. Johnson, *Lives*, 1:21; *T*, pp. 806, 1002; Piozzi 1861, 2:158–59; Piozzi 1801, 1:345. For Cowley and Davenant see McCarthy, "Davenant's Prefatory Rhetoric."

19. Piozzi 1789, p. 88.

20. *Comparison between the Two Stages*, p. 17; *T*, p. 402. See Gilbert and Gubar, *Madwoman*, p. 49.

21. Piozzi 1801, 2:227, 113.

22. *T*, pp. 797, 1000n, 748; Piozzi MS P P, 16 May 1800. See *T*, pp. 330–31. For Carter's earnings see Halsband, "Ladies of Letters"; for HLP's elegy on Carter see below, p. 252. HLP sent her attack on Hayley to a newspaper (*T*, p. 796); I have not traced it. For her denial of JB see Piozzi 1786, p. 161.

23. Chapone to W. W. Pepys, 24 August 1784 (in Clifford, p. 231).

24. Astell, *Reflections*, p. 172; Burney, *Diary*, 6:418; Piozzi 1798b, pp. 20, 16. On the dread of being monstrous see Gilbert and Gubar, *Madwoman*, pp. 29–36.

25. Barbauld, *Works*, 1:xix; Williamson, "Who's Afraid of Mrs. Barbauld?" p. 91; More, *Strictures*, 1:7; More to Walpole, 27 July 1789 (Roberts, *Memoirs*, 1:316). For More's earnings see Halsband, "Ladies of Letters."

26. *QL*, p. 109 (Burney to H. M. Thrale, 28 July 1785); Piozzi MS H P, 3:126.

27. Piozzi 1861, 2:257 (to Robert Gray, 2 December 1801), 323 (to Sir James Fellowes, 16 January 1816), 268–69 (to Gray, 13 November 1811).

28. Piozzi 1936, p. 129; Piozzi 1934, pp. 39–40.

29. Piozzi MS M M P, f53r; Piozzi 1801, 2:167, 59.

30. Piozzi 1801, 2:374–75; Piozzi 1794, 1:296.

31. Johnson, *Works*, 7:62; *T*, pp. 766, 248; Boswell, *Life*, 2:49; Piozzi MS H P, 5:f6r; Piozzi MS Mangin, 12 December 1817; HLP to Daniel Lysons, 10 December 1798 (in Bloom et al., "Portrait," p. 334). See also Piozzi 1794, 2:301.

32. Wollstonecraft, *Rights of Woman*, p. 183; Piozzi MS P P, n.d. August 1801. See Ry. 612.

33. Johnson, *Prose*, p. 366.

34. *T*, p. 799; Piozzi 1798b, p. 25; Piozzi MS Mangin, 25 August 1819.

35. Piozzi MS H P, 5:f2or; Piozzi 1861, 2:390 (to Fellowes, 23 January 1818); Mangin, *Piozziana*, p. 89. For her reading *Werther* see *QL*, p. 243. See also Goethe, *Conversations*, p. 81.

36. *T*, pp. 1097–98; Piozzi MS N C P B, f23v.

CHAPTER THREE

1. Pennington, "Death of Mrs. P."

2. Boswell, *Life*, 2:26; Tyers, "Sketch," pp. 72–73. The poem was reprinted often: *A Collection of Poems*, ed. George Pearch (1770, 1775, 1783); *Lady's Poetical Magazine*, 1 (1781):82–85; *The Three Warnings* (Kidderminster, 1792); *British Poetical Miscellany*, 2 (Huddersfield, 1797):5–8; and in several nineteenth-century anthologies as late as 1883 (*English Poetesses*, ed. E. S.

Robertson). Clifford (p. 61n) cites a chapbook, *Abbas and Mirza . . . to which is added the Three Warnings* (Chelmsford, n.d.). Public readings were given in 1780, 1784, and 1795 (Clifford, p. 61n; *T*, p. 592).

3. Reprints appeared in *EM*, 9 (1786):121–22, 203–4, 286, 362–63; *GM*, 56 (1786):699, and 57 (1787):3, 257–58; *LC*, 30 May–1 June, 22–24 August, 7–10 October 1786, and 14–16 February 1788; *World*, 5 and 11 February 1788.

4. Piozzi MS H P, 1:80–81. See Clifford, p. 458.

5. Browning, in Gilbert and Gubar, *Madwoman*, p. 539. See also ibid., p. 541.

6. Piozzi MS H P, 1:24, 1–2; Spacks, "Scrapbook," p. 228; *T*, pp. 402, 730. In Gilbert and Gubar see, e.g., pp. 3, 6, 9, 541–42.

7. *T*, pp. 778–79.

8. *T*, pp. 265–66, 242–43.

9. *T*, p. 9; *LSJ* 269; *T*, p. 223; Piozzi 1861, 2:80. The poem she thus introduces is a rondeau on the name *Burney*.

10. Johnson, *Works*, 6:292–93; *T*, p. 1040; Piozzi 1786, p. 115.

11. For these poems see *T*, pp. 74–77, 114, 626–27, 1048, 953, 972.

12. *T*, p. 1042; Sutherland, *Preface*, p. 162.

13. Spacks, "Scrapbook," p. 238n; Piozzi MS H P, 2:123–24. See Clifford, pp. 329–30.

14. *T*, pp. 1053, 55, 351.

15. Piozzi 1769; *T*, pp. 887–88.

16. Piozzi 1766. See Piozzi MS Ry. 624, f10v.

17. Piozzi 1786, pp. 85–86.

18. Piozzi 1788, 2:416; Johnson, *Works*, 6:314; Piozzi 1788, 2:417; Johnson, *Prose*, pp. 316–17.

19. Johnson, "The Fountains," pp. 137, 141; Piozzi 1788, 2:233. See also Clifford, p. 63.

20. *T*, pp. 752–53.

21. *T*, p. 836; Piozzi MS H P, 3:5, 6, 12, 8.

22. Piozzi MS H P, 3:15; *T*, p. 492; Piozzi MS Ry. 587.184, 14 May 1813.

23. Piozzi MS H P, 3:34, 42, 48; Piozzi MS Ry. 533.1.

24. Woolf, "Professions," pp. 236–38.

25. *T*, p. 651; Piozzi 1789, pp. 226, 228.

26. *T*, pp. 1058–59.

27. Bloom, *Map*, p. 96.

28. *T*, pp. 1085–87.

29. Piozzi MS H P, 4:ff51v–52r; Wordsworth, *Poetical Works*, p. 462.

30. Piozzi MS H P, 3:118, 4:f55r, 3:133.

31. Piozzi MS P P, 30 January 1820. Dated from N C P B, f57v. For "Moral Stanzas" see p. 15 above.

32. See Marshall, *Italy in English Literature*, pp. 173–80; Bostetter, "The

Original Della Cruscans"; and Hargreaves-Mawdsley, *The English Della Cruscans*, pp. 56–61, 97.

33. Piozzi 1850, p. 310 (27 July 1785); Piozzi 1785, p. 5; Piozzi MS H P, 2:52–53. See Bostetter, above. For the printing of the *Miscellany* see Clifford, p. 252.

34. Piozzi MS P P, 15 October 1791; Piozzi 1850, p. 621.

35. Piozzi MS H P, 5:f26r. For her dinner with Gifford see Mangin, *Piozziana*, p. 4.

CHAPTER FOUR

1. Johnson, *Works*, 3:79–80 (*Rambler* 14); Piozzi MS H P, 4:f28r.

2. *T*, p. 385. See Collins, "B's Contact with J."

3. Piozzi 1786, p. 141. For Greene's critique of the *Life*, see "'Tis a Pretty Book."

4. Clifford and Greene, *S J*, p. 16; Piozzi 1786, p. 156. See Balderston, "J's Vile Melancholy." For various responses see Greene, *S J*, p. 33; Wain, *S J*, pp. 287–91; Irwin, *S J*, chapter 3; and Bate, *S J*, pp. 384–89. In the following pages I concur generally with Irwin and Bate.

5. Johnson, *Works*, 1:140; *LSJ* 307.1 (my translation); *T*, pp. 386, 415.

6. Piozzi 1786, p. 86.

7. *LSJ* 350, 657; Burney, *Diary*, 1:128. See also *LSJ* 547 and *T*, p. 375n. For the French letter see Bate, *S J*, pp. 439–41.

8. Piozzi 1786, pp. 119–20; Boswell, *Life*, 4:282; *LSJ* 78; Burney, *Diary*, 2:171.

9. *LSJ* 287, 311.1a, 376, 311.1, 403a; Piozzi MS Conway.

10. Piozzi 1786, pp. 86–87.

11. *T*, p. 418; Reynolds, "Recollections," p. 272; Seward, in Broadley, *Dr. J and Mrs. T*, pp. 19–20, 14n; Burney, *Diary*, 1:82; *T*, p. 149; Seward to Wm. Hayley, 6 October 1787 (in Piozzi 1861, 1:255); Piozzi 1932b, p. 143. For chemistry see *T*, p. 174.

12. *T*, pp. 813n, 528; Piozzi 1861, 1:250; *T*, p. 55. The psychoanalyst is Irwin, *S J*, p. 128. See also Piozzi 1786, p. 156.

13. *T*, p. 321; *LSJ* 703.1; Piozzi 1786, p. 150; Burney, *Diary*, 1:67–68; Reynolds, "Recollections," p. 273. See also Boswell, *Life*, 4:239, and Johnson, *Works*, 1:289.

14. Burney, *Diary*, 1:128–30.

15. Piozzi 1910, p. 219; Piozzi 1786, p. 101 (cf. *LSJ* 489a: Expecting a visit from SJ she warns him, "I can't sit up at Night now"); *T*, p. 459; Piozzi 1932a, p. 101.

16. Piozzi 1786, p. 120; *T*, p. 476.

17. *T*, p. 487; Piozzi 1861, 2:43.

18. Piozzi 1788, 2:268–72 (= *LSJ* 850); Boswell, *Hypochondriack*, 1:285. For the scenes at Brighton see Burney, *Diary*, 2:108–9, 122.

19. See Hyde, *The Impossible Friendship*, and Lustig, "B at Work."

20. Boswell, *Correspondence*, pp. 140, 142, 143; Piozzi 1786, p. 133.

21. Raleigh, "J Without B," p. 49.

22. Piozzi 1852, p. 136. For the 1768 fragments see *T*, pp. xxi, 601–2; the 1777 account is *T*, pp. 158–215. The "character" is *T*, pp. 205–8, and Piozzi 1786, pp. 159–60. For the composition of *Anecdotes* see *T*, pp. 625–26; Piozzi 1850, pp. 165–70; Piozzi 1852, p. 232; and Clifford, pp. 240–45, 255–57.

23. *T*, p. 867. For Labov see Pratt, *Speech Act Theory*, chapter 2.

24. Beattie, *Essays*, p. 373; Campbell, *Diary*, p. 46.

25. *T*, p. 185; Piozzi 1786, pp. 88–89 (my italics). See *T*, p. 180.

26. Piozzi 1786, p. 135. See *T*, pp. 260, 261.

27. Piozzi 1786, p. 148. See also pp. 140, 71, 134.

28. Walpole, *Correspondence*, 25:636.

29. Piozzi 1786, pp. 63–64, 69.

30. Quoted in Piozzi 1861, 1:288.

31. Piozzi 1786, p. 66. For Rousseau-SJ parallels see *T*, pp. 12, 172, 183n, 197–98, 203–4, 765–66.

32. Bronson, "Double," p. 165.

33. Piozzi 1786, pp. 94–95, 131–32; Greene, *Politics*, p. 66; Bate, *S J*, p. 211. See also Krutch, *S J*, p. 160.

34. Piozzi 1786, pp. 126, 111.

35. See Bate, *Achievement*, pp. 68ff.

36. *T*, p. 466. See also Piozzi 1786, p. 120.

37. *T*, pp. 785, 421–22; Smith, *Theory*, p. 312; *T*, p. 1066; Piozzi MS Ry. 635, p. 17; *T*, p. 784; Piozzi 1794, 2:169.

38. Piozzi 1786, pp. 120, 90; Boswell, *Life*, 3:292. See Bate, *Achievement*, pp. 150ff.

39. Johnson, *Lives*, 2:207. See Boswell, *Life*, 2:78.

40. Piozzi 1786, pp. 89–90.

41. Piozzi 1786, pp. 97, 150, 153–54; Boswell, *Life*, 5:211. Some of the words given to SJ in *Anecdotes* are spoken by a different person in *T*, p. 466n.

42. *T*, p. 900. For SJ's turning of Milton and Swift against themselves in the *Lives* see McCarthy, "The Moral Art of J's *Lives*."

43. Boswell, *Life*, 5:382; Piozzi 1932a, pp. 99–100. "Keppel" is Admiral K, court-martialed for "failing in duty" at the battle of Ushant, 27 July 1778.

44. Piozzi 1786, pp. 132, 67.

45. *QL*, p. 109 (Burney to H. M. Thrale, 28 July 1785); Beattie to Sir William Forbes, n.d. 1786 (in Clifford, p. 259); Piozzi 1786, p. 86.

46. Moses Tyson, in Piozzi 1932b, p. 42.

47. Piozzi 1786, pp. 152, 158, 107, 131, 159, 149, 101.

48. Boswell, *Journal*, p. 257.

49. Blair to JB, 4 May 1786 (in Boswell, *Correspondence*, p. 154); Piozzi 1786, p. 125; Boswell, *Life*, 4:191; Bate, *Achievement*, p. 3; Johnson, *Works*, 3:78–79.

CHAPTER FIVE

1. *English Review*, May 1788 (in Clifford, p. 315).

2. Piozzi 1850, p. 170 (30 April 1785). Chapman tallies 369 letters from SJ to HLT and estimates about 50 more to her family (*LSJ*, 3:301, 297). His total count of SJ's letters is 1515. In this chapter I am much indebted to Chapman's edition.

3. JB to Thomas Percy, 9 February 1788, and Malone to JB, 8 March 1788 (Boswell, *Correspondence*, pp. 265, 272–73).

4. Burney, *Diary*, 3:366; More to her sister, n.d. 1788 (Roberts, *Memoirs*, 1:282–83); Sprat, "Account," p. 137; *T*, p. 704.

5. Mason, *Poems*, p. 6; Boswell, *Life*, 3:419, 436, 4:240. See *LSJ* 1004, with Chapman's note.

6. Mason, *Poems*, pp. 15n, 29n; *LSJ* 189. "Perhaps the best criterion . . . [of what to omit from a letter] is 'Would the author, in publishing, have left it out or not?'" (Saintsbury, *Letter Book*, p. 59).

7. *LSJ*, 1:xv; Piozzi 1788, 1:ii. She corresponds with Lysons about the edition in 1850, pp. 540–42. My count of 92 omitted letters is based on a comparison of Piozzi 1788 with *LSJ* and with Hyde, "'Not in Chapman.'"

8. Piozzi 1788, 1:iii. HLP made one really reprehensible change: the concealment of a paragraph in one letter by substituting for it a paragraph from another letter (Piozzi 1788 No. 114, = *LSJ* 408).

9. See, e.g., Moses Tyson in Piozzi 1932b, p. 49, and Clifford, pp. 317–19.

10. Anderson, *Life*, pp. 545–46; Piozzi 1788, 1:295 (= *LSJ* 428); Seccombe, in Broadley, *Dr. J and Mrs. T*, p. 46.

11. Piozzi 1788, 2:325–26, 100–101, 15 (= *LSJ* 900, 657, 559).

12. Ibid., 1:5, 2:376 (= *LSJ* 191, 972).

13. Ibid., 1:295 (= *LSJ* 428).

14. Piozzi 1786, p. 87; Piozzi 1788, 1:187. For her treatment of her own letters see Clifford, pp. 299–301.

15. *LC*, 1–3 April 1788; Piozzi 1788, 1:247–51.

16. Piozzi 1788, 1:96–101.

17. Wollstonecraft, *Rights of Woman*, pp. 102–3.

18. *T*, p. 496; Piozzi 1788, 1:82 (= *LSJ* 308); Burney to HLT, 14 February 1781 (in *T*, p. 496n); Seccombe, in Broadley, *Dr. J and Mrs. T*, p. 43; Johnson, *Letters of Mrs. T*, pp. 5–6.

19. Piozzi 1861, 2:276 (to the Williams family). See *T*, p. 972n, and Piozzi 1801, 2:511.

20. Piozzi MS P P, 1 August 1798; Pennington to M. Brown, 3 December 1821 (in Piozzi 1914, p. 373); Piozzi 1863, 2:343 (28 March 1811); Piozzi 1861, 2:280 (to the Williams family); Piozzi 1863, 2:396 (8 April 1815); Piozzi 1861, 2:419 (to Fellowes, 12 January 1819).

21. Piozzi MS Ry. 560.59 (18 September 1797); Piozzi MS Mangin, 25 August 1819, 9 July 1818.

22. *QL*, pp. 175, 193; Piozzi MS Ry. 546.14 (25 September 1788).

23. Piozzi MS Ry. 585.76 (4 October 1810).

CHAPTER SIX

1. Bloom, *Poetry*, pp. 123–24.

2. *T*, p. 717; Piozzi 1932b, p. 206; Piozzi MS Ry. 546.8 (11 August 1788). For the composition of *Observations* see *T*, p. 719; the draft is Ry. 619. Notes added at the end of Ry. 618 cite other travel writers; in a letter to L. Chappelow (Ry. 559.8, 28 June 1788) she requests botanical information about Italy. Between the MS sent to press (Ry. 620–22) and the printed text there are verbal variants.

3. Johnson, *Works*, 2:299, 300. See Batten, *Pleasurable Instruction*, pp. 91–96.

4. See Fussell, "Patrick Brydone."

5. Piozzi MS Ry. 618, 1:f41v; Piozzi 1789, pp. 147, 416.

6. Sharp, *Letters*, pp. 124–25.

7. Smollett, *Travels*, p. 56; Swift, *Gulliver's Travels*, pp. 514–15; Smollett, *Travels*, pp. 259–60.

8. Cole, *Journal*, pp. 45, 51; Swift, *Gulliver's Travels*, p. 242.

9. Boswell, *Life*, 3:236; Johnson, *Works*, 1:206; Piozzi 1932b, p. 117; Johnson, *Works*, 1:233.

10. Piozzi 1788, 1:139–40, 107, 120 (= *LSJ* 326, 318, 323).

11. Batten, *Pleasurable Instruction*, p. 74; Smollett, *Travels*, p. 60.

12. *T*, pp. 635–37.

13. *T*, pp. 638–40; Piozzi MS Ry. 618, 2:f103r.

14. Brownell, "H L P's Marginalia," p. 97; Smollett, *Travels*, pp. 294, 268, 242, 199. See Piozzi MS Conway.

15. Piozzi 1789, pp. 1, 2.

16. Ibid., pp. 38, 46, 52.

17. Ibid., pp. 92, 93.

18. Addison, *Remarks*, p. 162; Piozzi 1789, pp. 122–23.

19. Piozzi 1789, pp. 149, 331, 351–52.

20. Ibid., p. 137. See Fussell, *Abroad*, chapter 1.

21. *T*, p. 190.

22. Piozzi 1789, p. 148; Piozzi 1786, p. 150. For Batten, see note 11

above. For SJ's struggle to be pleased, see above, p. 105 and note 13, and Bate, *S J*, pp. 497–99.

23. Smollett, *Travels*, p. 202; Piozzi 1789, pp. 3, 4.

24. Piozzi 1789, pp. 11, 15–16.

25. Ibid., pp. 17, 20; Johnson, *Lives*, 1:178; Johnson, *Rasselas*, p. 113.

26. Piozzi 1789, pp. 23, 24, 25.

27. Ibid., p. 28; Smollett, *Travels*, pp. 294–95 (italics mine).

28. Piozzi 1789, p. 29.

29. Ibid., p. 35.

30. Ibid., p. 42.

31. Ibid., pp. 89–90.

32. Ibid., pp. 141, 168, 169, 171, 172.

33. Ibid., pp. 183–86.

34. Ibid., pp. 188, 189, 191, 192.

35. Ibid., pp. 196, 211, 212, 220.

36. Ibid., pp. 223–24.

37. Ibid., pp. 231, 235, 251, 254, 255, 257, 265.

38. Ibid., pp. 286, 280.

39. Ibid., pp. 281, 289, 290.

40. Ibid., p. 300; Moore, *View*, p. 165.

41. Piozzi 1789, pp. 303, 304, 305.

42. Ibid., pp. 310, 332, 333, 335.

43. Ibid., pp. 356, 284.

44. Ibid., p. 414.

CHAPTER SEVEN

1. Piozzi 1794, 1:317; Gilbert and Gubar, *Madwoman*, pp. 30–31.

2. *T*, pp. 729, 836. "I cannot imagine why I should not write a Comedy . . . but as I have not a Spark of Originality about me, I must take a French Model—it shall be *L'Homme Singulier*" (by Philippe Néricault Destouches; *T*, pp. 386–87, May 1779). She apparently did so: Ry. 650 is "The Humourist. A Comedy" (Act I only), in her hand; a slip pasted in identifies it as "Des Touches's Humourist." The first idea for "The Two Fountains" is *T*, p. 731; for its composition see pp. 752–53. For Kemble's reading it see *T*, pp. 771, 772, 820–21, 829.

3. Piozzi MS Ry. 546.19 (11 July 1789); *T*, p. 751. For her Scotch journal see Reynolds, "Mrs. P's 'Scotch Journey.'" Evidence of her reception in Scotland includes unsigned verses "To Mrs Piozzi on Her Visit to Scotland" (Ry. 656.54); they complain of SJ's treatment and express confidence that HLP will "bestow the praises due."

4. "The Adventurer" is Ry. 651–52: two drafts, one (651) in a different

hand with occasional alterations in HLP's hand, the other (652) in her hand throughout. (A draft of part of act 2, in her hand, is Ry. 629.71.) No indication of date or origin.

5. *T*, p. 813; Mason, *Poems*, p. 183n.

6. *T*, pp. 831, 837.

7. *T*, pp. 837–38.

8. For "usurper" see above, p. 45. For Whately see Egan, "English Synonymy," p. xiv. In this chapter I am much indebted to Egan, and also to Noyes, "Synonyms in England."

9. Piozzi 1794, 1:ii, iv, v, vi.

10. *EM*, 25 (May 1794):361; *British Critic* (1794), pp. 508–9.

11. *Critical Review* (1794), p. 121; *British Critic* (1794), p. xix.

12. HLP to H. M. Thrale, 22 August 1793 (in Clifford, p. 368); Piozzi 1789, p. 410.

13. See Emblen, *Roget*, p. 263. The rumor is mentioned and denied by HLP (*T*, p. 905); the *Monthly Review* also mentioned and dismissed it (p. 243), as does Clifford, p. 372.

14. *LSJ* 742a; Piozzi 1914, pp. 136–37; *T*, p. 144.

15. Egan, "English Synonymy," p. viii; Girard, *Synonymes*, pp. 392–93; Piozzi 1794, 1:2–3; *Webster's*, p. 1. Translation of Girard:

> *Abandonner* [abandon, desert, neglect] is said of things and of persons. *Délaisser* [forsake, abandon, neglect] is said only of persons. We *abandon* things for which we have no use. We *neglect* the unfortunates to whom we give no assistance.
>
> *Abandonner* is more frequently used than *délaisser*. The former is equally correct in the active and the passive. The latter has more grace as a participle than in other modes; & it has by itself a total force that can be given the former only by joining it with some term that precisely delimits it. Thus one says, He is a poor forsaken one, he is generally neglected by everybody. . . .
>
> Often our families *abandon* us sooner than our friends do. God sometimes permits us to be forsaken by men in order that we may be obliged to seek Him.

16. Piozzi 1794, 1:23; *Webster's*, p. 89; Piozzi 1794, 1:265–66, 347.

17. Piozzi 1794, 2:37, 1:131, 2:244–45.

18. Piozzi 1794, 1:92–93; Fowler, *Dictionary*, p. 77.

19. Fowler, *Dictionary*, pp. 112–13.

20. Piozzi 1794, 1:54, 2:254.

21. Crabb, *English Synonymes*, p. [ii]; Trench, *Study*, p. 30.

22. Piozzi 1794, 2:80–81.

23. Trench, *Study*, p. 138.

24. Piozzi MS P P, 13 June 1800.

25. Gifford, *Maeviad*, pp. v–vi; Walpole, *Correspondence*, 42:244, 11:21; Seward to HLP, 31 December 1789 (in Clifford, p. 344).
26. *EM*, in Clifford, p. 344; *Athenaeum*, p. 113; Pottle and Bennett, "B and Mrs. P," p. 422.
27. *Monthly Mirror*, p. 138; Wollstonecraft, *Rights of Woman*, p. 102; *British Critic* (1802), p. 355; *Anti-Jacobin Review*, p. 242.
28. Lakoff, *Language*, pp. 12, 15n, 53–54, 7, 6.
29. See Hiatt, *Way*, p. 113.
30. Baretti, *Journey*, 1:231; Piozzi 1801, 1:39; *EM* 39 (1801):188, 189; *QL*, p. 255.
31. Gregory, *Legacy*, pp. 31–32; Pennington, "Death of Mrs. P"; Mangin, *Piozziana*, p. 6; Boaden, *Memoirs*, p. 2.
32. Hiatt, *Way*, p. 77; *T*, p. 726.
33. More, *Strictures*, 1:134, 155.
34. *T*, p. 622; Piozzi 1801, 2:301–2.
35. Piozzi 1863, 2:369.
36. *QL*, p. 138; Piozzi 1794, 2:139; Piozzi 1786, p. 118; Piozzi MS P P, 19 September 1794.
37. Piozzi 1801, 1:17n, 2:198, 199.
38. Piozzi 1863, 1:9.
39. Fowler, *Dictionary*, p. 545.
40. Piozzi MS Ry. 559.24 (22 December 1794).
41. *Anti-Jacobin Review*, p. 241.
42. Piozzi 1801, 2:99, 1:376, 277.
43. Piozzi 1794, 2:202; Piozzi MS Ry. 635, p. 19.
44. Klingel, "Reform, Revolution and the Regency"; Piozzi 1794, 2:374.
45. Piozzi 1801, 1:200.

CHAPTER EIGHT

1. Wollstonecraft, *Rights of Woman*, pp. 147–48.
2. Piozzi 1850, p. 170; to Miss Williams, n.d. (in Clifford, "Mrs. P's Letters," p. 164); *T*, p. 241.
3. See Clifford, pp. 360–61, 395–96. For Macaulay see Boos and Boos, "Catharine Macaulay"; for HLT on Macaulay see *T*, p. 123n.
4. Piozzi 1762b; Piozzi 1801, 2:389; Piozzi 1762b; *T*, pp. 241, 423; Piozzi 1801, 2:427. My background for this chapter is chiefly Watson, *Reign of George III*.
5. Piozzi 1768; *LSJ* 556a; Piozzi 1798b, p. 13; Piozzi 1769; *T*, p. 317.
6. See Namier, *Personalities*, pp. 59–64.
7. Piozzi 1798b, p. 1; Piozzi 1801, 2:423–24.
8. Piozzi 1801, 1:39, 229, 415, 2:40, 1:359.

9. Paine, *Rights*, p. 448; Piozzi 1789, p. 19; Piozzi 1801, 2:406.

10. Piozzi 1789, p. 291.

11. Namier, *Personalities*, p. 19 (quoting Hume, *Essays Moral, Political, and Literary*, 1742); Piozzi 1798b, p. 5; Piozzi 1794, 2:136; Piozzi 1789, p. 14.

12. *T*, p. 722; Piozzi MS Ry. 635, pp. 55–56.

13. Swift, *Gulliver's Travels*, p. 430; *QL*, p. 173; Swift, p. 434; *T*, pp. 637–38; Piozzi MS Ry. 634, f2or.

14. Piozzi 1794, 1:98–99.

15. *T*, pp. 744, 864, 875; Piozzi MS P P, 13 June 1795; *T*, p. 897; Piozzi 1914, p. 100 (4 November 1793).

16. Piozzi MS P P, n.d. April 1800; Piozzi 1794, 2:165–66.

17. Piozzi MS Ry. 587.227 (11 June 1814); *T*, pp. 947n, 813n.

18. *T*, pp. 997, 842, 909, 919, 938.

19. *T*, p. 997; Piozzi MS P P, 21 August 1799; Piozzi MS Ry. 560.101 (19 September 1800).

20. *T*, p. 1016.

21. Piozzi 1801, 2:36, 394; Piozzi 1794, 2:368; Piozzi 1798b, pp. 21, 10. For Spanish conquest see Piozzi 1801, 2:120–21.

22. Piozzi 1798b, p. 4; Piozzi MS Ry. 635, pp. 34–35.

23. Piozzi 1794, 2:154–55; Piozzi 1801, 1:409.

24. Shaftesbury, *Characteristics*, p. 44; Piozzi 1794, 2:226, 1:144; Piozzi 1801, 2:317; *T*, p. 912.

25. *T*, pp. 713–14; Piozzi MS Ry. 635, pp. 47–48; Piozzi 1794, 1:193.

26. *T*, pp. 722, 744; Piozzi 1850, pp. 626–27; *T*, p. 980; Piozzi MS Ry. 559.55 (3 July 1797). See *T*, p. 966. In addition to Watson, *Reign of George III*, in this and the next paragraph I follow Lefebvre, *Napoleon*, and Ross, *European Diplomatic History*.

27. Piozzi MS P P, [8] December 1800, 30 November 1801; *T*, p. 1043.

28. *T*, p. 1093n.

29. Piozzi MS H P, 1:102; *T*, pp. 241, 753.

30. *T*, pp. 788, 792, 475–76.

31. Piozzi MS Ry. 635, pp. 68–70, 130; Paine, *Rights*, p. 488. Paine is often named in "Una" as the antagonist to be refuted.

32. *T*, p. 837; HLP to H. M. Thrale, n.d. March 1796 (in Clifford, "Mrs. P's Letters," p. 165); Piozzi 1801, 2:508, quoting Hannah More.

33. Paine, *Rights*, p. 288; Burke, *Reflections*, p. 91; Piozzi 1801, 2:447–48. See also Wollstonecraft, *Rights of Man*, pp. 26–27.

34. Piozzi 1798b, p. 36; Piozzi MS Ry. 647.37r; Piozzi 1914, p. 101 (2 December 1793); *T*, p. 898 (c. 1 November 1794); Piozzi 1798a. For other patriotic songs by HLP see Piozzi 1850, pp. 75–76 ("A Loyal Ballad," also in *T*, p. 753), and *T*, pp. 901–2, 1026–27. There are others, not traced: "I sent a Sheet to the Crown & Anchor for Distribution this Morning, a 3^dy Touch; but you shall not be told till you find out which is mine" (Piozzi MS P P, 7 February 1793); "earnest to shew my Zeal & write a Ballad for the Welsh

here to sing at ye Balloting Houses; I made 5 Stanzas. . . . I will print a . . . Copy" (*T*, pp. 1040–41, 25 July 1803).

35. Piozzi MS Ry. 641, f1; HLP to H. M. Thrale, 21 June 1805 (in *T*, p. 1065n). The "Address" is undated except by reference to the first French invasion of Italy "three Years ago" (Piozzi MS Ry. 629.19, f2v); that, if accurate, dates it to 1799. I find no evidence of publication. Invasions of England were particularly expected in June 1798 and the summer of 1801, and between July 1803 and February 1804. The Dumouriez translation was written in September 1803 (Clifford, p. 416); informed that an English translation had already appeared (in 1798), HLP laid hers aside. On invasion threats and defence see Glover, *Britain at Bay.*

36. Piozzi 1914, p. 94 (19 July 1793); Piozzi MS P P, [29] April 1798; *T*, p. 986.

37. Clifford, p. 397. See Pendleton, "English Pamphlet Literature," pp. 30, 32, 34.

38. Ibid., p. 31.

39. Piozzi 1798b, pp. 4, 7, 25, 21.

40. Wollstonecraft, *Rights of Woman*, p. 147; Piozzi MS Ry. 629.19, f1.

41. Wollstonecraft, *Rights of Woman*, p. 33; Piozzi 1798b, p. 17.

42. *T*, p. 800.

43. *T*, p. 873; Baretti, in Clifford, p. 134; *T*, p. 776.

44. *T*, p. 744.

45. *T*, pp. 854, 860, 880–81, 883.

46. Piozzi 1794, 2:129, 413–15. She quotes Barbauld's "Address to the Opposers of the Repeal of the Corporation and Test Acts" (1790); the original is in Barbauld, *Works*, 2:371.

47. HLP to H. M. Thrale (in Clifford, p. 379); *T*, pp. 951–52, 1005; Piozzi MS Ry. 560.99 (7 July 1800); HLP to H. M. Thrale (in Clifford, p. 393); Piozzi MS M M P, f33r (for an extract of that "review" see above, p. 44).

48. Gilbert and Gubar, *Madwoman*, p. 72; *British Critic* (1802), p. 355; Piozzi 1801, 2:396, 363.

49. See Clifford, p. 394. HLP states her hope that the book will be used in schools in Ry. 560.98 (30 June 1800).

50. *Critical Review* (1801), pp. 28–29; Piozzi MS H P, 3:60; Piozzi 1801, 2:499, 1:244.

51. *British Critic* (1802), p. 357, quoting Piozzi 1801, 1:80.

52. Piozzi 1801, 1:101.

53. Piozzi 1798b, p. 14; HLP to H. M. Thrale, 23 March 1796 (in Clifford, p. 393).

54. Hume, *History*, 1:243; Piozzi 1801, 1:271, 274.

55. Piozzi 1801, 1:272, 273; Hume, *History*, 1:247; Gibbon, *Decline*, pp. 2049, 1652; Piozzi 1801, 1:273.

56. Piozzi 1801, 2:463, 523–24, 376; Butterfield, *History and Human Re-*

lations, p. 136; Butterfield, *Christianity,* p. 22.

    57. Piozzi 1801, 2:345.

    58. Ibid., 1:416.

    59. Ibid., 1:399, 430, 2:239, 402, 46.

    60. Ibid., 2:431–33.

    61. Ibid., 2:374, 1:381, 420, 450, 2:28, 149, 239.

    62. Ibid., 2:312, 351, 374–75, 376.

    63. Hume, *History,* 2:482.

    64. See Clifford, pp. 404–5.

    65. Gilbert and Gubar, *Madwoman,* p. 3.

CHAPTER NINE

    1. Piozzi 1861, 2:321 (to Fellowes, 16 January 1816); *T,* p. 840 (1 June 1792).

    2. *QL,* p. 256 (30 September 1801); Piozzi MS Ry. 560.111 (18 June 1801); Piozzi MS P P, 30 August 1802; Piozzi MS Ry. 533.29 (to ?John Perkins, 9 October 1811); *T,* p. 1071n. She complained against the *Critical Review* in *GM,* 71 (1801):602–3. The Carter elegy was printed (unsigned) in *SJC,* 4–6 March 1806; it is claimed by her in Piozzi MS H P, 3:90.

    3. *T,* p. 1080n. "The Mysterious Bride," with her epilogue, was performed at Drury Lane Theatre, 1 June 1808 (*SJC,* 31 May–2 June); for the epilogue see *T,* pp. 1092–93. For the prologue to "Friends and Enemies" see Clifford, p. 416, and *T,* pp. 1050–51. She mentions Milman's request in a letter to Mangin, 12 December 1817; see also Piozzi 1932b, p. 40. She tried to sell "Lyford" through Mangin in March 1815 (Piozzi MS N C P B, f43r).

    4. Didion, "Why I Write," p. 17; Dr. James Currie to F. Trench, 1 September 1789 (in Clifford, "Mrs. P's Letters," p. 157). The argument is made in Brownley, "Publishing Career."

    5. Piozzi MS H P, 5:f7v, 4:f21v. "Poems on several Occasions," "Piozziana," and "Scrap & Trifle Book" are Piozzi MS H P 1–3, 4, and 5 respectively; the pocket diary is Ry. 616. The untitled miscellany of 223 poems is dated from the occasion of its latest poem, the funeral of Princess Charlotte (7 November 1817); the "Collection" is dated also from its latest poem. Both are in a private collection.

    6. Piozzi MS H P, 1:[1], 3:129, 133, 5:f26r (2 May 1814); Piozzi MS Ly R, 2:[1].

    7. Piozzi 1938, 2:105n; HLP to H. M. Thrale, 19 March 1799 (in Clifford, p. 414); Piozzi, diary, 21 April 1809 (in Clifford, p. 426).

    8. Piozzi 1977, p. 173; *QL,* p. xxiii (H. M. Thrale to F. Burney, n.d. 1813); *T,* p. 744.

    9. *QL,* pp. 145, 210–11.

10. Piozzi MS P P, 1 May and 13 June 1800. She quotes Piozzi 1794, 2:212–13.

11. *QL*, p. 253; Piozzi MS P P, 10 January 1798, 3 December 1803, 22 May 1801; HLP to W. M. Thackeray, 8 April 1809 (in Clifford, p. 424); *T*, p. 1099. The attack in 1791 is mentioned in Piozzi MS P P, 8 November 1791.

12. HLP to Lady Williams, 14 January 1799 (in Clifford, p. 392); Piozzi MS Ry. 585.2 (9 September 1807) and 14 (7 November 1808). See also *T*, p. 993.

13. Piozzi MS H P, 3:117.

14. Piozzi MS Conway; Piozzi MS Ry. 586.124 (3 November 1811); Piozzi MS Ry. 616.

15. Piozzi MS Conway; Piozzi MS Mangin, 15 March 1819, 7 October 1817 (her emphasis).

16. Piozzi MS Mangin, 4 September 1819.

17. Piozzi MS Fellowes, p. 32; Piozzi MS Conway.

18. Moore, diary, 28 April 1819 (in Piozzi 1861, 1:361); Bell, "Late View."

19. Ry. 656.20, 33.

20. HLP to Fellowes, 19 October 1815 (Princeton AM 17952, published with permission of Princeton University Library); Piozzi MS P P, 6 November 1819.

21. Piozzi MS Mangin, n.d. and 4 February 1818.

22. Piozzi MS P P, 29 October 1819; Piozzi MS Mangin, 13 November 1817; Piozzi 1862, p. 172 (n.d. October 1819).

23. Piozzi MS P P, 24 March 1820, 4 March 1821.

24. Clifford, p. 455.

25. Piozzi MS Ry. 616; Burney, *Diary*, 6:399–400.

26. *T*, pp. 386–87.

Sources

See also the list of abbreviations and short titles, p. 269 above.

PIOZZI, HESTER LYNCH: PUBLISHED WRITINGS

1762a "The Lamentation of Samoset, a Chief of the Oneydoes, over his Son, who fell in Battle. An Indian Fragment." (Unsigned.) *SJC*, 18–20 February 1762. (Identified by reference in *T*, p. 322, and fragmentary MS, Ry. 647.11.)

1762b (Letter concerning "Albion Manor," signed "Thomas _____.") *SJC*, 24 July 1762.

1763 "Imagination's Search after Happiness: An Allegorical Fable." (Unsigned.) *SJC*, 8–10 September 1763. (Also in *T*, pp. 351–53.)

1766 "The Three Warnings. A Tale." (Unsigned.) In Anna Williams, *Miscellanies in Prose and Verse*, pp. 74–80. London: Davies, 1766.

1768 (Epigram on John Wilkes, unsigned): "In proud _____'s Despight." *PA*, 20 July 1768.

1769 (Letter signed "Nurse Love-Child," and poem): "*A* was an Alderman." *PA*, 4 August 1769. (Also in *T*, pp. 122–23.)

1785 *The Florence Miscellany*. Florence: G. Cam, 1785. "Preface," pp. 5–6; "Translation" [of Ippolito Pindemonte, "Hymn of Calliope" from *Gibilterra Salvata*], pp. 19–23; "To W^m. Parsons Esqr.," pp. 43–44; "Imitation of the Foregoing Sonnet [by Giuseppi Parini] on an Air Balloon," p. 59; [Enigma] "Imitated," p. 60; [Arietta] "Imitated," p. 61; "Translation of an Italian Sonnet upon an English Watch," p. 62; "Song," pp. 92–93; "La Partenza," pp. 209–11; "Conclusion," p. 217.

1786 *Anecdotes of the Late Samuel Johnson, LL.D. during the Last Twenty Years of His Life*. Edited by Arthur Sherbo. London: Oxford University Press, 1974.

1788 *Letters to and from the Late Samuel Johnson, LL.D. to which are added some Poems never before printed*. 2 vols. London: Strahan and Cadell, 1788.

1789 *Observations and Reflections Made in the Course of a Journey through France, Italy, and Germany*. Edited by Herbert Barrows. Ann Arbor: University of Michigan Press, 1967.

1794   *British Synonymy; or, an Attempt at Regulating the Choice of Words in Familiar Conversation.* 2 vols. London: Robinson, 1794.

1798a "Extract of a private letter from Venice." (Unsigned.) *The True Briton,* 8 March 1798. (Acknowledged in Piozzi MS P P, 27 March 1798.)

1798b *Three Warnings to John Bull before He Dies. By an old Acquaintance of the Public.* London: Faulder, 1798.

1801   *Retrospection: or a Review of the most striking and important Events, Characters, Situations, and their Consequences, which the last eighteen hundred Years have presented to the View of Mankind.* 2 vols. London: Stockdale, 1801.

1850   (44 letters to Samuel Lysons, 1784–89.) *Bentley's Miscellany,* 28 (1850):73–82, 163–71, 307–15, 438–47, 535–43, 620–28.

1852   (9 letters to Thomas Cadell, 1785–88.) *GM,* n.s. 37 (1852): 135–37, 232–33.

1861   *Autobiography, Letters, and Literary Remains of Mrs. Piozzi (Thrale).* Edited by Abraham Hayward. 2d ed. 2 vols. London: Longman, 1861.

1862   "[14] Letters of Mrs. Piozzi to William Augustus Conway [1819–20]." *The Athenaeum,* no. 1815 (1862):169–72.

1863   35 letters to T. S. Whalley, 1784–1820. In *Journals and Correspondence of Thomas Sedgewick Whalley, D.D.,* edited by Hill Wickham. 2 vols. London: Bentley, 1863.

1910   Journal of her tour in Wales, 5 July–30 September 1774. In *Dr. Johnson and Mrs. Thrale,* edited by A. M. Broadley, pp. 158–219. London: John Lane, 1910.

1914   *The Intimate Letters of Hester Piozzi and Penelope Pennington, 1788–1821.* Edited by Oswald G. Knapp. London: John Lane, 1914.

1932a Zamick, M., ed. "Three Dialogues on the Death of Hester Lynch Thrale." *BJRL* 16 (1932):77–114.

1932b *The French Journals of Mrs. Thrale and Dr. Johnson.* Edited by Moses Tyson and Henry Guppy. Manchester: Manchester University Press, 1932.

1934   *Mrs. Piozzi and Isaac Watts: Being Annotations . . . of Mrs. Piozzi on a Copy of . . . the* Philosophical Essays *of Watts.* Edited by James P. R. Lyell. London: Grafton, 1934.

1936   (Marginalia in Nares, ΄ΕΙΣ ΘΕΟΣ, ΄ΕΙΣ ΜΕΣΙΤΗΣ, 1801.) Nicolson, Marjorie. "Thomas Paine, Edward Nares, and Mrs. Piozzi's Marginalia," *Huntington Library Bulletin* No. 10 (1936):103–33.

1938   (Marginalia in Boswell's *Life.*) Boswell, James. *The Life of Samuel Johnson, with marginal Comments and Markings from two Copies* annotated by Hester Lynch Thrale Piozzi. Edited by Edward G. Fletcher. 3 vols. 1938. Reprint. New York: Heritage Press, 1963.

1956   Allison, James. "Mrs. Thrale's Marginalia in Joseph Warton's *Essay.*" *Huntington Library Quarterly* 19 (1956):155–64.

1977   "The Children's Book or rather Family Book" (1766–78). In *The Thrales of Streatham Park*, edited by Mary Hyde, pp. 21–218. Cambridge: Harvard University Press, 1977.

PIOZZI, HESTER LYNCH: MS WRITINGS

Conway   Memoir and marginalia in a copy of *Observations* presented to W. A. Conway, 1819. Private collection, quoted by permission. (A printed text appears in *Atlantic Monthly* 7 [1861]: 614–23.)

Fellowes   Autobiography for Sir James Fellowes, December 1815. Princeton University Library AM 12475. (Published with permission of Princeton University Library.) (A printed text appears in Piozzi 1861, 2:6–30.)

H P   Harvard Piozziana. 5 vols. MS Eng. 1280, Houghton Library. (Quoted by permission of the Houghton Library.)

Ly R   "Lyford Redivivus or A Grandame's Garrulity." 2 vols. Private collection, quoted by permission.

Mangin   94 letters to Edward Mangin and family, 1816–20. Princeton University Library AM 14615. (Published with permission of Princeton University Library.)

M M P   "Minced Meat for Pyes." MS Eng. 231, Houghton Library. (Quoted by permission of the Houghton Library.)

N C P B   "New Common Place Book." Private collection, quoted by permission.

P P   Letters to Penelope Pennington, 1788–1804, 1819–21. 6 vols. Princeton University Library AM 14613. The letter of 7 February 1793 is AM 14675. (Published with permission of Princeton University Library.)

Ry. 533   Drafts of 41 letters to various persons, 1763–1818.

Ry. 536   Letters to H L S T P from various persons, c. 1762–1813.

Ry. 546   24 letters to Sophia Byron, 1787–89.

Ry. 559–61   165 letters to the Rev. Leonard Chappelow, 1786–1818.

Ry. 585–90   472 letters to John Salusbury Piozzi Salusbury, 1807–21.

Ry. 612   Catalogue of the books at Brynbella, 1806–13.

Ry. 616   Daily journals.

Ry. 618   Journal in France, Italy, and Germany, 1784–87. 2 vols. (The
          French portion is printed in Piozzi 1932b.)
Ry. 619–22   Drafts of *Observations and Reflections.*
Ry. 624   "Essay on Man a Translation from Racine. . . ."
Ry. 629   Miscellaneous prose fragments.
Ry. 634   Chapters on theological subjects. (Dated Milan, 13 August
          1786.)
Ry. 635   "Una & Duessa or a Set of Dialogues upon the most popular
          Subjects." "Begun in April & ended in July 1791."
Ry. 641   Translation, Charles-François Dumouriez, *Tableau Spéculatif de*
          l'Europe.
Ry. 646   "Select Manuscript Poems on Various Subjects and Several Oc-
          casions" (c. 1768)
Ry. 647   Drafts and fragments of poems, c. 1756–1820.
Ry. 650   "The Humourist. A comedy."
Ry. 651–52   "The Adventurer." A comedy in two acts.
Ry. 656   Miscellaneous poems. (Chiefly by other persons.)

OTHER SOURCES

Addison, Joseph. *Remarks on several Parts of Italy* (1705). In *Works*, edited by
    G. W. Greene, 2:131–375. Philadelphia: Lippincott, 1883.
Anderson, Robert. *The Life of Samuel Johnson.* 1815. Reprint. Hildesheim:
    Olms, 1973.
Anti-Jacobin Review 8 (1801):241–46. (Review of Piozzi 1801.)
Astell, Mary. *Some Reflections upon Marriage.* London, 1730.
Athenaeum, no. 1735 (1861):111–13. (Review of Piozzi 1861.)
Balderston, Katharine C. "Johnson's Vile Melancholy." In *The Age of Johnson*,
    edited by Frederick W. Hilles, pp. 3–14. New Haven: Yale University
    Press, 1949.
Barbauld, Anna L. *Works.* 2 vols. London, 1825.
Baretti, Joseph. *A Journey from London to Genoa.* . . . 3d ed. 4 vols. London,
    1770.
―――――. "Strictures on Signora Piozzi's Publication of Dr. Johnson's Letters."
    EM 13 (1788):313–17, 393–99; 14 (1788):89–99.
Barker, Jane. *A Patch-Work Screen for the Ladies.* 1723. Reprint. New York:
    Garland, 1973.
Bate, Walter Jackson. *The Achievement of Samuel Johnson.* New York: Oxford
    University Press, 1961.
―――――. *Samuel Johnson.* New York: Harcourt Brace, 1977.
Batten, Charles L., Jr. *Pleasurable Instruction: Form and Convention in Eigh-
    teenth-Century Travel Literature.* Berkeley: University of California Press,
    1978.

Beattie, James. *Essays on Poetry and Music*. London, 1776.

Bell, A. S. "A Late View of Mrs. Piozzi." *Notes & Queries*, n.s. 18 (1971):337–38.

Bloom, Edward A.; Bloom, Lillian D.; and Klingel, Joan E. "Portrait of a Georgian Lady: The Letters of Hester Lynch (Thrale) Piozzi, 1784–1821." *BJRL* 60 (1978):303–38.

Bloom, Harold. *The Anxiety of Influence*. New York: Oxford University Press, 1973.

———. *A Map of Misreading*. New York: Oxford University Press, 1975.

———. *Poetry and Repression*. New Haven: Yale University Press, 1976.

Boaden, James. *Memoirs of Mrs. Siddons*. Philadelphia, 1827.

Boos, Florence, and Boos, William. "Catharine Macaulay: Historian and Political Reformer." *International Journal of Women's Studies* 3 (1980):49–65.

Bostetter, Edward E. "The Original Della Cruscans and the Florence Miscellany." *Huntington Library Quarterly* 19 (1956):277–300.

Boswell, James. *Boswell, Laird of Auchinleck 1778–1782*. Edited by Joseph W. Reed and Frederick A. Pottle. New York: McGraw-Hill, 1977.

———. *Correspondence and other Papers relating to the Making of the* Life of Johnson. Edited by Marshall Waingrow. New York: McGraw-Hill, 1969.

———. *The Hypochondriack*. Edited by Margery Bailey. 2 vols. 1928. Reprint. New York: AMS Press, 1973.

———. *Journal of a Tour to the Hebrides with Samuel Johnson*. Edited by Frederick A. Pottle and Charles H. Bennett. 2d ed. New York: McGraw-Hill, 1961.

———. *The Life of Samuel Johnson*. Edited by G. B. Hill and L. F. Powell. 6 vols. Oxford: Clarendon Press, 1934–50.

British Critic 4 (1794):xix–xx, 508–12. (Reviews of Piozzi 1794.)

———. 19 (1802):355–58. (Review of Piozzi 1801.)

Broadley, A. M., ed. *Dr. Johnson and Mrs. Thrale*. Introductory Essay by Thomas Seccombe. London: John Lane, 1910.

Bronson, Bertrand H. "The Double Tradition of Dr. Johnson" (1951). In *Johnson Agonistes and other Essays*, pp. 156–76. Berkeley: University of California Press, 1965.

Brownell, Morris R. "Hester Lynch Piozzi's Marginalia." *Eighteenth-Century Life* 3 (1977):97–100.

Brownley, Martine W. "Samuel Johnson and the Publishing Career of Hester Lynch Piozzi." Paper presented at the annual meeting of the Modern Language Association, New York, 28 December 1981.

Burgh, James. *The Dignity of Human Nature*. London, 1767.

Burke, Edmund. *Reflections on the Revolution in France*. Edited by William B. Todd. New York: Rinehart, 1959.

Burney, Frances. *Diary and Letters of Madame D'Arblay*. Edited by Charlotte Barrett and Austin Dobson. 6 vols. London: Macmillan, 1904–5.

Butterfield, Herbert. *Christianity and History*. New York: Scribner's, 1950.

_____. *History and Human Relations*. New York: Macmillan, 1952.

Campbell, Thomas. *Dr. Campbell's Diary of a Visit to England in 1775*. Edited by James L. Clifford. Cambridge: Cambridge University Press, 1947.

Clifford, James L. "Mrs. Piozzi's Letters." In *Essays on the Eighteenth Century presented to David Nichol Smith*, pp. 155–67. Oxford: Clarendon Press, 1945.

_____, and Greene, Donald J. *Samuel Johnson: A Survey and Bibliography of Critical Studies*. Minneapolis: University of Minnesota Press, 1970.

Cole, William. *A Journal of my Journey to Paris in the Year 1765*. Edited by F. G. Stokes. New York: Smith, 1931.

Collins, P. A. W. "Boswell's Contact with Johnson." *Notes & Queries* (April 1956):163–66.

A Comparison between the Two Stages. Edited by Staring B. Wells. Princeton: Princeton University Press, 1942.

Cowley, Hannah. *Works*. 3 vols. London, 1813.

Crabb, George. *English Synonymes Explained, in Alphabetical Order*. London, 1816.

Critical Review 12 (1794):121–28. (Review of Piozzi 1794.)

_____. 32 (1801):28–35. (Review of Piozzi 1801.)

Didion, Joan. "Why I Write." In *The Writer on Her Work*, edited by Janet Sternburg, pp. 17–25. New York: Norton, 1981.

Egan, Rose F. "Survey of the History of English Synonymy." In *Webster's Dictionary of Synonyms*, pp. vii–xxv. Springfield, Mass.: Merriam, 1942.

Emblen, D. L. *Peter Mark Roget: The Word and the Man*. New York: Crowell, 1970.

English, Sarah. "The Project Up till Now: Methodological Problems and Decisions." Paper presented at the annual meeting of the Modern Language Association, New York, 29 December 1983.

European Magazine 25 (1794):361. (Review of Piozzi 1794.)

_____. 39 (1801):188–91. (Review of Piozzi 1801.)

Finch, Anne. *The Poems of Anne Countess of Winchelsea*. Edited by Myra Reynolds. Chicago: University of Chicago Press, 1903.

Fowler, H. W. *A Dictionary of Modern English Usage*. Oxford: Clarendon Press, 1937.

Frye, Northrop. *Anatomy of Criticism*. Princeton: Princeton University Press, 1957.

Fussell, Paul. *Abroad: British Literary Traveling Between the Wars*. New York: Oxford University Press, 1980.

_____. "Patrick Brydone: The Eighteenth-Century Traveler as Representative Man." In *Literature as a Mode of Travel*, edited by Warner G. Rice, pp. 53–67. New York: New York Public Library, 1963.

Gibbon, Edward. *The History of the Decline and Fall of the Roman Empire*. Edited by J. B. Bury. New York: Heritage Press, 1946.

Gifford, William. *The Maeviad*. London, 1795.

Gilbert, Sandra M., and Gubar, Susan. *The Madwoman in the Attic: The Woman Writer and the Nineteenth-Century Literary Imagination*. New Haven: Yale University Press, 1979.

Girard, Gabriel. *Synonymes françois, leurs différentes significations, et le choix qu'il en faut faire pour parler avec justesse*. 3d ed. Paris, 1741.

Glover, Richard. *Britain at Bay: Defence against Bonaparte, 1803–14*. London: Allen and Unwin, 1973.

Goethe, Johann Wolfgang von. *Conversations with Eckermann*. New York: Walter Dunne, 1901.

Gordon, Mary. "The Parable of the Cave." In *The Writer on Her Work*, edited by Janet Sternburg, pp. 27–32. New York: Norton, 1981.

Greene, Donald J. *The Politics of Samuel Johnson*. New Haven: Yale University Press, 1960.

———. *Samuel Johnson*. New York: Twayne, 1970.

———. "'Tis a Pretty Book, Mr. Boswell, But—." *Georgia Review* 32 (1978):17–43.

Gregory, John. *A Father's Legacy to His Daughters*. 1774. Reprint. New York: Garland, 1974.

Halsband, Robert. "Ladies of Letters in the Eighteenth Century." In *Stuart and Georgian Moments*, edited by Earl Miner, pp. 271–91. Berkeley: University of California Press, 1972.

Hargreaves-Mawdsley, W. N. *The English Della Cruscans and Their Time, 1783–1828*. The Hague: Nijhoff, 1967.

Hiatt, Mary. *The Way Women Write*. New York: Teachers College Press, 1977.

Hume, David. *The History of England from the Invasion of Julius Caesar to the Revolution in 1688*. 6 vols. Boston: Little, Brown, 1868.

Hyde, Mary. *The Impossible Friendship: Boswell and Mrs. Thrale*. Cambridge: Harvard University Press, 1972.

———. "'Not in Chapman.'" In *Johnson, Boswell and Their Circle*, pp. 296–319. Oxford: Clarendon Press, 1965.

Irwin, George. *Samuel Johnson: A Personality in Conflict*. Auckland: Auckland University Press, 1971.

Johnson, R. Brimley, ed. *The Letters of Mrs. Thrale*. London: John Lane, 1926.

Johnson, Samuel. "The Fountains: A Fairy Tale." In Anna Williams, *Miscellanies in Prose and Verse*, pp. 111–41. London, 1766.

———. *Lives of the English Poets*. Edited by G. B. Hill. 3 vols. Oxford: Clarendon Press, 1905.

———. *Prose and Poetry*. Edited by Mona Wilson. London: Hart-Davis, 1950.

———. *Rasselas*. Edited by G. B. Hill. Oxford: Clarendon Press, 1887.

———. *Works*. New Haven: Yale University Press, 1958–. Vol. 1, *Diaries, Prayers, and Annals*, edited by E. L. McAdam with Donald Hyde and Mary Hyde. Vol. 2, *The Idler and The Adventurer*, edited by W. J. Bate, J. M. Bullitt, and L. F. Powell. Vol. 3, *The Rambler*, edited by W. J. Bate and Albrecht B. Strauss. Vol. 6, *Poems,* edited by E. L. McAdam and George Milne. Vol. 7, *Johnson on Shakespeare,* edited by Arthur Sherbo.

Klingel, Joan E. "Reform, Revolution and the Regency in the Letters of Mrs. Thrale-Piozzi." Paper presented at the annual meeting of the Modern Language Association, New York, 28 December 1981.

Krutch, Joseph W. *Samuel Johnson.* New York: Holt, 1944.

Lakoff, Robin. *Language and Woman's Place.* New York: Harper, 1975.

Lefebvre, Georges. *Napoleon.* Translated by Henry F. Stockhold and J. E. Anderson. 2 vols. New York: Columbia University Press, 1969.

Literary Memoirs of Living Authors of Great Britain. . . . 2 vols. London, 1798.

Lobban, J. H., ed. *Dr. Johnson's Mrs. Thrale: Autobiography, Letters and Literary Remains of Mrs. Piozzi.* Edinburgh: Foulis, 1910.

London Chronicle, 28–30 March 1786. (Review of Piozzi 1786.)

———, 1–3 April 1788. (Review of Piozzi 1788.)

Lonsdale, Roger. *Dr. Charles Burney: A Literary Biography.* Oxford: Clarendon Press, 1965.

Lustig, Irma S. "Boswell at Work: The 'Animadversions' on Mrs. Piozzi." *Modern Language Review* 67 (1972):11–30.

McCarthy, William. "Davenant's Prefatory Rhetoric." *Criticism* 20 (1978): 128–43.

———. "The Moral Art of Johnson's *Lives.*" *Studies in English Literature* 17 (1977):503–17.

Mangin, Edward. *Piozziana; or, Recollections of the late Mrs. Piozzi, with Remarks.* London: Moxon, 1833.

Marshall, Roderick. *Italy in English Literature, 1755–1815.* New York: Columbia University Press, 1934.

Mason, William. *The Poems of Mr. Gray. To which are prefixed Memoirs of his Life and Writings.* 2d ed. London, 1775.

Monthly Mirror 5 (1798):323–25; 6 (1798):137–38. ("Biographical Sketch of Mrs. Piozzi.")

Monthly Review 15 (1794):241–51, 371–80. (Review of Piozzi 1794.)

Moore, John. *A View of Society and Manners in Italy* (1781). Boston, 1792.

More, Hannah. *Strictures on the Modern System of Female Education.* 2 vols. 1799. Reprint. New York: Garland, 1974.

Murphy, Arthur. "An Essay on the Life and Genius of Samuel Johnson" (1792). In *Johnsonian Miscellanies,* edited by G. B. Hill, 1:353–488. Oxford: Clarendon Press, 1897.

Myers, Sylvia H. "Breaking Away: Mrs. Thrale and the Bluestocking Circle." Paper presented at the annual meeting of the Modern Language Association, New York, 28 December 1981.

———. "The Ironies of Education." *Aphra* 4 (1973):61–72.

Namier, Sir Lewis. *Personalities and Powers: Selected Essays.* New York: Harper, 1965.

Newton, A. Edward. "A Light-Blue Stocking." In *The Amenities of Book-Collecting*, pp. 186–225. Boston: Atlantic Monthly Press, 1918.

Noyes, Gertrude E. "The Beginnings of the Study of Synonyms in England." *PMLA* 66 (1951):951–70.

Paine, Thomas. *The Rights of Man*. Garden City, N.Y.: Doubleday, 1973.

Pendleton, Gayle T. "The English Pamphlet Literature of the Age of the French Revolution Anatomized." *Eighteenth-Century Life* 5 (1978):29–37.

Pennington, Penelope. "Death of Mrs. Piozzi." Clipping from unidentified newspaper, Princeton University Library AM 14613. (The Bath newspaper, according to Clifford, p. 457.) Reprinted in Piozzi 1914, pp. 371–73.

Pigott, Charles. *The Female Jockey Club, or, A Sketch of the Manners of the Age*. New York, 1794.

Pope, Alexander. *Essay on Man*. Edited by Maynard Mack. New Haven: Yale University Press, 1950.

Pottle, Frederick A., and Bennett, Charles H. "Boswell and Mrs. Piozzi." *Modern Philology* 39 (1942):421–30.

Pratt, Mary Louise. *Toward a Speech Act Theory of Literary Discourse*. Bloomington: Indiana University Press, 1977.

Raleigh, Sir Walter. "Johnson Without Boswell." In *Six Essays on Johnson*, pp. 40–74. Oxford: Clarendon Press, 1910.

Reynolds, Frances. "Recollections of Dr. Johnson." In *Johnsonian Miscellanies*, edited by G. B. Hill, 2:250–300. Oxford: Clarendon Press, 1897.

Reynolds, Richard R. "Mrs. Piozzi's 'Scotch Journey,' 1789." *BJRL* 60 (1977):114–34.

Roberts, William. *Memoirs of the Life and Correspondence of Mrs. Hannah More*. 2 vols. New York, 1835.

Rogers, Katharine M. *Feminism in Eighteenth-Century England*. Urbana: University of Illinois Press, 1982.

Ross, Steven T. *European Diplomatic History, 1789–1815: France Against Europe*. Garden City, N.Y.: Doubleday, 1969.

Rowson, Susanna. *Charlotte Temple* (1791). Edited by Clara Kirk and Rudolf Kirk. New Haven: College and University Press, 1964.

Saintsbury, George. *A Letter Book*. London: Bell, 1922.

Scott, Mary. *The Female Advocate; a Poem*. 1774. Reprint. Los Angeles: William Andrews Clark Memorial Library, 1984.

Scott, Walter S. *The Bluestocking Ladies*. London: John Green, 1947.

Shaftesbury, Anthony, Earl of. *Characteristics of Men, Manners, Opinions, Times*. Edited by John M. Robertson. Indianapolis: Bobbs-Merrill, 1964.

Sharp, Samuel. *Letters from Italy, describing the Customs and Manners of that Country, in the Years 1765, and 1766*. London, 1766.

Smith, Adam. *The Theory of Moral Sentiments*. Edited by D. D. Raphael and

A. L. Macfie. Oxford: Clarendon Press, 1976.

Smith, James Edward. *A Sketch of a Tour on the Continent, in the Years 1786 and 1787*. 3 vols. London, 1793.

Smollett, Tobias. *Travels through France and Italy*. Edited by Frank Felsenstein. Oxford: Oxford University Press, 1979.

Spacks, Patricia Meyer. "Scrapbook of a Self: Mrs. Piozzi's Late Journals." *Harvard Library Bulletin* 18 (1970):221–47.

Sprat, Thomas. "An Account of the Life and Writings of Mr. Abraham Cowley." In *Critical Essays of the Seventeenth Century*, edited by J. E. Spingarn, 2:119–46. Oxford: Clarendon Press, 1908–9.

Stone, Lawrence. *The Family, Sex and Marriage in England, 1500–1800*. Abr. ed. New York: Harper, 1979.

Sutherland, James. *A Preface to Eighteenth Century Poetry*. London: Oxford University Press, 1963.

Swift, Jonathan. *Gulliver's Travels and Other Writings*. Edited by Ricardo Quintana. New York: Modern Library, 1958.

Trench, Richard. *On the Study of Words*. 2d ed. New York, 1852.

Tyers, Thomas. "A Biographical Sketch of Dr. Samuel Johnson" (1785). In *The Early Biographies of Samuel Johnson*, edited by O M Brack and Robert E. Kelley, pp. 61–90. Iowa City: University of Iowa Press, 1974.

Wain, John. *Samuel Johnson*. New York: McGraw-Hill, 1976.

Walpole, Horace. *Correspondence*. New Haven: Yale University Press, 1937–83. Vol. 11, *Correspondence with Mary and Agnes Berry*, edited by W. S. Lewis and A. Dayle Wallace. Vol. 25, *Correspondence with Sir Horace Mann*, edited by W. S. Lewis and Warren Hunting Smith. Vol. 42, *Miscellaneous Correspondence*, edited by W. S. Lewis and John Riely.

Watson, J. Steven. *The Reign of George III, 1760–1815*. Oxford: Clarendon Press, 1960.

Webster's Dictionary of Synonyms. Springfield, Mass.: Merriam, 1942.

Williamson, Marilyn L. "Who's Afraid of Mrs. Barbauld? The Blue Stockings and Feminism." *International Journal of Women's Studies* 3 (1980):89–102.

Wimsatt, William K. "Images of Samuel Johnson." *ELH* 41 (1974):359–74.

Wollstonecraft, Mary. *A Vindication of the Rights of Man*. London, 1790.

———. *A Vindication of the Rights of Woman*. Edited by Carol H. Poston. New York: Norton, 1975.

Woolf, Virginia. "Professions for Women." In *The Death of the Moth and other Essays*, pp. 235–42. New York: Harcourt Brace, 1942.

Wordsworth, William. *Poetical Works*. Edited by Thomas Hutchinson and Ernest de Selincourt. London: Oxford University Press, 1950.

Index

59, 260, 261
Pitt, William, the Elder, 213, 216
Pitt, William, the Younger, 215, 218, 219, 221
Plutarch, 5
Pope, Alexander, 15, 16, 21, 27, 47, 48, 55, 65, 68, 71, 77–78, 126, 135, 136, 146, 205, 225, 240; *Essay on Man*, xiii, 11, 13, 14, 63; *Windsor Forest*, 15; *Epistle to Dr. Arbuthnot*, 78; *Dunciad*, 237
Pottle, Frederick, and Charles Bennett, 197
Price, Richard, 235
Prior, Matthew, 123, 126; *Alma*, 123
Purcell, Henry, 17
Puttenham, George, 57

Quin, James, 5

Racine, Jean, 42, 55
Racine, Louis, 9, 11, 14, 80, 126, 240; *Épitres sur l'homme*, 11–13; *La Religion*, 13
Rapin (historian of England), 5
Reynolds, Frances, 105
Reynolds, Sir Joshua, 3, 24, 127, 254, 262
Richardson, Samuel, 65, 135, 142
Robertson, William, 64, 254
Roethke, Theodore, 71
Rogers, Katharine M., 43
Rousseau, Jean-Jacques, 9, 63, 155; *Confessions*, 65, 117
Rowe, Nicholas: "Colin's Complaint," 100–101
Royal Society, 62

St. James's Chronicle, 16, 20
Saintsbury, George, 136, 277 (n. 6)
Salusbury, Hester Lynch. *See* Piozzi, Hester Lynch (Salusbury) (Thrale)
Salusbury, Hester Maria, 4, 5, 6, 7, 18–28 passim, 85, 86, 99, 135

Salusbury, John, 4, 5, 7, 17, 18, 19, 85, 102, 104, 270 (n. 2)
Salusbury, Sir John. *See* Piozzi, (Sir) John Salusbury
Salusbury, Sir Thomas, 7, 17, 18, 19, 20, 21, 22, 25, 204
Savage, Richard, 122
Schiller, Johann Christoph Friedrich von, 67
Scott, Mary: *The Female Advocate*, 42
Scott, Sir Walter, 67, 68, 72, 145
Seccombe, Thomas, 139, 144
Selden, John, 10, 30
Seven Years' War, 17, 213
Seward, Anna, 70, 103, 197, 267
Shaftesbury, Anthony, earl of, 122, 126, 181, 222, 240
Shakespeare, William, 10, 11, 41, 196; *King John*, 10, 270 (n. 10); *Midsummer Night's Dream*, 83
Sharp, Samuel, 150, 155, 156, 169; *Letters from Italy*, 151
Shaw, George Bernard, 259
Shelley, Percy Bysshe, 62, 81, 87; *Alastor*, 15, 82, 85; "Mont Blanc," 84
Shenstone, William, 76
Sherlock, Martin: *Letters from an English Traveller*, 156, 158
Siddons, Sarah, 51, 52, 179
Skeffington, Lumley St. George, 252
Smith, Adam, 121–22, 214
Smith, James Edward, 52
Smollett, Tobias, xiii, 65, 156; *Travels in France and Italy*, 151–52, 155, 158, 161, 162, 164, 167, 169, 174
Southwark, 20–21, 33, 106
Spacks, Patricia M., 41, 71, 77
Spectator, The (Addison and Steele), 62
Spence, Joseph, 181, 271 (n. 38)
Spenser, Edmund, 10, 11, 48, 78; *The Faerie Queene*, 181
Sprat, Thomas, 135